CONTENTS

Acknowledgments 7

Introduction 7

The Rock — Its Discovery 9

Settlement 24

Man Takes the Rock 31

The Rock as a Fort 55

The Rock as a Military Prison 70

The Rock as a Federal Penitentiary 97

The End of an Era 123

Distinct Men of Alcatraz 197

Alcatraz and the Indians 225

Appendices:

    Afterword 242

    Commanding Officers on Alcatraz 244

    Army Units 245

    Escape Attempts 246

Bibliography 247

Index 252

Cover Design by Sam Payne, Seattle, Washington

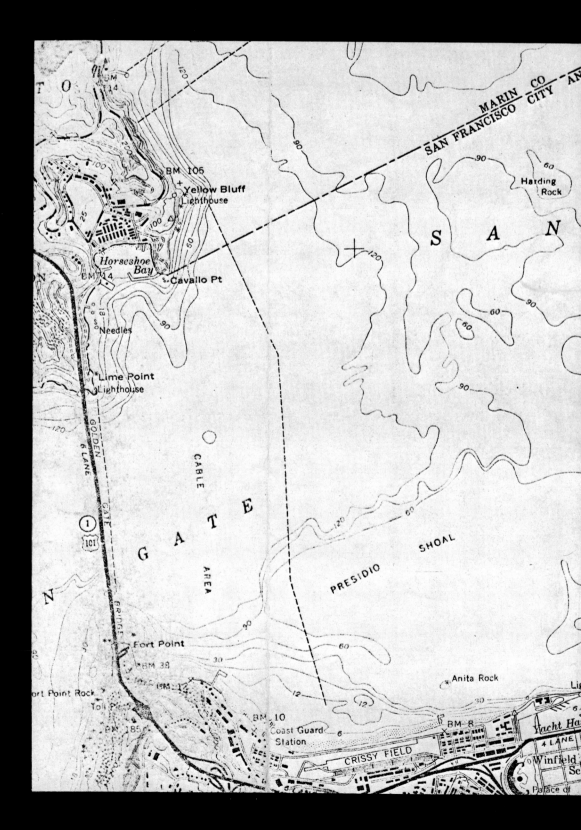

This book is dedicated with all my
love to my daughters

YVETTE DEBBI

A HISTORY OF ALCATRAZ
THE FORT/THE PRISON

BY
PIERRE ODIER

Published by L'Image Odier, Eagle Rock, California

6th Printing 2003

Library of Congress Catalog Card Number 81-80586

Book Trade Distribution by L 'Image Odier
1255 Hill Drive, Eagle Rock, CA 90041

ISBN 0-9611632-0-8

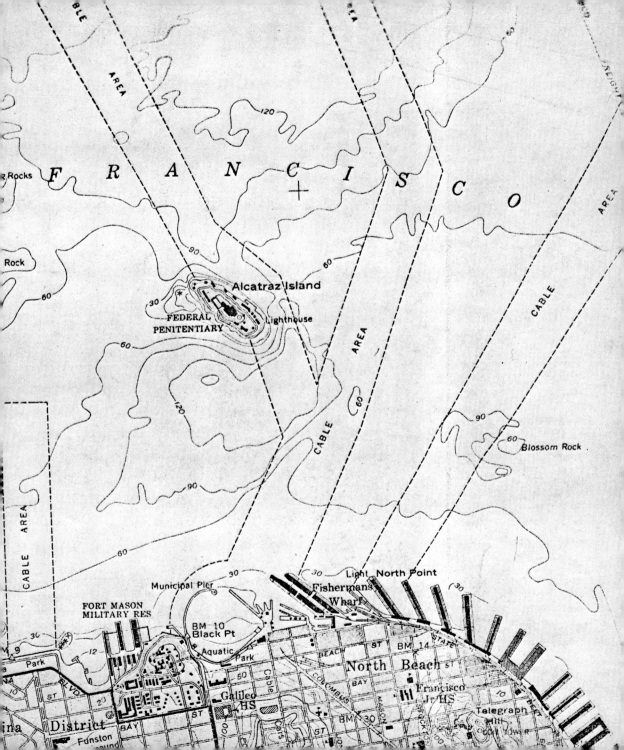

search
FOR
self
—
HigH

ACKNOWLEDGMENTS
INTRODUCTION

This book would not have been possible without the help of many people and I do fear neglecting a "thank you." Some are just voices on the other end of the phone and in archive rooms of some institution around the nation, and to them I want to express a most sincere thank you and gratitude. Most of the visual material came to me over the years without the identity of its originator. I can assure you that every effort has been made to locate and acknowledge the sources of the original material and photographs used in this book, which was a major task in itslef. All efforts have been made to verify stories as to their accuracy. I regret any instances of not acknowledging the correct source.

Material for this book was so sparse that in order to find any material one had to develop the insight and skills of a super detective. So many hours were spent searching through indexes and card files of archives that it was hard to maintain a clear view or a system to record, gather and later recall all this source material. I remember that, after four hours in the stacks at the Huntington Library research basement, I could not find my way out until I used little tape stickers to trace my way to the door I came in. It just all looked the same. Everybody else knew exactly where they were going, or did they? The staff was so patient and so helpful. To the Huntington staff and the rear bookroom attendant, much thanks.

Special thanks must go to the people who stood by through the long process of creating this book. A special thanks to Les Barnum, the National Parks Ranger of the Golden Gate Recreation and Parks Services in charge of Alcatraz, who first said, "Yes, let's do it," and then figured out how to bypass the government bureaucracy to make it all happen. To Les, a very special thanks from all of the students and myself. He was the key to the lock. During the follow-up research, much help came from the many people at the Parks and Recreation center at Fort Point and Fort Mason. Bob Kirky, who took Les Barnum's place, James Delgado, Historian, Jack Davis, Superintendent of Golden Gate Recreation Parks Services, and Charles Hawkins at Fort Point. They all gave freely of their time and advice and I thank you all.

The biggest thank you must go to a group of people that provided me with the most meaningful and direct insight into Alcatraz, the Prison. I am grateful to the many former inmates, guards, wardens and Alcatraz support personnel who granted interviews and with whom lengthy correspondences developed. That part of the book is *your* story and I hope that the trust you had in me was not used in a way to make you feel betrayed. To say thank you seems so little in return for your understanding, loyal help, but I hope the text in this book reflects my sincere appreciation for your contribution. To create that segment of the book without falling into opinionated documentation was very difficult. Again my sincere thanks to all of you.

The segment of this book that proved the most difficult to research was that part dealing with the 1969-1970 Indian Occupation. That part of the research ran into so many emotional opinions that it was difficult to relate a factual account of that time. Most helpful were the direct interviews with the Native American Indians who participated in that occupation. Many of you gave me the interviews with the understanding that I don't reveal who you are — well, I still want to say thanks to all of you.

A very special thanks must go to three individuals who helped me with the words on paper. Stacy Bennett, who for over one year took my terrible handwriting and transposed it to type. That labor of love was probably the most responsible for the completion of this text. At the end of this process when time was running out, I owe a special thanks to Michele Leffler who came to my rescue and helped Stacy with her task. The individual whom I relied on the most was Rudy Freno, who proofed and retyped my manuscript so it could be sent to the typesetter. I owe Rudy a great deal of gratitude for his loyalty for almost two years. The personal dedication and professional help I received at the Church Press in Glendale, made me feel at home in a new world of publishing. To all of you my warmest thanks.

For their patience with me as I was spending much time in the basements of libraries, bookstores and many odd places, searching for material and information, I thank both my daughters. A special thanks to my daughter Debbi for her continued support and encouragement, and who had to give up many of her days of fun just to let me pursue this project, so much love and thanks.

Left page: Indian sketch from the 1969-70 occupation of Alcatraz.

THE ROCK, DISCOVERY

photograph was furnished through the courtesy of the Environmental Research Institute of Michigan by James B. Cooper

The Landsat view of San Francisco and the Bay area was made with computer enhancement at an altitude of 570 miles.

SIR FRANCIS DRAKE.

Today, a visitor to San Francisco cannot avoid becoming aware of the existence of Alcatraz. In travel brochures, hotel posters, tour maps of the city, public relations material from the Chamber of Commerce, and souvenir stands all over the city, Alcatraz announces its presence. How much historical detail the tourist knows is hard to ascertain; but it could be said that San Francisco without Alcatraz would be like Paris without the Eiffel Tower or Egypt without the Pyramids. The Eiffel Tower and the Pyramids were the products of the societies settling in those areas. Alcatraz was there before any settlers. However, it became one of the main historical focal points as San Francisco developed into the metropolitan city it is today. San Francisco's Alcatraz, like Egypt's Pyramids, has a mysterious drawing power. This power directly challenges the visitor's imagination. Even a casual visitor must give in to many thoughts, fantasies and queries. Often undefinable feelings become part of that thought process. There is a power that lingers and affects the visitor to Alcatraz, "The Rock."

Today we use satellites to scan and record with pinpoint precision our earth's surface. There are almost no secrets from space. Information regarding rivers, mountains, food sources, and weather, so important to our modern mobility, is a luxury not shared by our ancestors. Any discovery made by our ancestors challenging the unknown was done at great risk. Time and manpower had to be given freely. The smallest gain in recording the "other side" was attached to the biggest risks. The making of records was very basic and subject to the opinions and interpretations of the discoverer. It was probably all done with the best of intentions but with limited factual information, thus allowing a lot of free interpretation and standing myths to be mixed in with the facts.

The method and tools for recording were very limited. What we have today is a very vague, hazy, and often disputed sequence of events. The evidence and pieces of the factual puzzle are few and often not quite authentic. Even with so-called hard evidence, one cannot avoid the debates and varied opinions on its interpretation. The debates will go on forever. However, one must collect as much data as possible in order to create a sequence of events that will allow us to construct a fair picture of our past.

California's and Alcatraz's history are no exception to all the debates. All the different viewpoints will probably keep the scholars busy forever. The fact that most of the early California history records were destroyed in the 1906 San Francisco earthquake does not make the researching of the historical facts any easier. This book is an attempt to trace the historical evolution of this island, Alcatraz, "The Rock," in San Francisco Bay.

The year 1559 marked the beginning. At that time King Philip II of Spain (1556-1598) urged the prosecution of Spain's early Philippine trade. "Go there," he ordered, "and to the adjacent islands. Discover a return route to New Spain with all possible speed and bring back spices and other valuable commodities."

Father Andrés de Urdaneta was in command of the Spanish galleon, the *San Pedro*. He followed Philip II's order and sailed from Manila in 1565. On board, the commander had with him a crude chart of the North American coast. His shoreline chart was based largely on the information provided by the exploratory voyage of the Portuguese, Juan Rodríguez Cabrillo, the only navigator who had sailed northward from New Spain.

In 1542, sailing in a little ship, the *San Salvador*, Cabrillo was the first white man to make the coast of Alta California. Lower (Baja) California had been discovered by Cortés in 1530 and was thought to be the first island in an archipelago reaching to the Asiatic coast.

Cabrillo and his men saw the California coast on Sunday, July 2, 1542. The log of Captain Cabrillo gives us a long record of their island hopping. On the 3rd of January, 1543, Cabrillo died on the island, Possession, as a result of a fall he had taken there on a previous stay. In that fall he had broken his arm near the shoulder. He left as his senior pilot Bargolomé Ferrelo, a native of the southeastern coast of Spain. The last order Captain Cabrillo gave to his senior pilot was to go and discover whatever they could all along the coast.

The name "California" first appeared in the romantic medieval novel *Las Sergas de Esplandián*. This land was described as "an island abounding in gold and other delights, located to northward of New Spain."

Father Andrés de Urdaneta reached the high blue coast at California. It had taken him a total of a hundred and twenty-nine days to reach "New Spain."

This trip marked the beginning of one of the most important trade routes affecting the California coast. In the next decade, trade between the Philippines and New Spain became established by the annual voyages of the Manila Galleons. The flow of spices and other valuable com-

Drake's voyage around
the world, 1577 to 1580

modities as ordered by Philip II was in full swing. So rich was this trade, yielding up to one thousand percent profit in the market of Acapulco, that merchants bid high for the privilege of shipping. The route appeared so safe that at last guns were sacrificed to the carrying of more cargo.

The word of this rich "Manila trade" began to spread. In February of 1579 word reached Master Francis Drake. He was sailing off the coast of Peru in his ship, the *Golden Hind.* On board he carried a large cargo of treasures. As he reached Paita, Drake heard that the ship *Cacafuego* or "Spitfire," aware of his presence, had sailed away for Darién. Drake decided to hoist all sails and pursue the *Cacafuego.* He told his crew, "Whoever first describes her shall have my chain of gold for his good news." The *Golden Hind* was a small ship and on board was Drake's nephew, John. On March 1st John, just sixteen sighted the galleon's topmasts swaying in the seas.

It is recorded that by "six of the clock" the *Golden Hind* came up beside the large ship, *Cacafuego,* shot down the galleon's mizzen, and racked her with arquebus balls. There was no resistance and Drake's men boarded to take the cargo. The loot was enormous: jewels, precious stones; thirteen chests of royals of plate; four score pound weight of gold; and six and twenty tons of silver. The attack took place off Cabo de San Francisco, one hundred and fifty leagues from Panama.

This marked the beginning of the naval battles that continued through the voyages of Cavenish, Woodes Rogers, Clipperton and Shelvocke up to the classic raid of Anson. The English made their presence felt. The Manila trade route was no longer the peaceful, no-risk, profit route it had been.

Captain Drake came the closest to the history of San Francisco Harbor. After taking the *Cacafuego* he sailed north in search of the Straits of Arian. The Straits of Arian was the fabled Northwest Passage that connected the Atlantic Ocean with the Pacific. Drake wanted to sail to England through the passage. His shop was overloaded with gold, jewels and silver, and presented Drake with a sense of urgency. Failing to find the Straits of Arian, he turned south, hoping to find a haven on the coast of California. He had to resurvey and maintain his ship before following the route of Magellan homeward.

Don Sarmiento had put out to sea after him with a fleet. Drake, aware of the value of his cargo, was constantly on the lookout for Spanish sails. He found a "faire and good Boye with good wind to enter" and anchored at a "convenient and fit harborough." Had he gone a few more miles south, he would have come upon as great an anchor

place the world has ever seen, today's San Francisco Harbor. At Los Reyes he erected a brass plate with the following inscription:

Be it known to all men by these present:
June 17, 1579
By the grace of God in the name of her Majesty, Queen Elizabeth of England and her successors forever, I take possession of this kingdom whose king and people freely resign their right and title in the whole land unto her majesty's keeping. Now named by me and to be known unto all men as Nova Albion.
G. Francis Drake

Six weeks later the *Golden Hind,* cleaned, caulked and pitched, sailed by way of the Cape of Good Hope around the world to England.

As soon as the brass plate was found on April 6, 1937, proponents and opponents of its authenticity went at it. Today one finds very little discussion, and the brass plate takes its place in history as hard evidence. However, the debate in scholarly circles continues.

Henry A. Wagner is the most vocal opponent to the brass plate as being authentic. He offers the following arguments to support his theory. On June 5, 1951, he wrote: "The primary objection to the plate lies in the fact that the only contemporary evidence states that the plate was of lead. Lead was cheap and easily inscribed. . . . All the brass in England at the time was made in Germany, as none was made in England until much later. . . . The brass of which this plate is composed might have been only sixty or seventy years old. All traces of age from vegetable growth or that sort were effaced when the plate was sandblasted in order to be able to read the inscription."

Here we have a classic point of debate, relating to a crucial part of California history. It may well be that in the future we will have a testing method that may settle this argument, but we would still have to deal with the opinion of Captain Reginald Hazelton that the actual writing on the plate from the paleographer doesn't match that of the English Elizabethan Age.

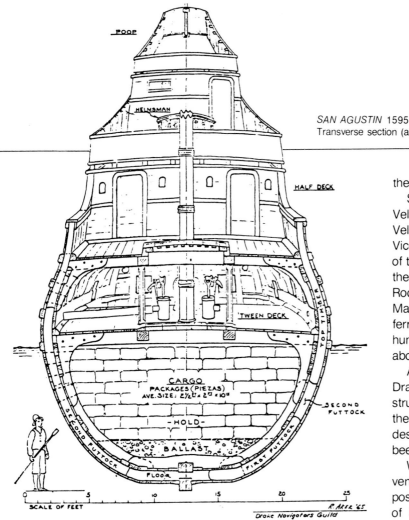

SAN AGUSTIN 1595
Transverse section (approximate)

POOP

HELMSMAN

HALF DECK

TWEEN DECK

TOP TIMBER

SECOND FUTTOCK

SECOND FUTTOCK

FIRST FUTTOCK

CARGO
PACKAGES (PIEZAS)
AVE. SIZE: 2½ˡᵗ x 2ᶠᵗ x 10ⁱⁿ

-HOLD-

BALLAST

FLOOR

SCALE OF FEET
0   5   10   15   20   25

R. ALLEN '65
Drake Navigators Guild

It is important to understand that the crucial link in the chain of events that would lead to the forming of California was in place. This crucial link was the deep intrusion of the English into Spanish territory. This Manila trade route was rich and it was that of the Spaniards. We find records of increasing threats and pirate activities on the vessels of this trade route.

The concerns of the Spaniards reached a state of alarm at the end of the fifteenth century. They felt that the safety of their rich Manila trade was at stake. The galleon *Santa Ana*, the richest ship ever dispatched from the Philippines, was taken by the Englishman Cavendish in his ship the *Desire*. The fierce sea battle lasted five hours. The loss of "thousands of marcos of gold; twenty arrobas of mush; an abundance of civit; many priceless pearls and the richest silkes and brocade" brought strong protest from the merchants in various places. These merchants urged that Spain find and establish safe ports for their ships — ports that would be safe from the pirates.

In 1591 the King of Spain, Philip II, and subsequently his successors, devised several schemes to tax the salt industries. One of the primary purposes of the salt levies was to raise funds for defending against pirates who began harassing Spanish colonies and shipping routes in the late sixteenth century. One levy was specifically earmarked for

the building of the "Flota de Barlovento" or Pacific Fleet.

Spain readied fast, and in 1594 the King wrote a letter to Velasco ordering the voyages of discovery. (Luis de Velasco had succeeded the Marquis de Villamanrique as Viceroy of New Spain in 1590.) Velasco, obeying the order of the King to "chart all harbors homeward," bought a ship, the *San Pedro,* and ordered the Porguguese Sebastián Rodriques Cermeño to sail. Cermeño left Acapulco on March 21, 1594. After arriving in the Philippines, he transferred to the *San Agustín.* On July 5, 1595, with one hundred thirty tons of cargo and about seventy men aboard, the *San Agustín* sailed from the Philippines.

After a storm Cermeño anchored the *San Agustín* in Drakes Bay, just under Point Reyes. He began the construction of a small boat with which he planned to explore the coast and its inlets. A storm changed that plan by destroying the large ship and losing the valuable cargo of beeswax, porcelain and silks.

When Captain Cermeño landed on the 7th of November, 1595, the following is recorded: "...he took possession of the Land and Port, which he named the Bay of San Francisco. Fray Francisco de la Concepción on order of barefoot Franciscans baptized it." This was the first mention of the name of San Francisco, but it was not the same area of today's city. He had given the name to Drakes Bay. It is unknown to us why he used the name of San Francisco, but the important fact is that the name San Francisco was later incorporated into the navigation handbook. This navigation book was written by J. González Cabrera Bueno and published in 1734.

The description of the bay in the navigation handbook was that the "Port of San Francisco was recognizable by its three white cliffs (*barrancas blancas*) and an area by an estuary with a good entrance, without any breakers, friendly Indians, and fresh water." There is at this time no document that tells us of the name change from San Francisco (Drakes Bay) to San Francisco, the city we know today. This change came about just by the usage of the name in that general area of reference for navigation. This change must have occurred by 1775.

His ship, the *San Agustín,* being wrecked, Captain Cermeño left Upper California on the 8th of December, 1595, in an open, makeshift boat to head south. There is a real historical question about the crew of the *San Agustín.* We know that the boat used by Captain Cermeño was much smaller and probably did not have the entire crew on board. It is very possible that some of the crew of the *San Agustín* made their way back to New Spain overland. This then could account for the news of the discovery of the

This spike is from the Estero-Cauley site at Drake's Bay. This crude, heavy wrought-iron spike is from the San Agustín shipwreck. Photo, Lowie Museum of Anthropology, University of California, Berkeley.

"Lost Port" and the use of the name San Francisco. The word spread fast of the new safe port at 38 degrees.

After the wreck of the *San Agustín,* the ships from the Philippines, full of merchandise, were forbidden to explore the coast. Eight years after the *San Agustín* incident, Sebastián Vizcaíno came northward in a caravel (a sailing vessel of the fifteenth and sixteenth centuries, of 80 to 90 tons). This vessel had a square stern, fore and aft castles, high bulwarks, a bowsprit, four masts, a square-rigged foremast and three lateen-rigged masts. It was used by the Portuguese especially in the westward voyages. Vizcaíno's special mission was to find a good port for the Manila galleons. However, there still was no deep commitment on the part of the Spaniards to expand their empire northwards.

In 1602 Vizcaíno arrived north from Mexico, rounded Point Pines and anchored at Monterey. The Bay of Monterey was his greatest discovery and he named it after the Mexican Viceroy who had sent him on the trip. He then sailed north. With him as his pilot was Bolaños, who had sailed in the region before with Cermeño. It was Bolaños

who recognized the point enclosing that bay that Cermeño had named Bahía, today's Drakes Bay. Vizcaíno probably headed straight for that point which he named Point Reyes. In his haste he bypassed the mouth of the Golden Gate. So it is that the great natural harbor remained hidden behind the coastal hills for another 167 years.

Vizcaíno, who had been unsuccessful on a previous trip, needed to bolster his ego and gave a glowing description of Monterey Bay. "I have found," he wrote, "a harbor that is all that can be desired as a station for the Manila ships." He continued writing, "a port sheltered from all winds . . . thickly settled with people . . . with great supplies of wood and water."

In the next century pathfinders of New Spain would trudge overland towards Vizcaíno's Bay. Spain at first in the 15th century had no reason to settle her bleak northern coastal region. Navigators wanted to sail north, but Spain was in no haste to invest in that venture. So the thought of the northwest passage and the "Lost Port" remained dormant.

That thought was changed as soon as the news reached

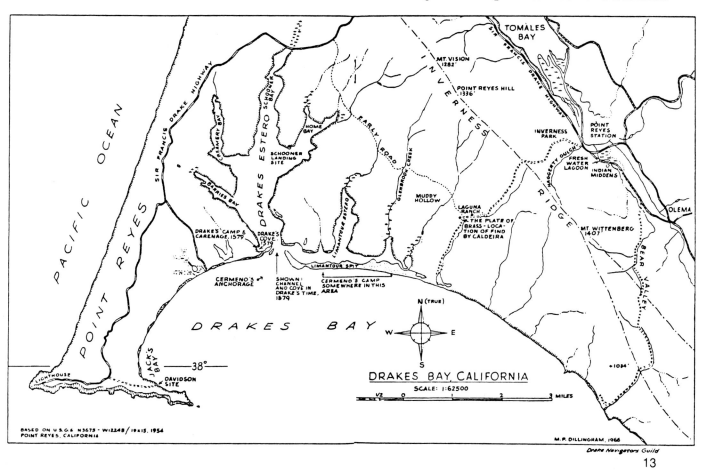

DRAKES BAY, CALIFORNIA
SCALE: 1:62500

BASED ON U.S.G.S. N3675 - W12248/19x15, 1954
POINT REYES, CALIFORNIA

M.P. DILLINGHAM, 1966

Drake Navigators Guild

FATHER
Junípero Serra

the government of Spain that the Russians were settling in Alaska and were preparing to sail south. This was a threat to Spanish land and Spanish supremacy. The King of Spain, Charles III and his farsighted Visitador General of Mexico, José de Gálvez, decided upon the start of the expedition.

The order went out: there was to be a major attempt at settling Alta California. The forming of four military divisions, including Indian auxiliaries of about 225 men, took place. Two divisions were ordered north by the sea route and two by a land route.

On January 10, 1769, José de Gálvez duspatched the first ships of the "Sacred Expedition" to colonize California. "May the Lord guide her prosperously," he declared, "for the enterprise is entirely His." Junípero Serra and his Franciscans took literally the statement of Gálvez that the salvation of souls and the propagation of the faith were the main objects of the California enterprise.

the conquest of Alta California was undertaken by Spain through the Franciscan Order of missionary friars. This was the most popular and effective religious order active in New Spain. The soul of their character was disinterestedness and self-abnegation. Their vows of chastity and obedience were well observed. The vow of poverty was particularly well observed and this made them very popular with the Spaniards as well as the Indians. The Franciscan Order appeared in Mexico in 1524. Sandal-shod and in flowing gowns of sackcloth, the Franciscans, a band of twelve, the apostolic number, arrived in the capital on May 13th and were reverently greeted by Cortez. The Franciscan Fathers were superb pioneers of civilization, spreading Christian faith among the heathen beyond the borders of settlements. They directed the labor of their charges toward bringing the frontier spaces under profitable cultivation. Serving as guardians of the borders to hold back hostile natives and intruding European neighbors, they left their permanent mark in the soil of California.

As explorers they left for us a body of records detailing the geographical and ethnological aspects of the world. The largest portion of the recollection of the discoveries is to be found in the diaries of these friars. The friar, often un-

attended, could go unmolested and without arousing hostility into areas where soldiers could not go, and thus was able to write the best diaries of early explorations.

With the dispatching of the ships *San Carlos,* with Don Vicente Vila in charge, and the *San Antonio,* Gálvez fully trusted that they would find the "Lost Port" and establish, in order to maintain Spanish supremacy and land control in Alta California, a new Spanish stronghold. The expansion, power and pride of Spain rested with this expedition.

Gálvez did not put the same trust in his land divisions. He felt that the land divisions did not have the same *viva fe.* But he wrought valiantly by exhortation to set them in motion.

Gálvez's first land division was commanded by Rivera y Moncada. In September of 1768 he gathered the following supplies for his first land expedition: cattle (200 head); horses (38 head); mules (144 head); pack-saddles, leather bags, sides of leather, bottles, wheat, flour, dried meat, lard, sugar, figs, raisins and wine. Blessed by Padre Lasuén and accompanied by Padre Crespi, at four o'clock in the afternoon of the 24th of March 1769, guided by the cosmographer, José Canizares, Rivera took up his march. The men from the garrison of Loreto, 25 cuirassed, 42 Christianized Indians, and three muleteers with 188 mules and horses took up the march with Rivera.

Gálvez's second land division was led by Governor Portolá. This division had 10 soldiers (cuirassiers) led by Sergeant José Francisco Ortega, 44 Christian Indians, four muleteers with 170 mules and two servants. When they departed on the 21st of May, 1769, Padre Junípero Serra joined the expedition.

The objective of the Gálvez expeditions was Monterey (Vizcaíno's harbor), but the four divisions had been ordered to meet at San Diego. All divisions had arrived by July 1st, but the expedition was totally deranged. The sea division had been badly taken by scurvy. It became very clear to all that if Monterey Bay was to be occupied, it had to be done by a land division. After the reorganization, a land party composed of Portolá, Rivera, Fages, Ortega, Costansó, Crespi and Gómez, 27 cuirassiers, 8 volunteers, 15 Christian Indians, 7 muleteers, and 2 body servants, 66 persons in all, set out for the north.

The only documents (maps) Portolá had to guide him were the two books of Miguel Costansó, the "Noticia de la California de Veregas," which contained the account of Vizcaíno's voyage of 1602-1603 and the writings (Navijalia Book) of Cabrera Bueno, printed in Manila in 1734, showing the port at the 37 degree mark.

On October 1, 1769, they gazed over a hilltop out over

the bay of the search. But where was the harbor, the *puerto*? What was to be seen was simply an open roadstead. *"Ni Puerto de Carmelo, ni de Monterei,"* sorrowfully records Portolá. On October 1st Crespi entered in his diary: "On this day after Mass had been said by us two priests and heard by the rest, we broke camp and following the same river we traveled one league approaching the beach ... soon after our arrival, the commander, the engineer, and I, accompanied by five soldiers, went to examine the beach. Ascending a small hill which is not far from it, we saw a great bay which we conjectured to be the one which Cabrera Bueno placed between Point Año Nuevo and the Point of Pines of Monterey, for we saw this point covered with tall pines, and it must be that the port of Monterey is near by."

At this point Portolá was concerned and he called a council meeting with the officers and padres. It was agreed that they should find (by God's aid) Monterey or perish in the attempt. In a letter written from San Diego, Crespi writes to Fray Francisco Palou: "Seeing that Monterey did not appear, it was decided with great eagerness, in view of the fact that the thirty-seven degrees had not been covered, to continue until it was found."

On October 8th they started northwards again. Food ran short; scurvy reappeared; men had to be borne in litters. Portolá and Rivera themselves fell ill. Crespi wrote on October 10th: "At about eight in the morning we set out northwest. We could not make the march as long as was intended, because the sick men were worse and each day their numbers increased, so we must have traveled but little more than one league, over plains and hills, well forested with very high trees of a red color, not known to us. They have a very different leaf from cedars, and although the wood resembles cedar somewhat in color, it is very different, and has the same odor; moreover, the wood of the trees that we have found is very brittle. In this region there is a great abundance of these trees and because none of the expedition recognized them, they are named redwoods from the color."

Slowly this expedition moved northward. This task was not easy. One does tend to forget the great personal stamina it took to undertake such a mission. We find many written passages in the diaries that refer to the hardship of the members of the expedition. On October 11th both Crespi and Costanzó gave the following report: "The sick were so very ill and near their end that, with several of them having been given the Sacrament, it became clear to us that by not giving them some surcease and rest we would risk their dying on the way."

This condition would be very burdensome on the expedition and forced the commander to slow down and change the plans for the forward push toward Monterey Bay. The condition of these men remained the same and the fathers gave most of their time and attention to caring for the sick. The slow pace northward continued and on October 20th we find an encouraging entry in the diaries of Crespi and Costanzó.

Crespi writes: "This day broke very cloudy and dark, with all the people wet and fatigued from loss of sleep for lack of tents, so that it was necessary to rest today and dry the clothing. Our greatest anxiety being that the poor sick persons with us might be harmed by the wetting. But exactly the contrary happened, and it seemed as though God had sent them health with the drenching, for to the surprise of everybody they began to improve, and in a short time were entirely recovered, thanks to God, to whom we attributed this special blessing. For this reason the valley was renamed La Salud."

Costanzó's entry reads: "At daybreak Sunday it was overcast and gloomy, with our people wet and sleepless from having no tents, so that it was necessary to give them a day of rest. But the remarkable thing on this occasion was that all of the sick, for whom we had feared that their having gotten wet would prove harmful in the highest degree, found themselves between night and morning relieved of their pains. . . ."

15

The other members did not want to accept the fact that they had missed Monterey Bay. There was a debate in camp as to whether or not they had passed Monterey Bay. "In order to clear it up entirely the commander ordered that during the stay Sergeant Ortega should go out with a party of soldiers to explore, and that we should wait until they returned," writes Crespi.

The next morning Portolá ordered two parties to leave camp. José de Ortega, rugged soldier and pathfinder, was sent northwards with a party of armed men to make certain of their location. The other party of some soldiers was sent up on the ridge to kill some of the deer they had seen silhouetted the day before.

The returning hunters were very excited as they returned to camp, for they had seen "an immense arm of the sea or estuary, which penetrated the land as far as the eye could reach." So Crespi tells us. Oretga's party came back with great excitement, firing their muskets. He reported seeing an uncharted body of water and that the Indians through sign language told them that two days' march northwards lay a ship. This news was sufficient to inspire the group to head northwards again, after the desperately needed supplies.

On the 4th of November the way-worn party descended to the bay (at Palo Alto). From here Ortega and eight men were sent out to explore the possible way to reach Point Reyes. He reached the most northern point in the neighborhood of Hayward. It is either from here or another point on the peninsula on that day that he saw the passage through the Golden Gate and the three islands within the strait, Alcatraz, Yerba Buena and Angel. This sighting is told about in a letter of Crespi to Fray Francisco Palou from San Diego on February 6, 1770, ". . . This great estuary or arm of the sea connects with the ocean between some high mountains which form, they say, three islands within the strait; but we could not see them from where we were because it was low." This marks the first sighting of this bay and Alcatraz, by white men.

Their disappointment was great when Ortega and his men returned from an expedition up the east coast only to report finding a bigger body of water that would take days to circle.

"After hearing the report of the scouts, the commander decided to call together his officers in order to resolve jointly upon the course that might be suitable to adopt in the present circumstances, bearing in mind the service of God, and of the King, and their own honor.

"The officers being assembled gave their votes in writing and resolved to return in search of the Port of Monterey

The group being in better health and spirits increased their pace and reached Montara Mountain on the last day of October. At that moment in Father Crespi's mind the view he shared with the rest of the expedition was none other than that of San Francisco Bay. He wrote in his diary: "Following the coast of the bay to the north some white cliffs are visible, and to the northwest is the mouth of an estuary which seems to penetrate into the land. In view of these signs, and of what is stated in the itinerary of the pilot, Cabrera Bueno, we came to the recognition of this port; it is that of our Father San Francisco, and we have left that of Monterey behind. Filled with these doubts and arguments, we descended from the hill and pitched camp in the middle of a small valley . . . not far from the camp we found a village of friendly heathen, who, as soon as we arrived, came to visit us with their presents of *tamales* made of black seeds. . . . All the signs that we find here we read in the itinerary of the pilot, Cabrera Bueno, from which we concluded that this is the Port of San Francisco; and we are confirmed in this by the latitude in which we find ourselves, which is a full thirty-seven and a half degrees. . . ."

which they knew, from consideration of the signs they had noted along the coast, must lie behind them. The missionary fathers, Crespi and Gómez, likewise attended the meeting, and their opinion was asked for courtesy's sake. They concurred in the decision, recognizing that the return in search of the Port of Monterey, which they also knew must lie behind, was necessary. The resolution was put into effect; in the afternoon the camp was moved two leagues from the stopping place at the estuary, retracing our steps on the return from the Port of San Francisco." This was the entry in Constansó's diary for November 11, 1769.

The lack of supplies prevented Portolá from establishing a mission in San Francisco at this time. The information given to a Portolá scout by an Indian, that there was a ship in a port near them, was wrong. It is clear that the scout misinterpreted the sign language. But these men were desperate and any sign of possible supplies was not challenged too much. So desperate was the Portolá expedition for supplies that, on the way back, after they had reached fog-covered Monterey, they waited for this supply ship. The *San José,* the supply ship, that was sent out to bring supplies to Portolá, had sunk in a storm off the coast of Baja California months earlier.

The return trip was the hardest on the expedition. The time came when they were living on mule meat and rainwater only. They lit big fires in hope of attracting the supply ship. Their hope that such a ship would spot them gave them the strength to make it to San Diego.

We find the following entry in the diary of Constansó for Wednesday, the 24th of January: "We were reaching San Diego and varied were the opinions among us about the condition in which we should find the new settlement that we had left at its very beginning, more than six months ago. Each one discussed the matter according to his temperament and the mood affecting him. Some, seeing things in a favorable light, expected to find there every comfort and help; others grieved, considering its weak state and the few resources we had left it.

17

Discovery of old
San Francisco Bay
October 31, 1769

"In truth, all of us were returning with a misgiving lest, through the continued force of the maladies and the mortality among the people, the settlement had become a place of solitude. On the other hand, there was every reason to fear the evil disposition of the natives of San Diego whose greediness to rob can only be restrained by superior power and authority, and we feared lest they had dared to commit some outrage against the mission and its small garrison. As we had obtained no news whatsoever along the coast concerning the ship, notwithstanding our efforts in that direction, we had fears in anticipation that in San Diego we should meet with a like disappointment."

As the Portolá expedition approached San Diego they discharged their arms and were immediately greeted with joy and open arms. They found out that in August the Indians did indeed attack the mission and wounded Fray Vizcaíno. At that time Fray Junípero Serra was in charge of the mission aided by Fray Juan Vizcaíno and Fray Fernando Parrón.

Don Pedro Fages had succeeded Don Gaspar de Portolá as military commander of Upper California after the latter's departure following the founding of the presidio and mission at Monterey. Crespi, sharing the sense of disappointment with Portolá, writes to the Viceroy, asking him to give thanks to Portolá for the expedition. "The Governor has treated us with all possible courtesy and conducted himself toward all with great wisdom. Will you, Reverence, please thank him, a thing which will delight him greatly? He has worked hard like a true and faithful servant of the King to find the Port of Monterey."

Fages led a party of explorers (six soldiers and one muleteer) on November 17, 1770 northwest from Monterey to the Santa Clara Valley, down the valley to the head of the bay. Fages realized that he could not cross the water to reach Point Reyes and his final entry in his diary reads: "This day, November 29, 1770, seeing that we were unable to cross to the other side — that of the Punta de Los Reyes — without spending many days, and because of the anxiety which I felt for the camp, the cultivation of the land, and the raising of the stock, it was decided to go back. . . ."

After his arrival in Monterey on December 4, 1770, he found out that the Mexican Viceroy, Croix, was preparing to send another expedition north. His purpose was to establish a mission so that such an important place as San Francisco would not fall into foreign hands. This order was dated the 12th of November, 1770 and reached Monterey the 21st of May, 1771.

This expedition finally got underway in March of 1772, almost a year after Croix gave the order to Fages. Captain Pedro Fages was accompanied by Father Crespi. In Fages' diary we find very factual reporting. In Fray Crespi's writings we find a different feeling for this expedition. Crespi was feeling left out and lonely as seen in his letter to Fray Juan Andrés, asking him to send his friend, Fray Cruzado, to Monterey. His friend never arrived, and in a letter to Father Andrés he writes: "I am not writing this because I think that you have not replied to me. But to speak frankly, I have not received any letter in reply. Since we are exiled here in another world, as it were, the letters have perhaps been lost." So this second expedition into the same area may have caused Crespi to give deep thought as to the reason and methods in obtaining this objective.

Crespi was part of this expansion program from its conception, so his writings have the deepest insight as to the reasons and setting of these expeditions. He gives us perhaps the closest view as to how it was. This next entry seems almost like a summary, a telling of his perception of the true reasons for this particular expedition.

"The famous Port of San Francisco, named in the navigation route of Admiral Cabrera Bueno and in the expedition of General Don Sebastián Vizcayno as intermediate between the Port of Monterey and Cape Mendocino, was seen confusedly by those who went on the expedition of the year 1769 when we were seeking the Port of Monterey," wrote Crespi. "As soon as we saw the *farallones* which indicate it and Point Reyes which incloses it in the inlet it forms with Cape de las Almejas, from this place the expedition turned back, assured now from the signs that Monterey lay behind. The year following, in the month of November, the mission and the Royal Presidio of Monterey being established, an attempt was made by Lieutenant of Volunteers Don Pedro Fages (now Captain), Commandant of the said Royal Presidio, with an adequate number of soldiers, to go and examine the said port, but there was little or almost nothing he could add to the first reports. That which was gained was that he discovered a straighter road, level and easy.

"Later there arrived the vessel, *El Príncipe,* in the month of May, bringing ten religious from the Apostolic College of San Fernando for the founding of five missions in this vast heathendom, and among these (missions) was named that of Our Seraphic Father San Francisco in his port, the excellent Viceroy ordering first an examination made by the sea or by land, so as to carry out the said foundation, and with the occupation of that important Port for the Crown of Spain. The ship was not able to go at that time because of reasons given by its captain. For the landsmen neither was it possible to go because the founding of other missions was urgent, and the said commander went to San Diego to bring persons and mules for those foundations. Meanwhile, the Reverend Father President went with what he had to found Misión San Antonio de Padua, in the valley of the Oaks, about twenty-five leagues distance from this one of Monterey. These things finished, and the heavy rains over, it now seemed necessary to undertake this expedition to take care of the foundation ordered as quickly as possible."

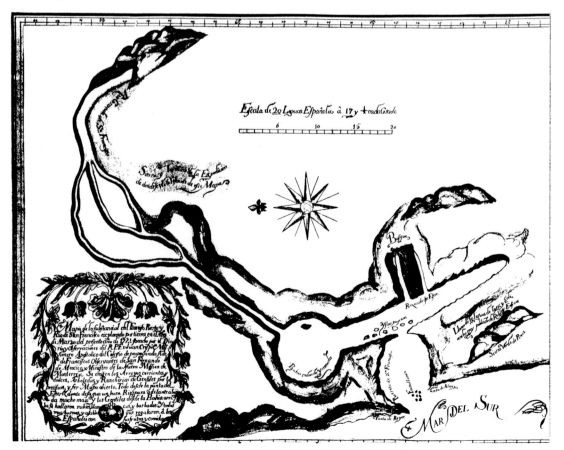

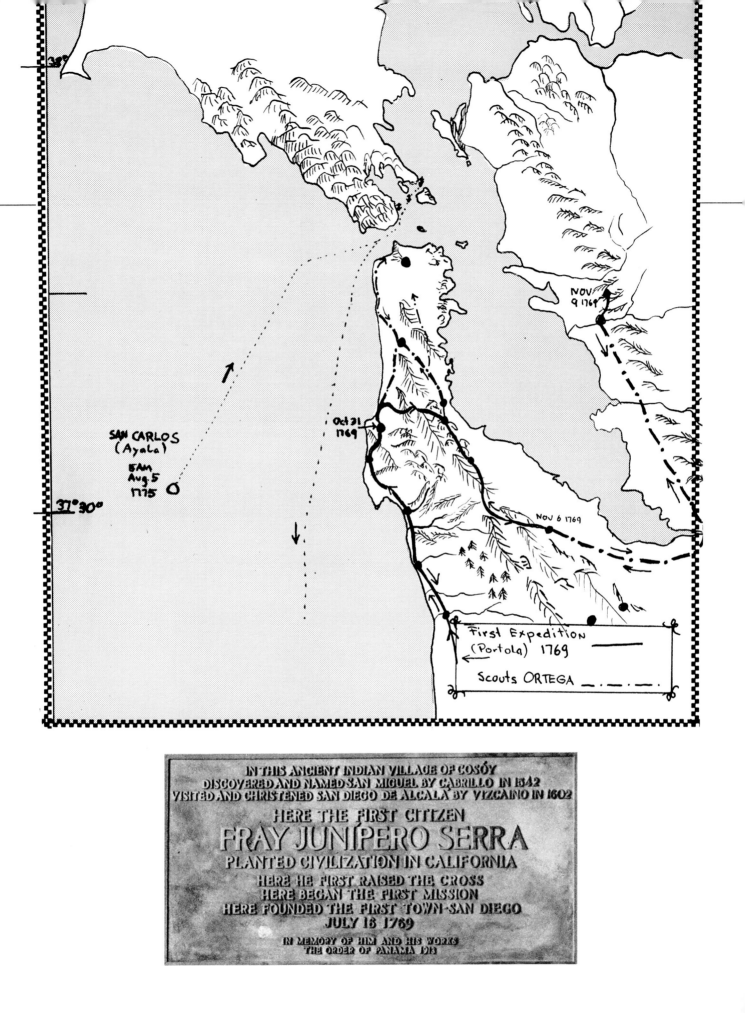

38°

37°30°

SAN CARLOS
(Ayala)

5AM
Aug. 5
1775

Oct 31
1769

NOV
9 1769

NOV 6 1769

First Expedition
(Portola) 1769 _____

Scouts ORTEGA _ . _ . _ .

IN THIS ANCIENT INDIAN VILLAGE OF COSÓY
DISCOVERED AND NAMED SAN MIGUEL BY CABRILLO IN 1542
VISITED AND CHRISTENED SAN DIEGO DE ALCALA BY VIZCAINO IN 1602

HERE THE FIRST CITIZEN
FRAY JUNÍPERO SERRA
PLANTED CIVILIZATION IN CALIFORNIA

HERE HE FIRST RAISED THE CROSS
HERE BEGAN THE FIRST MISSION
HERE FOUNDED THE FIRST TOWN - SAN DIEGO
JULY 16 1769

IN MEMORY OF HIM AND HIS WORKS
THE ORDER OF PANAMA 1913

This next expedition failed to reach its goal. The water mass prevented them from crossing to Point Reyes. On the 30th of March, 1772, Crespi expressed an opinion in his diary: "From all that we have seen and learned it is inferred that if the new mission must be established on the way to the Port of San Francisco or in its vicinity, neither provisions nor stock can be taken by land; nor if it is founded will it be able to maintain any connection with this port of Monterey unless several canoes and some sailors are provided with which to go from one place to the other, to transport the necessities, and in this way make communications easy."

What came out of this expedition, however, was a map, the first of the bay. We don't know if Crespi prepared the map, but it is known as the "Crespi Map." Much is distorted and we see the proportions through the eyes of the explorer. Still, it gives a good idea as to the structure of San Francisco Bay.

The time had arrived when the decision regarding the missions had to be made. Father Serra was convinced that this area was not the true Port of San Francisco. However, he states in a letter to Father Rafael Verger, Guardian of the San Fernando College, that ". . . the evident result is . . . from here it is impossible to reach the Port of San Francisco . . . it is far better to consolidate what we have begun than to reach out for further acquisition."

The Crown of Spain now was getting this message from several different sources; the bay area had to be settled. In January 1773, the Viceroy received royal instructions to strengthen the northern defenses. "Finally," read the document, "his Majesty directs particular attention, as the regulations and instructions indicate at length, to the old and new establishments in California, for in their possessions rest the extension of his dominions, the security of the Province (of New Spain), and, above all the propagation of the Faith and the light of the Gospel. Take his royal order as the special charge of your Excellency so that the said establishments be supported and supplied; that they will not decline, but will rather grow by means of voluntary conversion of the Indians."

It must be mentioned that what might have pushed the Crown to issue this order at this time was the fact that the Minister of the Spanish King to the Russian Court in St. Petersburg, Conte de Lasy, was informing the King that the Russians had sent expeditions into the North Pacific and might soon be reaching California.

All these events in the spring of 1773 were the turning point in the history of Spanish California. The "Defensive Expansion" was in full swing and the events occurred in

rapid succession. Land routes leading northwards were opened by Juan Bautista de Anza. His second expedition ordered by the Viceroy in November 1774 was to both explore and colonize. At the same time the maritime phase of this exploration brought the first Spanish vessel into San Francisco Bay. This naval activity started in the summer of 1774 with Juan Pérez, Bruno de Eceta, and Juan de Bodega Quadra, and lasted until the spring of 1775.

There was a serious lack of harmony between the military and the missionaries. Father Serra wrote thirty proposals to the Viceroy on this matter. He was very concerned, especially since he was so committed to the matter of expanding the missions system in Upper California. He created a friendly relationship with the Viceroy in order to get an increased supply of food. He was capable of obtaining this commitment; and over land and by sea the supplies started to flow towards the San Francisco Bay area. Settlers were needed and encouragement was offered in promises of free transportation to California. Bucareli's determination to extend the mission system, especially in the San Francisco Bay area was very encouraging to Father Serra. He was convinced of the intentions of the Viceroy and left in 1774 for the San Francisco Bay area.

Food arrived in great quantities and the mission fields yielded encouraging crops. Settlers arrived and the Native Americans remained peaceful. In a letter of June 21, 1774, Serra wrote to Viceroy Bucareli: "In this mission alone, where but yesterday there had never been pronounced the name of God nor of Jesus Christ, there are more than two hundred souls, counting Christians and catechumens. Three times a day they eat from what we provide them; they pray, sing and work; and from the labor of their hands we can boast of fields of wheat, corn, beans, peas, and a garden chock-full of cabbage, lettuce and all kinds of vegetables. When we have completed all our preoccupations connected with the boat, we will be able to increase the number of Christians almost at will. Why then should I not be anxious for the number of our mission foundations to be multiplied, when the field is so large and uncultivated? If the hand be only put to work the same results may be expected as have been accomplished here, both on the spiritual and on the temporal side.

"The livestock is the only subject which still leaves something to be desired; but for us it is enough that Your Excellency should know it, because we are sure that, in knowing it, you will find a remedy, whether it be by ordering that the concordat with California should be put into effect, straightforwardly, as it ought to be, or by seeing to it that livestock comes from Sonora. One urgent reason is that, once we have the animals in our possession, breeding is a simple matter in these fertile lands, and additional help will not be needed. Even if our conquest should be extended farther north for many hundred leagues, there will be no difficulty in supplying any such extension of our conquest from the regions we now possess."

It is clear from these words that the system needed for this "Defensive Expansion" was firmly in place. Of special interest to us are the thoughts of Father Serra on the conversion of the Native Americans to Christianity and his confidence, once receiving the livestock, in supplying new missions with the needed supplies. The thinking, between the military and the Fathers, in the matter of expansionism, is now the same.

Bucareli gave orders to Lieutanant Diego de Marique to sail north to survey the Port of San Francisco. Marique went "mad" and had to be replaced with Lieutenant Don Manual de Ayala. The ship he took command of was the "packet boat" San Carlos, alias Toisón de Oro (Golden Fleece). Marique in his state of madness had left several weapons loaded in the cabin, and as Ayala was removing them, one of those discharged and injured his foot. This caused him great pain but he managed to go forward with this mission.

"The Captain of the packet boat, Don Juan de Ayala, tells me he has orders from Your Excellency to go immediately after the boat is unloaded to make an inspection of the Port of San Francisco and of all its surroundings and the bays nearby; and that, after arranging for it with the Captain Commandant, Don Fernando de Rivera y Moncada, a number of soldiers shall go at the same time by land as an escort for the launch, the getting ashore, etc. The plan seems to me an excellent one. I have added an item to it myself — that Fathers Palou and Peña should go with the troops," so writes Father Serra to the Viceroy on July 2, 1774.

In the early morning of the 5th of August, 1775, the San Carlos approached the entry of San Francisco Bay. Ayala ordered his pilot, Don José Canizares, to enter the bay to find a good place to anchor. As the sun was setting and the pilot had not returned, Ayala decided to sail his ship into the bay. The strong outgoing tide slowed his entry, but he sailed with favorable winds through the entrance to "one league within the mouth and a quarter of a mile from shore." Anchor was dropped, and it held in a sandy bottom at a depth of twenty-two fathoms. The time was 10:30 on the night of August 5, 1775.

At 6:00 a.m. the next morning his pilot returned to the ship. It was the strong currents and the fatigue of the men that prevented them from reaching the ship the night before.

The San Carlos anchored off today's Hospital Cove from the 13th of August until September 8th. It is from this position that Ayala and his pilot explored and charted the bay. During the 42-day stay in the bay, Ayala collected all

The Franciscans founding their Mission

California's presiding missionary, Father Junipero Serra, statue as it stands in Mission Dolores cemetery today.

the information needed and used, to create the now famous map of San Francisco, the Ayala Map. The entry and description of the Island of Alcatraz in Ayala's log is of particular interest to us because it gives a lasting flavor to this island. Ayala writes: "On the 12th the launch was lowered to look for a better anchorage near Angel Island, which is the largest in the bay, and many good places were found. It was also thought a good idea to examine another island, which was found to be very steep and barren, so barren and craggy that it could provide no shelter even for small craft and it was called Alcatraces (Pelicans) because of the large numbers of them that were there." This description is the link between an island and a name. On the map of Ayala we find that the name Alcatraces was given to the present-day Yerba Buena, and the present-day Alcatraz was left unnamed. The only explanation for this fact is that when the pilot, Canizares, prepared the map from his notes, he incorrectly identified the island on the map. The identical description by Ayala and Canizares of the island Alcatraz may have preserved the name for us.

Upon his return from this mission Ayala reported to his Viceroy, Bucareli: "Your Excellency, I have finished the orders under which I took command of the San Carlos, returning to this Port of San Blas today, November 6th, after having visited the Port of Monterey and San Francisco.

"It is true that this port is good, not only for the beautiful harmony that it offers to the view, but because it does not lack very good fresh water, wood, and ballast in abundance. Its climate, though cold, is healthful and free from those troublesome fogs which we had daily in Monterey, because the fogs here hardly reach the entrance of the port, and once inside the harbor, the weather is very clear. To these many advantages is to be added the best: and that is that the heathen Indians around this port are so constant in their good friendship and so gentle in their manners that I received them with pleasure on board several times, and I had the sailors frequently visit them on land; so that from the first to the last day, they remained the same in their behavior. This made me present them with trinkets, beads and biscuit; the last they learned to ask for clearly in our language. On September 17th, I decided to leave the Port of San Francisco, as I considered the reconnaissance completed."

SETTLEMENT

On January 4, 1776, Anza arrived in Monterey. He had received orders from the Viceroy, Bucareli, to proceed to Monterey and from there to establish a presidio and mission in San Francisco Bay.

After a few days' rest he proceeded to the lagoon which they named Laguna de Nuestra Señora de los Dolores, since they arrived there on the feast day of Our Lady of Sorrows. They planted a cross at the spot where the presidio was to be built. This was the formal claiming of the land, and the settlers started the construction of the presidio and mission.

Tents were set up and the soldiers started the cutting of lumber for the presidio buildings. The two priests in charge of the founding of the mission were Father Francisco Palou and Father Pedro Benito Cambón. The Mass held by Father Palou in a makeshift shelter on June 29 marked the official beginning of the City of San Francisco. This took place five days before the signing of the Declaration of Independence. The formal establishment of the mission of Saint Francis was delayed until the arrival of the necessary church documents, and took place on October 9, 1776.

The flags of Spain and the Catholic Church were firmly planted in the soil of California. Settlers started to form a community and the King of Spain, in gratitude for his soldiers, started passing out large land grants. Families started to set up ranchos and worked hard at cultivating the land. Livestock were tended by the *vaqueros,* and Indians became servants occupied with household tasks, grinding corn, cooking, washing, sewing and servicing guests.

Life in Alta California took on a colorful style. A gracious, free spirit prevailed. Hospitality was lifted to an art. The visitor, without exception, was moved and impressed with the California spirit. Every home in the long chain of ranchos was open to visitors. All had extra rooms for visitors. This gracious hospitality of friars and rancheros was inborn from Spanish ancestry.

The curiosity spread and travelers started to make California part of their travel objectives. The first Englishman to arrive in the Port of San Francisco was George Vancouver. In 1772 he anchored his ship "Discovery" in the bay. He was overwhelmed with the hospitality and he wrote in his diary: "I believe the pleasure they got was not so much from the society of their visitors as from their own power to give comfort and assistance to others." The essence of the California character is no longer the dominant part of today's California. The California character and spirit became world known and was referred to as the the "true spirit of California." Vancouver was at a loss, however, to explain why the Spaniards had settled in a region so far from Mexico and the rest of the civilized world.

Many of those visits by these foreigners passed without notice to history, but that is not true of all these visits. The Russian Count Nikolas Rezanov, needing supplies for the Russian settlement at Sitka, Alaska, landed his ship and went ashore. He started to deal with the Comandante Argüello who at the time did not trade with him. As the time passed and Rezanov realized that it was futile to hurry the Spaniards, he joined the life of the colony. It is during that time that he fell in love with Concepción, the daughter of the comandante. Her indulgent parents gave in; the Franciscans finally consented, pending sanction by the Czar and the Pope. Rezanov would return to San Francisco after going to St. Petersburg. He sailed away, promising to return to marry Concepción, but on his way to Russia he fill ill and died.

Upon learning of his death, ten years later, she still refused to marry, and spent her life in caring for the sick. The story of Concepción's love and her life of sacrifice was known to the Californians, and her name was revered by everyone.

Several of the early visitors left their marks in the Spirit of California. We find a fitting passage in the correspondence of the botanist, Adalbert von Chamisso, who arrived on board the Russian frigate Rurik in 1816. "How inspiring to have in my nostrils the tang of salt, mingled with the good herb. . . ." In his visit to the Valley he was charmed by the poppy blooms. He declared this to be the one flower he had seen that fully expressed the beauty of the country. The poppy today is the official state flower of California.

California was the "new" place to visit. It was full of new things. Scientists from all over came to collect specimens of new trees and herbs. The Scottish horticulturist, David Douglas, from Glasgow, Scotland, made the first gold discovery in California. At the time he found the nugget, while collecting sample firs for shipment, it did not create a stir but it was the first gold found. Gold was to be the major factor in the development of California.

Douglas had a watch made from the sample ore, but the major contribution to California came in the form of his name being attached to a tree he was successful in growing, the Douglas fir, the Douglas spruce.

If one had to pick the most influential visitor to California, one would have to say it was Captain Frederick Beechey. He was the first to make a complete survey of the bay. He renamed the islands and gave them their permanent names. The maps and charts of Captain Beechey gave courage to the sea captains who had not yet ventured

to this faraway place. It took one year to sail from Boston to California, quite an investment of money and time without a sure and accurate map. With this survey available to the captains, the traffic increased tremendously, and this traffic changed this remote port fast.

The social structure of Alta California was made up of all but the normal aristocratic, democratic strata that normally can be found in a growing society. At the top were the European Franciscans and Spanish governors. Below them came the officers' corps, of which none were Spaniards. The early settlers were of mixed origin: native American, negro and Mexican. The mixed marriages between the soldiers and the native Americans (Indians) was common practice. The last class category were the *Cholos,* or Mexicans of the lowest social categories, who accompanied the soldiers as servants and handymen.

The Californians had it too easy and had not yet focused their attention on politics, so when in 1821 Mexico declared its independence from the Spanish Crown, it did not really faze them too much. The new flag went up and the Mexican Government appointed its first governor, Luis Antión Argüello. He was well liked and life in the ranchos and pueblos went on as before.

The mythology of California as a land of opportunity has its origins in the soldiers turned rancheros who established a way of life to which many persons still aspire. Their service to the Crown and economic conditions of the Mexican Government permitted them to amass these large land holdings, and within a generation had trans-

formed themselves into a powerful provincial aristocracy. We find sufficient evidence that the California presidial society was disaffected toward the civil government, the mission fathers, and the Mexicans; no movement for independence even began before 1822.

The missions flourished, and they could report staggering holdings. Misión Dolores could boast seventy-six thousand head of cattle, nine hundred and fifty tame horses, two thousand breeding mares, seventy-nine thousand sheep, eighteen thousand bushels of wheat and barley, and thirty thousand dollars in merchandise. This certainly confirms the projections of Father Serra, when he urged the Viceroy to provide him with the initial breeding stock.

The Mexican Government started to secularize the California missions. All the property and the control over the Indians was taken from the Fathers. The government ordered the Fathers to attend to the spiritual needs of the people and gave them their church for it, but that was all they retained. The Indians were to receive the land and cattle. Town councils that were to govern matters of law and order were established. The final order to convert the missions into pueblos came in 1834 from the sixth governor, José Figueroa.

The soldiers who had come from New Spain because of lack of opportunity at home, married and remained on the lands, once their tour of duty was finished. These persons formed clans and expanded their holdings once the missions were secularized. This gave them a tremendous opportunity to become big landlords. There was nothing to stop them, since there were no major influxes of settlers

Above: The Monterey Custom House Seal, a wood cut that was used to validate sealed papers. Below: Raising the Bear Flag, finished Mexican rule of SAN FRANCISCO, April 1846.

until the 1849 gold rush.

The time that followed for California was grim indeed. The Mexican Government was in no position to pay the governor on a regular basis and, in turn, the governor could not pay his cavalrymen. This condition forced the governor to take private loans from the citizens, mostly foreigners. As this condition of near bankruptcy continued, it was impossible for the governor to pay back his loans. Consequently, one of the methods he used in paying his debts was in giving land grants.

The year 1846 for California was the most significant year prior to the gold rush. In April of 1846 the Revolutionary Party led by Ezekiel Merritt and William B. Idle were planning to declare California a republic. In Sonoma they captured the Mexican General Mario Vallejo and all his aides. As military prisoners they were sent to Sutters Fort. A flag for the new republic had been made from a piece of unbleached cotton. In the upper left-hand corner was painted a five-pointed star in red. Facing this was the figure of a grizzly bear, emblem of strength. He was colored black with pokeberry juice. A stripe of red flannel was sewed to the flag's lower edge and lettered in black, "California Republic." This was the bear flag, and it finished Mexican rule of San Francisco. This republic lasted only twenty-six days.

On May 3, 1846, the United States had declared war on Mexico. The news reached Yerba Buena that Commodore John Drake Stout had raised the American flag over the customs house in Monterey on July 7th. The following day, on July 8th, the Vice-Consul of Yerba Buena (San Francisco) received a note from the commander of the U.S.S. Portsmouth. The commander, John B. Montgomery, announced that he would lead a body of armed men ashore at seven o'clock the next morning. They would march to the flagstaff in the plaza, where the flag of the United States would be hoisted under a twenty-one-gun salute from the *Portsmouth*.

Next morning, July 9, 1846, the citizens of Yerba Buena watched as the men of the ship marched to the plaza. Fife and drum played "Yankee Doodle" as Commander Montgomery stepped to the flagpole and gave the order to raise the Stars and Stripes.

After the reading of the proclamation, the commander gave the signal to his ship, from which a twenty-one-gun salute roared through the air as the U.S. flag, whipped by a brisk wind, displayed its colors. California now was part of the United States of America.

John H. Brown, one of those present, said afterward, "When we heard that fife and drumbeat, there was great rejoicing among the few of us whe were in the village. Before, we were friends from different countries. Now we were brothers whose hearts swelled with pride and patriotism at thoughts of being under the protection of the United States Government."

The American takeover created some confusion. Nobody in San Francisco was any longer sure who owned what. Alcatraz was no exception in the general real estate confusion.

The Spaniards and the Mexicans had no interest in Alcatraz. From 1775 to 1845 the island belonged to the birds from which it derived its name, the pelicans. The soft sandstone, the absence of vegetation and fresh water, and its 130-foot cliffs were sure to discourage any settlers from occupation. The nearby mainland was so rich in the natural resources and so large in space that there was no need to tackle this island.

In 1893 a Mr. W. H. Pratt in a letter to H. T. Gordon stated that he had found an alleged grant of the island of Alcatraz by Governor Manuel Micheltorena dated 18 December, 1843, to José Ives Limantour, which was rejected in 1858 by the United States District Court. This grant was undoubtedly an effort by the Governor to pay off his debts to some of these foreigners.

This period of land-granting in exchange for debts created a terrible mess in the U.S. courts. The land grant in regard to Alcatraz that occupied the courts the longest was that of Julian William Workmann, granted to him by then Governor Pío Pico.

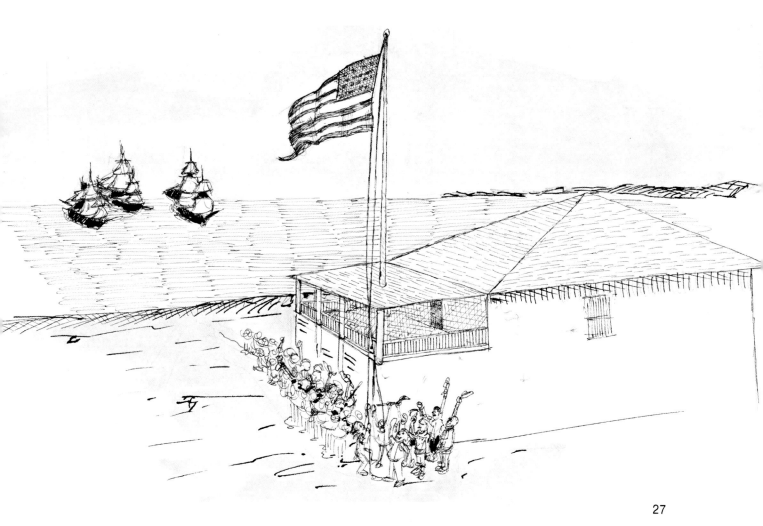

U.S. Ship Portsmouth
Yerba Buena July 8th 1846

Sir,

At passed seven o'clock to morrow
morning I propose landing a considerable
body of men under arms, And to march
them from the boats to the flag staff,
in Yerba Buena, upon which, at 8 o'clock,
I shall hoist the Flag of the U. States,
under a salute of twenty one guns, from
the ~~ship~~ Portsmouth, after which, the
Proclamation of the Commander in Chief,
Commodore Sloat, will be read in both
languages for the information of all class.

I will thank you therefore to have
it translated and ready for that purpose
at the appointed hour - And be pleased
to present my compliments to the Alcaldy, and say, ~~to him~~ if agreeable to him
I shall be gratified to see him present
on the occasion, that I may, under the
authority of the Proclamation, confirm
him in his official position - until
the pleasure of the ~~Commander~~ in
Chief shall be known.

Very Respectfully
&c &c
Jno B. Montgomery
Commander

To
Willm A Leidesdorff Esqr
Vice Consul of the U. States
Yerba Buena

Workmann, a naturalized citizen, had petitioned the governor for this island. The real reason as to why he wanted this completely bare, useless piece of real estate is unknown. One must guess that his reasons for wanting this "worthless" island were in speculation of selling it to a government. Even then it was clear that eventually this island would have an important strategic position in the defense of this harbor.

Pío Pico, on June 8, 1846, granted the island of Alcatraz to Julian Workmann, in order to settle two loans of amounts that were never established. There was a condition the governor attached to this grant. He wrote: "Under the sole condition that he (Workmann) cause to be established as soon as possible a light which may give protection on dark nights to ships and smaller vessels which may pass there."

Workmann accepted the condition as a face-saving device meant to mix a private transaction with a little civic purpose. there is no record of Workmann ever having set foot on the island. He certainly did not erect a light on the island or anything else, for that matter. He transferred ownership of Alcatraz to his brother-in-law, Francis Temple. The why and when Workmann "conveyed" Alcatraz is not clear.

Francis Temple is said to have sold the island to the newly-installed governor, John C. Fremont, for $5,000. As is later stated, Temple claimed he never received the $5,000 from Fremont. Fremont stated he had given a bond for the purchase money in his official capacity as Governor of California. The federal government, however, claimed that Fremont had been designated "legal representative of the United States" when he made this purchase, and promptly rejected this sale on the grounds he did not have proper authority to make it.

After that decision by the government, Fremont figured that the island then, indeed, belonged to him and eventually, through Simon Stevens of New York, paid $5,000 to the holder of the bond (Francis Temple).

In the 1850's the name of Temple disappeared from the records, but not so that of Fremont. In 1855 the San Francisco law firm of Palmer Cook and Company, which seemed to specialize in land litigation that involved the federal government, entered the case either on behalf of Fremont or in partnership with him.

The engineer in charge of the works on Alcatraz, Major Zealous Bates Tower, notified Chief Engineer Joseph Totten that, "Messers Palmer Cook and Company have commenced suit against him personally for trespassing in occupying Alcatraz." The U.S. Government was convinced that Alcatraz was U.S. property and proceeded to fortify it.

Through the years there have been many claims in the courts for the land in the San Francisco area, including Alcatraz. The most formidable one must have been that of a Mr. L. M. José Y. Limantour, an ex-captain in the French Navy. He had lived in Mexico and showed up in California in 1852 with claims to 620,000 acres of land, which included three-quarters of San Francisco, Alcatraz, Yerba Buena, Angels Island and the Farallones. His claims were so incredible that they reached all the way to today's Stockton.

The San Francisco claim alone was valued at $15,000,000 — and everybody called him "The Mad Man." All were not so sure of his madness when handwriting experts pronounced the signatures on his documents genuine.

He retained John B. Felton as his legal brain and promptly won the first legal round. The Land Commission granted his two most valuable claims, San Francisco and the bay islands, including Alcatraz. The property owners hired the great lawyer, Edward M. Stanton, to face the legal brain of Limantour.

The break did not come from legal maneuvers, but, instead, it came from an ex-partner of Limantour who blew the whistle on him and testified to the alleged fact that the documents were false.

The final twist came to this incredible claim when the testimony which Limantour's ex-buddies had given was proven to be as phony as his claims. The signatures on the documents were genuine but the grants were not. They had been fabricated by Mexican officials — including President Mariano Arista — after they had already lost California, probably as revenge.

Drawer 95.
Sheet 107.

Note   This Island is chiefly composed of
irregularly stratified sandstone
covered with a thin coating of
guano.   The stone is full
of seams in all directions   which
render it unfit for any
building purposes & probably
difficult to quarry
the island has no beach &
but two or three points where
small boats can land

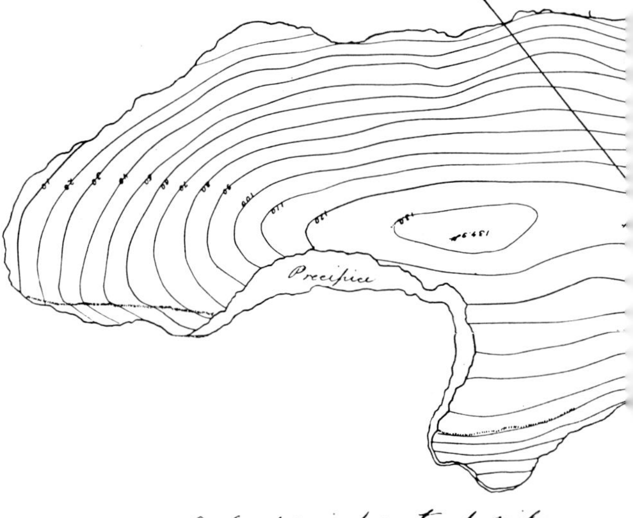

Precipice

Scale 40 inches to 1 mile

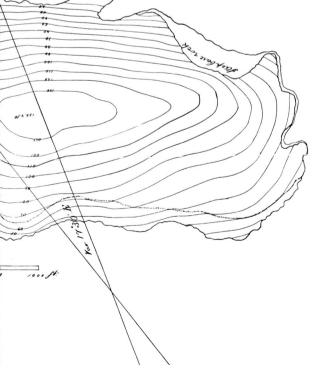

'Field Map
of
"Isla de los Alcatrazes" San Francisco Harbor
Surveyed by
Lieut. W. H. Warner U.S. Topl. Engr
assisted by
Mr. N. S. Beston Washington D.C.
May 1847

(sd) W. H. Warner
1st. U. Topl. Engr

The shape of the land, the product from it and its make-up always seem to be the key to man's evolution. Some of the geological features were responsible for many of the events that shaped nations. Alcatraz Island was once just a rocky sandstone hill in one of the fertile Coast Range valleys now occupied by the Bay of San Francisco. The Sacramento River flowed through these valleys, emptying into the ocean outside the Farallone Islands. Ages ago several hundred square miles of rich valley lands were washed away and submerged by the sea. As a result of that natural disturbance, several of the higher rocky hills were now entirely surrounded by water and became islands.

Alcatraz Island was first surveyed in May of 1847 by Lt. William Horace Warner, Corps of Topographical Engineers. This land survey is one of the very first land surveys conducted by the newly formed Tenth Military Department on the Pacific Coast. This Tenth Military Department was created per General Order No. 49, War Department Adjutant General's Office, November 3, 1846, and was actually established in Monterey in February of 1847. In many ways it becomes clear that the Federal Government was looking at Alcatraz as a vital strategic point on the Pacific Coast.

Warner's map, as it is referred to, does become the basic document for a 20 year planning of the bay defense. The Military Department's desire for the survey map supports the yet unwritten realization that Alcatraz would play an important part in the scheme of defense.

The Federal Government considered itself the rightful owner of Alcatraz. President Fillmore in 1850 ordered Alcatraz Island reserved from future sale. The Army Board of Engineers for the Pacific Coast confirmed that belief in 1851 when it wrote it was under the impression "that our government had succeeded to the right of property in that and other islands — which had been vested in the Mexican Government."

For California and San Francisco the years of 1846-1852 are probably the most active years of any state during development. Besides the political growth and the establishing of working systems for a state, California had to start with the pressure of speculators, prospectors, and investors, all hoping to get rich from the gold discoveries. When you have wide open land that overnight becomes attractive and desirable by everybody, the worst in man surfaces. Greed and dishonesty are the rules that govern the course of action, until the power structure can establish laws and agencies to keep order.

It was generally assumed that upon the signing of the treaty of peace with Mexico (February 2, 1848) Congress would enact territorial legislation for California. Congress, however, was too deeply involved in other matters and neglected California. As a result of the inaction of Congress, the people of California adopted their own Constitution, elected their own governor, legislature, judiciary, and other civil officers. The final legislature of California met December 15, 1849, and adopted laws for the government of the state.

☆ ☆ ☆ ☆ ☆ ☆

H.R. 685

December 20, 1848

Mr. Caleb B. Smith, from the Committee on Territories reported the following bill:

A bill to establish the territorial government of upper California.

Be it enacted by the Senate and House of Representatives of the United States of America in Congress assembled, that from and after the first day of April in the Year of Our Lord eighteen hundred and forty-nine all the part of the territory of the United States, known and designated as Upper California, shall be organized into and constitute a temporary government by the name of the territory of Upper California.

✨ ✨ ✨ ✨ ✨ ✨ ✨ ✨

California is unique among the states in that it had its own government in operation before it was legally recognized and accepted into the family of states by the Congress of the United States. California was admitted into the Union by an Act of Congress on September 9, 1850.

During this period of development Alcatraz lay waiting to become a major key in the overall development of the San Francisco territory and its defense. Had not gold been the major attraction during this time of development, things in the bay area might have developed differently. One of the major problems during that time was the shortage of labor. Sailors arriving on board of long journey ships would desert and head for the gold. The problem was so severe that it prevented ships from sailing, for lack of crew.

The first law put on its books by the Town Council of San Francisco addressed itself to this problem:

U.S.S. Portsmouth (A), transports, a schooner and a merchantman anchored in SAN FRANCISCO Bay, formerly Yerba Buena Cove, 1847

The problem of deserting seamen greatly affected the joint Board of Engineers surveying the San Francisco Bay Area in early April of 1849. This Board of Engineers came into being after the U.S. Congress appropriated funds for the examination of the Pacific Coast. The members of this joint Board of Engineers and Naval officers were three Army engineers: Maj. John L. Smith, Maj. Cornelius A. Ogden and First Lt. Danville Leadhelter; and three Naval officers: Comdr. Lewis M. Goldsborough, Comdr. G.S. Van Brunt, and Lt. Simon F. Blunt. Blunt had been in San Francisco Bay before as a member of the Wilkes Expedition.

The task of this board was to recommend what to do with lands reserved for public use. At the end of March, 1850, the board recommended that the three islands in San Francisco Bay, Yerba Buena, Angel and Alcatraz, be reserved for public use. Their thinking was clearly reflected in their final report dated November 1, 1850, which read:

The first consideration in connection with defense would be to prevent the passage of hostile vessels through the channel of entrance (Golden Gate). This would be difficult as the narrowest part of the entrance is about a mile wide and a vessel might pass through with the speed of 10 or 12 knots if favored by a strong fair wind, not unusual there, and the flood tide, estimated at 3 knots. The difficulty might be obviated by having, in addition to a strong battery on each shore, at the narrowest part . . . a third battery on Alcatrazos Island which lies within the Bay . . . and which, although about two miles from the other batteries would in cooperation with them and with a temporary battery on Point Jose at the South and another on Angel Island at the North, concentrate the fire of so many guns upon any vessels that might get past the front line batteries, that they would be destroyed or so disabled as to become harmless.

After submitting this recommendation the officers urged the immediate fortifications of Fort Point, Lime Point and Alcatraz. With this recommendation they were confident that the Bay Area would be protected from any intrusions. Alcatraz had already been declared reserved for a military reservation by President Fillmore. The cost of a battery on Alcatraz would be $600,000.

Activity around the Bay Area increased at a fast pace. Gold was discovered at Sutter's Mill in the spring of 1848, but the news did not reach the East Coast until September of 1849. This news immediately set off the thousands of hopefuls, young and old, obsessed with the dream of becoming rich. Everybody clamored for passage to the gold fields. Maybe it's hard for us today to envision what that meant. Today we go to the airport and in several hours we are on either coast. In 1849 it meant sailing around Cape Horn. This voyage took 240 days and would include 2 to 3 weeks of stormy sailing to negotiate the Straits of Magellan. Men who risked these hardships were motivated by the dreams of profit.

33

The early seekers for wealth in
California were called the "FORTY NINERS"

Not all these dreams were based on finding gold but having the supplies to sell to those settlers searching for gold. Food supplies were scarce in the Bay Area. The current supply from Mexico and local sources were inadequate and needed to be reinforced from the east.

The San Francisco Market in 1849 was wild. To best illustrate the profit range, let us consider the following price samples. In the summer of 1849 Franklin A. Buch disposed of two prefabricated houses for two thousand eight hundred dollars. He had purchased them in Maine for less than three hundred dollars. Hemlock boards bought in Belfast for ten dollars per thousand feet were sold for three hundred dollars per thousand feet, a three thousand percent profit.

In 1849 there were only ten sawmills active in California with an estimated annual production of five thousand board feet. No local brick industry was yet developed. Those were the two main building materials the mainland needed. A ship arriving from the east could only carry a certain amount of materials, obviously a small part of what was actually needed. A typical load of a vessel, as seen from the manifest for the brig North Carolina which dropped anchor in San Francisco on June 4, 1850 was:

571,000	feet white pine boards for frames
199,000	shingles
49	kegs nails
25	boxes window frames
24	boxes house materials
10,000	boards
8	tons mill gear
3	hundred weight dried apples
20	boxes tin
17	bundles wire
94,000	bricks

This kind of reality must have weighed heavily on the minds of those men responsible in making any recommendations for the defense development of the Pacific Coast.

On June 17, 1851 the defense of San Francisco Bay moved forward when Chief Engineer Totten established a Board of Engineers for the Pacific Coast. They did their planning from Washington D.C. Totten then prepared a report on the national defense of the United States. In this report he agreed with the old joint commission's recommendation on what should be done with Alcatraz: mainly, that Alcatraz is a "First Class" defense position and should be developed at once.

In October of 1851, in Washington, D.C., the planning of the defenses of San Francisco formally started. The board members consisted of three members from the old joint Board and two new members. The former members were Smith (the senior member), Ogden and Leadbetter (the recorder). The two new members were Capt. James J. Mason, a veteran of the Mexican War, and Capt. Frederic A. Smith, who died two months after the plans were completed.

Major John Lind Smith, a member of the original board, did not agree with the recommendations of the current board. As the procedures allowed, he filed a separate minority report. The main objectives of this board were to consider the following:

First, to prevent the passage of enemy ships into the harbor; secondly, to be in a position to destroy such vessels should they gain entrance; and, lastly, to have an interior line of batteries that could block the three passages with gunfire. The three passages are between Alcatraz and San Francisco, between Alcatraz and Angel Island, and through Raccoon Straits.

Considerations had to be given to the range of the weapons available in the U.S. Arsenal. The main range that had to be considered for effective fire power were 1_4 miles and 2 miles. The board addressed itself to that question in the following paragraph:

Nature seems to have provided a redoubt for this purpose in the shape of Alcatrazes Island — situated abreast the entrance directly in the middle of the inner harbor, it covers with its fire the whole of the interior space lying between Angel Island to the North, San Francisco to the South, and the outer batteries to the West . . . . It is just three miles from each of the Entrance forts and consequently takes up the fire dropped by them at the 1_4 mile range. A vessel pass-

Sunset over San Francisco Bay, 1880
Alcatraz Island on the right

ing directly to San Francisco must pass within a mile; and the center of the city is about two miles distant. A vessel approaching the city from the north by the Riley channel (east of Angel Island) must pass within two miles of Alcatrazes — thus the main object of preventing an anchorage in the harbor within range of the town may be accomplished from this position and Rincon Point.

On August 4, 1852, the board submitted its plans, estimates and memoirs to Totten. The main recommendations for Alcatraz were all based on Warner's 1847 survey map and were signed by the majority (four-fifths) of the board. The barbette battery, one for each end of the island, a caponier (a small, strongly-built structure with guns mounted internally to provide flanking fire for the protection of the guns of the barbette battery), a defensive barrack and a guard house could complete the works.

The island being high and provided with a natural scarp (almost vertical cliffs) in many places, it has been decided to complete this escarpment (by removing the gentler slopes) so as to secure a perpendicular height of 25 feet all around . . . .

A battery of 20 guns is proposed to cover the passage to the North in conjunction with Angel Island, and a battery of 23 guns to cover the Southern passage. Three guns of this latter battery are designed to prevent a fleet flying to the east of the island.

By blasting a small triangular ditch from the solid rock of which the whole island is composed, for a length of 690 feet (principally in front of the batteries), a height of at least 25 feet is secured (for the natural scarp), flanked for the greater portion of its length.

A ramp (or road) at the wharf (to be built on the east side of the island, out of sight from the Golden Gate) is excavated from reference (10) to reference (30) (that is, from an elevation of ten feet above sea level near the wharf to a point 310 feet distant that was thirty feet above sea level): — on the upper end of this ramp a wall being constructed on the inside . . . .

A guard house is placed at the upper end of the ramp enfilading it with 4 mountain howitzers or other small pieces: this guard house also enfilades the ditch on the other side (the "ditch" here became a covered road that led to the northwest battery).

A defensive barrack capable of accomodating

Military Reservation Alcatraz Island.

This Island is situated in San Francisco Bay, and was preserved for Military purposes by the Presidents order of Nov. 6. 1850.

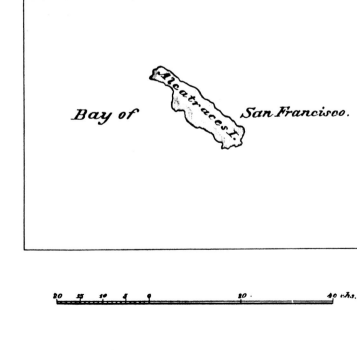

comfortably 100 men in bunks, is placed on the Southern end of the island having a good view of the Southern battery, and seeing the northeast slope of the island as far as the Northern caponier. This barrack is provided with a parapet on the top & the windows of the second story are to be provided with iron bars, thus securing a height of about 33 feet.

The defensive barracks were designed to house enlisted men's rooms, officers' quarters, a guardroom, and cells. Next to the building was located a cistern capable of supplying water to 200 men for six months. The water problem was of great concern since Alcatraz did not have its own water supply. The powder would be stored under each caponier. The total estimated cost as submitted by the board came to $300,000.

Masonry:

Brick:
South Caponier . . . . 5,005 cubic feet
North Caponier . . . . 5,005 cubic feet
Guardhouse . . . . 2,237 cubic feet
Defensive Barracks . . . . . 44,056 cubic feet
    56,303 cu. ft. at 36 cu. yd. $75,060

Brick and Concrete:
South Caponier . . . . . . 27,975 cubic feet
North Caponier . . . . . . 32,970 cubic feet
    60,945 cu. ft. at 18 cu. yd. 56,425

Concrete:
South Battery . . . . 54,159 cubic feet
North Battery . . . . 33,380 cubic feet
Wall of Ramp . . . . 2,700 cubic feet
    90,329 cu. ft. at 18 cu. yd. 60,030

Excavation of rock:
    267,500 cu. ft. at $3 cu. yd. 29,733

Asphalt: 638 sq. yds. at $2 sq. yd. 1,276
Stone Steps: 10 at $20 each 200
Finishing 2 magazines 2,000
Embrasures in caponiers: 16 at $120 each . . 1,600
Iron girders for barracks: 36 at $120 each . . 4,320
Loopholes in barracks: 110 at $20 each 2,200

Finish of barracks, including wooden floors and stairs, plastering part of walls, kitchen arrangements, doors, windows, grading of yard, etc. . . 25,000

For wharf, roadway to top of island, making inaccessible such points of the precipices as are not so, and for unforseen expenses 37,856

                                 $300,000

With these recommendations and cost factors the general course of action was established. This was the first serious commitment for the work necessary in building up Alcatraz to fulfill the defense position needed for the San Francisco Bay. A lot of changes and helpful recommendations by various engineers would be forthcoming, but the program of fortification of Alcatraz was now established.

With all the recommendations completed, all that really was needed now was the money from Congress. The gold rush had greatly changed this silent bay and brought in a tremendous increase in population and commerce, yet San Francisco in 1853 was still without any permanent protection. This prompted the correspondence between Totten and Maj. John L. Smith where we find the latest estimates by the majority and minority (Smith).

Majority estimate

Fort Point, ...107 guns $1,000,000
Lime Point, ... 80 guns 600,000
Alcatraz Island, ... 43 guns 300,000
Total $1,900,000

Minority estimate

Fort Point, ...205 guns $1,400,000
Lime Point, ... 80 guns 600,000
Alcatraz Island, ...120 guns 340,000
Total $2,340,000

The entire board concluded that the works could be completed in five years.

On February 7, 1853, the Congress appropriated $500,-000 for fiscal year 1854 to begin the fortification of San Francisco Bay. We should note here that the army did not obtain possession of Lime Point for fifteen years, thus giving Alcatraz more priority in the total development.

Action was relatively swift and we can read in the correspondence from Totten that he wanted fast action on Alcatraz. In one letter to James Mason he writes, "Any delay not inevitable, will be a fault of ours exclusively; and a very great fault — the cause, possible, of a great calamity."

Totten selected all the members for the board and one of the new members was Zealous Bates Tower who transferred in June 1853 from Portland, Maine. Tower was in charge of Alcatraz. Assigned to him as assistant was Frederick E. Prime.

Upon arriving in San Francisco on August 5, Tower found Mason sick with "Panama Fever." This was unfortunate since Tower was anxious to start on Alcatraz. Before calling a board meeting he went to Alcatraz. His first impressions are recorded in a letter he sent to Totten on August 15, in which he writes:

"The island is rougher than I had anticipated — very rough, steep, and broken on the Eastern portion of the (proposed) Northwest Battery and where the 3 gun battery is designed to be placed. I have commenced the survey of the North West and South East portions of the island. The constant prevalence of high winds delays this work much. . . . The sandstone composing the island is very friable, even where hardened on the surface it can be cut with a hatchet. Wrought iron spikes can be driven into the rock without much trouble."

August, 1853, Alcatraz was taken from the birds. Man had started to change this natural habitat to a man-made fortification. In the operation journal of Tower it is written that he had procured a whaleboat, hired civilian masons, carpenters, and laborers and was starting the construction of the temporary buildings. Tower and Prime with the help of hired laborers were busy completing a new survey of the island. This survey was done in 5-foot contour lines and considered more accurate than Warner's map.

In most of the correspondence to come we find a lot of dialog on the cost of this undertaking. This is understandable since the prices of East Coast goods and services were considerably different. The first recommendation Tower made to Totten was for additional storerooms and barracks. He also expressed a concern for a too-low cost estimate by the 1852 board. The typical wages at that time were as follows:

Masons . . . . $10 to $12 per day
Carpenters . . . . $7 to $8 per day
Blasters . . . . $4 to $5 per day
Laborers . . . . $3 to $5 per day
Lumber . . . . $50 to $60 per M
Best brick . . . . $25 per M
Rubble stone . . . . $5 to $8 per ton
Stone for work in courses — perhaps . .60¢ a foot

There was a slowing down of progress on Alcatraz. This was due to the available appropriations. In December, 1853, Tower was informed by Totten that armament was being sent to Alcatraz. This first shipment consisted of thirty-three 8-inch and 10-inch columbiads. This prompted the start of construction on the permanent terrepleins. The parapets (a low wall) could be built later. On the map prepared by Tower in September, 1854, one can see a temporary battery of Navy 68-pounders. The reason for this was that then Commander Birg. Gen. John E. Wood was growing uneasy and impatient with the delay in the ship-

Drawer 95.
Sheet 18.

Longitudinal Section and Elevation of North Carponnier.

Section and Elevation on 1.2.
Scale 1 Inch to 8 Feet or 9½

ALCATRACES ISLAND.
North Battery Sheet No 2.
showing details and progress of work on 30th Sept 1856.
drawn under the direction of Maj Z.B. Tower Corps of Engs.

Zo. B. Tower
1st Lt. Major Engs

Section and Elevation
on F F.   Scale 1 Inch to 4 Feet or fee

Section and Elevation on 3.4.
Scale 1 Inch to 8 Feet or 9½

Section and Elevation on 5.6
Scale 1 Inch to 8 Feet or 9½

Section and Elevation on 9.10.
Scale 1 Inch to 8 Feet or 9½

Section and Elevation on 7.8.
Scale 1 Inch to 8 Feet or 9½

Elevation of Embrasures.
Scale 1 Inch to 4 Feet or fee

Recess as constructed.
Scale 1 Inch to 4 Feet or fee

Recess in Angle.
Scale 1 Inch to 4 Feet or fee

Engineer Department
Received this day transmitted with Major
Tower's letter of 29 Oct (343) 1856 on't just any

95—18

ment of those columbiads. Gen. Wood insisted that Tower erect a temporary position for the guns available at that time.

The temporary battery had five Navy 68-pounders; another temporary battery on the west side contained three 24-pounder siege guns; a single Navy 68-pounder on the northwest peak, and two 24-pounder siege guns on the southeast peak, were the beginning of Alcatraz as a fortified place.

There was a fear in 1854 that either the Mexicans or the French would storm the harbor. The French threat was not unfounded; but on June 13, 1855, a battle near San Diego harbor settled that score. A Russian frigate, 83 guns, sank the French Corvette Egalite, 23 guns, that was to attack San Francisco. This fear helped speed up the fortification process of Alcatraz.

The news in March, 1854, that Fort Point would receive two-thirds of the appropriated $500,000 aggravated Tower, and he objected strongly to this unequal distribution. Tower's rationale, as expressed to Totten, was, "I urge equal distribution from my desire to see the work under my charge finished so that the Dept. may say San Francisco has one work mounted with guns ready to receive a garrison to stand between hostile ships and this large commercial city." He felt that Alcatraz could be ready before Fort Point and that was where more of the funds should go.

The newest member of the Pacific Board, Capt. John G. Bernard, called a meeting with Tower and Halleck to reconsider Alcatraz's defense. They agreed that the 1852 estimate of $300,000 was too low. They worked out some modifications of development plans and recommended a new budget of $600,000. Tower was notified that the modifications were approved. Orders came along with this approval that the caponiers be designed for 24-pounder howitzers, which had now been adopted for such a purpose.

The first annual report by Tower in 1854 showed a lot of construction had taken place. Alcatraz with its temporary Battery now became habitable, no longer a rock just for the birds.

Roads, wharves, batteries and buildings all started to give this island a new skyline. The "temporary building" built just for the construction workers remained also for some of the garrisons. Tower in his report of 1854 gives us a good description of these first buildings on Alcatraz:

Carpenters' Shop
This shop was 30 by 20 feet, with a tool room in the hall basement. It was situated on the edge of the road leading to the southeast battery. A wooden cistern, 12 by 10 by 6 feet stood outside the building at its northwest end.

Blacksmith Shop
This shop was 30 by 20 feet, had two forges. This stood near the main wharf, on a leveled spot on the cliff. A flight of steps led down to the wharf.

Two Storehouses
These storehouses were used for cement and lime, one 40 by 26 feet, the other 40 by 20 feet. Both were located leading to the northwest battery.

Stable
The stable was 30 by 20, with a hayloft above and grain room attached. It accommodated eight animals, and it stood by itself on the southwest side of the island.

325. Pirates Cove - Alcatraz Island

View of
Alcatraz in 1865

Messhouse

This building was 66 by 21 feet, with a kitchen attached, and was used for mechanics and laborers. Located at the southeast end of the island, adjacent to the five-gun temporary battery.

Laborers' Barracks

This barracks was 75 by 22 feet, with three tiers of bunks accommodating 96 men. It stood across the road from the messhouse.

Mechanics' Barracks

This barracks was 81 by 21 feet, with accommodations for 50 persons. It was located above the southeast barracks.

Office building

This 1½ story building also contained rooms for the master mason, the master carpenter, and the principal overseer. Its dimensions were 24 by 14 feet, with an ell 20 by 20 feet. It crowned the southeast peak, where the citadel would eventually stand.

Kitchen and Mess Room

This building was 26 by 12 feet, for master mechanics and principal overseer. The boarding housekeeper occupied the attic. This structure was not identified as such on Tower's map; but it may have been an unidentified building below the office, on the southwest side of the island.

Powder House

This structure was 10 by 10 feet and located just below the northwest peak.

Water Tank

This tank, made of plank, had a 23,000-gallon capacity. It stood between the storehouses and the wharf area. Water for general purposes, including concrete mixing, was secured under contract from the Sausalito Water Company.

A major problem during this first year of construction was the building material available in the San Francisco area, the availability of brick and stone being the main problem. One purpose for stone was to face the scarp walls. Quarries had already been opened in the bay, the major quarry being on Angel Island, but the blue sandstone was only available in limited quantities. At that time the engineers were sure this sandstone would be fit for facing the scarp walls.

Tower's concern on this matter made him consider other alternatives. The slow availability of this granite from Point Reyes and his doubt about the durability of sandstone alone made him decide to build the scarp walls of the southeast battery with sandstone and a concrete backing. In a letter from Totten to Tower ideas and ways of dealing with masonry were shared. By May, 1854, Tower was using blue sandstone. "The blue stone has been adopted for the South Battery . . . , I should not hesitate to use brick could the hard bricks of the East be obtained."

The west coast brick industry was still almost nonexistent. These eastern army engineers could not find any local brick hard enough, nor the desired quantity and price. Tower sent samples of local brick back east for testing. Totten, in July, 1854, wrote Tower that the large bricks from Contra Costa County seemed "rather tender from being underdone and too sandy . . . the small bricks from Contra Costa County were pretty hard and could be used for inside work." The bricks from Sacramento were the best. At a later date when the works on Alcatraz changed from sandstone to brick nearly all the bricks used came from Sacramento.

Today an incredible amount of brick is still visible on Alcatraz, walls up to 5 feet thick made from brick. The entire basement of the old citadel, powder storage rooms and archways are all brick. The brick and its use in this fortification played a major role. One must remember that Fort Point and Alcatraz were not the only buildings being built. A major world city was growing overnight, consuming an incredible amount of building material. The shortage of brick manufacture was somewhat alleviated by the state using prison brickyards and a brickyard established by the engineers themselves at Fort Point.

The problem of rocks and bricks caused Tower friction with his superior, Totten. There was also dissatisfaction on the part of the engineer at Fort Point, Bernard, who subsequently was transferred to Charleston, South Carolina. Bernard was replaced by Lt. Col. Rene E. de Russy. It was de Russy who gave Tower the needed support to deal with this building material problem.

After inspecting Alcatraz, de Russy wrote Totten, "I have visited Major Tower's work on Alcatraz Island and am gratified to find it progressing, in spite of the difficulty of procuring stone in this vicinity." The promise by him to Tower to visit the Bay Area quarries in an effort to work out better prices must have been a tremendous relief.

A change recommended by Tower in the position of the three guns pointing eastward and the building of a connecting wall between the two batteries was agreed upon by de Russy and forwarded to Totten. Totten readily approved this change of plans.

One year of activity had passed and Tower was reflecting on his early stated objectives. His objectives for that year were to bring the three batteries toward completion and to mount the first permanent guns on South Battery. In his report he states that the breast-high walls and the semi-circular walls for the wooden platforms were finished. The entire three-gun battery, with the exception of the coping on the scarp wall, was completed and that the North Battery scarp wall, except for the coping, was also complete. This in all is a remarkable accomplishment, considering the struggle with material and funds.

ALCATRACES ISLAND.

The international scene and friction would dominate the Congress. The major concern was that Spanish warships were in the Philippines and that was only a few thousand miles away from San Francisco. The conflict was over Cuba. In April of 1854 the Spanish authorities in Cuba seized a U.S. ship, the *Black Warrior*. Some members of Congress wanted to "wrestle it from Spain," this causing great concern to Spain. As chief engineer in charge of the fortification and security of the west coast, and specifically San Francisco, Totten's concern over the security and readiness of the bay against enemies grew. In a confidential letter to de Russy in San Francisco, Totten writes:

"You will have noticed in the newspaper that our foreign relations wear a somewhat threatening aspect . . . but a principal object, not yet touched upon in this letter is to direct your attention to efforts for making the utmost of the armament of thirty-three 8 and 10 columbiads, now on its way to your harbor. I fear that with the exception of the South Battery of Alcatraz Island perhaps only a part of that permanent provision will not have been made for the reception of these guns in battery . . . .

As to expenditures on batteries to be thrown up to supply a sudden need, you will not hesitate as to them, in any exigency that may present itself before a heavy armament shall have been accommodated in its proper place."

Late in 1853, Totten had written Tower that 43 columbiads would arrive on Alcatraz as soon as possible. Some of these prominent weapons left the New York Arsenal in the fall of 1854. The following request for shipment to Alcatraz and the West Coast Arsenal of Benicia, California, was made to the Quartermaster Department:

        4 10-inch columbiads
7 8-inch columbiads
8 8-inch barbette top carriages
8 8-inch barbette chassis
8 8-inch barbette platforms
13 boxes of pintle stone
96 10-inch shot
430 8-inch shot
384 10-inch shell
750 8-inch shell

As the first columbiad arrived on Alcatraz, Tower reported he could mount 53 guns in six months — if the funds were available. At the same time in Washington, D.C., Secretary of War Davis assembled a board of affairs to determine the up-to-date need of the sea coast's armament. There was some concern with the amount of firepower located in the bay area. Tower was informed that the guns on Alcatraz would eventually amount to ten 10-inch columbiads, thirty-three 8-inch columbiads, and ten 42-pounder guns with 24-pounder howitzers. Totten included a description on how to mount the 42-pounders. The columbiads could not handle "hot shot," thus the reason for the howitzers. The "hot shot" is meant to burn the ships, as this red hot piece of metal lands on deck. A special War Department order in 1855 ordered a set of 15-foot shot furnace irons shipped to Alcatraz. This was to heat up the solid shots.

The total 1855 allotment of guns to Alcatraz is as follows:

South Battery
        Right face (or long branch)
                4 10-inch columbiads
                4 8-inch columbiads
                5 42-pounders
        Left face (or short branch)
                2 10-inch columbiads
                2 8-inch columbiads
                5 42-pounders
        Caponier
                8 24-pounder howitzers
                        (4 on each side)
North Battery
                2 10-inch columbiads
                18 8-inch columbiads
        Caponier
                7 24-pounder howitzers

Correspondent of the London *Times* inspecting a 10-inch columbiad at Fort Pulaski

Proposed Eight-Gun Battery, Now Called West Battery
North Battery
        2 10-inch columbiads
        18 8-inch columbiads
    Caponier
        7 24-pounder howitzers
Proposed Eight-Gun Battery, Now Called West Battery
        2 10-inch columbiads
        6 8-inch columbiads
Three-Gun Battery
        3 8-inch columbiads

These batteries represented the first permanent American fortification on the Pacific Coast to have their guns mounted. On April 15, 1855, Tower had seven 8-inch columbiads mounted on the left face of South Battery. For Alcatraz this marked the beginning of permanent firepower. This was six years before the Civil War and just at the time when only the foundation at Fort Point had been completed.

The columbiads on Alcatraz were the 1844 model and were mounted on wooden barbette carriages. The 8-inch columbiad was 124 inches long and weighed 9,200 pounds. Its maximum range was 4,812 yards at an elevation of 27 degrees 30 minutes; the 10-inch columbiad on Alcatraz had a range of 5,654 yards at an elevation of 39 degrees 15 minutes. These columbiads were designed to fire shells but on Alcatraz they were used to fire solid shots too.

In March of 1855, Congress passed the appropriations for the coastal defense for the year 1856. This was early but may have been due to the increasing international tension. The new fiscal year would show a tremendous increase in armament on Alcatraz.

The recommendation from Tower to Totten regarding funds for Alcatraz reflects the concern for the defense posture of San Francisco:

Since the fortifications at this point will be almost entirely useless until finished, and would be liable to be seized by a boat attack from an enemy's squadron, further, as there is no fortified point in this important bay and harbor, I would earnestly recommend that $400,000 be appropriated by the next Congress to finish the defensive works upon Alcatraz Island. This amount will be expended in building the north battery, the 368-gun batteries, the barracks, and defensive line around the island, and should be available as soon as appropriated.

I would earnestly recommend that Congress appropriate $400,000 for finishing the defenses commenced upon Alcatraz, so that there may be one fortified and inac-cessible point in the important bay and harbor of San Francisco.

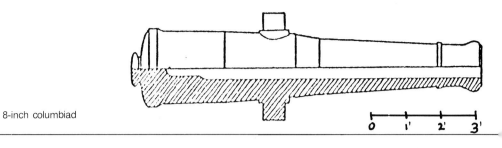

8-inch columbiad

0   1'   2'   3'

Based on these recommendations, Totten addressed the Congress with the following letter to accompany S. 659:

SENATE

33rd Congress   Mis. Doc.
2d Session   No. 14.

IN THE SENATE OF THE UNITED STATES

February 13, 1855. — Ordered to be printed.

(To accompany bill S. 659.)

LETTER
from
JOS. G. TOTTEN
Brevet Brigadier General and
Colonel of Engineers, with estimates for

Continuing the operations at the fort at Fort Point, and for continuing the operations on the defensive works at Alcatraz in the State of California.

ENGINEER DEPARTMENT
Washington, February 12, 1855.

SIR: On the subject of your letter of this date, addressed to the Hon. Secretary of War, I have the honor to furnish herewith estimates of the officers in charge at Fort Point and Alcatraz, for their respective works.

The estimate for the fort at Fort Point, San Francisco bay, for the year ending June 30, 1856, is $650,000; the officer requests "that this sum be asked from Congress for the fiscal year commencing July 1, 1855," and should this sum be now granted, the engineer expresses his belief that the work may be finished in the next fiscal year without difficulty.

One hundred and fifty thousand cubic yards of rock have been excavated from the site, and the officer in charge expected to commence the masonry foundations of the fort and of the 10-gun battery in January — this being the last report from him. We shall remit to him today, on his call, all the balance ($54,000) now remaining in the treasury for this fort.

The officer in charge of the works at Alcatraz recommends, "that Congress appropriates $400,000 for finishing the defences commenced upon Alcatraz."

He reports the left face of the south battery ready for eight guns, and the flanking caponnier high enough to be left for the present; so that the whole force may be turned upon the right face of the battery.

For this work there are in the treasury $29,500. Operations both here and at Fort Point have been much impeded by the smallness of last year's appropriations.

I have the honor to be, very respectfully, sir, your obedient servant,

JOS. G. TOTTEN
Brevet Brigadier General and
Col. Engineers.

Hon. Wm. M. Gwin,
Senate of United States.

P.S. —On the subject of the condition of the defences at San Francisco, the Engineer Department reported on the 18th of January, in answer to a resolution of the Senate, and this report has been printed.

The Pacific board met in April, 1856. From this meeting came a full review of Alcatraz and its role and development. The board in considering the total picture of the bay defense concluded that Alcatraz needed additional armament. "The most prominent position of this secondary line is Alcatraz Island. Its guns sweep a larger expanse of waters than those of any other point and it lies upon the two passes of ingress and egress most readily navigated. It has additional importance at this time from the advanced state of its batteries as compared with those of the outer line."

The strategic location of Alcatraz prompted the board to make additional recommendations. These had a more permanent ring to them. The guardhouse should be enlarged and fortified. The recommendation of a drawbridge and ditch (or moat) has a medieval ring to it but illustrates their concern with the possibility of enemy foot soldiers here on the island. The basement was to be used as a "prison."

Also recommended by the board was the enlargement of the barracks so as to house a war garrison. The inclusion of a hospital was mentioned in the place of office portions of the building. So we see a tremendous increase in desire to establish a major fortification post on Alcatraz. Tower received the approval by the Secretary of War for all recommendations except for the expansion of the barracks. The approval of de Russy's recommendation for ten additional guns would bring Alcatraz' gun total to 75.

Congress appropriated another $200,000 for Alcatraz for fiscal year 1857. With this Tower planned to finish the three existing batteries because he could not follow through with his goal. Colonel de Russy was found to have a serious lung disease and transferred to Fort Delaware. Tower succeeded him at Fort Point as engineer in charge and senior engineer for the Pacific Coast. Tower's assistant

Major-General James B. McPherson, U.S.A.

engineer, Lt. Fredrick Prime, rose from the shadow of Tower to take charge of Alcatraz.

Prime was in charge of Alcatraz for less than one year. During the summer and fall of 1857, he made several requests for a transfer. It finally came. And in December of 1857 he turned over charge of the fortification to 2nd Lt. James Birdseye McPherson.

In one of Prime's progress reports, he lists the labor force he employed on the island at that time.

    1 master mason & overseer
   11 masons
    4 stonecutters
    3 carpenters
    2 blacksmiths
    1 captain of sloop
    1 seaman
  101 laborers
    1 clerk
    2 sub overseers
    1 office attendant

In his annual report, he elaborates on the progress of the construction of the Guardhouse. This provides us with many details. The lower part of the Guardhouse was being built with the blue sandstone and with Chinese granite. This granite was part of the 2,000 tons ordered by Barnard in 1854 for Fort Point. The upper part of the Guardhouse was to be all built with brick. The brick walls of the gun room on the waterside already stood nine feet above the roadway. Work on the revetment wall on the inside of the road from the Guardhouse to the wharf area was in progress. This particular work brought some tragedy to the construction site. On the 9th of July, 1857, a massive landslide of crumbling rock, approximately 7,000 cubic feet, buried two workers. Daniel Pewter, 50, from Ireland, and Jacob Unger,

25, from Germany, died instantly under the weight of all this rock. The coroner's report made it clear that there was no blame to be attached to any parties for the deaths. There was a second slide in the same area, so Totten wrote Prime, giving him instructions on how to change the construction. Despite all the trouble with this wall, a large portion of it still stands.

Prime, in his report, expressed a concern with the state of deterioration of the main wharf; and before he left, he recommended a permanent iron piling wharf. The wharf subsequently became a major objective of McPherson.

McPherson arrived on Alcatraz, but he was depressed about his assignment. McPherson, born in Sandusky County, Ohio, on November 14, 1828, entered West Point in June of 1849 at the age of 20. He graduated at the head of his class.

Alcatraz Island was not really what this top-of-the-class graduate had in mind as a career. He had three years of experience building harbor fortifications around Wilmington, Delaware and New York. His mood and feelings about his assignment were not enhanced after he arrived in San Francisco. He arrived on the wooden side wheeler, *Golden Gate*. To arrive at the Golden Gate on the ship *Golden Gate*, and to be in charge of engineering the defense of the Golden Gate holds a certain irony.

The ship *Golden Gate* was a three-decked steamer built for the Pacific Mail Steamship Company at a cost of $482,844. It entered service between the Pacific Coast of Panama and San Francisco in November, 1951. The *Golden Gate* burned on July 27, 1862, off Manzanillo, Mexico. Today the Mexican Government is supporting Cedam, Mexico in the excavation and retrieval of fragments of the *Golden Gate*.

McPherson started living on Alcatraz and only went to San Francisco on weekends. In a letter to a friend in Wilmington, Delaware, he shares his feelings and impressions:

My dear "Major,"

Perched upon a little rocky Island the summit of which is one hundred and forty feet above the water and while watching the sun as he dips into the broad Pacific, or listening to the never ceasing roar of the breakers dashing against the rocks, I often think of my position one year ago, and instinctively draw a comparison between it and my present one — Candor compels me to state that in everything appertaining to the social amenities of life the "Pea Patch" is preferable to "Alcatraz," and were it not, that being here in charge of this work is very gratifying to my professional pride I should regret the change deeply, as it is all my pride is scarcely sufficient at times to keep my spirits up — though I am determined to make the best of the matter, looking forward joyfully to the time when I can return to the Atlantic States.

I have made but few acquaintances as yet in San Francisco, though I go over every Saturday evening and remain until Monday morning, and frequently at other times during the week when I get tired of playing the hermit —

Fate or circumstances, or perhaps both combined have arranged it so that I am doomed to live on Islands, and though it may sound very poetical in the distance to speak of the "Gems of the Pacific" and all this manner of thing, I have not attained that sublime height of sentimentality, which places me above the practical unromantic incidents of every day life, and consequently hear something besides music in the deep sea's roar, especially as I get a good wetting about every third time I go over to Town — San Francisco beats all the cities I have ever been in, in the way of Drinking Saloons, Billiard Tables, Cigar Stores and idle men — "loafers" genteely dressed, and if you happen accidentally (sic) to make the acquaintance of

one of them, before you are aware of it, you will be introduced to any number more — for they have the greatest way of introducing folks I have ever seen —

I often congratulate myself when I am in Town, that I have a place to flee to, where the air is pure and where I can avoid meeting people whom I do not care to know — for the more of them you know the worse you are off —

There is the most heterogenous mixture of people in this country, that you can possibly imagine — In a short walk through most any of the streets of San Francisco you will meet Americans, Englishmen, Frenchmen, Russians, Germans, Sandwich Islanders, Chinamen, Sepoys and various nondescript races to (sic) numerous to mention and the confusion of tongues will rival "Babel" of old —

The climate of this country is perfectly delightful at this season of the year — scarcely cold enough for frost, and the atmosphere perfectly transparent — I have seen no snow except on the distant mountain tops since I arrived— . . .

Your sincere friend

"Mac"

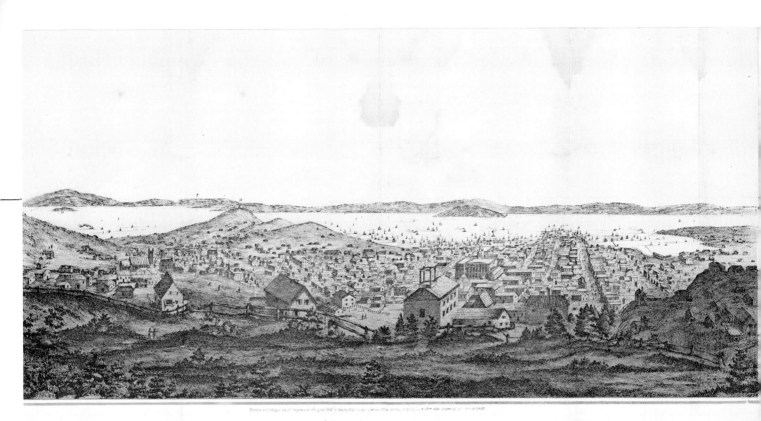

SAN FRANCISCO.
1857.

Published for the History of the World by Henry Bill New York

1 North Bay
2 Contra Costa
3 Yerba Buena Island
4 California Exchange
5 Plaza
6 Leonards Warehouse
7 Rincon Point

1 Market Street Pier
9 California Street
10 Central Wharf
11 Catholic Church
12 Marine Telegraph
13 Angell Island

McPherson was immediately involved in the work on Alcatraz. First he bought a new boat to help with transport from the mainland. The bricks stacked on the top of the hairpin road constructed by Prime were a constant reminder to McPherson of the job ahead of constructing the defensive barracks.

A thrilling moment must have occurred on April 19, 1858, when McPherson got to fire the 8-inch columbiad in a 21-gun salute. This salute was in honor of the British corvette, *Satellite*, entering San Francisco Bay. McPherson was chosen to give the salute; and since no military was on Alcatraz, it is not clear who helped him fire those columbiads. It could well be the masons and carpenters. He writes to Totten, "Last Saturday I had to awaken to echoes of the Island by returning the salute of the English corvette, *Satellite*. I fired twenty-one guns from 8-inch Columbiades which require something like twelve pounds of powder for a load, so you can imagine what kind of report they mack (sic)." One wonders if this ship's captain knew that no army was on Alcatraz. The *Satellite* was a screw-corvette, one of the largest wooden corvettes ever built for the Royal Navy: 1,042 tons, 400 horsepower, 21 guns and 206 men. This ship played a major part in the conflict that developed later in July of 1859 in the Pacific Northwest over the dispute of the San Juan Islands.

One of McPherson's major projects was the building of the defensive barracks. In his first annual report he stated the condition of this building. The excavation for the barracks and the cistern had been completed. All walls up to the main floor were standing and the brick arches for the

basement had been turned and "leveled up" with the concrete. All iron girders for the main floor had been set. McPherson estimated his completion time at seven more months.

The name, "Fort Alcatraz," as used by McPherson, was never formally used. The technically correct name was "Post of Alcatraz Island," but we find many references to a Fort Alcatraz.

The report prepared by McPherson showing the guns on hand gave a distinct feeling of Alcatraz being a fortified place. This armament reflected the views of Washington, that Alcatraz was a primary rather than secondary defense power for the Bay Area. The total allotment of guns for Alcatraz was 63 columbiads, twelve 42-pounders, nineteen 24-pounders; on hand 49 columbiads, six 42-pounders, 15 Howitzers; and needed 4 columbiads, six 42-pounders and four 24-pounders. So we can see that the total allotted was almost met.

In the year 1859 McPherson went full force toward the completion of the barracks. It did not progress without problems. Material, mainly the iron travers, arrived with different dimensions than ordered. McPherson had to solve that problem on Alcatraz by filing down the irons. To him this was an aggravating, unnecessary delay, but his willpower and loyal help from his crew kept him close to his time line.

The description of the barracks and guardhouse in his 1859 annual report are fine in detail and reflect a first-class accomplishment on his part. McPherson's other accomplishments that year were as impressive as the completion

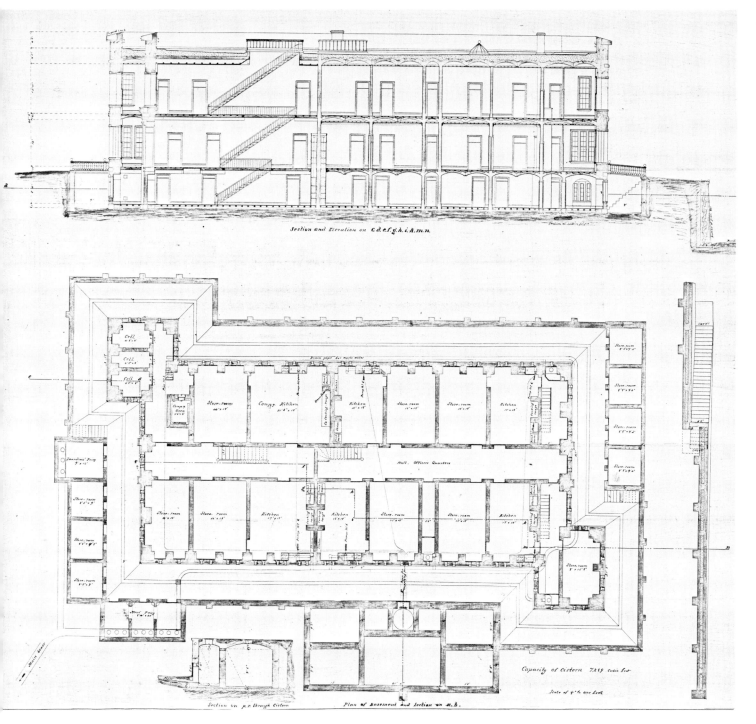

PLAN and SECTIONS
of
Defensive Barracks
Alcatraces Island   Jas. B. McPherson
Sept 30ᵗʰ 1859.   1ˢᵗ Lieut. of Engrs

Right: Granite blocks as found today on Alcatraz. These two pieces were never used. Note the holes, drilled to split the rock.
Bottom: Portion of iron fence for defensive barracks, September 1, 1859

of the barracks. He mounted four 42-pounders on the right face of the North Battery and eight on the West Battery. He mounted two 8-inch columbiads on top of the caponier. Many smaller construction projects were completed to render the island ready for military occupation. At the end of November, McPherson declared the barracks ready for occupancy. On December 1, 1859, a board of officers headed by Lt. Col. Thomas Swords inspected the barracks and wrote, "The interior arrangements are admirably adapted to wants and convenience of occupants, and the building, as a whole, reflects great credit upon the Engineer Officer under whose charge they have been erected."

Twenty-nine days later on December 30, 1859, Company H, Third Artillery, commanded by Capt. Joseph Stewart, occupied Alcatraz, beginning 77 years of military administration.

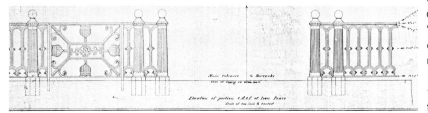

As today, the water supply on Alcatraz presented a major problem. McPherson built a water storage next to the barracks. A 50,000-gallon cistern was the main water supply for the troops on Alcatraz. This cistern was filled with water brought from Sausalito, three miles away. But in 1862 this was changed and cisterns with the capacity of 175,000 gallons were completed. With the help of a 2½-inch pipe from the wharf, water was pumped to these cisterns. But, for now, the supply was sufficient.

The crisis in the Northwest was responsible for the visit of several officers from Washington. Maj. Gen. Winfield Scott traveled to the West and by chance Colonel Totten was sent to assist him, should he need it. This gave Totten a chance to visit a project he had been very much involved in — Alcatraz.

Totten was very pleased with what he found. He made several minor recommendations, but must have surprised McPherson when he said, "The guns should be increased in numbers at this position, until all the contour of the island that looks towards the entrance, and toward Angel Island, shall be occupied by making an addition to its armament of some 25 or 30 guns."

The frustration must have been great for McPherson, a list of corrections, improvements and additions to be fulfil-

led and his request for the $132,000 cut down to $25,000. He made a detailed expense estimate on how he proposed to spend the small sum:

Defensive barracks 2,000
Weight for drawbridge 325
Fort Keeper's wages and forage for animals 3,000
Office in San Francisco and employee wages 5,500
Permanent storehouse 7,000
Service magazine left face North Battery . . 6,000
General repairs to Wharf 1,115

Even more changes to his plans were ordered. He was to use most of this $25,000 to build a new battery between the North and West batteries. In September, 1860, McPherson and his men were already excavating for the 12 guns in this new battery. Matters did not get better; and even as McPherson was in the process of delaying for lack of funds, he received orders from Totten to stop the works. "Under instructions from the Secretary of War, I have to direct that all operations of construction upon the works under your charge be at once discontinued . . ."

There was uneasiness all over the country, and shortly thereafter the Confederate States of America would be formed. This approaching hostility brought great concern to San Francisco. Union officer, Brigadier General Albert S. Johnston ordered 10,000 muskets, model 1855, their accoutrements, a supply of percussion caps and 150,000 cartridges with elongated balls moved from Benicia Arsenal to Alcatraz for better safekeeping. There was no space and the muskets had to be stacked in the officers' quarters and in rooms on the main floor. McPherson used this event to write to Totten informing him of the urgent need for a permanent storehouse.

By April, 1861, Alcatraz still is the only site in the Bay Area with permanently-mounted guns, 86 of them. The garrison of Alcatraz grows. A detachment of engineers and three additional artillery companies make Alcatraz their home. The force now is up to eight officers and 361 enlisted men. McPherson was hoping that the men in the Engineers Company would be under his command, but they were assigned to Captain Stewart as part of the military force. He did get an assistant by the name of Lt. Edward Porter Alexander.

In his last report McPherson announced the correction of most of the deficiencies Totten had observed. As for the new 12-gun battery, the breast height walls and the six small shell rooms were completed. He also installed a flagstaff on the south tower of the defensive barracks. For many years to come, the flag would wave from that point.

MAJOR-GENERAL M'PHERSON.

JAMES B. M'PHERSON, Major-General of Volunteers and Brigadier-General of the Regular Army, whose Portrait we give on our first page, was born in Sandusky, Ohio, November, 1828. He graduated at West Point in the year 1853, standing at the head of a class which numbered among its members the rebel Generals HOOD, WALKER, and ROSS; General SCHOFIELD, Commander of the Army of the Cumberland; General W. S. SMITH, General R. O. TYLER, General SHERIDAN, General TERRIL, who fell at Perryville; and GILL, who was killed at Stone River. Entering the army as Second Lieutenant of Engineers, he was immediately, although hardly twenty-five years of age, appointed as an assistant instructor of practical engineering at West Point. In 1854 he was employed as assistant-engineer on the New York harbor defenses; in 1857 he superintended the construction of Fort Delaware; also the fortifications on Alcatrus Island, San Francisco Bay, California. December 13, 1858, he was appointed First Lieutenant, and until August, 1861, was engaged as Chief of Engineers on the Pacific Coast.

When General HALLECK assumed the command of the Department of the West he selected M'PHERSON as an Aid-de-Camp, with the rank of Lieutenant-Colonel. He was GRANT's Chief Engineer in the operations against Forts Henry and Donelson, and also against Vicksburg. May 15, 1862, he was promoted to the rank of Brigadier-General of Volunteers, and during the following summer superintended the military railroads in the Department of West Tennessee. When our army at Corinth was cut off from its supplies, in October of that year, he succeeded in bringing up reinforcements to its assistance, and for this service was made Major-General of Volunteers.

It is not, however, merely as an engineer that M'PHERSON has distinguished himself in this war; now he was appointed to guard the rear in a retreat, and now to lead an assault. He and SHERMAN were GRANT's great allies in the capture of Vicksburg.

When General GRANT recommended his various officers to the Government for promotion for their services at Vicksburg, he wrote as follows about General M'PHERSON:

"He has been with me in every battle since the commencement of the rebellion, except Belmont. At Forts Henry and Donelson, Shiloh, and the siege of Corinth, as a staff officer and engineer, his services were conspicuous and highly meritorious. At the second battle of Corinth his skill as a soldier was displayed in successfully carrying reinforcements to the besieged garrison, when the enemy was between him and the point to be reached. In the advance through Central Mississippi General M'PHERSON commanded one wing of the army with all the ability possible to show, he having the lead in the advance and the rear retiring. In the campaign and siege terminating with the fall of Vicksburg, General M'PHERSON has filled a conspicuous part. At the battle of Port Gibson it was under his direction that the enemy was driven, late in the afternoon, from a position they had succeeded in holding all day against an obstinate attack. His corps, the advance always under his immediate eye, were the pioneers in the movement from Port Gibson to Hawkinson's Ferry. From the North Fork of the Bayou Pierre to Black River it was a constant skirmish, the whole skillfully managed. The enemy was so closely pressed as to be unable to destroy their bridge of boats after them. From Hawkinson's Ferry to Jackson the Seventeenth Army Corps marched roads not traveled by other troops, fighting the entire battle of Raymond alone, and the bulk of JOHNSTON's army was fought by this corps, entirely under the management of General M'PHERSON. At Champion's Hill the Seventeenth Corps and General M'PHERSON were conspicuous. All that could be termed a battle there was fought by the divisions of General M'PHERSON's corps and General HOVEY's division of the Thirteenth Corps. In the assault of the 22d of May on the fortifications of Vicksburg, and during the entire siege, General M'PHERSON and his command took unfading laurels. He is one of the ablest engineers and most skillful Generals. I would respectfully, but urgently recommend his promotion to the position of Brigadier-General in the regular army."

The appointment was given to date from August 1, 1863.

On the 12th of March, 1864, on the promotion of Lieutenant-General GRANT to the command of the United States armies, and General SHERMAN to the command of the military division of the Mississippi, General M'PHERSON was placed in command of the Army and Department of the Tennessee, embracing the Fifteenth, Sixteenth, and Seventeenth Army Corps.

In SHERMAN's advance on Atlanta M'PHERSON has conducted some of the most gigantic flank movements of the war. At Powder Spring, near Dallas, he obtained an important victory, driving the enemy and inflicting on him a loss of 2500 killed and wounded. After crossing the Chattahoochee he held the extreme right of SHERMAN's army at Decatur, and was here killed in the battle of Friday, the 22d. He was shot while riding along his lines, superintending the advance of his skirmish line, by a band of rebel bushwhackers in ambush. Then occurred the most notably disgraceful act which has ever blackened the annals of civilized warfare. Having shot M'PHERSON, the rebels took the body and stripped it of its clothing. Colonel STRONG, however, led a charge and secured the body. Thus the Army of the Tennessee lost its brave commander.

McPherson was a strong supporter of the Union, and when news reached him of the surrender of Fort Sumter he wrote Washington, volunteering:

The intelligence that the "Confederate States" have commenced hostility against the General Government, and threatened to seize the Federal Capital, has aroused (sic) a feeling of Patrotism in the breast of every true and loyal citizen. The Union element of this state irrespective of party, has come out in the most decided manner — and today there is one of the grandest and most enthusiastic *"Union Demonstrater"* in this city that I have ever witnessed. So that I think there is no danger to be apprehended on this coast . . .

I wish *you*, and also the Department to understand that I am ready and anxious to go wherever I can be of the most *service*.

McPherson left California on August 1, destined for fame and death. Replacing McPherson was 1st Lt. George Henry Elliott.

In 1846, when Pio Pico granted the deed of Alcatraz to Workman, he stated that one of the conditions was that he install a light on Alcatraz. It was not until 1854 that the first light started guiding the navigator. It took years for the realization to dawn, that one of the original intents of the use of Alcatraz was as a light station.

Top: Lighthouse in operation after 1854
Bottom: 1854 plan for the Alcatraz
lighthouse

as was mentioned in the personal correspondence of McPherson: "This beats all countries for wind I ever inhabited . . ." The wind was responsible for most of the damage. On New Year's, 1855, a storm blew the metallic roof off. It was replaced with pine shingles.

Part of the navigational warning aid was a fog bell. This fog bell weighed 1,000 pounds, and was struck four successive blows at intervals of ten seconds, followed by a pause of 30 seconds. The hammer weighed 30 pounds and was attached to a two-foot arm. This whole system worked on a weight and pulley system. Fourteen cast iron dishes weighing 3,640 pounds, provided the tension on the mechanism. When fully wound the system lasted for five hours. One man could wind up the machine, and it took him three quarters of an hour to do so. The public was informed with an article in the *Daily Alta California* of May 19, 1858. The article explained the bell and the light:

> Beneath the south wall, and jutting over a bay-washed rock, stands a little frame building enclosing the machinery connected with the fog bell, suspended on its outer edge. This bell is of clear, sonorous tone, and its close proximity to the bay enables its silver-tones to be heard a long distance over the waters on that side of the island. But there is some complaint heard from pilots . . . that it is impossible to hear the bell at all on the upper side of the island. They state that in foggy weather the sound never reaches them until they clear the lower end.

> The fog bell is struck by the clapper eight times a minute, and the chain is three hours and a quarter unwinding. It takes an hour and a quarter rapid turning of the crank to wind it up, and in foggy weather the bellman oftimes presses into the service a merry party to help him in his labors, which are as arduous as those of the *bona fide* "chain gaing," for four thousand revolution's are required to wind up the chain.

The Congress in 1850 appropriated $120,000 "for the completion of lighthouses in California and Oregon." From a precise, natural point of view, Alcatraz Light is situated at 37° 49.6′ N, 122° 25.3′ W. Alcatraz Light was the first on the West Coast. Six lighthouses were provided for and the contract for the Alcatraz Light went from the Treasury Department to a treasury clerk. This clerk sold the contract to the Balitmore contractors, Francis X. Kelly and Francis Al Gibbson. The original date of completion was to have been November 1, 1853, at a cost of $15,000.

It is the classification of the lighthouse that determines the amount of money allotted for operation. Alcatraz lighthouse was classified as a third-order light. The salary of the first principal keeper was only $750 per year. It is assumed that the low salary forced the principal light keeper to take on a second job. The inspector reminded Michael Cassin, who was appointed principal keeper on August 15, 1853, that if he would not spend more time at work he would be dismissed. Cassin did not live up to the inspector's wishes and was dismissed in October of 1855.

John Sloan, the assistant keeper, held the job for one month until he was replaced by Underhill van Wagner. The salary was changed to $1,100 per year. His assistant keeper, Nathaniel Blackstone, was replaced by Edward E. Swan.

This light was inspected on a regular basis. We can read the official reports and they reflect a smooth operation on Alcatraz. One of the problems, however, was the weather,

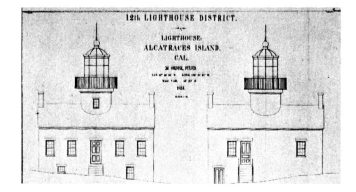

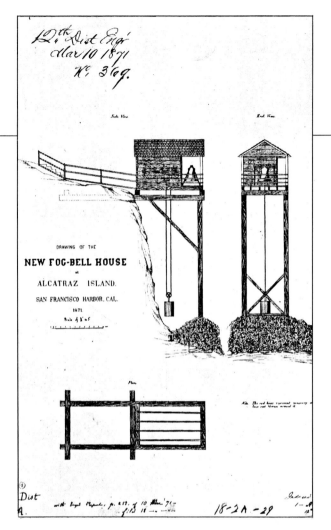

Fog bell located on the southeas end of the island in 1871

On the highest eminence is situated the light-house, that bright beacon of safety to the port seeking sailors. The lower part of the building is very conveniently and nicely arranged as a dwelling for . . . Mr. U. Van Wagener and his family. At the top of a second flight of stairs the visitor enters the mammoth lantern, the walls of which consist of immense plates of flint glass, which are so extraordinarily transparent as often to lead one to imagine nothing intercepting an unobstructed view without. The hydraulic pressure lamp within is the third order of Fresnel light, and burns with remarkable clearness and brilliancy . . . . The house is lit at sunset, in order that the light may shed its full effulgence by the time darkness sets in. It is not extinguished until sunrise. Two quarts of sperm oil are consumed nightly.

A new bell was installed in 1881, 15 feet farther out. It weighed 3,340 pounds. This change was to accommodate the concern of the sea captains who could not hear the bell until they cleared the lower end of the island. Changes were also made in the structure, such as a new roof, kitchen, outhouse, and a fence.

The light itself went through some changes in 1884. The land burners were replaced with mineral oil lamps. The entire complex was painted and declared in "excellent condition." A nice personal touch was added when Capt. Leeds became the Alcatraz keeper. He built a small wall to retain soil in order to plant flowers and trees. The lighthouse building was the first home of the first Alcatraz post office.

There were several lights guiding ships at sea around the mouth of the bay, but the two main signals were the red and white flash lights at Fort Point and the steady white light on Alcatraz. These two lights guided all the ships into San Francisco Harbor. They were called the range lights.

Over the next years more changes were made. The outhouse was removed, more living space provided, a brick oil house was built in 1900 and the fog bell was moved again. By the end of the following year a second bell was put in place of a gun on the northwest end of the island. All these changes were gradual improvements of the navigational aids.

A story in the *San Francisco Call* on April 26, 1896, sums up the condition of the light on Alcatraz in an excellent way:

The Alcatraz Island lighthouse consists of a stone tower forty feet high, with a keeper's residence of the same material built around it. The walls of the structure are about two feet thick, stuccoed and painted a pure white. The lantern is reached by a spiral stairway in the tower.

Alcatraz Island station is of the third order and has one of the finest lenses ever built. It was made by Sautler & Co. of Paris, France, in 1852, under the direction of Thomas Corwin (U.S. Secretary of the Treasury, 1850-1853). The glass used is most peculiar, as it is so soft that a pocket knife will cut it. The advantage of this glass is its remarkable clearness. With a seventy-four candle-power Funk lamp the light can be seen nineteen miles at sea, while Point Bonita which has nearly double the candle-power and an ordinary lens, can be seen only seventeen miles. The reason more of these lenses are not used is on account of the cost. Alcatraz Island lenses cost $8,000, and at the same rate a first-class lens like Point Bonita would cost . . . $20,000 . . . .

At present the lamp burns mineral oil, which is supplied to the wick from a reservoir and regulated by a float feet attachment. The lamp cleaning room is just beneath the lantern. Everything about the place is as clean and as orderly as possible. All of the brasswork shines like gold.

Alcatraz Island is also supplied with a fog signal. It is

51

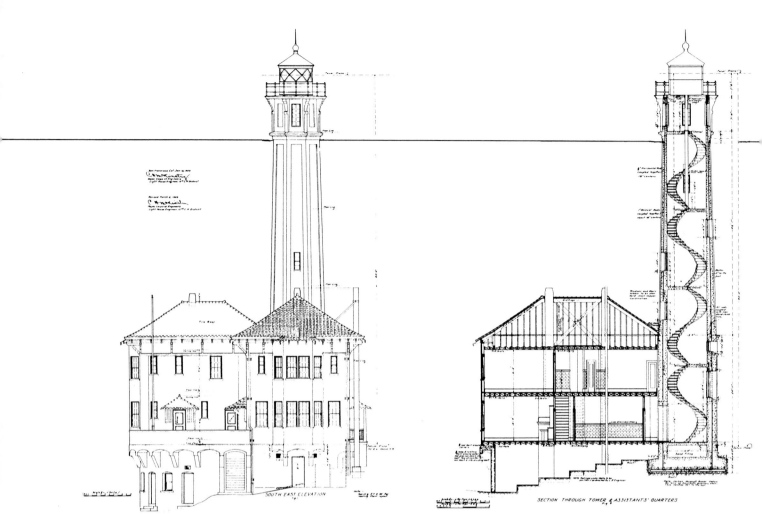

SOUTH EAST ELEVATION

SECTION THROUGH TOWER & ASSISTANTS' QUARTERS

In 1909 the present stately tower was built. Only the foundation under the grand, two-story lightkeeper's house now remains from the fires of 1969.

located at the base of the cliff on the southern end of the island, and is reached by a flight of steps. The bell is operated by a machine that will run four hours with one winding . . . .

In 1902 the third-order steady Hearn light was replaced by a fourth-order flashing lens. Some navigator complained that the steady beam light looked like a street light. When the great San Francisco earthquake occurred four years later, in 1906, there were only minor damages to the light on Alcatraz; it never stopped operating.

The relatively small structure with its light tower was to be changed to the lighthouse structure we find today, but not without some struggle.

Turner, then in charge of the military prison, wanted the light to be mounted on the roof of the new expanded prison under construction. Plans made by Major Charles H. McKinstry were to prevail, and the new lighthouse was built slightly to the east of the previous one. The old fourth-order lens was moved to the new light tower and started flashing on December 1, 1909. At that time the intensity was estimated at 22,000 candles. The light was furnished by a 25-millimeter double-tank incandescent oil vapor lamp. The

structure was an 84-foot tower built of reinforced concrete.

Again we find one of the best impressions of this new lighthouse in a public newspaper. On December 13, 1919, Albert J. Porter gave the reader a personal view:

The keeper first raised the yellow curtains which cover the octagonal windows of the tower. This action displayed the apparatus . . . . Technically it is called a fourth-order light. With its resplendent brass and glittering crystals, which curve in semi-circles on either side of two central bullseyes, it would seem to be more of an object of admiration than for practical use. In the center of this canopy of crystals the lamp is set.

Removing a covering which shields the appartus . . . the keeper took a small brass lamp from a sideboard and lighted it. "This lamp," he said, . . but when it gets inside its intensity is increased to 2,000-candle power."

That crystal structure you see," continued the keepr, as he began to wind a small crank, as one might a phonograph, "is operated by seventy-pound weights, which are regulated by clockwork. It makes one revolution every thirty seconds, and, as it has two faces, the flare can be seen from any point once every fifteen seconds.

The final phase of the Alcatraz light is not very glamorous. 1963 could be called its "year of automation." A certain amount of romance was taken from it when the conversion to fully automatic operation took over. The keeper and his assistant were no longer necessary. A last major change was to a new double-drum reflecting light.

The light on Alcatraz temporarily stopped shining on June 2, 1970, when members of the Indian occupation party burned down the building, damaging the lighthouse. The Alcatraz Indian Council denied responsibility for the fire, and claimed to have started the light again by hooking up a small generator. After the removal of the Indians occupying Alcatraz, the light again faithfully guided sailors into San Francisco uninterrupted.

For Alcatraz, in 1859, there was a three-part operation functioning. These operations ran simultaneously and, for the most part, in harmony. The first function for Alcatraz was to act as an important light station guiding the ships. The second function was to house the engineers, completing what had been planned on paper, building the fortification capable of defending San Francisco. Thirdly, Alcatraz had to be a garrison home for an artillery company of 86 men and two officers. It was like breaking in a new shoe. What was planned and built now was being tested and used.

Lighthouse as it looked before the 1969 fire

319 *French Admiral Cloué at Alcatraz*

323 . *1670 & 1870 at Alcatraz Island*

"THE ROCK" AS A FORT

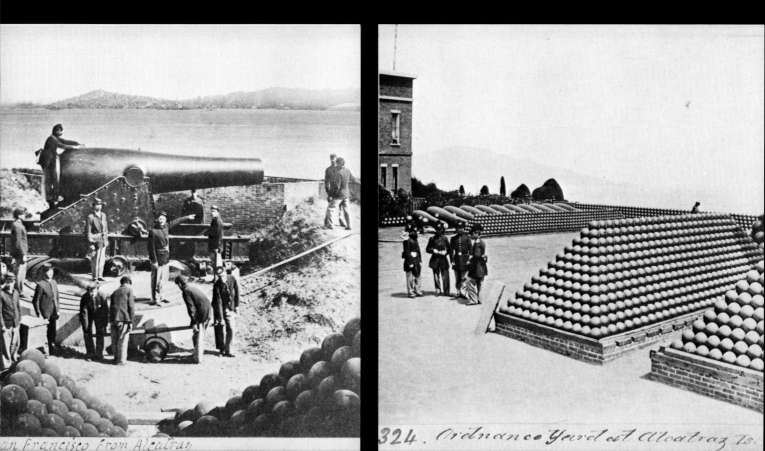

an Francisco from Alcatraz

324. Ordnance Yard at Alcatraz Is.

"The Rock" in 1862

THE ROCK AS A FORT

and even though the Civil War was not in Stewart's background, he managed to mix up a simple 21-gun salute in honor of a foreign flagship. Stewart received a communication from his commander that read: "The General commanding wishes me to inquire if you fired 21 guns in replying to the salute of the British steamer *Plumper*, and in case you did not, he directs that the deficiency be fired forthwith." Alcatraz was being used at that time as a salute post for foreign warships entering San Francisco Harbor.

The times were tense and, in order not to shake the civilians up, Stewart was ordered not to practice his artillery. However, he was ordered in a firm way to defend the Rock against all efforts to seize it:

> . . . Maintain your post and defend Alcatraz Island against all efforts to seize it, from whatever directions such efforts may be made," Stewart was directed. "No interruption will be given to the commerce of the harbor by hailing boats passing in any direction, or at any distance, or even coming to the island, unless, in this last case, from the numbers and appearance of the persons on board an attack from them may be feared, and then, be the answer what it may, no gun must be fired; the sentinel or guard must report without delay. The only conditions on which you will be justifiable in using your arms will arise when an organized attack is made on your post, and of this fact you must be the sole judge, and are forbidden to delegate the authority to fire, or to order any party to be fired on, to any officer, non-commissioned officer, or sentinel.

With the military on Alcatraz, history would be recorded in a somewhat orderly manner. Every post and a fort commander had to send in monthly returns to Washington. These returns reported the personnel on hand and the status of these men, who was on leave, who was sick or who was detained for some kind of punishment. The official activity on Alcatraz now was being recorded. This is good in looking back at history, but it still leaves a big gap in the personality of the men on the Rock. Ironically, this holds true all the way up to the Indian occupation in 1970. One has all the information of the official life on Alcatraz, but to put the pieces together as to how it was for the individuals who experienced this life on Alcatraz is a task that probably never will come to a firm, factual conclusion.

The military days present the hardest challenge at looking into the detailed evolution of Alcatraz, for much of the record that could be used as evidence is missing. The monthly post returns do provide us with a lot of material and recorded activities.

The first commander on Alcatraz was Capt. Joseph Stewart. He commanded 86 men of Company H of the Third Artillery. Stewart did not have an exciting army career. He graduated 18th in the class at the U.S. Military Academy in 1842, and retired in 1879 as Lieutenant Colonel.

To be the first commander at a newly built defense post must have been a challenging task. All had to be broken in,

Alcatraz Island from Black Point

The engineer on Alcatraz, Elliott, was also concerned with the possibility of foreign powers attacking the Pacific Coast. He wrote Totten of this concern and expressed himself forcefully in saying, "I conceive it to be absolutely necessary, that not only the fortification in this harbor, but those for the defense of Puget Sound and the Columbia River, should be constructed without delay . . ."

Totten requested an update of the armament on Alcatraz, and Elliott sent him the following report. Alcatraz had 77 guns mounted, three guns and two mortars with beds ready to be mounted and six more guns without carriages, for a total of 86 guns and two mortars. Funds allocated for Alcatraz had been frozen by the chief engineer and finally in February, 1862, Elliott was advised to resume the operations on Alcatraz. With this communication came the instructions to change four emplacements on Alcatraz to be able to mount 15-inch Rodman guns. This news must have been good for the annual report of 1861-1862. It had been the shortest yet and read: "Nothing had been done on this work for want of funds during the year, beyond the necessary repairs on the Wharf and the cutting of the columbiad platform stones." The lieutenant did have some ideas, some new and some old, but the one that is of special interest is the recommendation for a permanent prison in the vicinity of the guardhouse. He also mentioned the need to enlarge the water cisterns. The idea of the cistern may have been prompted by the fact that in April of 1861 the garrison on Alcatraz grew to 361 men and eight officers.

Mechanics' barracks were turned over to the Army and plans were made for temporary quarters at the southeast end of the island. Company H was joined by Comapanies A, I, and M, all of the Third Artillery. Stewart was superseded as Commander by his senior officer, Capt. Henry Burton, also of the Third Artillery. Burton wasted no time resuming practice firing of the guns in 1861, when the ban was lifted. One of these practice shells was thought to have started a fire on Angel Island.

Under the command of Capt. Burton, we find that 15 of his 268 privates were locked up. This may well be the start of a pattern that eventually led this post to become an exclusively military and then federal prison. The facilities were located in the basement of the guardhouse. The rooms measured 10x12, and were dark and gloomy. A trap door provided the only entrance. The windows were narrow musket slits. There were three more cells in the basement of the Citadel on top of the island. These cells included a dark cell, "the hole." Each cell measured 8 feet by 4 feet 8 inches.

As stated earlier, this period is well recorded as far as the official activities are concerned. We know that civilian prisoners have been transferred to Alcatraz but no record has been kept as to who and how many. So only the military personnel were recorded. This prison activity was a casual affair. Nobody knew that that was the beginning of a 73-year history of military penology. The exact date was August 27, 1861. The subject of prison on Alcatraz during military days will be dealt with in a later chapter of this book.

These were difficult times for any military operations. Many soldiers went east to fight and, consequently, a lot of guns were manned by volunteers. This, of course, did not give the same firm command control as if it were all regular army. The strength of the army on Alcatraz during the Civil War fluctuated from 150 to 433 men in February, 1865. Some of these volunteers were from the Washington territory and were held and trained on Alcatraz before being transported north.

In May of 1862 Burton was transferred to the east to take part in the war. His replacement, to be in command of Alcatraz, was Capt. William A. Winder, Third Artillery. The Civil War never directly affected any commander on Alcatraz, but Capt. Winder may have come the closest. He had received a confidential message concerning the possibility that there were some Confederate raiders in the Pacific Ocean around the Bay. Except for the March, 1863 incident, nothing was recorded or can be found in any correspondence relating to Civil War activity in San Francisco Bay.

In March of 1863, 15 Confederate sympathizers were seized on the schooner, *Chapman*. They had a cannon and ammunition on board. This 90-ton schooner had been secretly outfitted as a raider. All the men had been taken to Alcatraz to be interrogated by Capt. Winder. It is not known what was told to Capt. Winder nor how long they were detained on Alcatraz. Orders had been given to the commander not to permit anybody other than the officers to see them. The conspirators were brought to trial and found guilty of treason. The leaders were sentenced to 10 years in prison, but not on Alcatraz. So ended the only real Civil War excitement for Alcatraz.

The fortification construction on Alcatraz under Elliot was being rushed to completion. The batteries between West and North Battery, and his new battery between West and South Batteries were nearing completion. The identification of these batteries became confusing to all the parties concerned, so Totten finally wrote Elliott, instructing him to find a system of designation for the various batteries: "Their

FINISHING TRUNIONS

number has become so considerable that they require to be designated by names."

Elliott was not bound by the common practice of naming batteries after deceased military men. He employed names of engineer officers "who have been distinguished in the present war":

Battery Halleck consisted of all of the right face and the first 16 positions to the left of the caponier of the former North Battery. It was named in honor of Henry Wager Halleck, a member of the first Board of Engineers for the Pacific Coast, now Commander-in-Chief of the Army.

Battery Rosecrans consisted of the five positions on the extreme face of the former North Battery. It was named in honor of the then Maj. Gen. William Starke Rosecrans, Union Army.

Battery Mansfield. This new 12-gun battery was nearing completion on the northern peak of the island. It was named for Maj. Gen. Joseph King Fenno Mansfield, who had inspected the works on Alcatraz in the 1850's.

Battery Stevens. The new work on this battery consisted of six positions which were stepped like a staircase immediately to the northwest of old West Battery. It was probably named for Maj. Gen. Isaac Ingalls Stevens, formerly an engineer and first Governor of Washington Territory; killed in the Battle of Chantilly, Virginia, in 1862.

Battery Tower consisted of both faces of old West Battery. It was named in honor of Alcatraz's own Zealous Bates Tower, now a brigadier general in the east.

Battery McPherson comprised the four new positions immediately to the southwest of Battery Tower. It was also named for a former Alcatraz engineer, now Maj. Gen. James Birdseye McPherson. Why Elliott decided to split the eight guns of this new work between Battery McPherson (four) and Battery McClellan (four) is not at all clear.

Battery McClellan consisted of all of old South Battery and the adjacent four emplacements of the new work between former West and South Batteries. It was named in honor of Maj. Gen. George Brinton McClellan, Halleck's predecessor as Commander-in-Chief of the Army.

Battery Prime was formerly the old Three-Gun or Southeast Battery. It was named, of course, for Alcatraz' Lt. Frederick Edward Prime, now a captain in the east.

Elliott's annual report of 1863 offered a view of the current armament on Alcatraz. One must say it is very impressive. This report reflects a strong effort indeed to make Alcatraz an artillery power to be respected. On June 30, 1863, Alcatraz had the following armament:

Guns mounted

 3 8-inch columbiads center-pintle stone platform
37 8-inch columbiads center-pintle wood platform
 8 10-inch columbiads center-pintle wood platform
12 42-pounders, front-pintle stone platform
19 24-pounders, flank howitzers in casemates
 2 24-pounders, siege carriages
___
81

Ordinance on hand, not mounted

 6 8-inch shell guns, Navy pattern
 5 42-pounders, front-pintle carriages
 2 10-inch mortars, with beds and carriages

Presently under construction

 8 center-pintle stone platforms, for Parrott guns or 8-inch and 10-inch columbiads
17 front-pintle stone platforms, new pattern
 1 platform for a 15-inch gun

Elliott in the correspondence with Totten expresses his views on the columbiads. He states that few of the 48 mounted columbiads were really serviceable. Some time before, in old North Battery, an 8-inch columbiad had burst and Elliott wrote: "A large portion of the columbiads now in

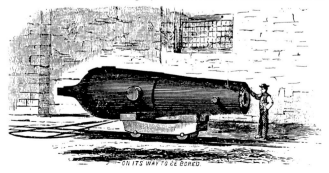

ON ITS WAY TO BE BORED.

58

A NEW MAP OF
ALCATRACES ISLAND
SAN FRANCISCO HARBOR
Scale 1 Inch to 50 ft
Respectfully forwarded to Chief Engineer
with letter of this date
San Francisco California
February 12th 1863

position can hardly be called serviceable, for the Ordinance Department several years ago directed that they be used only as shell guns and with reduced changes. They belong to a lot made at Boston which passed the inspection and were afterwards condemned." Wlliott desperately tried to get information on these guns and wrote requesting any and all data from the Benicia Arsenal. He received information explaining the bad reputation of these guns and that some had burst on the east coast. Elliott was then advised not to experiment with these guns, especially not with heavy charges:

> . . . The guns in the harbor (of San Francisco) are from Algiers & West Point Foundries if I remember aright, and they carried their iron too high the year in which they were cast destroying a portion of the fibre.

At that time there was a glimmer of hope among all this depressing news, and that was that the Ordnance Department was aware of the armament needs of the Pacific Coast and was preparing to send for the defense of San Francisco a new gun, the 15-inch Rodman. It was not until July 20, 1869 that the first 15-inch Rodman was in operation ready to fire on the northwest side of Battery Mansfield. This event, the mounting of the first 15-inch Rodman on the Pacific Coast on Alcatraz, was cause for celebration. Two soldiers became so drunk from the free liquor that they lost control and fell off a 40 to 50-foot-high wall

and were killed. These casualties were not listed in the monthly returns. This information was in the correspondence of the Post surgeon. This writer cannot find the original documents and it is strange that the deaths were not recorded by the commanding officers.

The guns on Alcatraz, though impressive and strong, never fired a shot in anger. These guns were used for many salutes that varied greatly in purpose.

One incident that is recorded in great detail is the ordering by Capt. Winder of an empty shell to be fired. On October 1, 1863, a blank shell was fired toward the British warship, *Sutlej*. This ship was the flagship of the British Pacific Squadron. Rear Adm. John Kingcome was both surprised and angry. The federal post regulation requires that all vessels be brought to, and their character ascertained. Normally, this is done by a government steamer which, for some reason, was not present that day. The commander of the land batteries had orders that all vessels be stopped and examined before passing the forts.

This was all a very delicate international issue and the Rear Adm. was not pleased and requested an answer from General George Wright. Wright came to the defense of the Alcatraz post commander, But Capt. Winder spoke well for himself, as seen in his own report:

> Thursday the officer of the day reported an armed ship towed by small boats in the direction of Raccoon

59

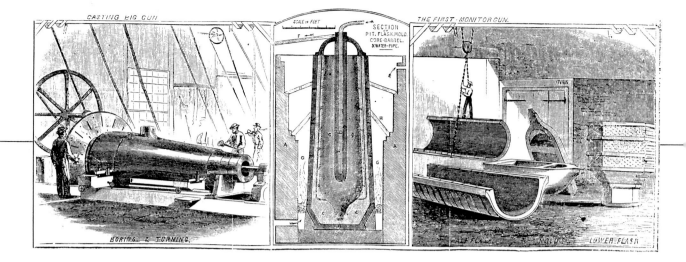

Straits. I discovered her under the land near Lime Point. I could distingquish a flag flying at the peak, but there being no wind, I could not tell her nationality. The ship's direction was so unusual I deemed it my duty to bring her to, to ascertain her character. I therefore fired a blank charge, which apparently not attracting her attention I directed a gun to be loaded with an empty shell and to be fired 200-300 yards in front of her. This was done and the ship rounded to.

The ship just waited there. And since Alcatraz could not send soldiers to inspect the ship for lack of a small boat, time passed. Finally, the ship fired the international salute of 20 guns. This salute was returned from Alcatraz.

Alcatraz was the designated post and when Fort Point returned the salute, the rear admiral must have been confused. He was still upset as he left San Francisco. The extensive correspondence on this matter lasted until late March, 1864, six months after the incident.

The war was in full swing and Alcatraz guns were used to support the victories of the Union. September 26, 1864, in honor of Sheridan's victories in the Shenandoah Valley, and again in December, 100-gun salutes were fired in celebration of Sherman's capture of Atlanta. The presidential election in November, 1864, put the Alcatraz soldiers on alert, just in case there was trouble in San Francisco, "to be held in readiness for service at a minute's warning."

The soldiers of Alcatraz did go to San Francisco at the request of the mayor for the army to help preserve peace. Companies F and G, 9th U.S. Infantry, and 6th California Volunteers were moved to Harrison Street in San Francisco. This was in the aftermath of President Lincoln's assassination. In accordance with army regulations, the half-hour gun firing for the mourning was performed by Post Alcatraz.

During that period a major change took place in the value of paper money versus gold and silver coins. This was a serious problem on Alcatraz because the engineers employed workers that received paper money for their work. Elliott paid $4 per day for a mechanic in notes, but when the mechanic converted it into gold or silver, he re-

ceived only $2.40 in purchasing value. This caused a problem and the only way to solve it was to pay the workers in coin. This was attempted, but the Treasury Department could not follow through, and had to raise the pay. Elliott called his workers together and informed them of that news and he had to watch workers walk off the job. Ten days after the Secretary of War had been notified, the workers returned to work with the promise that they would get paid according to San Francisco wages. These engineers desperately needed these workers in order to complete the fortification and defenses of a city that was capturing the spotlight of the world.

For the next few years the work on Alcatraz concentrated primarily on modernizing the Post. The recognition of obsolescence came early in the war at Fort Pulaski, Georgia, where great breaches were opened in the masonry by rifled guns, smooth bores and mortars, causing the fort to surrender. Alcatraz, not having been under fire, could only learn from the demise of other posts and forts. The recommendations from the engineers came constantly to the War Department. Slowly these changes recommended by the post engineer were accepted. One of the recommendations by Elliott considering the war lesson read:

I have thought it might be well, while constructing the platforms and parapet, for the 15-inch gun in the salient of Battery Tower to continue the earthen embankment in front of the scarp. . . . The scarps of this Battery are constructed of sandstone facing . . . and appear to be in good order. The height of the scarp varies from two to 16 feet and . . . I think the thickness to be rather thin to resist the projectiles which are now used, one section of 5-foot height shows a thickness of three inches. The earthen embankments which I propose will prevent in a manner the breaking of the scarps . . . I would increase the thickness to 15 to 16 feet.

Some of the changes were also made from the recommendations of the artillery officers and the soldiers manning those guns. One such recommendation dealt with the wall behind the gun. If a projectile hit this wall, it would

Right: Brick arch built in 1866

fall off into the area where the soldiers were operating the guns. To solve that problem, a small 2-foot-wide brick wall was placed 4 feet away from the natural rock, thus catching anything rolling down this back wall.

The 1864 appropriation for Alcatraz of $200,000 was a great incentive to work on various projects. Elliott had a large working force: a master mason, a boat crew, two blacksmiths, a carpenter, seven stone cutters and 59 laborers were carried on the payroll. This work force in a way was economical because they could make on Alcatraz things they normally would have to buy in San Francisco. Ventillation doors, copper hinges for the magazines, and iron grating for the prison windows did not have to be transported from San Francisco. This saved time and money. Laborers repaved the ditch around the Defensive Barracks (Citadel). The carpenters relocated the fog bell and, all in all, Elliott must have been pleased with the progress and the 1865 appropriation of $90,000.

Before being replaced by Capt. James Madison Robertson, Winder caused an explosion in the War Department by giving permission to photograph Alcatraz. The commercial photographers Bradley & Rulofson photographed the batteries and buildings. This venture was cleared by his superior, De Russy, at Fort Point. After a trip to Oregon the senior engineer, Elliott, looking at the photographs, wrote to the chief engineer describing the project:

I have thought that you would be glad to obtain copies to illustrate the condition and the progress (of the works) . . . and I append a list, and include two specimen copies (stereoscopic size). The price asked is $200 in Notes for the entire series which is rather less than $100 of the currency of this coast . . . . The entire number of views is about 50. The views enclosed show a part of the work I was carrying on at the time, viz., No. 1. Remodeling the Magazine in Battery Tower, decreasing the inclination of the superior slope of the parapet, and putting iron plate on the Breast high wall, and No. 2 filling outside the old scarp so as

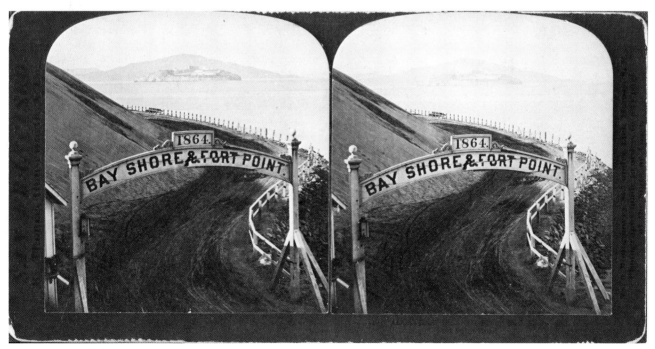

Alcatraz from Fort Point Road

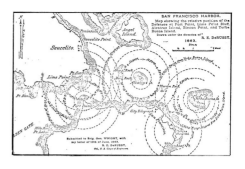

to strengthen the parapet in Battery McClellan . . . . Had I been here there are some (other) views which I would have suggested.

The following list is the only record of what those snapshots of the 1860s showed, and the historic value of those pictures would be tremendous today. Many details have been lost to us that a photograph could reveal. The list includes:

The Barracks
Light House
Mortar Battery
Battery Prime
Battery McPherson
Battery Rosecrans
View of side of island (under Battery Mansfield)
View of side of island (showing part of Battery Rosecrans)
Battery Mansfield
Battery Halleck
Battery Stevens
Battery Prime from the north
Battery Prime from the west
North view of the barracks
View of same showing parade ground and engineers and adjutant offices
South view of Battery McPherson
North view of Battery Tower
View of Battery McClellan, soldiers' quarters and caponier
View showing Battery Tower and city of San Francisco in distance
View of Battery Rosecrans and bay towards Sausalito
View of Battery Halleck and Angel Island
View of wharf

The order from the War Department to Elliott was that nobody be allowed to have the photos: "You will immediate-advise with Colonel De Russey to the end that they be instantly suppressed." A lot of correspondence over this matter with a notation that "the provost marshal-general has all the negatives and all the copies, except those (two) Capt. Elliott sent to the Engineers Department."

Out of this incident came the Department of Engineers order No. 32 that directed that no photocopy of any military objects be made except "such as required to explain . . . reports of officers." The photographers were still trying to collect money from the government for property seized.

Life on Alcatraz started flowing into the day-by-day routine necessary to maintain the Post. The engineers were still completing the remodeling but the garrison of Alcatraz was now ready for drills, routines, and inspections. Visiting dignitaries started to arrive on Alcatraz for inspection. The new commander, Capt. James Madison Robertson, who arrived on Alcatraz in October of 1865, gave several dignitaries an inside view of Alcatraz.

Queen Emma of Hawaii and the Civil War general, Maj. Gen. Henry Halleck, who had returned to San Francisco as Department Commander, arrived on Alcatraz to review and inspect the troops. The guns, saluting the visitors, always reminded the citizens of San Francisco of the the importance of this Post. Thirteen guns for Maj. Gen. Halleck boomed the traditional order of Rank.

Alcatraz now was indeed a settled, permanent military post. Its commander, Capt. Robertson, was very much interested in penology, and with Robertson the idea of Alcatraz as a prison started growing into firmer commitments leading to the construction of prison buildings.

In 1865 Alcatraz had few prisoners, 20 as reported, and there was room for them. Alcatraz was not a prison even

Steps leading to D-block   Rooms of first floor military barracks under B-block   Rifle windows of original barrac

[NOVEMBER 23, 1861. THE FIRST TELEGRAPHIC MESSAGE FROM CALIFORNIA.

though the thought was constantly on the minds of many officials. The change was now that a lot of buildings and facilities on the island were designed for the daily life of officers, soldiers, and families. School houses and bowling alleys, bakery and library all are evidence of life of a normal style rather than just supporting war efforts.

At the same time we find an increase in armament on Alcatraz. At times one wonders about the need to fortify at such a rate. An English tourist by the name of Harvey Tower, who was given a tour of Fort Point, remarked, "Twenty large guns . . . would have been quite enough." By mid-year of 1864, the total weight of metal that could have been discharged simultaneously on Alcatraz was 4549 pounds; and by the end of the year, the total was 6949 pounds, a constant increase in armament. By the end of 1865 the total armament on Alcatraz was 106 guns, but by 1868 this increased to 154, a steady growth.

Despite this growth, a faster development than the primary defense of Fort Point, there were some who felt that Alcatraz was not yet up to its potential. Alexander, a member of the Pacific Coast Board of Engineers, wrote in detail the exact placement and conditions of Alcatraz' armament. He included into this report an opinion that Alcatraz could not withstand an enemy fleet:

The defenses at Alcatraz Island are very imperfect. It is my opinion that the broadsides of half a dozen powerful men-of-war would render the island, in its present condition, entirely untenable.

The defense is so unsatisfactory that the Board of Engineers for the Pacific Coast has several times taken up the subject with a view of trying to suggest some important improvement, but as often has laid it aside again, as a problem too difficult for immediate practical solution.

The great difficulty is that the whole island is a mass

of rock, and rising as it does immediately behind the guns, it is to be greatly feared that the batteries would be so insecure from splinters of stone that the gunners could not serve their guns.

1869 would be the start of major revampment of the Alcatraz defense systems. Ideas, recommendation and cost were discussed on a regular basis, and from these discussions came recommendations that eventually were used by the engineers on Alcatraz. The recommendations that would influence the Alcatraz developer were: specific distances between the guns, sand to be used instead of clay for the parapets, traverse for every two guns and service magazines to be built with well-tamped concrete. These were relatively small projects compared to the major recommendations of the leveling of the southeast end of the island to 62 feet. This meant changing the surface of one fourth of the island. The board estimated that this would be an excavation of 430,000 cubic yards at a cost of $215,000. Of special interest here was the recommendation of using military prisoners as labor force.

In January of 1869 Mendell requested from the Post Commander a prison labor force. It was in March of 1868 that Alcatraz was designated a military prison. At the time of Mendell's request to Robertson, there were 90 to 125 prisoners on Alcatraz. Mendell did get a force of 30 to 50 prisoners but later reported that he was not happy with this work force. "The men are not industrious and they are

Brick floor of military barracks   Storage space west end   Steps leading up to A-block

Left: Alcatraz Island as seen in 1862
Bottom: Arsenal and
Ordnance Yard

careless and at times malicious in their treatment of public property . . ." This, however, marks a beginning of the use of prisoners on Alcatraz as an official part of the work force.

The defense project as recommended by the board was approved in 1870, and the works on Alcatraz would drastically change the topography of the island. It was the picks and shovels of the military prisoner that would cause the greatest change in appearance. This labor force developed out of need for cheap labor and, later, to keep a large number of men occupied while confined.

These major changes occurred over a period of several years. The first estimates were sent forward from Alcatraz in April of 1870:

100,000 yds. of rock excavated at 75¢ . . .	$ 75,000
35 front-pintle 15-inch gun platforms	
with breast-high walls	42,000
5 center-pintle 15-inch gun platforms	
with breast-high walls	10,500
20 magazines (in the traverse)	116,000
earth filling on slopes and parapets	26,400
moving platforms; and moving guns	
and buildings	12,500
miscellaneous construction, drains	
sinking covered ways, etc.	11,000

		294,000
	add 10%	29,400
	total	$323,400

In his annual report for 1870 Mendell lists his prisoner work forces at 45 under two civilian supervisors. He seemed pleased with the accomplishments, the removal of the 15-inch platforms in old Battery Mansfield and the removal of 13 columbiads in the left face of Battery Halleck. These prisoners were now used for the dismantling of the now obsolete shot furnace. The excavation of the near Batteries 2, 3, and 4 at the northwest end of the island were completed. The progress of the excavation of the southeast part of the island was progressing satisfactorily. A crew of prisoners were rebuilding the road that passed over the top of the near rooms of the bomb-proof barracks.

The armament on Alcatraz was to change too. The columbiads were to be replaced by the 15-inch Rodman. For lack of funds the platforms for this change would have to be built out of wood. The wood recommended by Washington was the Oregon fir or pine that had performed well on the Columbia River. In January, 1871, Mendell

received the necessary permission to install the wooded platforms and to fire test shots.

On June 28, 1871, such a test was conducted. The *Daily Alta California*, on June 29, 1871, had a full description of this new setup and its testing:

In place of stone, as used heretofore, this one (platform) is constructed from Oregon pine, unpreserved. Ths cost of timber and entire construction was about $500, while one of stone would cost $2,000. The wooden one is equally effective. . . .

There are 7,000 feet of timber used in its construction. It is built on solid rock and riveted with two and a half inch bolts, four feet in the rock. The bolts are filled in around with hot lead in order to insure solidity. The width of the platform on (behind?) the breast-high wall is thirty-four feet; from the breast-high wall to the outside it is twenty-two feet. In depth it is twenty-eight inches, and is filled in with concrete. . . .

The firing was commenced about ten o'clock under the direction of (Bevel) General (James M.) Robertson, who has charge of the island. The supervision of the gun was under Lieutenant (Thomas T.) Thornburg. . . .

Right: Cannon Balls
Bottom: Gunpowder barrel in blocked-off tunnel

The shots discharged were solid, and 448 pounds each in weight. Mammoth power was used. The first shot was fired off with fifty-five pounds of powder, at point blank range, and in the direction of Point Blunt (Angel Island). The shot struck the water about a mile and a half off, and made a number of ricochets. Upon examination, it was discovered that the gun had bounced back upon the counter hoisters with considerable force. The transom of the platform was slightly sprung near the pintle, also sprung a little near (were) the hind wheels of the carriage.

Testing went on and the gun was eventually fired 26 times. The platforms held up well and only some nails to an iron plate needed to be added.

The Post Commander now was housing 150 military prisoners. The work force he gave Mendell ranged from 80 to 100 men. This force was very instrumental in the speed with which things progressed on Alcatraz.

The Congress for 1872 appropriated $75,000 for Alcatraz. The 1871 work was carefully listed in a journal kept by each engineer who would hand it down to the next person in charge. Work such as plastering and laying brick; cutting, coping the magazine of Battery 2.

Making magazine doors (measuring 6 feet by 6 by 2 feet by 10 by 4 inches)
Laying flooring in North Caponier
Battery 6, excavating and drilling on bluff
Battery 4, excavating on slope
Battery 1, excavating and drilling on slope
Filling in caponier and rear of "fort"
Battery 2, excavating on slope and asphalting magazine
White washing magazine roofs
Battery 3, cutting out brick
Painting crane on wharf
New barracks, clearing off arches, painting embrasures (most iron was "painted" with coal tar), shutters, and pipes
Prisoners employed in smithing, carpentry, clearing brick, excavating, etc.

Mendell's annual report for 1872 was a busy one. Lots of work and changes had been done on Alcatraz. Not all the changes were of a military nature. The visual senses now were being addressed by having sod brought over from Fort Point and Lime Point. One must remember that there had been no natural growth on Alcatraz and all soil and vegetation had to be brought over from the mainland.

Clover seed may have been the first real attempt at planting on Alcatraz.

Today a lot is said about some underground tunnels throughout the island. There is no real tunnel visible today, but we find some records indicating that around 1872 Mendell covered some traverses, thereby creating tunnels. These passageways were considered bombproof. There was one tunnel, carved through lime rock. Mendell had a 180-foot long bore cut through the island from the northeastern end to Battery 4 on the west side. Many legends have grown: that Alcatraz was laced with underground tunnels built in the days of the Spanish Empire. We know that not to be true.

During this intensive redevelopment period, the soldiers on Alcatraz had an opportunity to go to school on Alcatraz. In the morning the children would attend school and in the afternoon the garrison soldiers had a chance to attend school. The post library had been established. The hospital was built by 1873, and the post surgeon took up residency on Alcatraz. His duty was to attend to the health of the people on the post. His report would list the number of sick and diseased.

He performed for us the greatest service, by keeping a very fine record of daily events on Alcatraz. Not all his journals have survived but the information proves to be of immense value in reconstructing the daily life of the people of that post.

In order to construct another battery at the southeastern end of the island, Mendell had to level the barracks. The soldiers moved to the hospital where they were very happy. The doctor wrote into his journal that on January 28, 1874, this company had a ball, "social entertainment," celebrating moving into these new quarters.

The hospital did not last long, for in April of 1874, fire, a worse enemy than soldiers, destroyed the hospital on this waterless island. The surgeon set up his hospital in the guardhouse and the men had to strike up tents on the island. They lived in those tents until the fall, when an extremely ugly building was built on top of the unfinished casements behind the wharf.

There had been a proposal by the Board of Engineers in 1872 to build a permanent four-company, two-story brick barracks on top of this unfinished casemented barracks. Their reason was that the barracks were directly behind Battery McClellan and on the site of Battery 10. They were made of wood and therefore could burn down easily. In 1873 the engineer was informed that he could not build this permanent barracks: "The present unfinished casements will be reserved for completion, and the Pacific Board will at once proceed to project the necessary peace quarters located in some (other) position or positions."

Coastal fortifications no longer were on the top of the list of Congress. In 1875 the allotment for Alcatraz was only $20,000 and in 1876, $25,000 was appropriated. In 1877 Congress would not pass any appropriation for Alcatraz. For several years following there were no monies for the fortification construction on Alcatraz. The work now was limited to maintenance. Mendell's labor force was composed of prisoners and the funds for maintenance came from a separate appropriation called, "Preserving and Repair of Fortifications."

The daily activities of the garrison were in full operation. General Robertson was succeeded by Major Charles Hale Morgan in December, 1872. On a hunting trip to the Sonoma Valley he suffered an attack of apoplexy. On Alcatraz there was a frantic attempt by several army surgeons to save his life, to no avail. He died on December 20th. He was to be shipped east, but for lack of embalming capacity, he was buried on Angel Island. His replacement was Capt. John Egan.

Activities on Alcatraz included the customary greeting of foreign visitors, such as the visit by Japanese naval officers and midshipmen, and the firing of the gun salutes for special occasions. Once the eight officers on Alcatraz gave a party for the officers stationed at the various posts around the bay. It was called an "informal matinee hop."

Births and deaths were very much part of the daily events. Soldiers and prisoners died on the island. Babies were born, too. However, the record is not complete on this matter. Some deaths were accidental, like the two privates who drowned when their small fishing boat capsized off the island. Other deaths were caused by disease, suicides and murder. All this information was recorded by the post surgeon. He was so diligent in his recording that we have an outline of the routine of January 1, 1878:

Mondays, Wednesdays, Fridays 8-9 a.m., Battalion drill. First call 7:45 a.m. All on duty to attend except post guard, provost sergeant, two sergeants on duty at prison, baker, and one cook from each company.

Tuesdays and Thursdays 8-9 a.m., Artillery drill; Daily 2 p.m., Drill call for such company exercises as the company commanders may direct.

Tuesdays, Thursdays and Saturdays, 4 p.m., Guard mount preceded by a Dress Parade.

Drawer 95.
Sheet 51.

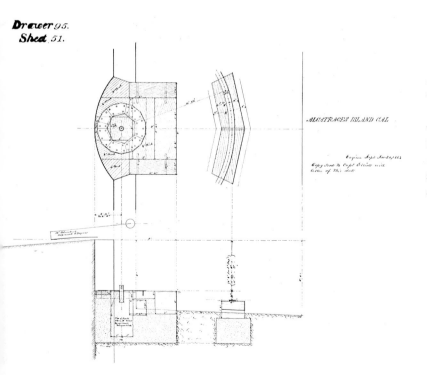

ALCATRACES ISLAND CAL

Right: Annual Report for 1889
Bottom: Photograph of guns in place from a family album

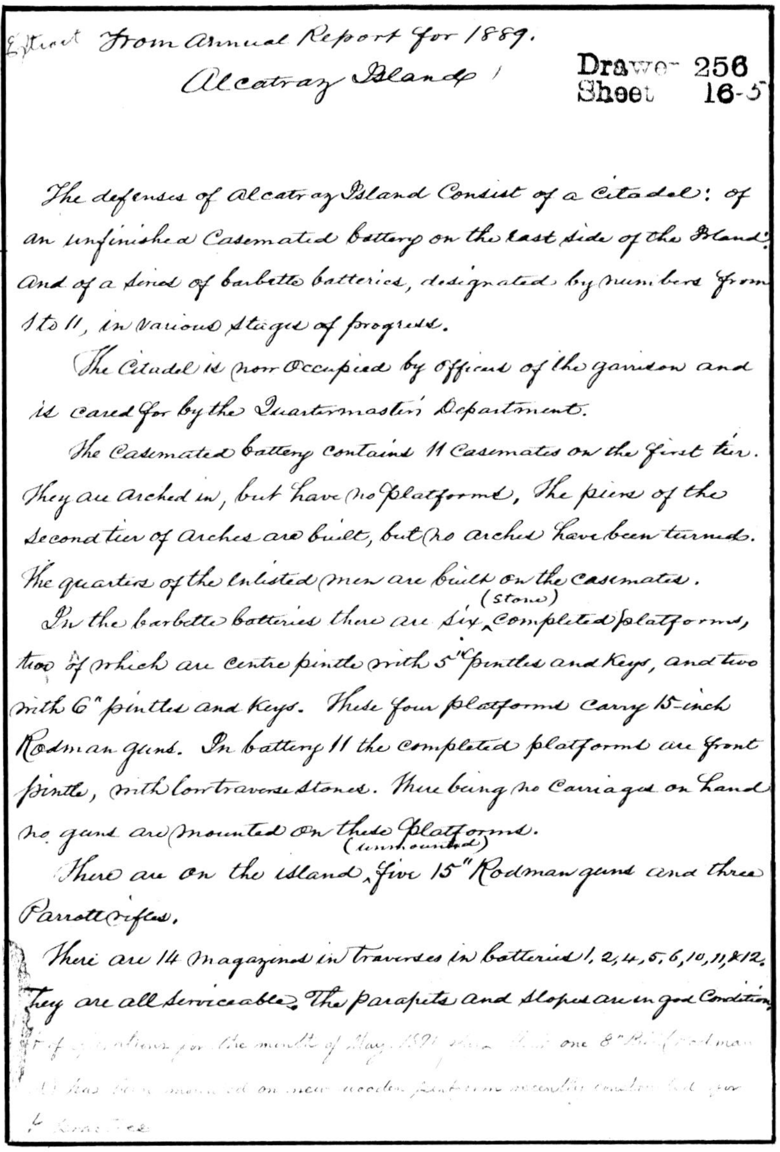
Extract from Annual Report for 1889.
Alcatraz Island.

Drawer 256
Sheet 16-5

The defenses of Alcatraz Island Consist of a Citadel: of an unfinished Casemated battery on the East side of the Island: and of a series of barbette batteries, designated by numbers from 1 to 11, in various stages of progress.

The Citadel is now Occupied by officers of the garrison and is cared for by the Quartermaster's Department.

The Casemated battery contains 11 Casemates on the first tier. They are arched in, but have no platforms. The piers of the second tier of arches are built, but no arches have been turned. The quarters of the enlisted men are built on the casemates.

In the barbette batteries there are six (stone) completed platforms, two of which are centre pintle with 5" pintles and keys, and two with 6" pintles and keys. These four platforms carry 15-inch Rodman guns. In battery 11 the completed platforms are front pintle, with low traverse stones. There being no Carriages on hand no guns are mounted on these platforms. (unmounted)

There are on the island, five 15" Rodman guns and three Parrott rifles.

There are 14 magazines in traverses in batteries 1, 2, 4, 5, 6, 10, 11, & 12. They are all serviceable. The parapets and slopes are in good Condition.

[illegible] of operations for the month of May 1891 [illegible] one 8" [illegible] Rodman [illegible] has been mounted on new wooden platform recently constructed [illegible]

Sunday 9 a.m., inspection.

While the garrison was active and busy on Alcatraz, the post engineer, Mendell, had virtually no construction going on at either Lime Point or Alcatraz. It was the post quartermaster on Alcatraz who had some construction funds. He wanted to remodel the citadel into officer's quarters. The citadel now was considered a post structure and no longer a fortification structure. Doors were cut into the main floor, the loopholes were enlarged to create windows and dumb waiters were installed to the basement kitchens. The cells in the basement were blocked off. The outside did not change and remained part of the skyline for San Francisco residents.

There were just no monies, and the other buildings did not get as much attention as did the main Citadel. Two buildings, the stables and laborers' quarters, were lost in the March 25, 1888, fire. Some money came to Mendell for him to prepare some casements in order to store submarine mines. The post commander objected, for he feared they would explode and harm his men. He was convinced that these mines did not contain the explosives, and he then went along with this plan.

By June 30, 1884, Mendell had received 451 mines. He had them painted and stored on scaffolding. The practice of storing mines lasted until the end of World War II. Mendell did not find this a satisfactory situation. The storage facilities were damp, dark and practically unventilated. He had to use prisoners to scrape the rust off the mines and paint them. He prepared a plan for a permanent storage shed on Yerba Buena Island.

The approval did not reach the Pacific Coast until 1889, and Mendell wrote his activities regarding the mines in his monthly report: "During the month 128 torpedoes were cleared and scrapped and 153 torpedoes were painted with one coat of red lead and one coat of white lead." He was alarmed when he received notice that 120 more mines were coming his way. His request for postponement was granted until November, 1890, at which time the storage facility on Yerba Buena was completed.

The mining of a harbor was a new concept for San Francisco Bay, and Alcatraz was part of this development. Alcatraz had one of the control rooms. From this room, upon a given signal, an electric impulse was sent to the mine, causing it to explode under the ship. The room on Alcatraz was completed; and, after that, not much information is found in the correspondence, except that seven years later, when the Spanish-American War broke out, the harbor was mined for the first time.

The Spanish-American War did bring a flurry of activity to San Francisco. For Alcatraz, however, there was no increase in armament. By this time in history it was clear that the era of smooth-bore guns was coming to an end. More flexible, modern weaponry was being produced and appearing on the West Coast. On December 31, 1901, the annual report of arms on Alcatraz revealed that no coastal guns whatsoever stood mounted on Alcatraz. In 1920 we find an article in *Popular Mechanics* that reads as follows:

WRECKING OLD NAVAL GUNS

One of the Old Naval Guns, Condemned to be Broken Up, About to be Rolled from Its Emplacement by Means of a Steel Cable Attached to a Windlass, and Then Lowered to the Place of Its Execution—an Abandoned Tunnel. The Gun Weighed 52,000 Pounds

The Barrels of the Old Guns were Loaded with Dynamite in Layers from Breech to Muzzle, Tamped Down by Thick Layers of Clay between the Charges. The Sketch at the Right Shows the Arrangement

TAMPING
POWDER

The Fragments Which Look So Much like Building Stone Are the Pieces of the 17 Guns, Reduced to Scrap and Ready for Shipment

The First Gun to be Rolled Down the Terrace is Seen Lying in the Cut Leading to the Mouth of the Tunnel, Which Yawns in the Background. The Next Step Was to Get It into the Tunnel

The Blasting of the First Gun Was Largely Experimental, and the Resulting Fragments Were Rather Large. Heavier Charges were Used Later

Breaking Up the Guns Incidentally Nearly Wrecked the Tunnel. The Walls Were Intact before the Blasting

WRECKING OLD NAVAL GUNS
WITH DYNAMITE

"What to do with 17 antiquated 15-in. guns, at the military post on Alcatraz Island in San Francisco Bay, which had outlived their usefulness, was the problem that confronted the War Department recently. The guns, cast in 1862, were of an obsolete smooth-bore type, known as "Rodman rifles," and could be used only for firing round shot. As each gun weighed 52,000 lb., the task of removing them from the island intact would have involved operations more costly than their value as old metal. Cutting up the old cannon with acetylene torches was suggested, but, after a trial, was found impracticable. Exploding the guns appeared to be the only remaining alternative, but to do this without wrecking the buildings on the island or losing the gun metal, appeared impossible.

"Leading away from the power house which supplies electricity to the military post and the Federal prison on the island, there was an old tunnel, once used as an aqueduct and power conduit, but for the past ten years abandoned. This tunnel was stripped of its fittings. Then a corps of carpenters went in and lined the hole — top, sides, and bottom — with 6 by 6-in. timbers.

"One of the guns was jacked out of its emplacement, and rolled into the tunnel. Here 100 lb. of 70-per-cent dynamite was loaded into the breech. This was tamped down with 26 in. of clay. Another charge of 75 lb. of 70-per-cent dynamite was then placed on top of the first, and tamped down with more clay. The dynamite and clay were then tapered down to the muzzle with a third load of 75 lb. of dynamite; then loads of 50, 40, and 30 lb., respectively, until, in all, 370 lb. had been stuffed into the gun. A final muzzle seal of clay and white lead closed the mouth of the cannon. Meanwhile, to protect the island power house, the carpenters had constructed a barricade of 6 by 6-in. timbers about 100 ft. from the mouth of the tunnel, which happened to be in a direct line with that building. An ignition wire was strung from the gun to a safe distance away from the side of the tunnel, and when all was ready, the handle of the blasting machine was shoved down.

"The explosion that followed was terrific. Alcatraz Island and all of San Francisco trembled. Every window in the power house and other near-by buildings was shattered. When the engineers went into the tunnel, after the smoke and dust had cleared away, all that was to be found were scraps of the gun, splinters of the planks that had lined the tunnel, and tons of loose rock that had formerly been the tunnel wall. When the debris was all cleaned out, the biggest piece of the gun that could be found weighed 840 pounds.

"Profiting by the experience gained in the shattering of the first gun, heavier charges of dynamite were placed in the breech of the next one. The second gun was reduced to bits, the largest of which weighed only 360 lb. The third gun was broken into portions all under 300 lb., and the remaining 14 were reduced to fragments of less than 290-lb. weight.

"With the completion of the blasting operations, there was little difficulty in collecting the remnants of the old guns. The metal was then transferred to the hold of a vessel and shipped by way of Panama to the Atlantic coast. In an eastern arsenal these old cannon, which "did their bit" in the Civil War, will be melted up and recast into modern harbor-defense mortars, or possibly into high-power naval guns to bristle from the turrets of one of our best and newest fighting ships.""

The modernization of costal fortifications was studied by the newly established board in 1885. This was done under the Secretary of War, William C. Endicott. The board was called the Endicott Board. The Army Engineers made their recommendations of 200 modern rifles and mortars, but the Endicott Board recommendations for San Francisco were more grandiose: 110 guns and 128 rifled mortars.

In 1890 the recommendation was made by Thomas Casey, Chief Engineer, to the Senior Engineer on the West Coast, that he temporarily install 8-inch guns on Alcatraz. Mendell questioned the value of this decision for temporary

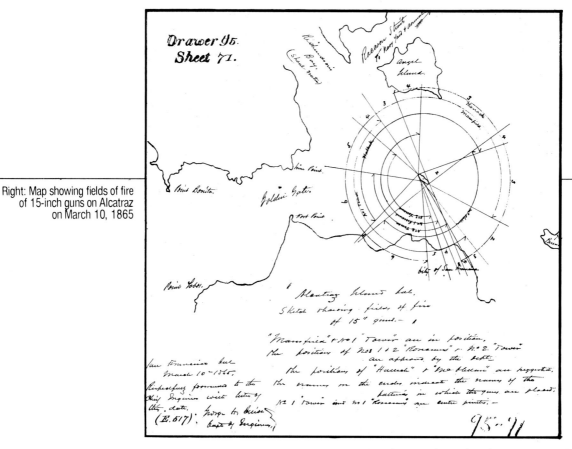

Right: Map showing fields of fire
of 15-inch guns on Alcatraz
on March 10, 1865

guns, and especially the cost. Casey felt that Alcatraz was still important in the defensive scheme, even though the main defense system was constructed with the placement of mines. He wrote to Mendell: "I think that Alcatraz, although deprived by modern advances (in weapons) of the high importance with which it has been invested in the past discussion of the defense of the harbor, will always have value for its fire into the Golden Gate." There is no record of these 8-inch guns ever having been placed on Alcatraz.

The needs on Alcatraz had changed drastically. The steady increase in the number of prisoners made it necessary to give more attention to the facilities needed to deal with a large contingent of prisoners. The debate went on, and those who favored the heavy fortifications, as did Maj. Gen. Arthur MacArthur, expressed themselves eloquently. We read in a letter written in 1905 by the father of the famous Gen. Douglas MacArthur:

As a purely defensive proposition there can be no question that the installation of high power guns on Alcatraz Island would not only greatly strengthen but would make the defense of San Francisco Bay absolutely invincible against any combination that the entire world could bring against it. . . .

Effective defense of the harbor is of course all that is required, but when experts differ. . . it is impossible to make an error on the side of prudence. For example, if we have many more guns than are needed the national interests are safe, but if we have one gun less than necessary at the critical moment the honor of the nation may be jeopardized and all the money invested on existing works are as good as thrown away.

Since. . . all my convictions in the premises have

been confirmed and strengthened and are now most emphatically to the effect that all of Alcatraz should be devoted to fortification. Personally, I favor high power guns and as many of them as can be installed on the island, but the question of the weight of the guns, for the time being, considered as secondary to the proposition that the island shall be dedicated exclusively and for all time to the purpose of defense.

This was a noted attempt to convince everybody of the need for Alcatraz, but, as we know, it was just a few years after 1905 that the chief of engineers stated that Alcatraz would not be armed, especially due to the fact that Congress was considering suspending appropriations for additional batteries. 1907 was the official year that Alcatraz lost its role in the defense of San Francisco. In that year the Secretary of War selected "the Rock" as the site for a large, permanent military prison. That was the end of the role of the corps of engineers who had been the first to deal with this "Rock." The office of engineers with Alcatraz Island was officially terminated January 29, 1907.

Fifty years had passed since Alcatraz started to guard the Golden Gate. For fifty years "the Rock" had to endure the constant rearranging of its surface, molding it into a platform supporting the most powerful armament of the nation. Alcatraz was the first post to have guns mounted, and it was the only post ready when the Civil War began. In 1898, had the Spanish approached San Francisco, Alcatraz would have played the major role in the defense of San Francisco. This all now is passed, and this colorful development fades into the background of history, only to give the spotlight to the grim story of a military prison and federal penitentiary.

MAP
OF
PACIFIC BRANCH
UNITED STATES MILITARY PRISON,
ALCATRAZ ISLAND,
CALIFORNIA.

Scale 1in = 50 ft.

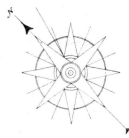

P X

Stockade

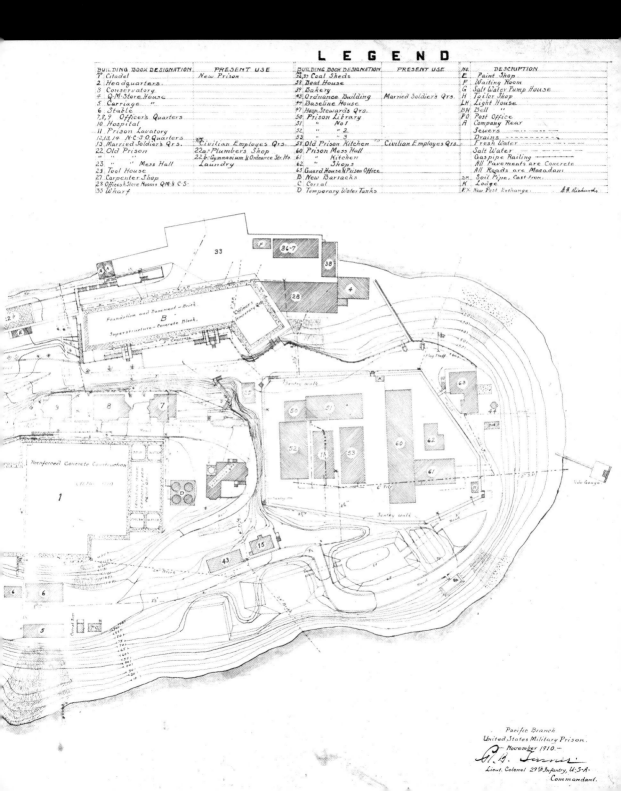

LEGEND

BUILDING BOOK DESIGNATION	PRESENT USE	BUILDING BOOK DESIGNATION	PRESENT USE	NO.	DESCRIPTION
1 Citadel	New Prison	36,37 Coal Sheds		E	Paint Shop
2 Headquarters		38 Boat House		F	Waiting Room
3 Conservatory		39 Bakery		G	Salt Water Pump House
4 Q.M.Store House		43 Ordnance Building	Married Soldier's Qrs.	H	Tailor Shop
5 Carriage "		44 Baseline House		LH	Light House
6 Stable "		47 Hosp. Stewards Qrs.		BH	Bell "
7,8,9 Officer's Quarters		50 Prison Library		P.O	Post Office
10 Hospital		51 " No 1		A	Company Rear
11 Prison Lavatory		52 " " 2			Sewers
12,13,14 N.C.S.O. Quarters		53 " " 3			Drains
15 Married Soldier's Qrs.	Civilian Employes Qrs.	58 Old Prison Kitchen	Civilian Employes Qrs.		Fresh Water
22 Old Prison	22 a. Plumber's Shop	60 Prison Mess Hall			Salt Water
22 " "	22 b. Gymnasium & Ordnance Str. Hs.	61 " Kitchen			Gaspipe Railing
23 " Mess Hall	Laundry	62 " Shops			All Pavements are Concrete
25 Tool House		65 Guard House & Prison Office			All Roads are Macadam
27 Carpenter Shop		B New Barracks		sr.	Soil Pipe, Cast Iron.
28 Officers Store Rooms Q.M.& C.S.		C Corral		K	Lodge
33 Wharf		D Temporary Water Tanks		P.X	New Post Exchange. B.A.Richards

Pacific Branch
United States Military Prison.
November 1910
G.A. Ferrier
Lieut. Colonel 29th Infantry, U.S.A.
Commandant.

Alcatraz, 1891

THE ROCK AS A MILITARY PRISON

Alcatraz Island more by accident than design became the first army long-time prison. The inception of the prison was as mentioned earlier, a casual affair. The records, as far as the prison operations are concerned, are scarce. The type of punishment and all the details have not yet been found.

All Army posts had a place and provisions for the confinement of military offenders. There was no exception on Alcatraz. The guard house served in that capacity. This was, however, only for minor short-term offenses. The standard facilities usually consisted of general prison rooms for compliant prisoners and a few individual cells for those who did not go along with the discipline asked for. Alcatraz had both of those facilities. The location of these facilities were separate on Alcatraz. The cells for the more severe prisoners were in the basement of the Citadel on top of the island. The regular prison room was located in the basement of the defensive guardhouse, just 500 feet up from the wharf.

Early in the Civil War the garrison grew in numbers and so did the soldiers violating Army regulations. In 1861, out of a command of 268, fifteen were in confinement. From the start, the prisoners were a problem for Alcatraz. On September 10, 1862, Capt. Winder wrote the Department Headquarters that the "caponiere at the entrance of the fortification defending the approach from the wharf, is occupied by the guard and prisoners; the latter being so numerous they entirely fill the casement on the right of the entrance, rendering it necessary that the guard should occupy the corresponding one on the left. For this reason the howitzers intended for the defense of this approach have never been mounted, nor can they be until some other arrangement is made for the care of the prisoners." At that time we find a request by Winder that a suitable prison be built.

The imprisonment of 13 prisoners from the Presidio on Alcatraz marked the formal start of Alcatraz as a prison. At that time nobody could see that that move indeed was the beginning of 73 years of military penology on Alcatraz. On August 26, 1861, the Department Adjutant General wrote; "Any prisoner sent to your post by Lt. Col. Merchant (commanding officer at the Presidio) . . . will be used on the Island for police purposes until a court is ordered for their trial." The post commander on Alcatraz was concerned with this kind of order but did not envision that this was the formal start of a program that would be the only continuous one until the close of Alcatraz in 1963. In 1861, the adjutant general wrote: "Since August 27, 1861, Alcatraz Island in the Harbor of San Francisco, has been the point for collecting prisoners on the Pacific Coast."

The problem grew. And in the fall of 1861, the close quarters and lack of proper sanitation caused an outbreak of illness and forced the commander to house the prisoners in tents until a cleansing of the prison room was completed. Finally, between 1861-1863, a wood structure measuring 21 by 50 was constructed behind the guardhouse. The exact figures are not available, on how many prisoners, etc., and we find only scattered accounts of individuals confined on Alcatraz.

Prisoners from Army units were sent to Alcatraz, the first arriving in January, 1862. Some of the prisoners sent to Alcatraz represented a large cross-section of the population. In the same year orders were issued that Alcatraz was to accept any prisoner sent there by the U.S. marshal.

C.L. Weller, former governor and chairman of the Democratic State Committee, found himself confined on Alcatraz for a speech he made. Others who did not fit into the existing political structure were also sent to Alcatraz, such as State Assembly representative E.J.C. Kewen and Ben Walher, who organized a group to go and fight for the Confederacy. As mentioned in a previous chapter, the crew and passengers on the schooner *J.M. Chapman*, were at that time the largest group of Southern sympathizers to occupy the guardhouse.

As mentioned earlier, the prison became a major part of the work force on Alcatraz. Following the Civil War that population of prisoners changed. During the years of 1865-1868 the average number of prisoners was only 20. The concept of Alcatraz having prisoners was alive and would start to grow again with the building of a 30-foot x 50-foot brick cell block on the same spot where the temporary wood frame building had stood.

The idea of a permanent prison for long-term confinement for the Western Military Department, which included California, Nevada, Oregon, and the Territories of Arizona, Washington and Idaho, was mentioned by Maj. Gen. Henry W. Halleck. There was an interest in this idea, and everybody who had to make decisions went along. The adjutant general of the Army, Brig. Gen. Lorenzo Thomas, was interested in establishing military prisons around the country. The engineer in charge of Alcatraz (Mendell) went along with the idea, as long as it would not interrupt the firing of any gun.

1868 marked an increase in prisoners from 34 to 93 on Alcatraz; and by January, 1869, the population climbed to 127. This was a firm direction in the growth of Alcatraz, but did not meet with the endorsement or approval of everybody. Chief Engineer General Humphreys wrote his

Sallyport, Alcatraz guardhouse. The original sallyport is from the arch to the letter "A". Beyond the second arch the ceiling is the floor of two of the cellblocks. The gun room past the first arch to the left was the one used as the "dungeon" for the first prison. The two holes above the arch were used for the drawbridge chains and pulleys.

concern on this latest development:

It is now proposed to add to the establishment a mess room and kitchen for the use of prisoners confined in the building, and as a measure of security to protect the garrison and works from a danger of a rising of the prisoners. While there is not the same degree of objection to a general on Alcatraz Island that applies to the case of an enclosed Fort (as the Fort of Fort Point) it must still be urged that a permanent Fort for the defense of the seaboard is a most unsuitable place for the establishment for a general or departmental military prison. Guard duty for the prisoners always exacts large details from the garrison, while the works are not adapted to accommodate any troops beyond those necessary for the service of the guns. Hence, in case of emergency, the garrison will probably be found insufficient for its special duty; while the danger is at all times threatening — of a rising of prisoners.

Humphreys' point of view was shared by the adjutant general and the Secretary of War, but the prison would stay and ironically outlast the fortification.

The growth was very rapid. 1870's post return had listed 153 prisoners. More were on the way, and the post commander urgently pushed for new housing. Wooden cell blocks, on the northwest side of the guard houses were proposed. Very primitive cells, indeed, 2-inch plack floors, overlaid with sheet iron, 1/3/4-inch thick and covered with 1 1/4-inch flooring. The ventilation would only be a 4-inch span over each cell door and a 2-inch span below. The doors were to be solid wood. This was a three-tier cell structure.

Mendell, after some prisoners were housed in the

Only existing gunport on Alcatraz. U.S. Army armory room

northern Caponier, expressed his concerns: "There could scarcely be found a place more unsuitable for quarters. The room is comparatively without ventilation, and the health of those confined therein must suffer."

Not only was there concern on the part of the engineer as to the prisoners, but also on the part of the commanding officer and Washington. It was in 1870 that the first official records were kept on the military prisons. Flogging, a common practice, was stopped. The entire aspect of prison confinement took on a more regulated professional approach.

There had to be a mixing and blending of this life of freedom and life of confinement. The prisoners made up the bulk of the labor force, and it was with their labor that much of Alcatraz took shape. A 16-foot-wide and 120-foot-long building was to become the prison's own mess hall and kitchen. Up to this time the food was prepared by the garrison. The mess hall used was "an old, rotten place built for and formally used as a water tank." Time, place and quality of meals is probably the most crucial event in the daily routine of both prisoners and soldiers. A letter from Corporal Trim to the Army and Navy Journal in December of 1870 gives us a rare insight into the feelings and thoughts of this cohabitation on Alcatraz of prisoners and garrisons:

Sir: Believing that a few items from the "Pride of the Bay" might prove interesting to your readers, here goes. The post is garrisoned by Battery B., Second Artillery, whose commanding officer also commands the post. Having been designated by the division commander as a general prison for all prisoners in either of the three departments, who may receive any

lengthened term of sentence, there are at present writing 147 "scallawages" or rather "birds of passage" for they are nearly all deserters, serving out their sentences and doing good service for our "uncle" under direction of the engineer department, in improving the island.

On Thanksgiving Day the battery, and prisoners as well, were treated to one of those old-fashioned dinners usually given on such days. The bill of fare ranged from turkey and fixings to pudding, pies and fruit. In the evening the Dramatic Association gave one of their inimitable performances in their cosy little theatre, winding up the day's festivities with a dance, all of which combined to cause the boys to wish that Thanksgiving Day might come as regular as Sunday inspections do.

The performances of the Amateur Dramatic Association prove a source of great amusement to our "little world," and for an amateur association they deserve great credit for the creditable manner that they have followed in fitting up their theatre; it is well appointed, and some of their scenes are really good. They have a good orchestra of five pieces, and although only "buck soldiers," their actors may safely challenge comparison with those of any kindred association, "mariners" not excepted.

Corporal Tim.

All activities on Alcatraz started to take on a resemblance to daily life routine, rather than a constant combat-ready defense posture. The guardhouse had been expanded greatly by the addition of both frame and brick buildings that housed the military prisoners and their mess facilities. But the visible growth could be seen in the facilities set up for the garrison and their offices. Near the lighthouse was the bakery and the valued bowling alley. The school for the children and enlisted men could be found near the engineer's office on the northwest peak of the island. In 1866 this post was declared a chaplain post,

Military prison building

which meant that Alcatraz was allowed to have a permanent chaplain. This must have been a great help in stabilizing a civil social fabric. The chaplain and post surgeon had minimal alliance with the stiff military and prison format and, therefore, could deal with the individual human needs better. This in any situation as military or prison structure was a great relief factor. It is in the records of chaplain post surgeon that we find information so valuable in reconstructing the life of Alcatraz.

In the reports of the post surgeon we find a constant pushing for better facilities for the men. The deplorable sanitation facilities were a constant point of contention by the post surgeon. The post quarter master contributed to this record by reporting on the public buildings. In 1881 we find the first full written report on the prison complex on Alcatraz:

The military prison is situated on the northeastern part of the island. It is a collection of buildings, the center of which is an old caponier (guardhouse) which is considered useless at the present time for the defense of the post. It contains in the basement (originally the prison room) a washroom and bathroom for the prisoners, on the first floor the guard room and on the opposite side 10 single cells and four dungeons (dark cells?). This part of the prison is now only used for temporary confinement of refractory prisoners. On the top of the caponier (actually to the northwest) a strong frame building had been erected resting on the south side on a parallel building of brick. The brick building contains 45 single cells in three tiers (an 1879 description said it had two rows of cells, with two tiers in each row), a room for the non-commissioned officer of the guard, and the printing office (Alcatraz Prison Press); the frame building contains 42 double cells in three tiers.

A third building at right angle with the two former (and resting directly on top of the guardhouse) built of stout plank, contains 48 single and four double cells in two tiers. Galleries run along the tiers and connect the buildings. The average size of the cells is 8 to 12x6x3½ feet, thus giving to each an air space of 161 cubic feet. They are ventilated by air tubes in the walls and by open spaces in the top and bottom of the door of each cell.

The wing, a building in front of the guardhouse extending toward the wharf, had many uses through the years. Court martial, prison tailor shop and book binder's shop were all in this building. Chapel and library also found their

way into this structure. The fire in 1874 forced the post surgeon to move some of his patients into this temporary hospital ward. The Prison Dramatic Association, mentioned by Corporal Tim, probably held their performances here. The last use of this space was used in the later years as a pistol range.

The last prison building was added to this complex in 1887. This brought the number of cells to 185. This frame structure was added to a second frame structure built in front of the brick building.

Order N.R. 99 from Major Randal, 2nd lieutenant, first Artillery Post adjutant, complied with orders from Headquarters of the Department of California and issued the first regulation for the government of military prisons. These orders were printed in the printing office on Alcatraz. They read as follows:

Regulation and Existing Orders
for the Guidance of Prisoners

Every prisoner on admission will be placed in a reception cell and minutely and strictly searched and deprived of everything except his clothing. He will then be taken to the bathroom and thoroughly washed and clad in the prison dress, his hair cut close to his head, and his beard, whiskers and moustache trimmed.

Each prisoner on his admission will receive a number by which he will be known while in prison.

Prisoners will be divided into three classes, to be known as the first, second and third classes. Each class will be designated by a distinctive badge, to be attached to some conspicuous part of the outer garment of this prison dress.

Privileged members of the first class will be distinguished by a red band with a white stripe in the center; the first class by red band, second by a blue band, the third by a yellow band; the band of each man to be worn around the paper hat.

On being assigned to a class, each prisoner will be made acquainted by the person in charge, with the rules relating to the conduct and treatment of prisoners.

A copy of these rules will be kept posted in each prison room.

On their admission, prisoners will, except in very special cases, be placed in the second class, and may be reduced to third class for misconduct, or promotion to the first class for good conduct.

Reduction to the third class may be for any of the following reasons: (1) insubordination, or mutinous conduct; (2) misconduct; here even in comparatively unimportant matters, when it reveals the continued ill disposition of the

Right: Brick casemates. The first tier was completed in 1865, before work was suspended due to obsolescence of brick fortification. Temporary barracks stands on top of the casemates. Smaller buildings are the first sergeant's quarters and barbershop. Far right: Interior of temporary barracks. Bottom left: Hospital building. Bottom right: Prisoners at work on site of Battery 2 in 1910.

man; (3) quarreling when it culminates in an assault or a fight; (4) such disregard of rules or proprieties as shows in indifference to progress, or great want of self control, if continued for three months or more.

A strict rule of silence among prisoners of the third class, will be rigidly enforced.

Prisoners of the third class have not the privilege of the library, neither will they be permitted to write or receive letters or visits. When not at work they will be locked in their cells.

So reads in part Order 99, and from this document we can see that the formal approach, rather than the casual handling of prisoners, is firmly implanted on Alcatraz. The opinion of the post surgeon who inspected the prison in 1890 did not reflect a formal, efficient system in handling prisoners. He wrote that from the standpoint of modern penology the prison was "totally unequal to fulfill its legitimate purpose." Most of this concern stemmed not necessarily from the system of operation but rather from the facilities. Even Brig. Gen. Nelson Mills, commander of the Department of California, was alarmed at the condition of Alcatraz prison. He was so alarmed that he ordered immediate steps to be taken to change this situation. A special requisition passed and 193 strong iron doors were installed to replace the wooden ones, that provided no proper ventilation.

The method of punishment in the 70's did leave an impression on the entire system that never really disappeared. True, the flogging was outlawed for military prisons, but we find the wearing of a 12-pound ball and chain a part of the system. It vanished from Alcatraz in the mid 70's. Prisoners who violated the rules did receive additional punishment, such as lockup and unpleasant work assignment, such as working at the dump.

One must understand the type of prison the Army would have. The men serving in the 70's were poorly recruited. During the Civil War men were allowed to enter the service in spite of possible physical or mental defects. This was done in order to fulfill the authorized allotment of men. All types of crimes would be responsible for the confinement of soldiers, but the most prevalent one was that of desertion. After having been found guilty by a court martial, they started their sentence. Some of the other frequent offenses involved assault, theft, larceny and murder.

We find by checking the Alcatraz register of the 1870's that most prisoners served five years in confinement. The average age was 24 and the longest sentence was 20 years. The military broke their prisoners down into two major categories. One was the general prisoners and the other the military convicts. The general prisoners were those serving a sentence while still in the Army, and would return to their unit after completion of the sentence. The military convict would be released back to the civilian population with a dishonorable discharge after completing his sentence.

Alcatraz had many more military convicts than general prisoners. In that sense, we see the start of a reputation of a place for the worst on Alcatraz. The post returns made the distinction between the two groups up until 1912, when the term "military prisoners" was dropped and all convicts were referred to as general prisoners. The prisoners were broken down into the three groups mentioned earlier.

Left: Garrison on Alcatraz. Bottom left: Part of the sentry walk that ran around the stockade. The building in the background is the guardhouse. Bottom right: Prisoners making little rocks out of big ones.

These markings of groups later changed to general prison markings. Around 1906 a "P" was painted on the seat of their pants and a number was put on their hat. Civilian prisoners in other prisons wore the familiar black and white stripes. There was a time when each prisoner that had deserted the Army was branded, and later this was replaced by tatooing him with a "D" or "T" on the hip.

In 1889 the order came to Alcatraz that the prisoners were to wear regular Army clothes with all the brass removed. A sergeant, noting that they looked like the regular garrison, wrote: "Seeing them about in this way, or lounging around the wharf, a visitor naturally takes them for soldiers and is surprised when he is told they are convicts."

The military convict's life was not nearly as harsh and brutal as that of the federal prisoners that followed this period. A fair description of that time is found in an interview given by Sgt. John Lowder:

Alcatraz is not a prison in the sense of a penitentiary. In the Army the island ranks only as a military post, and is not a recognized prison, it being only an unusually large guardhouse, where men are kept for longer periods than at ordinary guardhouses. It has been largely built by convict labor at a trifling cost to the Government. The convicts are allowed the regular Army rations, and are clothed in condemned Army clothing. The officer of the day at the post attends to daily inspection, under the officer in command, who has general supervision. Guard duty is performed by the regular post guard, mounted each morning at 9 o'clock, and composed of men with whom many of the prisoners have served, side by side, for years. . . . The

guard, consisting of a sergeant, corporal and eight men, is changed each morning, the sentries being on the post two hours at a time only. One sentry paces to and fro on the top of the citadel, from which point he can see any small boat that may approach the island . . .

No craft can land anywhere at Alcatraz without the sergeant of the guard or a sentinel being on hand when the landing is effected. Even the Government steamer, *General McPherson*, cannot stop at the little wharf without the officer of the day and the guard being there to receive all who land. A second sentinel paces the wharf, while the third guards the way up the hill. The fourth guard's beat is along the top of the library and over a bridge connecting with the top of the cellhouse. This prevents all escapes and guards against either the soldiers or outside parties smuggling liquor in for the convicts . . . .

The cells are used only for sleeping purposes, and no convict is allowed to remain in his cell under any circumstances during the day. These wardrooms (corridors in the cellblocks) are the common assembly places indoors, where the prisoners have unrestricted social intercourse . . . .

There is no wall or fence around the prison buildings and when not at work the convicts are allowed to go at will anywhere about the prisongrounds or island except into the soldiers' quarters on the upper levels . . . .

The daily life on Alcatraz for soldiers and convicts begins with first call for reveille at 5 o'clock in the

Good view of sentry walk

morning. At the next call, fifteen minutes later, all turn out for the officer of the day. The prisoners do not return to their cells again until night, but file into the messroom for breakfast. When that is over, the small detachment that is now sent under guard to the Presidio to work on those grounds prepare to take the boat. Those who have work on the island go to do it, followed by a sentry who acts more in the capacity of a foreman than a guard. The unemployed pass the morning in the yard, wardrooms or library, which is open to them until 9 o'clock at night. Dinner is at 12 noon, and at 4 o'clock the General McPherson returns to the island with the batch taken to the Presidio in the morning. Supper is over by 5 o'clock, and the time until retreat is passed as the men choose. Generally they collect in groups about the outside or congregate in the library. At 6 o'clock all turn out for retreat, when the officer of the day again comes round. Dismissed from retreat, the first and second class men are locked in the library and the "yellow-bands" are locked in their wardroom. At tattoo the officer of the day again goes round, and every prisoner, standing at attention at his cell door, is counted, then locked in for the night.

Reading the prison register of 1870-1879, we find that most prisoners were in jail for desertion. One point of interest is the way some of these offenders were described. Of the 537 mentioned some stand out, such as:

Samuel McCullogh, First Cavalry; desertion — dishonorably discharged and drummed out. He was marked indelibly with the letter "D": sentenced to five years of hard labor, wearing ball-and-chain. Despite the sentence, he was employed as Alcatraz baker.

Napoleon Labeare, First Cavalry; desertion — five years hard labor, wearing ball-and-chain, he was placed in the dungeon for four days for refusing to work and for using obscene language to a sentinel.

David Allen, 23, Infantry; desertion — "A rascal." Swindled the Catholic Priest out of $75 after his discharge.

Dennis J. Daly, Jr., First Cavalry; desertion — "A perfectly worthless character. An excellent penman."

Martin Burke, First Cavalry; desertion and theft — sentenced to three years. He was a very good workman, but was drunk on two or three occasions from alcohol procured from the paint shop.

Among all of these characters there was also a large civilian population on Alcatraz. The children of the Army personnel on the island reflected a rough average of 20 boys and girls. Chinese servants made up the largest civilian population. It was a common practice for military officers who had their families with them to employ Chinese servants. This practice was common on western Army posts from Idaho to Arizona. This large Chinese population on Alcatraz may have been the reason for the visit of the Chinese consul general of San Francisco to the the island in 1887.

The hospital matron, usually the wife of an enlisted man, was another civilian employee. She was responsible for doing the hospital laundry. When that chore was sent to San Francisco to do, there still was the appointing of a matron.

As the prison part of Alcatraz started pushing itself into the forefront, so did a more relaxed civilian, military style. The first recreation was restricted for lack of flat space but after the prison labor leveled the southeast end of the island, baseball became part of the social fabric of this island. The soldier had an amusement room up until 1890 that provided him with pool. 1890 brought a major improvement to the after-work hour. The Post Surgeon reported: "The canteen recently established is an appreci-

78

ated innovation, and will undoubtedly tend to render the enlisted man more contented with his monotonous life upon this rather circumscribed and lonely isle."

These civilians and the children must have offered a change in mood for the soldiers. Someone to talk to, other than military, and to hear the innocent laughter of the children. However, in March of 1888, a fire that destroyed two of the oldest frame structures on Alcatraz, the old engineer's stable and mechanic's quarters, broke out. This fire was attributed to some children. "The children of the post have been in the habit of using this building (the stable) as a secret playhouse, making their way therein through an opening known only to themselves." The children played with matches and started this fire. The fire in the San Francisco paper was reported as follows:

About 6 o'clock yesterday afternoon the attention of residents of the south end of town was attracted to Alcatraz Island, as dense volumes of smoke there betokened the fact that the fortress was on fire. As the fire for some time seemed to be beyond the control of those fighting it, the excitement of the thousands of spectators who from Telegraph Hill and other elevations watched the progress of the flames became intense. Some of the more imaginative half expected a terrific explosion, while others fell to speculating on the chances of the military prisoners, either for escape or for baking in the cells.

The question of escape was a prevalent one. The security on Alcatraz could not have been under the classification of maximum security, but most of the escapes in those days occurred from the work details on the mainland.

This was not something a Commander would pride him-

self in, so we don't find all attempts recorded in the post returns. There have been many attempts, and most of them demonstrated some degree of inventiveness. The prisoners escaping Alcatraz had the bay to contend with. In May of 1878, two prisoners commandeered a boat to make their escape good. Again in 1884 an unspecified number of prisoners stole a boat belonging to the engineer department. The engineers got their boat back from a farmer but the prisoners vanished. A newspaper report tells of another boat escape:

Two more military prisoners escaped Alcatraz yesterday morning. The men chose their time wisely. After making a hearty breakfast at 5:30, they went down to the slip, appropriated engineer Thomas' boat and pulled out toward Lime Point. The sentry could have shot them, had he been so minded, but as the steamer Sonoma was expected every second, it was thought she could overhaul and recapture the fugitives before the shore was reached. The Sonoma did appear and did give chase, but the men had a long start and succeeded in reaching Lime Point. They jumped ashore, and, clambering up the bank, were soon lost to sight. The Sonoma took the boat back to Alcatraz.

A desperate attempt happened in 1906, when four prisoners stole a butter vat from the bakery and attempted to put it to sea. The current and wind made it impossible for them to go far, so they returned to Alcatraz, where they hid in a powder magazine.

There was some violence connected to escape attempts. In 1892 a guard shot a prisoner attempting to flee the work party on the mainland. In 1900 another prisoner was shot attempting to flee. Escaping from

Left top: First military prison. The original cellblock is the dark brick unit with a door and five windows. At the time of this picture it was used as a guardroom.
Bottom right: View of bottom prison with paint shop in foreground.

Alcatraz was probably on the mind of all prisoners by the military. Considering the lack of security in those days, comparatively few escaped.

During this period most of the money for work on Alcatraz came from the quartermaster account. It was the quartermaster who received the $570 to repair the retaining wall leading from the wharf to the Citadel. Almost all the construction changes had to do with the expanding population of the prisoners, not the military defense fortification.

The Spanish-American War and the Philippine Insurrection were responsible for the next set of major changes on Alcatraz. Both the activities and the physical changes occurred fast. Consider the fact that between 1898 and 1900 Alcatraz had 13 commanding officers. Now for the first time since the Civil War did Alcatraz house California Volunteers: thus doubling Alcatraz' garrison. The prison population jumped to 441 at the same time. Almost overnight the facilities were totally insufficient. The soldiers were put into every nook and cranny; every available space was used. This put a strain on Alcatraz that had everybody concerned. All of this triggered the greatest burst of activities on Alcatraz since the major changes took place in the early 1870's.

The gymnasium was torn down to make room for a wing on the hospital. An operating room, laboratories and a 16-bed ward with barred windows were built. The parade ground soon fell to the construction of a new, temporary prison.

Barracks for the garrison, enlarging the hospital and many small improvements were the main activities of the day. The main laborers' force were the prisoners. In order to house the constantly arriving new prisoners, all space available was used to erect new prison buildings. The commanding general at San Francisco, Maj. Gen. William "Pecos Bill" Shafter, recommended a third cell block for the prison. The War Department approved; and by putting two men in a cell, the total that could be housed was 480. The buildings and the cells were ready upon the arrival of the shipment of prisoners from Manila in 1900.

The new cell buildings were frame and the roofs contained skylights. A wooden walk around the top of the stockade allowed the sentries to pace all around the prison. The problem of sanitation was solved with a chute from the prison to the water's edge. This new prison was a far cry from the first lower prison. This prison building was a nightmare for many on January 6, 1902. A lamp had melted the soldered connection and fell to the floor. The oil scattered and only a "cool, quick-witted man", a guard, saved the

lives of the prisoners by yelling "fire" and by putting the fire out. The fear was immense and the post quartermaster said: "The prisoners are crazed with fear every time any unusual outside noise is made at night, fearing fire and that they will be burned to death."

It was time for a permanent prison building on Alcatraz. The department quartermaster argued that the prison should be on Angel Island. Both the Department Commander, Maj. Gen. S.B.M. Young, and the Commander of the Army, Lt. General Nelson A. Miles, wanted the new prison on Alcatraz. Their recommendation was that it should be constructed "as soon as possible."

Reams of paper were used in the planning of this permanent prison building. The old prison was inspected many times in order for everybody, it seems, to make their recommendations. Attempts were made at projecting the number of prisoners to be housed on Alcatraz. Recommendations kept pouring in and the inspection reports gave a good opinionated description of the conditions. Capt. A.M. Fuller gave a description that reflected a lot of people's opinions: "rotten and unsafe; the sanitary conditions very dangerous (sic) to health. They are dank and damp and are fire traps of the most approved kind." The

Bottom: North end of prison. The sentry in the sentry box
was the only obstacle for prisoners
wanting to go to the west end of the island.

mess hall, he said, was "an absolute apology." The mess hall seating capacity was 200, and so the 450 prisoners had to eat in two and one-half shifts. The prisoners with 40, 20, 15-year sentences had to be walked ¼ mile through the post to the mess hall. Many guards were needed for that; and this was a dangerous method, especially in the winter, in early darkness. Fuller further pointed out that prisoners had escaped from their marching columns.

Others who investigated the prison agreed with Fuller. A Lt. Col. Thomas H. Hardburg had thoughts of moving the prison to Angel Island, but in his final decision he agreed to have the prison on Alcatraz. A probable consideration was the fact that Alcatraz could be guarded easily and that escape was very difficult. A concern was also with the fire power on Alcatraz. Everybody was convinced that the structure would not interfere with the 6-inch rapid-fire gun batteries. The role of Alcatraz as an important defense position of San Francisco was fading away.

Even though work was going on to improve the upper prison, the thought of a permanent prison dominated the planning phases. In April of 1907, the War Department decided to build a permanent prison on Alcatraz. The change of the entire garrison would take place and the regular garrison would be replaced with prison guards.

The four companies of the 22nd Infantry, Alcatraz garrison, was being replaced by the newly formed Third and Fourth Companies, U.S. Military Guard. Maj. Abner Pickering, the commanding officer of the 22nd Infantry, a West Point graduate, turned over the command of Alcatraz to Maj. Reuben B. Turner, also a West Point graduate.

Maj. Turner became the first Commander of the Pacific Branch, U.S. Military Prison. He was no longer referred to as the "commanding officer," but became now a "commandant." The island itself was no longer referred to as just Alcatraz Island but became "Pacific Branch, U.S. Military Prison, Alcatraz Island."

Maj. Turner and the year 1907, in the history of Alcatraz, mark the final change from military defense post to prison. Later, the military prison became a federal prison and Alcatraz remained a prison until its formal closure. Even though Maj. Turner was in charge of the personnel, his major accomplishment as far as Alcatraz is concerned is that he was in charge of designing and building the main prison.

Before all the plans were completed, in 1908 he started the preliminary work of installing a railroad. This railroad moved construction material from the newly completed steel dock to the building site. A lot of building material had to be shipped to Alcatraz, but much of the material already

on Alcatraz was to be used. Turner, a bright, dynamic commandant, demonstrated a high degree of enthusiasm for this project. His plans were well thought out, and he incorporated some of the old building's features into the new. For example, he used an iron staircase from the Citadel between the cell block and the mess room, down to the lavatory. He also hooked up the new drain to the already existing ceramic pipes.

The most disturbing part of Turner's building project was the demolition of the 59-year-old Citadel. This building made the skyline of Alcatraz a very identifiable landmark. The building itself was a clean-cut, beautiful brick building.

Turner wrote, "The most difficult part of the work has been wrecking of 'Citadel' and the necessary forming over basement walls and the 'moat' to carry cell room floor on utility corridors, and also forming over fresh-water cisterns so as not to interfere with their present use. This is completed and rough concrete floor is in place." The ditch and the basement of the Citadel were preserved under the prison and used as punishment cells. These cells were referred to as Spanish dungeons. The irony is that the Spanish never even set foot on the island. These cells were to be "ventilated artificially by means of a fan and proper ducts."

Preserved were the two original granite entrances to the Citadel: "The main entrance to the hall at the front, and entrance to the cell room at the NE corner are contemplated to be constructed from the material used in the entrances to the old citadel, which is a fine granular gray colored granite, finely cut and moulded. It is on heavy block work in jambs with solid piece pilasters at the sides and neat moulded entabular across the top. There are but two of these entrances in the citadel which it is deemed suit-

able to use." Both were used: one as the private entrance of the commandant's office, the other at one corner of cell block.

As time passed, in the 1960's, the discussion of what to do with Alcatraz was tossed around. The question of preserving the main building was a point of debate. The people who wanted to keep the building were faced with a monumental cost factor. The cost factor played a major role in the closing of Alcatraz in 1963. A key point of discussion in the preserving of the main building and its cost was the point as to how it was built, the material used. It is clear that the cement structures were falling apart and much of the blame goes to the way it was built in the first place. The complete history of the construction is not available, so we don't know if the cement was mixed with fresh water or salt water, a point that would affect the longevity of this material.

The best Portland cement was used, and the quartermaster's department urged the use of waterproof compound in the mixing. Fresh water was available since delivery was on a daily basis. The boat *General McDowell* made the daily water runs, stopping at Alcatraz as its first stop around the harbor. This went on until the acquisition of a water boat, in 1910, called the *El Aquador*.

Turner's labor force was composed of prisoners, but he had several civilians on the job. These civilians employed included three carpenters, one cement finisher, the iron workers, and one plasterer. In 1909 Turner reported the building 40% complete. The walls and floor for 168 cells were in place. The forms for the hospital walls and the near wing were in place, awaiting the cement. In November of 1909, a War Department inspector wrote: "A great deal of work has been done on the prison building. The Western half, containing dining room, kitchen, etc., is under roof; the cells in the east end are partly finished, and the forms for all walls are in place. The concrete work is splendid and a very satisfactory exterior finish has been obtained by the use of cement wash, composed of one part cement to two parts sand, mixed thin and applied with a brush."

Top right: Interior of a first prison cell block. The strap-iron doors on the three tiers of cells replaced solid wooden ones that allowed very little ventilation.

San Quentin was used by Turner as a model in the construction of cell fronts and locking devices. He was sent a set of blueprints from the Pauly Jail Building Company in St. Louis. The quartermaster general also recommended the use of the Flushometer-type toilet bowls. This type was eventually installed.

The hospital, one of the first parts completed, caused some negative reactions from the surgeon. He felt that the hospital was not big enough and did not have all the necessary facilities, such as an operating room, laboratory and darkroom. He urged that a separate building be built. His boss, the surgeon general, disagreed and stated the hospital and its space was adequate. Other construction directly related to this new building was the building of an electric and steam power plant. These two buildings were built on the northeastern side of the island on top of the Battery Halleck. All of this construction, except the walls around the boiler, was of brick.

Turner was proud of this work and wrote many good descriptions of the structure. He wrote: "This is a combination of structural steel and reinforced steel concrete, the former being used where necessary to carry unusually heavy loads, such as reservoirs on roof . . . it will have accommodations for six hundred (600) military convicts (one to a cell), heated by steam, lighted by electricity, ventilated by a modified system of forced ventilation with a steam cooking aparatus installed in kitchen."

The permanence of these buildings changed some of the ways prisons were ruled. The arrival of larger groups of prisoners forced the system to deal with the management of prisoners on a large scale. The traditions that remained were not really recorded for anybody's consumption, leaving the rumors and various accounts as to prisoner handling, just that, rumors. However, the construction of a permanent prison, the development of professional guards and the change from a departmental prison to a branch of military prison must have been the major factors for this development.

The regulation governing the daily procedures only told what had to be done. No process ever confirmed that it was done; no guard ever wrote down what he actually did. Up to this writing, no written account of a military prisoner has been found. It is hard to guess what the prisoner went through. Just because something was written on paper didn't guarantee the prisoner that that is what he had coming. The frustration of the guards would be reflected in the way they interpreted the rules. Horrors and brutality, surely part of everyday routine, went unrecorded. The mental health of some prisoners under these conditions must have been affected. There is one report in the *San Francisco Chronicle* of a prisoner who had mental problems. George Bender, who had set fire to homes in the Philippines, also set a fire on Alcatraz; and on the ceiling of his cell he had burned "Bender the Firebug will burn this jail tonight." This prisoner was carrying a ball and chain, and was sent to Kansas State Penitentiary "in an iron cage."

We have a better record of what the prisoner did for work than how he felt. Maj. Gen. George B. Davis, who inspected Alcatraz Prison in 1905, leaves us with a good report of the employment of the 271 prisoners:

105 in Quartermaster Department, working on the new barracks, getting out rock on Angel Island, etc.

32 on police work at different posts around the harbor

54 constructing the new departmental rifle range at Point Bonita (Fort Barry)

36 in the prison — cooks, waiters, room orderlies, barbers, tailors, etc.

15 sick (8 in hospital, 1 in quarters, and 6 on light duty)

1 waiting release

6 third-class prisoners not at work (third order was the lowest class of prisoners; these six were possibly kept in their cells)

6 awaiting trial

General Davis made several observations that are very valuable to us today. In his report he mentioned that Lt. Lawrence Halstead (the officer in charge) had been able to organize the filing system of the prisoners which until that time had been totally without a system. He mentions that Halstead "has arranged and filed the prison records, which were in considerable confusion, and has installed a very complete and well-considered method of identification by thumb and finger marks, in which the experience of the French police authorities and those of Scotland Yard in London has been fully utilized." Only since 1891 has the use of finger-printing as means of identification been in

View up California Street after 1906 San Francisco earthquake

use. Davis' comments on the general prison population reads as follows:

The prison rules are strict; obedience is rigidly enforced; no partiality is shown and the prisoners are taught that their future largely depends upon a faithful and conscientious observance of the prison rules. There are a few "trusties" employed, but all are engaged upon public work; none are allowed to be used as servants by officers, or others, or to work in or about the officers' quarters. Most violations of prison rules are met by reductions in grade, or by deductions from good conduct time. No solitary confinement on bread and water diet has been imposed for a year or more; and as that form of punishment has been found unsatisfactory and not productive of good results, the dungeons (in the guardhouse) in which this was executed have been abandoned. To replace these an iron cage has been constructed in one of the rooms on the second floor of the (lower?) prison; but this has been used but once in eight months . . . .

The moral condition of the prisoners is better than was to be expected, when it is considered that it is impossible to establish schools among them, to teach trades, or to apply modern prison administration . . . . Obscene practices are of rare occurrence and are severely punished. But two prisoners are known to be addicted to the use of opium; one being a pronounced case.

The general was impressed by all of what he saw, to the point of recommending the prisoners' way of building blocks to be used on the reconstruction at the Presidio. However, he did not feel Alcatraz was a good place for a prison. He mentioned that escaping from Alcatraz would not be too difficult.

The issue of who should be on Alcatraz to guard these prisoners was discussed many times, but the best account on this topic is given by Lieutenant McElroy in a report called "New Military Prison in the Pacific Division." He felt that permanent guards should be on Alcatraz. "With regular organizations guarding general prisoners, we have the recruit thrown in daily contact with the prisoner; no worse condition could exist and the recruit will eventually look upon him, not as a man serving a just sentence, but simply an unfortunate, a man misjudged, and he, the young recruit, may sometime be a fellow sufferer." He further states, "A guard should be as far removed from (the prisoner) as possible. He should be the guard and the prisoner the prisoner at all times and under all conditions. There should be no community of interest between them, no fellow feeling." His opinion doesn't only deal with the guards but with the commanding staff as well. He feels that the noncommissioned officers should have four months' instruction to learn how to oversee.

In his final recommendations he lists three ways with which to form a permanent guard. Hire a civilian guard, form a special enlisted service corps (his least favorite way), or form a detail from organizations. This last method was the one used to form the guard companies that arrived on Alcatraz one year later.

Most of the prisoners on Alcatraz at that time were military prisoners with military offenses. Following the Spanish-American War, San Francisco took on the role as one of the Army's most important ports of embarcation. Sea traffic was heavy and a side effect of this traffic was the stowaway. The stowaways boarded the steamers of Nagasaki. Arriving in the United States, these stowaways were detained on Alcatraz. The record showed five Japanese stowaways from the U.S. Transport *Logan* detained on Alcatraz for "safekeeping." Recorded in the post returns we find a total of two Russians, one Chinese, and 15 Japanese stowaways on Alcatraz. Another group of prisoners on Alcatraz were several Indians. The history of the Indians on Alcatraz is in a separate chapter in this book.

April 1906 was probably the most significant April in the history of San Francisco, the day of the great earthquake. San Francisco burned to the ground and here is not the place to deal with that phase of history, except as it related directly to Alcatraz. After the Broadway Street Jail was closed, all the prisoners were ferried to Alcatraz. The duration of their stay is not recorded in the post returns.

Conscientious objectors and political prisoners started to arrive on Alcatraz in the years of World War I. At that time other prisons had strikes and the leaders were sent to Alcatraz. An interesting report of prison news is to be found in the *San Francisco Chronicle* of June, 1919, regarding political prisoners. The story is related over several days and was part of a national hysteria against spies, German-

Top right: North end, showing structural steel to carry water tanks and mess hall and basement
Bottom left: Alcatraz, April, 1902

sounding names and conscientious objectors. Some University of California, Berkeley Campus, students took advantage of the customs of Sunday visitors for prisoners on Alcatraz. These "radical" students passed out "Bolshevik literature," urging a prison strike. Small stickers demanding the release of political prisoners were confiscated by the guards. This "Red propaganda" was part of a total movement but found its way into the prison, for here were those political prisoners around which an issue could be formed.

We can feel, even at the beginning of Alcatraz as a prison, that it was a different type of prison. Maybe it was just a feeling by all concerned, but it governed the actions of many. To go to Alcatraz was special; the "worst" would be sent there.

On July 1, 1908, the records show 330 prisoners confined. 526 were processed during that year. These military prisoners came from:

Department of California	168
Department of Columbia	106
Department of Texas	24
Department of Luzon	126
Department of Mindanao	59
Department of Visayas	42
Philippines Division	1

The crimes of that year were larceny, perjury, assault and burglary. The prisoners submitted 117 applications for clemency, of which 19 were granted by the War Department. 309 of this year's prisoners were native, 27 foreign born. They wrote 3,650 letters, received 7,300 pieces of mail. A prison school had been started and the first group of volunteer students numbered 26. They studied reading, writing, spelling, arithmetic and geography. Their school day was just one hour: from 6:30 to 7:30 p.m., and for 5 days a week. The library now hosted 228 books, magazines and periodicals. The occupations of these prisoners ran the scale; every occupation was represented.

During the day the average work force was 302, of whom 30 worked on Angel Island, in the stone quarries.

The rest were employed as follows:

Inside Stockade		Outside Stockade	
2	barbers	3	barbers
2	in bath and lavatory	1	blacksmith
1	breadman	4	blacksmith helpers
7	cooks	6	carpenters
3	dishwashers	6	dockmen
3	room orderlies	1	at sterilizing plant
1	shoemaker	1	engineer, pumping plant
1	tailor	1	engineer hoisting
4	vegetable men	12	laborers
8	waiters	1	lamplighter
2	yardmen	14	laundrymen
37		6	teamsters
		6	messengers
		4	painters
		1	plumber
		4	plumber helpers
		1	printer
		4	police party
		76	

A large labor force was employed on the construction of the main cellhouse. The commanding staff listed as following: The commandant, the adjutant (books and records), the quartermaster (supplies, equipment, and construction), the commissary (food), the surgeon (hospital), the chaplain (chapel, library and school), the executive officer

Construction of main cell block, west side

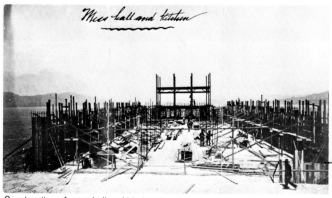

Construction of mess hall and kitchen

(direct charge of prisoners and cells), the exchange officer, and the ordnance and signal officer (weapons and communications). Some of the officers had other minor duties, such as athletic officer or mess officer.

A long set of rules now were enforced and governed all aspects of prison life. Some of their rules were instituted earlier on Alcatraz and listed in an early part of this book. We start the list after rules with solitary confinement.

Prisoners received 18 ounces of bread a day and as much water as they desired during their stay in solitary confinement.

Convicts were kept off hard labor six days a week and were allowed time off on seven national holidays. The commandant could suspend labor during unusual weather to protect the health of his prisoners. They engaged in every kind of police, maintenance, and construction activity, as well as clothing manufacture and rock breaking, not only on Alcatraz but at other posts around San Francisco.

Prisoners could make complaints, either in person or in writing, provided they went through the proper channels, but frivolous or untruthful complaints could bring punishment. Mass petitions or protest were not allowed.

Every cell was inspected daily for cleanliness, contraband articles, or escape attempts. Weekly inspections of the convict and the prison were also held.

All these rules were there to control an environment that was not pleasant for anybody.

Violations of the rules would be punished with the following official acts:

Reprimand
Deprivation of a meal
Deprivation of tobacco privileges
Deprivation of letter privileges
Reduction in class
Solitary confinement on restricted diet
Solitary confinement on restricted diet and handcuffed to
　door
Loss of part of good conduct time
Loss of all good conduct time

Many other things could have been done by individual guards against a prisoner but those acts are not recorded and are lost to us. For example, the rules state that solitary confinement was limited to 14 days at a time and there was an interval of 14 days between successive periods of confinement. The guard could "lose track" of the days or he could not honor the 14 days in between the times actually spent in the confinement. This practice was still very much in use in the modern penitentiary on Alcatraz up to its close.

The act of trying to escape was always most severely punished. The prisoner would lose all good time earned and could be court martialed, in addition. One of the most sacred things to a prisoner is his mail. In the military prison on Alcatraz he could send one letter a month to his family or friends. This letter was inspected. The mail received could be held unopened until his release. Lots of mail was lost that way. Personal contact with non-prisoners could take place once a month, providing there was written approval by the commandant.

July 4th and Thanksgiving marked the days the commandant had to notify the War Department of those convicts who, after 18 months of service, had the best good conduct record. At the time the prisoner was released he received a $10 suit of clothing and $5 cash. He received fare to his home, providing it was not farther than his place of enlistment.

February 6, 1912, the new prison building received its first dwellers. The cells completed, locks in place, steam plant furnishing steam heat, the power on, the lights working and the rules and routines clear, the history of the rock turns another corner. One wonders of the personal feelings of all these men, military prisoners, building their own detention facilities. It must have felt strange to walk into a cell, call it home just days after one was freely moving in and out of it with materials and tools, building it. There it stood, ready to deal with questionable ideology and characters.

The voices of objection, other than from the people confined, were still to be heard. Maj. Gen. Enoch H. Crowder concluded in 1913: "The buildings on Alcatraz constitute

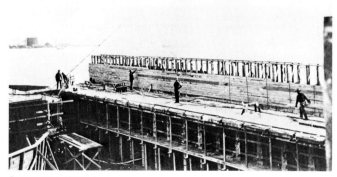

Construction of cells in progress

Construction materials for main cell block. Note sentry house on right side.

Construction of administrative section. Note granite door frame in place.

model detention barracks, and the sole objection to continuing it as such is, first, the sentimental one that their prominence in the harbor advertises, in a way unfair to the military service, the discipline of the Army, and, second, the more substantial objection that there are . . . no facilities for outdoor drill and instruction of prisoners confined therein." He wrote clearly, when he stated, "It is somewhat difficult to understand how the War Department came to recommend and Congress to appropriate the large sum of $250,000 for a new prison building on such a site as Alcatraz." At the same time the Bureau of Immigration preferred Alcatraz over Angel Island as an immigration station.

Crowder, however, had many more points of contention. To him the most objectionable fact was that on Alcatraz the military prisoner shared confinement with prisoners guilty of common law and statutory offenses. He recommended other changes and special legislation.

On March 4, 1915, Alcatraz Prison became officially designated as the Pacific Branch, United States Disciplinary Barracks (PBUSDB). The same year the Secretary of War ordered the establishment of a school of instruction. This order prompted a different type of publicity for Alcatraz, and we read in the University of Washington newspaper a reprint of the *Seattle P.I.* account on January 16, 1917:

Educating Prisoners

Two years ago the Secretary of War ordered the establishment of a school of instruction at the military prison at Alcatraz Island, California, and directed that steps be taken to ameliorate the condition of the prisoners. The prison became known as the United States Disciplinary Barracks,

Coustruction of main cell house

and many of the harsh, humiliating measures in vogue before the reforms were undertaken were abolished. The military authorities, in short, began treating the prisoners like men, and the result of the two years has shown it pays.

The school of instruction established at Alcatraz Island has three departments: department of graded school education, department of vocational training and department of military training. Every prisoner received instruction of some sort, and in many cases the improvement in the men, both physically and mentally, was marvelous.

There are fewer than 500 prisoners at the disciplinary barracks and more than half of these are between 21 and 25 years old. The majority of the prisoners are deserters or offenders against military regulations. The opportunity for making useful citizens of those who under old reform had been hardened or crushed by prison life was splendid. In many cases the military offenders were returned to the Army as good soldiers, and in other cases, not a few were sent into civil life with honorable discharges from the Army, with positions secured for them.

The new policy in force at Alcatraz Island indicated the trend of the times throughout the country. Vocational training and instruction in the common school branches give the prisoners self-reliance and equipment which will enable them to make places in the outside world. The old system with its cruelty and its humiliation, seems to have passed out of fashion nearly everywhere. Occasionally, one hears of a prison where the tortures of the Spanish Inquisition are still in vogue, but these places happily are few and far between. Society has adopted better methods for protecting itself. It endeavors nowadays to shape the bent twig in its proper course.

When this education opportunity started on Alcatraz, only 26 voluntarily enrolled. In June of 1917 the grade school boasted 227 enrolled men. The number of those who qualified in May and advanced to the next grade were as follows: Reading 76, Writing 35, Arithmetic 27, History 25, Grammar 34, Geography 24. Ninety men were taking university extension courses. The subjects covered a large area of interest. Spanish led with 24 enrolled, shop arithmetic 16, stenography 10, bookkeeping, free hand drawing and electrical engineering all had 8; French 7, penmanship 4, English composition 3; mechanics and salesmanship had one enrolled each.

The mission of the Alcatraz department of Graded School of Education; in accordance with paragraph 28 of the regulations for the governing of the Pacific Branch of the United States Disciplinary Barracks was to supply the deficiencies along general education lines of all men in the institution. From what little information is available, it seems that this mission was successful. A letter by a former prisoner in the vocational program on Alcatraz reveals some of that success:

Dear Sir,

I have the pleasure in writing you a few lines to let you know that I am well and working everyday and making twenty-five dollars a week. I arrived home Monday night at 6:25 p.m. and Tuesday I got a job as an automobile mechanic and am doing fine. They all like me at the garage and I am on my way for advancement which I am in hopes to secure in about five weeks if nothing happens.

Sincerely yours
(no signature)

The Vocational Training Department mission was to teach the men various trades. The goal was to enable prisoners to get jobs upon release. Deserving men were granted certificates of merit to assist them in securing employment. In addition, the authorities made special efforts on behalf of the men to secure them employment.

The concept as reflected in the following article only lasted on Alcatraz until 1934.

A man serving in the Disciplinary Barracks has an ever ready means of self improvement in the school of

instruction which is held here, and there is no reason why one who has worked conscientiously at these barracks in this school cannot become a much more efficient man whether he returns to civilian life or the Army.

In addition to the theoretical instruction which he receives in the Graded School Department he receives practical instruction in the Department of Vocational Training. This department corresponds very much to the manual training department in any school or college where a man learns to become handy in manual work connected with his profession.

U. S. Alcatraz Island, a Military Prison in San Francisco Bay.
Mt. Tamalpais in the Distance.

1934 marked the end of this type of effort to restore the man to normal life. That year was the last year of the military type prison. It became a federal prison.

"Regulations for the Government of the United States Disciplinary Barracks and its Branches" were published in

Top right: Cells in upper prison, 1902
Bottom right: Interior of new cell house, 1910.
Cell block "A" with still no concrete on the floor.

1915. Most regulations remained the same as those previously stated. There were some changes and modifications. No longer were the inmates called "military convicts," but were referred to as "general prisoners." The staff was enlarged, a prisoner's mess officer and a parole officer were added to the commandant's staff. Food was improved and the number of letters per month a prisoner could write was unlimited, but they were still inspected.

The handling of the two types of prisoners was spelled out in the 1916 orders:

General prisoners enrolled in disciplinary companies will be designated by name and not by number; will not be required to work in the same party with general prisoners not enrolled in disciplinary companies; will be quartered in a separate section of the barracks; will be seated at separate tables in the diningroom and in a section in the chapel; will be permitted the privileges of rendering the prescribed military salute; and when under arms, at work, or at meals, will be permitted to converse with each other under the restrictions that govern enlisted men while similarly engaged.

Those orders also spell out the training these prisoners would get in Army matters, such as rifle training. Significant, however, was the constant attempt at upgrading the individual prisoners. General Crowder came up with the concept of restoring the prisoners to better classes and eventually to return him to full military duty. In June of 1924 it is recorded that 1,396 men who had been on Alcatraz were "returned to the colors as soldiers by restoration or re-enlistment after training of this institution." The process used was that of a training process period. When a prisoner served one-third of his sentence, he automatically came before the Enrollment Board. He was given a chance to enroll in the training program. After the prisoner committed himself to this training program, the board would investigate his background and military records. No man was recommended "unless the board believes that he will be an asset to the Army."

The training session lasted four months and the prisoner was referred to as the "disciple." After this training period, he appeared in front of the board for consideration. This system worked well and 70% of those restored to duty "made good." In those days Alcatraz was at times referred to as "A Common-Sense Prison." Naturally, this is the official version as to how good it all worked on Alcatraz. Many areas have not been revealed to us and may be lost forever.

No matter what method is used to control man there will never be a solution that guarantees results. Compared to the later years of confinement on Alcatraz, there was then a better way to resolve one's predicament. However, education, help from the officials, and opportunity for self-improvement was still not enough to keep the prisoner from attempting to beat the system.

Probably the most memorable method used by prisoners trying to beat the system was when the system itself was used. The most skillfully planned escape was perpetrated on Alcatraz. At that time on Alcatraz there was a way that would allow a prisoner to apply for leniency and be granted early dismissal. This process was well known to the inmates. Alcatraz did not provide much for these men to do. A person wanting to plan an escape would have the

Top right: View looking out from military powder storage room under today's recreation yard.
Bottom left: Four pictures of the inside of powder storage rooms usde during the military days. Note the granite stone used to center the hinges and door latches. Bottom left picture shows an original door still on its hinge.

time needed to attend to the details. Such a plan was used by four prisoners in the mid 20's. These four men found the time to draw up and print an official document, the same used by officials in the city when filing the prisoners' applications for leniency. After printing these documents they proceeded to forge the signature of the commanding officer on Alcatraz.

"The documents bore all manner of splendid reasons for executive clemency, and are all of them written as though they were the recommendations of the commandant of the prison island."

All mail on Alcatraz was censored but these papers managed to slip into the mail bag leaving the island. All details were attended to and these papers traveled the road of bureaucracy to its final destination — Alcatraz. The route was long, first to department headquarters, then from bureau to bureau, and finally to the commander. The forged strong recommendation by the island commandant led the commander to sign an order, ordering the release of those men.

The order for pardon arrived back on the island and the dismissal process started. No soldier would question this, for he is not to question. So the men were processed, given a suit of clothes, as was the custom. They each received a check for $5, and boarded the Alcatraz boat for the mainland. Their freedom lasted only three or four years. This was not the end of the plot. $125 worth of checks in the name of the Alcatraz quartermaster were cashed in San Francisco. All the forms were forged, but were so authentic looking that their cashing presented no problems.

The conclusion of this well planned and executed escape ended when one of the escapees was arrested for drunkenness in a bar. He was identified and sent back to Alcatraz. The remaining three escapees vanished. In the press this escape was covered with headlines referring to Alcatraz as "Uncle Sam's Devil Island": a title used many times when describing this island in the San Francisco Bay.

In reality lives on those two islands have very little in common. But the myth, the exotic and the unknown make both these islands a mystery to the average person. Life on Alcatraz was very organized and the process well implemented. The reconstruction of life on Alcatraz in the late 20's is not easy, but we have sufficient clues to create a fairly accurate record.

Besides the strict routine it appears that sound psychology was used to govern the daily life on Alcatraz. Mass frustration most often leads to unreasonable action and there was no difference on Alcatraz. At one point the prisoners promoted the rumor that during outside work, on a given signal, all the prisoners were to rush to the water's edge, dive in and take a chance of swimming to San Francisco or Oakland. The prisoners understood that many would be drowned, more captured, but enough would make it. Here comes to play the peer pressure, the friend would convince a friend, and on and on. Nobody would be left out. The drama and danger would be sufficient motivation and reason would not prevail. Colonel G. Maury Crallé had just taken command of the Disciplinary Barracks. Crallé got wind of this rumor and in his reactions demonstrated the soundest possible way of dealing with a potential disaster.

"GO AHEAD, SWIM!"
With these words Col. G. Maury Crallé, commandant, quashed a revolt at Alcatraz.

Had he turned to the prescribed routine handling of this rumor, there would have surely been a stand-off situation. The routine way would have been to double the precautions, eliminate privileges and smash the potential revolt by singling out the leaders and punishing them. Col Crallé did not take this action. Rather, he had all prisoners gather on the parade ground. Instead of having armed guards surround the prisoners, he posted unarmed guards that could have been overpowered without a problem by the mass of prisoners. The fact in itself must have taken the first wind out of the prisoners. Each prisoner expected force power and authority to be flaunted. To their surprise the commandant casually walked in front of the men and started talking to them. In his brief comments he told them he was aware of the planned mass escape and gave his opinion as to how stupid this escape concept was. He stared at the prisoners and told them that now was the time and that he would not stand in their way. He made it clear he wanted it settled one way or another. The fact that he would not give pursuit and not notify the police or the mainland was enough for the prisoners to act. The prospect of a cold, dangerous swim and the reality of the unexcited colonel took the glamour, charm or thrill out of their plan. This was a daring and unusual solution by what must be called a common-sense or psychologically-wise commandant. The bonus for the commandant was that he gained a certain amount of respect from every prisoner.

91

Brick archway leading behind military barracks

G. Maury Crallé is a typical Army officer of varied background. He was born on a plantation near Blackstone, Virginia in 1898; a West Point graduate, he served in administrative positions. His duties took him to Cuba, Alaska, Panama, with service in the Philippines Insurrection and on the Mexican border. After the World War, he was detailed to the War Department, Board of Appraisers, and later to the War Claims Board. Study at the Infantry School and graduation from the General Staff School preceded his appointment as commandant at Alcatraz in 1926.

The daily routines on Alcatraz were aimed at giving each prisoner the intensive and intelligent consideration needed toward a law-abiding decency.

The process, however, was rigid. Here is the daily schedule used in the first thirty days of confinement.

First call	5:50 am
Sick call	6:30 am
Breakfast	7:00 am
Work starts	7:30 am
Recall from work	11:45 am
Dinner	12:00 noon
Work starts	1:00 pm
Supper	5:30 pm
Sick call	6:00 pm
Motion pictures	7:00 pm
Entertainments	7:00 pm
Lights out	9:00 pm
School for illiterates daily	1:00 to 4:00 pm
Saturday aftenoon and Sunday	no labor
Sunday outdoor recreation	morning and afternoon

The work for the entering prisoner meant that pick, shovel and wheelbarrow were his tools for seven and a half hours a day. Sunday was for rest and recreation. On Alcatraz we find the following recreations: baseball, handball, soccer, football and boxing. The food was fairly good and these were some of the foods served:

Breakfast

Cream of wheat and milk
Fried link sausage
French toast
Butter
Syrup
Bread and coffee

Dinner

Split pea soup and crackers
Boiled ham
Boiled cabbage
Boiled beans and bacon
Mashed potatoes
Banana pudding
Bread and coffee

Supper

Fried beef steak
Fried onions
Hashed browned potatoes
Brown gravy
String beans
Bread and coffee
Jam

Most prisoners had spent time in Army confinement. Usually this was in what was called the guardhouse. There the guards watched closely and were armed. Here on Alcatraz their only weapon of defense was a light wooden baton. This baton was no thicker than a broomstick and about fourteen inches long. There was one armed sentry on the island during the daylight hours, and he was guarding the landing wharves. All arms are left at the front desk where a guard entered the cell house. This practice lasted until the day Alcatraz closed. These guards knew that they had the backing of the entire U.S. Army, but did not parade this power in front of the prisoners.

After completing his first thirty days, the prisoner is scheduled for a session with the Medical Corps. A psychiatrist must judge the present mental condition, the capacity for improvement, and the odds of survival of each prisoner. The psychiatrist's office was a very special place, a place detached from the rest of the Army life. Here a prisoner could express himself freely, "get it off his chest," so to speak. The setting was informal and would provide an opportunity to express whatever was on one's mind. This place was very important, for the doctor in charge of this office would ultimately have a large say-so in the outcome of the prisoner's future. There is no question that some men tried to play games in order to influence or persuade the doctor one way or another. But each man entering the office was told of the game-playing and its effect on any outcome. The doctor would then not provide the sympathy but, rather, would blister that prisoner with the way he looked to others, and how he had to quit his nonsense and grow up.

The prisoners were given psychometric tests and rating. Most had reasonably average intelligence, but even the

zone between normality and insanity plagued each doctor assigned to deal with those evaluations. Today in our modern penal system nothing much has changed. We have more data, but there is still that gray zone.

There was another avenue for a prisoner to talk without the military formalities, and that is with the chaplain. He held open house for every prisoner who wanted to talk with him. In 1928 the chaplain had a bodyguard, Lobo, a police

dog, who was never more than six feet behind the chaplain. The chaplain attended to the spiritual needs of the men, but was also in charge of the recreational activities. The chaplain carried the griefs, regrets and confidences of hundreds of prisoners as part of his burden. The chaplain, on an overall basis, wanted to eliminate brooding and self-pity in those men, and went to great lengths in organizing activities on Alcatraz. In those days the aim was for the most humanitarian environment possible under the circumstances, a policy totally abandoned in 1934.

The systems on Alcatraz seemed to work, but there were questions. The predominant one was that of the cost factor. Alcatraz did not have to contend with unions and, therefore, could use its large labor force very economically. The construction of the industrial building demonstrates a clear process of sound financing. The commandant did not wait for approval for the funds; he went out and borrowed $2,500 from the Farm Colony Fund at Fort Leavenworth, Kansas. This loan was immediately paid off. With this small sum he built a model industry system, and with prison labor built an all-concrete, 50x136-foot three-story building at a cost of $15,000. The industry employed fifty-three men; paid them $2 a month each. This industry took in $13,000 a year. We find that the cost of operating the Disciplinary Barracks was less expensive than comparable civilian institutes. The next cost, after deducting actual earnings and taking a credit for prisoner labor performed off the island at the rate of twenty-five cents an hour, was $167,419 for the year ending June 31, 1929. This was a per capita average of $311, a figure that compared favorable with Sing Sing at $335, or Great Meadows at $400.

The cost was always a major factor in the history of

Alcatraz. The only advantage of the military prison days was the use of prisoners as laborers. The U.S. penitentiary days could not use the same system of discipline and flexibility needed in using the manpower confined on this rock.

Attention by the Army to landscaping on Alcatraz was minimal. Flower gardens can be seen around some office quarters, but no significant effort was made to beautify Alcatraz. In 1924 a group of prisoners was used to man the shovels in a planting program. The California Spring Blossom and Wild Flower Association had an agreement with the Army on a beautification plan for Alcatraz. The chair-person of this association was Mrs. George R. Child, a landscape gardener herself. Donations by the members of this association enabled the planting of 300 trees and shrubs and various flowers and herbs. The Army had neglected the planting of trees and flowers on Alcatraz; and, possibly this was due to the lack of a natural water source. Today we find many plants on Alcatraz that survived on just the moisture of the fog and the rain. Some grass seeds and flower seeds did get to Alcatraz via the birds' diet.

During the Federal Bureau of Prison tenure there was practically no new planting. When the Army left, the care given to these plants by the prisoners came to an end.

400 Gardens on Alcatraz Island

Today we find quite a variety of plants on Alcatraz:

Trees
Apple — *Malus sp.*
Eucalyptus
Fig — *Ficus carica*
Monterey Cypress — *Cupressus Macrocarpa*
New Zealand Cabbage Tree — *Cordyline Australia*

Shrubs
California Blackberry — *Rubus vitifolius*
Dwarf Coyote Brush — *Baccharis pilularis*
English Ivy — *Hedera helix*
Fuchsia — *Fuchsia hybridia*
Geranium — *Pelargonium zonale*
Pride of Madeira — *Echium fastuosum*
Yellow Brush Lupin — *Lupinus arboreus*

Succulents
Century Plant — *Agave americana*
Ice Plant — *Mesembryanthemem edule/chilense*
Purple Carpet — *Mesembryanthemum floribundum*

Flowers
Bear's Breech — *Acanthus mollis*
California Poppy — *Eschoscholzia california*
False Garlic — *Nothoscordium inodorum*
Honeysuckly — *Lonicera japonica*
Iris — *Iris*
Ithuriel's Spear — *Brodiaea elegans*
Lily of the Nile — *Agapanthus africanus*
Montbretia — *Crocosmia crocosmaeflora*
Nasturtium — *Tropaeolum majus*
Periwinkle — *Vinca major*
Pincushions — *Scabiosa atropurpurea*
Red Hot Poker — *Kniphofia uvaria*
Sour Grass — *Oxalis pes-capre*
Valerian — *Centranthus ruber*
Watsonia — *Watsonia angusta/rosea*

"THE ROCK" AS A FEDERAL PENITENTIARY

THE ROCK AS A FEDERAL PENETENTIARY

Warden James A. Johnston, 1934-1948.

In May of 1933 the wheels of a process started to grind away towards the ultimate fate of Alcatraz. The War Department let it leak that it was intending to abandon the U.S. Disciplinary Barracks on Alcatraz. Once that idea became known, everybody stepped forward with ideas as to what should happen to Alcatraz.

In June of 1933 Secretary of War George H. Dern wrote Attorney General H.S. Cummings, asking if the Justice Department would be interested in taking over Alcatraz. The first response by the Director of the Bureau of Prisons, Sanford Bates, was "No!" He felt that Alcatraz was not suitable as a federal prison. Bates reversed his opinion in three weeks and recommended that the most desperate, irredeemable type could be housed on Alcatraz. He felt that only 200 of them should be on this island. That was all it took — the opinion of Bates — for the Attorney General to notify the Secretary of War that indeed they were interested in obtaining Alcatraz from the Army. The signature of Secretary of War Dern on the permit was dated October 13, 1933.

Several reasons underscore the thinking of the Bureau of Prisons leading to the acquisition of Alcatraz. A primary reason had to be the fact that the then current federal facilities were overcrowded. One has to think of the specific time in history to understand these conditions. Bank robberies, kidnapping and the gangster era were in full swing. The nation was shocked and frightened. The pressure mounted for the law enforcement people to do something. Laws were passed and federal authorities had broader range in fighting crime.

The punishment increased, and the war against gangsters, racketeers and desperados was fierce — many shoot-outs, many deaths, but also many more arrests. This breed of criminal was considered terribly dangerous to society, and the authorities felt a need for special institutions of maximum security and minimum privileges for the confinement of such ruthless individuals.

No time was wasted. In October, 1933, the man to be in charge of refining the present structures to fit into the philosophy of maximum security/minimum privileges accepted his appointment as the first warden of Alcatraz. Warden James A. Johnston, a small man in stature, started the process of inspection and recommendations for the needed changes.

The citizens of San Francisco started their fight in opposition to Alcatraz becoming a federal penitentiary in their front yard. The local papers were full of back-and-forth arguments, recommendations and appeals. The San Francisco *Chronicle* ran editorials, articles and letters on October 14, 16, 17, 19, 20, and 21 of 1933, all against such action. Individuals, as well as groups, had something to say. The Chairman of the Chamber of Commerce, J.W. Malliard, Jr., stated: "I don't think an influx of such prisoners is at all desirable."

The fear that these prisoners on Alcatraz would escape to San Francisco was very audible. The Chief of Police, William J. Quinn, the Police Commission, and the San Francisco Board of Supervisors voiced their opposition to having these gangsters so near. The history of military escapees was brought to the forefront, and Doris McLeod and Gloria Scigliano swam successfully to the island. A peace statue on the island was one of the many recommendations for its use.

The protest was not only voiced in the Bay Area. Commissioner William J. Ellis of New Jersey feared the promotion of "grave danger . . . of cruelties and repressive measures," should a separate institution open on Alcatraz. Commissioner Walter N. Thayer, Jr., of New York felt that "prison officials should be able to handle dangerous criminals by segregation within their own walls."

During all of this debate many facts were distorted and many myths were perpetuated. Consider the letter by Philip O'Farrell:

To the Editor: I am inclined to think that your article in the November Midmonthly Survey on the use of Alcatraz prison in San Francisco Bay for vicious and irredeemable criminals is based on insufficient information. Alcatraz is an ideal prison site, according to Medieval standards. It was an ideal prison site when the first prison was established there by the Spanish. For at that time an ideal prison was a place where prisoners could be kept in dungeons hollowed out of the rock. Today the dungeons are not in use but they are still there.

Neither the size nor the topography of the island lends itself to the development of "facilities for educational, recreational and industrial therapies which are an accepted part of modern penology."

Alcatraz Island, 1932

The old myth that "escape by swimming away is impossible," has recently been exploded by three girls, one of whom swam from the island to the mainland; another of whom swam from the mainland clear around the island and back to the mainland. The feat of the third I have forgotten.

The question as to whether Alcatraz will become a second Devil's Island we can dismiss as most improbable. But the real objection to the use of the island is that its size and topography render it unsuitable for a modern prison.

Philip O'Farrell

Nothing changed this course of history for Alcatraz. The Justice Department continued with its plans. During this transition period the activities on Alcatraz were intense: the military closing up and the federal government opening up for business. The plan called for the immediate leaving of the Army, but that could not be carried out, for the laundry industry had to continue its service for the Army posts in the Bay Area. It was clear to everybody that it would take time to convert the facilities over to the maximum security facility needed and, in the meantime, the laundry had to keep operating. The military stayed and their prisoners kept the laundry industry operating. During that period the Bureau of Prisons revamped the prison facilities.

These two agencies had to work well together in order to make this type of a transition smooth. There were many details to consider to keep this island operational. One main point was that of the water supply and transportation. The Army turned over its motor launch, *General McDowell*, to the Justice Department, thus assuring transportation between the mainland and Alcatraz. The water was to be supplied by the Army from its normal Bay Area water run, with part of the cost paid by the Justice Department. Civilian personnel necessary to run Alcatraz were also transferred over to the Justice Department.

Many experts and companies were consulted and sent to Alcatraz. All this activity was designed to provide the Justice Department with an accurate account of what was necessary to turn their island into a maximum security penitentiary. Sanford Bates, Director of the Bureau of Prisons, came up with the idea of installing gas canisters and metal detectors all over the island. He requested the Prison Equipment Bureau in Cincinnati, Ohio to send an expert to Alcatraz.

The report that followed the visit of this expert, Robert C. Burge, was completed in November, 1933. This report was full of recommendations and changes that needed to be made. The entire island was affected by these recommendations. The main reason for its effect was that the new prisoners were to be in the area of the prison building only, and that that required tremendous security, something not needed for the much freer Army prisoners. The entire eastern side of the island, from the powerhouse to and including the southeastern end of the island, would be off-limits to convicts. "The tunnel that runs from the powerhouse across to building No. 84 (cleaning plant) must be made escape-proof, as it forms a direct connection from the walled area to the outside part of the island. This can be done by installing a tool-proof, grated door in either or both ends of the tunnel." The list of recommendations was long. The main recommendation was that all windows on the cell house receive tool-proof window guards. Tool-proof window guards were to be installed on all windows in any area where the prisoners had access: shower room in the basement, mess hall, hospital and all hallways.

Bunge's recommendations were in detail and it is clear he understood the concept of maximum security. He called for the installation of new durable plate and grating doors between the cell room and the outside stairway on the northwest corner of the cell room. This was to become the door leading all prisoners to the industrial area, the only door prisoners would use to leave the main building. All doors were to receive observation panels. The individual cells were to receive new, modern cell fronts and locking devices made of tool-proof steel. The area of these cell blocks between the top of the upper cell and the underside of the roof slab were to be enclosed with tool-proof steel grating.

Removal of the four sets of spiral stairs and the construction of a new stairway in the open space where the cell blocks are divided was recommended. The list was long and in great detail. Most of these recommendations were carried out, and Alcatraz was turning into a maximum security facility.

The main life support system on Alcatraz was inspected by Thomas F. Butterworth in January, 1934. Here is what he found on Alcatraz:

Boiler Plant: Three 130-horsepower B and W water tube boilers, and one 208-horsepower Erie City bent water tube boiler.

Electric Generators: Two 50-kilowatt, compound steam-engine-driven 125/250 volt, three-wire, direct current generators; and one 150-kilowatt, diesel-engine-driven, 125/250 volt three-wire direct current generator.

Water System: The salt water system consisted of a pumping plant located in the power plant and a 100,000-gallon storage tank on the roof of the prison. Fresh water was pumped to a 100,000-gallon storage tank also on the prison roof. There was a new 250,000-gallon soft-water storage tank on the northwest end of the island that had just been completed by the Army. The cisterns located below the prison were still in use. The weekly amount of water that would be used by 600 prisoners and the laundry would be 110,000-gallons, which would cost $34,000 per year.

Lighting system: Electricity was generated in the power plant at 125/250 volts D.C., three-wire systems, 125 volts for lighting, 250 volts for power. Butterworth recommended an emergency lighting system be installed in the building being used as a morgue.

Fire protection: Fire hydrants were on Alcatraz and water would be pumped to them after closing a valve at the "detention buildings." He recommended an entirely new system of fire mains. He listed the existing fire-fighting aparatus: 1 one-cylinder, hand-drawn, wheel-type extinguisher

3 two-cylinder, hand-drawn, wheel-type extinguisher

4 hand-drawn hose carts

14 one-quart pyrene extinguishers

99 2½-gallon soda extinguishers

1250 feet of 2½-inch double-packet, in poor condition

Completed powerhouse, 1934

Top and bottom interior views of boiler room as seen today

A water softener, bake oven and ice machine were also part of the recommendations resulting from his inspection tour. These systems were vital to a life totally self-sufficient and in no way connected to the mainland. All the work was given out to civilian firms under contract. The Stewart Iron Works Company, Cincinnati, won the contract for new steel work and other alterations. The total sum of that contract was more than the original cost of the prison. The major items in that contract were the doors and locking devices for the individual cells.

Removing cell fronts and pointing face	$ 4,675
Removing doors and closing openings	1,858
Doors	23,667
Cutoff grating with door	12,122
Grating top of cells to ceiling	10,000
Wire screens	2,925
Window guards	25,662
Cell fronts	56,510
Locking device and control boxes	62,258
Gun gallery	12,572
Stairs	2,056
Drilling holes for new work	2,582
	$216,927

All these improvements were the recommendations of Robert C. Bunge. Many firms received contracts for the various alterations. People came to inspect and offer their own recommendations but in the end it was all under the direct control of the warden. During this modification stage, he was very much a part of this process.

One of the main jobs of Warden Johnston was to scout the nation for the qualified personnel he needed to start the maximum security operation on "the Rock." He received a list from the Civil Service Commission. The list contained names of employees laid off during the depression who were entitled to reemployment, and names of officers at other institutions that were available for transfer to Alcatraz. Johnston wrote to McNeil, Leavenworth, Lewisburg, Chillicothe and Atlanta, interviewing applicants. Thirty men were selected, formed into a class and sent to McNeil Island Penitentiary for training.

As the final preparations for building and staff were in progress, the warden was summoned to Washington, where he was informed of the way the department wanted to use the island. The Island of Alcatraz was to be a maximum security prison with minimum privileges. They wanted to be sure that Alcatraz could handle the type of prisoners they wanted to send there. Warden James A. Johnston was not new at this. He was known by reputation as a tough disciplinarian. He was responsible for carrying out reforms at state institutions such as Folsom and San Quentin. He was enthusiastic and assured Attorney General Cummings and Director Bates that he fully understood his mission on Alcatraz.

Warden James A. Johnston took office on January 2, 1934 and moved into his home on Alcatraz on April 5, 1934. This home, not standing today, was a first-class home. The description by the Assistant Director for Fiscal and Business Administration, W.T. Hammack, describes it: "Today I inspected the house which has been recently

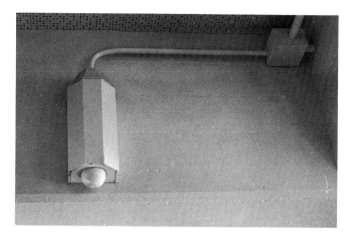

Left: Mess hall gas release control box. This control box was on the outside of the mess hall. Bottom: Gas canister mounted in the mess hall.

vacated by Col Weeks. It is the best house on the island and should be used by the warden. It is enormous, plenty large enough for two sets of quarters. There are five big rooms and a porch around two sides of the house on the first floor. There are five bedrooms on the second floor and two on the third. There are four bathrooms." This building was built in 1929 on the site of the commandant's home. The photographs that remain attest to the beauty of this home, elegant in style, true to its time period and generous in its comforts.

The commandant of the post, Colonel Webb, was rushing to complete the necessary work to get the Army out, while the warden was rushing to get the facilities ready for the first shipment of convicts. All the contracts had been awarded by the department and all that was left were the various inspections to confirm the completion and readiness of all structures. The first Bureau of Prsions person to move onto Alcatraz was the Chief Clerk, L.O. Mills. He was, so to speak, the overseer of all the transition detail. He had a long correspondence with his friend, Hammack.

The tool-proof steel bars, the greatest expense item,

underwent a test, In one of the cells, a bar was attacked with three hacksaws. After 20 minutes of sawing, only the outside softer steel could be penetrated. The inside hard steel would not allow the blades to penetrate. A bar was put into a vise and sawed at with a piano wire and was cut in half. But, despite this half success, the steel bars were accepted as satisfactory.

One of the final items to be worked on was the gas guns. Johnston did not agree with the recommendations that gas be put all over the place, including the cellhouse. He recommended the messhall. "It is impossible to predict what will happen or when or where, but experience has shown that the messhall is generally the place where agitators focus mass action." He did not want gas in the cellhouse and said that if it would be needed, it could easily be thrown in via grenades.

The installation of the gas guns in the mess hall was completed on August 14. All these gas guns were installed on the ceiling and were operated by remote control. A guard on watch on the outside of the mess hall could push the buttons that would release the gas. Two other gas guns in the entrance corridor could be released by the armorer, who had a view of that area through a vision panel set in the wall.

The telephone system was installed and operational by the end of July. The radio system was installed by the Coast Guard, who gave the guards their final instruction on the operation of the equipment on July 30, 1934.

On August 11, 1934, Alcatraz was ready for inspection. Hammack inspected the completed work. He found several details not satisfactory. Most of these were later corrected. But ready or not, the U.S. Penitentiary, Alcatraz Island, was open for business.

Right: Dock guard tower.
Bottom: The warden's house.

June 21, 1934

Mr. James A. Johnston, Warden,
Alcatraz, California.

My dear Mr. Johnston:

I am leaving Alcatraz this day, my work as Commandant being completed on turning over the Island to you as representative of the Department of Justice.

Before I go, I wish you to know how much I appreciate the thoughtful, considerate methods you used in assisting in the solution of the many problems that confronted us during the somewhat difficult period of reconstruction and joint occupancy just past.

Wishing you success in your new responsibilities as Warden of the United States Penitentiary at Alcatraz, I am

Most sincerely yours,

WILLIAM C. WEBB
Colonel, Field Artillery, Commandant.

James A. Johnston was fully in charge of Alcatraz. All was in place. The orders could go out for the shipment of convicts to be sent to the ultimate holding place of the U.S. Government's "Devil's Island," Alcatraz — "the Rock."

The character of Alcatraz was clearly established and outlined in simple but firm language.

Alcatraz was to be operated on the principle of very limited privileges to inmates.

The privilege of having visitors was to be earned, no visitors were to be allowed during a convict's first three months, and then only one visit per month.

Regular meetings of a parole board were not to be scheduled, and no parole officer was to be appointed.

No welfare work was to be undertaken.

There would be no direct commitments from the courts to Alcatraz. Prisoners were to come by transfer from other institutions.

Inmates could attain lawyers only after the written permission of the Attorney General.

The usual institutional library would be provided, along with limited educational facilities.

Mail privileges were to be limited. No original letters were to be delivered to prisoners, only typed copies of letters received.

Newspapers, magazines, radios, and other forms of entertainment were all prohibited.

It was up to Warden Johnston to draw on all his experience to create and maintain a foolproof system. His men were specially selected and all reasonable precautions and training were given. He organized Alcatraz into a precision institution. His guards were given strict orders and pro-

the entire process of being bad, outside in a community and inside in confinement: persons who would stop at nothing. A rigorous course of physical training — gymnastics, marching, drilling, boxing, wrestling, jujitsu, use of gas and the handling of firearms were part of this training. This was the physical part, but the mental part was also attended to. Lectures in sociology, psychology, penology, criminology and role-playing situations were the training that would be needed by a seasoned guard. This training program lasted until 1942 and was only stopped because of the War and the shortage of men.

cedures to follow. The shifts were organized into three groups. Each shift was given a color code.

Day-yellow . 7:00 am to 5:00 pm . . . ten hours
Night-red . . 5:00 pm to 12:00 pm   seven hours

Morning-green   12:00 to 7:00 pm   seven hours

Not all stations were manned all three shifts. Each guard on each shift had his own number. By August, just before the first convicts arrived, Alcatraz had 52 guards on the payroll. The guard stations were as follows:

Dock Guard . . . . Power House Tower
Transfer Guard . . . . Road Tower
Guard Truck Driver . . . . Gun Galley East
Main Gate . . . . Gun Galley West
Main Gate and Patrolman   . . .   East Island Patrol
Armory . . . . Industries Mech Guard
Cell House . . . . Policing and Gardening
Cell House Plumber . . . Utility and Special Detail
Officers Mess, Kitchen, Mess Hall .One day in seven
Dock Tower . . . . Annual Leave
Hill Tower . . . . Sick Leave

These guards, correctional officers (as some would correct you) or "hacks" (as called by the inmates) were Johnston's main instrument of control.

As the number of prisoners increased, so did the number of guards present during lockups, unlocks and counts. Twelve guards were present in the main cell house four times a day: 6:50 pm, 12:00 noon, 12:20 pm and 4:50 pm.

These guards, especially selected, received special training. One of the rules on Alcatraz was that no arms were allowed inside the cell house. The guards could not rely on fire power to control these prisoners. There must have been an added factor to the thinking process of these guards. The men confined on Alcatraz were types that would not hesitate to kill. The type and character was special. They were hardened criminals that went through

DEPARTMENT OF JUSTICE
BUREAU OF PRISONS
In-Service Training Certificate

This is to certify that
EUGENE D. FORBES
has satisfactorily completed the course required for BASIC
TRAINING : FOUR WEEKS

E. E. Buchner
Instructor

ALCATRAZ, CALIFORNIA
Institution

Warden

James V. Bennett
Director Bureau of Prisons
Washington, D.C.

DECEMBER 19, 1950
Date

The first list of arms needed on Alcatraz was as follows:

Arms
10 Shotguns — 12-guage
30 Pistols automatic — 45-cal
12 Rifles automatic — 30-cal Browning
12 Rifles, 30-cal Springfield, M 1903

Ammunition
15,000 cartridges for 45-cal Colt automatic pistol
6,000 cartridges for 30-cal Browning automatic rifle
6,000 cartridges for 30-cal Springfield rifle
1,000 cartridges for 12-guage shotgun, brass, loaded with 00 buckshot

Top right: Alcatraz switchboard. Bottom left: Two duty instruction folders with a Winchester 12-gauge riot gun of 1897.

Assessories (incomplete list)
      30 holsters for 45-cal Colt pistol, right hand
150 magazines for 45-cal Colt pistols, right hand
  30 bolts for 45-cal Colt pistols, right hand cleaning
       equipment, repair kits, extra parts

Gas
      6 Federal gas riot guns 1½-inch caliber
100 gas projectiles

A carefully detailed procedure for every aspect of Alcatraz life was drawn up by the warden. Attention was

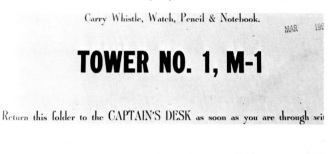

Carry Whistle, Watch, Pencil & Notebook.

MAR 196

TOWER NO. 1, M-1

Return this folder to the CAPTAIN'S DESK as soon as you are through wit

Carry Whistle, Watch, Pencil & Notebook.

MAR 1962

LIEUTENANT

MORNING WATCH

Return this folder to the CAPTAIN'S DESK as soon as you are through with it.

given to each detail and to holding true to the intended image of maximum security, with no privileges. The locking and unlocking of the cells was of immense importance. This was the most established foolproof way of count and control.

1. The deputy warden is in command and gives the signals. He takes a position at the east end of the cell house, between blocks B and C.
2. The lieutenant of the watch takes a position at the west end of the cell house, between blocks B and C; there he receives reports of count from the guards.
3. The guards take their assigned positions, ready to take

the count when the signal is given. On signal, the count is started on the south side of block B and the north side of block C.
4. As each guard completes his count he goes to the west end of the cell block and the report must be made as soon as it is ready.
5. After his report of count, each guard returns quickly to his position. Upon the whistle signal, guards open the cells in the same order of movement as when taking count.
6. After the prisoners have stepped out of their cells, the deputy warden and the lieutenant give hand signals for locking the cells. The second whistle is the signal to start prisoners moving in an orderly manner to the dining hall or yard.

No matter how well the structures were designed, the final control and safety factor was the man on duty. This guard had to be able to evaluate any situation, notice anything different and, most of the time, be able to anticipate the mood or action of each inmate. The warden, aware of this fact, went to great lengths to establish and write down the rules that would guide the guards in any situation. The list is a full description of his special duties:

UNITED STATES PENITENTIARY
ALCATRAZ, CALIFORNIA

SPECIAL DUTIES FOR OFFICERS
DURING COUNTS AND UNLOCKS
MEALS, LOCKUPS AND COUNTS

Visiting Room Officer: Officer on duty will be alert for any indications, being exhibited by officers at the Dining Room Gate, and of any disturbances in the Dining Room. In case of receiving or observing any signs that there is a disturbance in the Dining Room, he will immediately notify the warden and associate warden, and officer of highest authority who may be available; and will put out a general alarm and assemble all available lieutenants and officers

on the island.

Gallery Counters: Counts will be started when the count signal bell has stopped ringing. Look into each cell, counting every inmate on your assigned gallery. Observe each door to see that it is properly closed. Do not try to see how fast you can circle the gallery, but make sure that every man is standing up at the door. Make a written report on form No. 63, of each instance of failure to stand at the door. A miscount is a very serious error, and reflects on an officer's efficiency report, to his disadvantage. All counts and unlocks (except Sunday yard unlocks) will start at the west end of the cell house. All lockups will start at the east end of the cell house.

Officers Assigned to Duty in the Dining Room: Thoroughly familiarize yourself with the location of the different dining room positions, as indicated on the attached chart showing the location arrangements. Take up your position before inmates march into the dining room, or as quickly as possible after completion of your cell house duties. After taking your position in the dining room, check all knives, forks, spoons, cups, table equipment, and portions of food that may be on the tables, in order that you may be assured that there is the proper quantity of each for the number of inmates to be seated at each table. Observe the conduct of inmates marching into the dining room, maintain order in the line, observe the seating, and prevent any unnecessary loud talking. Report, on Form No. 63, any inmate who deliberately stalls, or wastes food.

Handling of Keys: The safeguarding of keys is a paramount duty of each custodial officer who is entrusted with

them. Under "Safeguarding," there are several outstanding precautions which must be strictly adhered to, *viz.*:

1. Never permit inmates to get possession of any keys other than those issued to them for use in connection with their work.
2. Never drop keys. Keys which have been dropped are likely to have their points bent, and subsequent use may injure the tumblers of the locks.
3. Never throw keys from one officer to another. Either pass the keys from hand to hand, or fasten them securely to a line, or to other means of conveyance to and from galleries and towers.
4. Carry and use keys in as inconspicuous a manner as possible. Do not allow inmates to become familiar with the numbers and identities of keys.
5. Never insert a wrong key in a lock. Always check the key number to make certain that it is the proper one for the lock to be opened. Practically all injuries to locks have been caused by using a wrong key. Never attempt to "force" a key to turn a lock. A very light pressure is sufficient.
6. Never relieve a post without first making a thorough count and check of the keys. Never turn over a post until you are sure that your relief officer has checked the keys and has agreed that he has counted and accepted them.

Handling of Padlocks: Padlocks are, usually sturdy pieces of mechanism, but abuse and inconsiderate handling will cause trouble or mechanical breakdown. Observance of the following precautions will tend to lengthen the life and usefulness of padlocks:

1. NEVER OIL PADLOCKS. The use of oil in padlocks tends to cause the mechanism to collect and hold dust and grit, which will gum a lock and obstruct its proper operation. Always use graphite for lubrication.
2. NEVER DROP OR HAMMER A PADLOCK. Either of these actions is likely to so deform the lock as to make it useless.
3. NEVER LEAVE A PADLOCK HANGING OPEN ON ITS

STAPLE. When a padlock is operated, always snap it closed on the staple, while the door, gate, cabinet, etc., is in use.

4. NEVER ATTEMPT TO REPAIR A PADLOCK. When a padlock seems to be out of order, report the condition, in writing, to the lieutenant of the watch or to the captain.

SHOP BREAKDOWN

What to Search For: Contraband (any and all articles not regularly issued or specifically authorized are contraband); preparations for escape attempt.

How to Search: Formulate a plan which will assure that no area of the shop will be overlooked. Apparently innocent places are often the most logical hiding places for contraband articles.

Caution: Bear in mind the possibility that coverings of openings, even though seemingly securely fastened, may be removeable, and that openings made in preparation for escape attempts may be concealed or covered. Authorized articles are often utilized for the concealment of contraband articles. Be alert to watch for and guard against the misuse of tools or materials to make saws, wrenches, jacks, spreaders, bombs, explosives, knives, guns, or other appliances which could be used to aid in escapes.

FRISKING OF INMATES

What to Search For: Contraband of all kinds.

Where to Search: Over *entire* body, from head to foot, and into the pockets and other concealed places.

How To Search: With sufficient pressure to fool even the smallest foreign object, pass the palms of your hands over the inmate's entire body. Run your thumbs under his waist band. Reach far up under his crotch.

Caution: Unless the search is thorough and consistent it is useless. An inmate will know, after a few searches, which places you are missing, and these are the places in which

he will hide the contraband articles. A seemingly innocent package of tobacco may, and quite often has, concealed contraband.

What to Search For: Contraband, specific articles.

How to Search: Formulate a plan of search that will cover every square inch of the cell and its contents.

Caution: The mark of a good shakedown officer is his ability to make a thorough search and yet leave the cell in the same condition it was when he began the search. Do not mess or upset a cell. Do not leave it in such condition that the inmate will know from its appearance that it has been searched.

BAR INSPECTIONS (WINDOW AND CELL BARS)

What to Look For: (1) broken welds, (2) cracked bars, (3) cut bars.

How to Find:

1. Tap ends of bars, and listen for distinctive rattle of bar ends striking against spreader plates.
2. Tap bars along length, and listen for dull ring.
3. Pass a thin metal instrument, such as the back of a knife blade, along the length of bar, feeling for cuts and depressions in the bar.

Caution: A bar which has been cut is likely to have the cut filled with soap, dirt, putty, etc., to conceal the cut. If you find such a spot, dig into it; and immediately report to the lieutenant, captain, or associate warden.

Inspection of Cell Blocks: During meals, officers

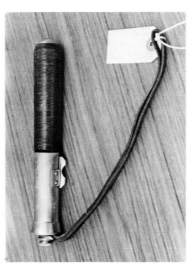 

assigned to "3-6" and "9-12" galleries will inspect the entire block and report, at the gate, any inmate remaining in his cell. Any such inmate will be locked in by these officers.

Kitchen Officer: During the serving of meals this officer will take position behind and at center of the steam table, and observe the serving of all food; assist the captain in taking the count, by counting the inmates on "C" side of the dining room; watch the conduct of the waiters; prevent unauthorized food or utensils being passed from the kitchen to the dining room.

Cell Lockups: After meals, officers assigned to this duty will see that all doors on positions assigned to them are locked as soon as all inmates remaining in the cell house are in their cells.

Officers in Gun Galleries: During the unlocks and lockups, the officer in the east gun gallery will observe the conduct in aisle "A-B" corridor. Officer in the west gun gallery will cover "C-D" corridor until inmates are ready to enter the dining room, and he will then cover the dining room, and, upon inmates returning from the dining room, cover "B-C" corridor until last inmate is at lowest step and then cover "C-D" corridor until lockup is complete.

Magazine Table: See that magazines are piled on the table and not taken into the dining room. Move table to its customary position after all inmates are in the dining room.

General: It is important for all members of the custodial force to know all of the duties of these various positions. At any time you may be called upon to perform them. No loud talking or other noises will be permitted at any time while passing through the cell house or dining room. Do not smoke while in the cell house or dining room. Learn the numbers of the dining room and cell house positions so that you will know your assignment.

(Signed) H.W. Weinhold, Captain
Approved: E.J. Miller, Associate Warden

The work systems were refined, all conceivable instructions were put on paper, the warden and his staff went over those instructions, orders, guidelines and procedures until in their minds all aspects were covered. Some of these instructions and guidelines were the same as in other federal institutions, but Alcatraz was a special place, a place that was to use a new method to deal with the nation's worst criminals — criminals who had in many cases beaten the rules and system so well established. This Alcatraz was to be the unbeatable, maximum security end-of-the-line option for all that violated the system.

Alcatraz and its system must have been used as a threat for all that were thinking of not following the rules, in any institution. The staff and the warden must have been clear on the fact, that whatever the systems they established they would be challenged and tested to the ultimate. That added pressure must have weighed heavily on all their thinking. It was like waiting for the ultimate showdown, the championship of the heavyweight. The system with its

Top right: Posted warning sign on east side of Alcatraz. Bottom right: Sign on west side of Alcatraz.

promise to society and the gangsters with their track record of defying regulations and abusing privileges granted in other prisons. No big shots on Alcatraz, just a home (prison) of maximum custody, security and with minimum privileges.

To all, this message was to be clear. From a boat, a casual onlooker circling the island would immediately upon reading the signs posted understand the intenseness and serious business mood emanating from this island. On the northwest end of the island by the model industry building, a 30x7 foot sign read:

W
A
R
N
I
N
G

Persons procuring or concealing escape of prisoners are subject to prosecution and imprisonment.

On the bulkhead wall between the lower and upper roads the 20x18 foot sign read:

Warning — Keep Off
Only government boats permitted within 300 yards of Alcatraz. Persons attempting to enter without authority do so at their peril.

And a sign over the registration office on the dock eight feet square read:

United States Penitentiary
Alcatraz Island — Area 12 acres
1½ miles to Transport Dock
Only government boats permitted. Others must stay off 300 yards. No one allowed ashore without pass.

Alcatraz was in its last stages of preparation for a phase that was to affect a select few but in a very lasting way. The question as to who would go to Alcatraz now was being dealt with. First there was no court that could directly send any convicted criminal to Alcatraz. (This practice changed at a later date.) The convict had to "earn" his way, so to speak, to "the Rock." To start the population on Alcatraz, Director Bates in October, 1933, wrote to the wardens of Leavenworth, McNeil Island and Atlanta, asking them to search their facilities for men who could be classified as desperate or difficult. One of the objectives would be to give those other institutions a better chance to deal with the

West tower with searchlight.   West tower on industrial building.

general population, once the main agitators were removed. In a way this must have been just what every warden wanted, to pick the worst and send them away.

Alcatraz Penitentiary did not stay empty long. When the Army left on June 19, Warden Johnston started to house and take care of 32 prisoners the Army left behind. These men had various sentences and became the first inmates of the official Federal Penitentiary: Alcatraz. These prisoners had various sentences and were not considered in the same league as the future shipments of prisons but their total sentences added up to 415 years' confinement and, looking at their records, one realizes that most of their offenses were sodomy and robbery.

		Years
F.B.	Sodomy	5
C.C.	Robbery & attempted assault	17
L.G.	Robbery & assault A.W.O.L.	10
J.H.	Sodomy	5
F.H.	Robbery & assault	17
C.H.	Sodomy	6
R.H.	Robbery & assault	25
A.H.	Robbery	5
A.H.	Sodomy	5
F.H.	Sodomy & false enlistment	15
E.H.	Robbery	15
C.J.	Sodomy	5
L.J.	Robbery & assault	25
W.L.	Robbery	5
M.L.	Forgery	5
J.M.	Robbery & escape	10
J.M.	Robbery & assault	22
W.M.	Manslaughter	10
J.M.	Disposing of military property	3½
A.P.	Sodomy	10
W.P.	Sodomy	5
J.P.	Felony & assault	5
L.P.	Sodomy & escape	5
J.R.	Robbery & disobedience	15
F.S.	Robbery	15
J.S.	Rape	Life
H.V.	Robbery	10
E.W.	Sodomy	15
G.W.	Attempted rape & assault	5
G.W.	Robbery	10
G.W.	Robbery & assault	17
H.W.	Robbery & assault	17

The really difficult question that immediately plagued Warden Johnston and Director Bates was how best to ship these hardened criminals to Alcatraz. The Kansas City Massacre was still fresh in their minds. Officers were killed as they were transporting escaped convicts back to prison. How best to move these convicts from other facilities to Alcatraz became a story in itself.

Finally they agreed that the best way would be to build special railroad cars and send large shipments. The risk and chances would be all at once and would minimize a failure from a long, drawn-out process. Secrecy, speed and efficiency would increase the chances of a flawless operation. No information could leak, for the conspirators would be sure to wait to derail or wreck the train in order to free the captives, regardless of the consequences.

The stakes were high. The calculated risks were plenty. This all had a sense of drama. Steel train coaches were being equipped with special safety features, steel bars installed on the windows, screens with close-mesh wire attached to the bars. Wire screened cages at the end of the car, for the guards, were put in place. Only the guards had access to the air brake card signal and no prisoner was allowed to move from his seat during any stop. Armed guards would station themselves on the platform at each end of the car any time the train stopped rolling. The baggage car had additional arms, with a guard acting as armorer.

These specially outfitted coaches with a baggage car for equipment, diner, club car with baggage and tourist sleeper for officers were linked to an engine and tender. Nobody but the train crew knew the route, and the location of the

Patch worn by Alcatraz officers.

stops. Special agents were assigned to switching areas and any stop stations.

All was ready for the first trainload, railroad officials, train crew, guards and prison officials. And now came the time to load and depart. All prisoners were removed from their cells, stripped, searched and outfitted with new clothing, marched to the cars, loaded, handcuffed and leg-ironed. Their records, files, staff and doctor were on board. The special train at 5:00 a.m. on August 19, was on its way and all the planning and secrecy paid off. It arrived at Tiburon, the final stop before loading on a barge at 8:20 on August 22nd, without any problems.

The coaches holding the prisoners were backed onto a barge, under the watchful eyes of the Coast Guard Commander, Meals, who was on board the Patrol Boat *Daphne*, and the barge was ferried to the Alcatraz dock. All went well and the only pressure put on the transfer operation was the news media with their telephoto lenses trying to get close to the action. News boats 300 yards away were scrambling for a glimpse of the nation's worst.

The process that was used to reassign each inmate to Alcatraz had been tested before on 14 prisoners sent to Alcatraz from McNeil Island on August 11. This small contingency was just right for Johnston to take all the planning from the drawing board and put it into real application.

One must wonder what went through the minds of all those prisoners looking out of the windows, barred and wired, feeling the slow back-and-forth rocking of the barge as it crept closer to this island. They were hot, dirty from the long ride, depressed, desperate and surely felt that as the

island came closer, they were at the end of the trail. All hope for any chance at anything was slowly drawing to a close.

Guards took off the men's leg-irons and grouped them in pairs. Flanked by guards, they marched to the yard. Passing the armed guards in the towers, and the unarmed guards at every road intersection must have given a feeling of a no-nonsense place. (Maybe in some, here and there, their inspection of possible escape routes preoccupied their minds.) The thought of escape was always on their minds and all that they saw on the way up from the

Top left: Leg irons. Bottom right: VIP's touring Alcatraz. L. to R.: Angeleo Rossi (mayor of San Francisco), Cummings, Johnston, and police chief Wm. Quinn of San Francisco.

dock had to be memorized in detail, for that would be the last time they would see any of that part of the Rock.

The registration process took place in the cell building near the rear entrance from the yard. Warden Johnston of Alcatraz would call out the name of a pair of prisoners as they had been brought from Atlanta. They would enter from the yard and stand in front of the desk where they had been escorted by an Atlanta guard, and their handcuffs would be removed. Warden Aderhold of Atlanta would identify the men and hand over his commitment papers to Deputy Warden Shuttleworth of Alcatraz. The papers were inspected and the clerk would verify the Alcatraz number and make out a ticket with each name, Alcatraz number and cell number.

An Alcatraz guard was assigned to each man to take him to the bath house. This was his first clean shower since leaving and must have felt good. His clothing was given back to the guards from Atlanta and new clothing from the clothing room with Alcatraz identification stamped on it was given to each man. Before he dressed and after the shower, he was given a medical examination by the chief medical officer and his assistants. The Alcatraz guard then would take the prisoner to his cell — his new home.

After all prisoners were processed and all looked in order, the Atlanta people left and the prisoners on Alcatraz were briefed in the signals and routines used to control them. Upon completion of final count after their meal, the warden sent a telegram to Attorney General Cummings and Director Bates in Washington: "Fifty-three crates furniture from Atlanta received in good condition — installed — no breakage." One wonders why the word furniture was agreed upon to describe the prisoners.

A hard reality for some, the maximum-security, no-privilege prison, the United States Penitentiary, Alcatraz, California, was in full operation. So starts another rich historical phase of "the Rock," Alcatraz.

During these first few months of operation, Alcatraz was constantly visited and inspected by all of those connected with the system. On some occasions the press went along. On August 18, Mayor Rossi and the chief of police, Quinn, of San Francisco went with Attorney General Homer S. Cummings on an inspection visit. Press people went along and gave the public a final view of a place that would be closed to the public.

One of the reporters even copied the menu in the mess hall: Breakfast: Oatmeal, milk, fried bologna sausage, cottage-fried potatoes, toast, oleo margarine and coffee. Dinner: Bean soup, gravy, stringless beans, mashed potatoes, oleo margarine and coffee. Supper: Pork and beans,

corn bread, potato salad, apricots, bread, oleo margarine and coffee.

The 8-by-4-foot cells were described as being equipped with a steel cot that folded against the wall, two seat-like steel shelves, a narrow steel shelf with three hooks for clothes, a toilet, and a small basin. The articles visible to that reporter were two towels, tooth powder, and a cup. This changed within the year, and we will see in a later cell inventory that indeed the cells were changed to a less austere environment.

A place of concern and debate in earlier inspection was the medical facilities. The reporter described the hospital

area as having two barred one-bed wards, two three-bed wards for the seriously ill, and a 12-bed ward. After this inspection tour, Cummings seemed satisfied and said this prison was ideal for its "somber purpose."

Until mid-September, Alcatraz was receiving its main population. The main activities were registering and establishing the work system to deal with these "worst" of all prisoners. During that time some of the big-name criminals arrived on Alcatraz. Alphonse "Scarface" Capone, George "Machine Gun" Kelly, Albert L. Bates, Harvey L. Bailey, Hugh A. Bowen, Frank Chapman, Frank B. Brownie, Ray Gardner and the list goes on, a "who's who" in crime. The Alcatraz staff worked very hard to establish the hard line tone, so that these crime "heroes" could not establish status identity. All were the same on "the Rock," no privileges for any reason.

The daily routine quickly established the patterns for all, a simple but rigorously enforced routine. Each prisoner from the first word he spoke as he entered the "island of silence" (a no-speaking rule was in force at that time), tried to establish his character. Most of this initial personal sizing up went unrecorded and is left up to our imagination. There is some, however, that has been recorded and can shed a light on the type of dialogue and sizing up that went on.

The prisoner that interested the public the most was Al Capone. He was a "big shot" and had generated lots of publicity. Everybody wanted to know about him and, especially, how he was on Alcatraz. He was known to be a "wheeler-dealer" and reports of him living a luxury life in prison were widely circulated. True, before he arrived on Alcatraz he had a certain amount of power and control and the public was well informed through the media, so it is normal for the public to want to see if a "big shot" would be able to pull the same strings on Alcatraz.

He was processed like all the other prisoners and was assigned his Alcatraz NR. 85 and his cell. Capone wanted to engage the warden in a conversation, but was moved along without success. He did ask for a meeting with the warden and, as Warden Johnston recounts, the following was said by Capone: "Well, I don't know how to begin, but you're my warden and I just thought I better tell you I have a lot of friends and I expect to have lots of visitors and I want to arrange to see my wife and my mother and my son and my brothers." Johnston, calm and stern, replied, "You will be able to see your wife and your mother and your son. Your brothers may visit you, that is, all your brothers except Ralph, who has a prison record. Now, I'll explain the regulations regarding visits, so that you may inform your family." He went on to say, "You may receive one visit a month from blood relatives, but only two persons may visit you at the same time." Capone would not accept that and tried to insist that he could have more visitors. "Warden, I got a big family and they all want to see me." The Warden told him that the rules would apply to him like to every other prisoner without favoritism.

One must wonder what went through the mind of the warden. In a way, he was dealing with a legend in his own time, an individual person who had control over vast amounts of money and who always considered himself beyond the law. It was important that at Alcatraz he would be kept from forming a chain of command. No deals, no connections. Just a number NR. 85. That's all.

There were many characters and personalities on Alcatraz and we will deal with them later on in this book, but all of them were given the same routine, rules and regulations. There were some changes in the later years but the initial impact and flavor of the first rules and regulations were felt to the end. Everybody on Alcatraz knew these routines by heart.

RULES

6:30 a.m.: Morning gong, prisoners arise, make beds, place all articles in prescribed order on shelf, clean wash basin and toilet bowl, wipe off bars, sweep cell floor, fold table and seat against the wall, wash themselves, and dress.

6:45 a.m.: Detail guards assigned for mess hall duty; they take their positions so as to watch the prisoners coming out of cells and prepare to march into the mess hall with them. The guards supervise the serving and the seating of their details, give the signal to start eating, and the signal to rise after eating.

6:50 a.m.: Second morning gong, the prisoners stand by the door facing out and remain there until the whistle

signal, during which time the lieutenants and cell house guards of both shifts make the count. When the count is found to be correct, the lieutenant orders the cells unlocked.

6:55 a.m.: Whistle signal given by deputy warden or lieutenant; all inmates step out of their cells and stand erect facing mess hall. Upon the second whistle, all inmates on each tier close up in single file upon the head man.

7:00 a.m.: Third whistle signal; lower right tier of block 3 (C?) and lower left tier of block 2 (B?) move forward into mess hall, each line is followed in turn by the second and the third tiers, then by the lower tier on the opposite side of their block, followed by the second and the third tiers from the same side. The block 3 line moves into the mess hall, keeping to the left of the center of the mess; block 2 goes forward at the same time, keeping to the right. Both lines proceed to the serving table; the right line served from the right and occupies the tables on the right; the left line to left, etc. As each man is served, he will sit erect with his hands at his sides until the whistle signal is given for the first detail to begin eating. (Director Bates did not agree with this last, saying that it simply could not be enforced.)

Twenty minutes are allowed for eating. When they are finished eating, the prisoners place their knives, forks, and spoons on their trays; the knife at the left, the fork in center, and the spoon on the right side of the tray. They then sit erect with their hands down at their sides. After all of the men have finished eating, a guard walks to each table to see that all utensils are in their proper place. He then returns to his position.

7:20 a.m.: Upon signal from deputy warden, the first detail in each line arises and proceeds through the rear entrance door of the cell house to the recreation yard. Inside detail, or those not assigned any detail, proceed to their work or cells.

7:25 a.m.: Guards and their details move out in the following order through the rear gates: (1) laundry, (2) tailor shop, (3) cobblers, (4) model shop, (5) all other shops, (6) policing, gardening, and labor details. The guards go ahead through the rear gates and stand opposite the rear gate guard. There they count prisoners passing through the gate in single file and clear the count with the rear-gate guard. The detail stops at the foot of the steps on the lower level road and forms into two ranks. The guard faces them to the right and proceeds to the shops, keeping himself in the rear of his detail. Upon arrival in the front of the shops, the detail halts and faces the shop entrances.

7:30 a.m.: Shop foreman counts his detail as the line enters the shop and immediately phones his count to the lieutenant of the watch. He also signs the count slip and turns it over to lieutenant making his first round.

7:30 a.m.: Rear-gate guard makes up detailed count slip, phones it to the lieutenant of the watch, signs it, and proceeds with it to the lieutenant's office.

9:30 a.m.: Rest period during which the men are allowed to smoke in places permitted, but are not allowed to congregate.

9:30 a.m.: Foreman or the guard gives whistle signal; all of the men on each floor of shops assemble at a given point and are counted, and return immediately to work. This assembly and count is quickly done, the count is written on a slip of paper, signed by the foreman or guard, and then turned over to the lieutenant making his next round.

11:30 a.m.: Prisoners stop work and assemble in front of the shops. The count is taken by the foreman or the guard. The foreman phones in the count and signs the count slip, turning it over to the guard, who proceeds with the detail to the rear gate and checks his detail in with the rear-gate guard.

11:35 a.m.: In the recreation yard, the mess hall line is immediately formed in the same order as in the morning. The details proceed in the same lines to the mess hall.

11:40 a.m.: Dinner routine is the same as for breakfast, except at the completion of dinner, when the details immediately proceed to the cells.

12:00 noon: Noon lockup cell count; the detail guards remain in front of cells until the prisoners are locked up and the count made.

12:20 p.m.: Unlock and proceed the same as before going to breakfast, except that the prisoners march in single file into the yard 3 cellblock first. Shop details again form in front of their guards.

12:25 p.m.: Details are checked out of the rear gate the same as in the morning.

12:30 p.m.: Details enter the shops and are counted by the foreman and the guard. Procedures are the same as at 7:30 a.m.

2:30 p.m.: Rest period; the procedure and count are the same as in the morning.

4:15 p.m.: Work stopped; the procedure and count are the same as at 11:30 a.m.

4:20 p.m.: Prisoners enter the rear gate, with count.

4:25 p.m.: Prisoners march into the mess hall, with count.

4:45 p.m.: Prisoners return to their cells.

4:50 p.m.: Final lockup.

5:00 p.m.: Standing count in the cells by both shifts of the lieutenants and the cell house men.

8:00 p.m.: Count in the cells.

9:30 p.m.: Lights out count.

12:01 a.m.: Count by the lieutenants and the cell house men of both shifts.

3:00 a.m.: Count in the cells.

5:00 a.m.: Count in the cells.

UNITED STATES PENITENTIARY
ALCATRAZ
California

GRIM WALLS AND BARS A PRISON MAKE

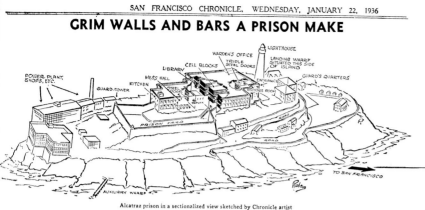

Alcatraz prison in a sectionalized view sketched by Chronicle artist

Top left: Headline from a San Francisco paper of January 22, 1936. Bottom right: industry building as seen in 1937.

These days just started to tick by in the dullest monotone. Time was totally regulated and soon just became a repetition of itself. Day in, day out — in the same routine. The only break came in the variety of foods or the different books the inmate had access to. The food, normally a prime source of complaints on Alcatraz, was fairly good. Alcatraz soon received a well-earned reputation for high-quality foods. There was a wide range of foodstuffs: beef, bologna, frankfurters, pork, pork loin, pork sausage, bacon, liver, lamb, veal, luncheon meat, ham, dired beef, beef hearts, liver sausage, salt pork, and corned beef.

The rules in the mess were not liked by the prisoners but were needed, since mealtime in the mess hall, here as in other penal institutions, was used to organize and start disturbances. On Alcatraz special precautions were taken, such as the gas canisters in the mess hall and armed guards outside the windows. No chance was to be taken. Johnston gave the prisoner full freedom as to the choice at the serving table — all they could eat — but the rule was: no food left on the tray. Breaking this rule did often result in the prisoner missing the next meal.

The rule of complete silence in the mess hall was a source of bitter complaint by the inmates. At one point this rule became public, and Johnston had to defend his rules. He stated that they were exaggerated in the press. To the prisoner, a bright spot in an otherwise drab, dull, monotonous routine was the library. Alcatraz' library was fairly well stocked. Its collection started with the donation of the books in the Alcatraz Army library. Books were purchased through bids, and there was a small budget for the library. Established writers were represented on Alcatraz: Cervantes, Conrad, Daniel Defoe, Alexander Dumas, Hamlin Garland, Zane Gray, Washington Irving, Jack London, and Lewis Sinclair — just to mention a few. The magazines were widely circulated, even though they were censored, especially anything dealing with sex.

Regulations regarding mail was very strict and probably the most disliked rule. For a person who is totally isolated from the rest of the world, any life sign from out "there" takes on a different, much more significant meaning. A bird chirping on a window bar will get the attention of even the most hardened, tough and cold individual. The most glamorous example is the story of Robert Stroud, who wrote several celebrated books on the care of birds while he was in confinement. So anything from outside became a treasured, sacred possession.

An inmate was allowed to correspond only with immediate relatives. One letter per week for the first grade prisoner, and two per month for the second grade prisoner. Three sheets of lined paper were given to the inmate by the cell house officer and he could write on one side only. His full name and number had to be on the page, and any person referred to in the letter had to be as a full name, no nicknames. These unfolded letters then were given by the prisoner to the guard for mailing. Special letters to a lawyer had to be approved by the deputy warden.

Another source of relief from the routines was the availability of religious services. Protestant services were held on the first and third Sunday of each month by a pastor from San Francisco; Catholic Masses were said on the second and fourth Sunday. The men on Alcatraz could not be classified as church-going citizens, but in the fall of 1936, 47 attended the Catholic Masses and 12 attended the Protestant service. In 1936, a Protestant chaplain, W. L. Hunter, was added to the penitentiary staff.

As the first year drew to a close, 242 prisoners called "the Rock" their home. Warden Johnston reported that now there was a staff of 88 needed to run Alcatraz. Even though some of the mechanical equipment failed to live up to what was expected, the island prison in the San Francisco Bay was declared a success. In a Bureau of Prisons publication, the following statement confirmed these views on the success: "The establishment of this institution not only provided a secure place for the detention of the more difficult type of criminal but has had a good effect upon discipline in our other penitentiaries also. No serious disturbance of any kind has been reported during the year."

Top right: There were two Alcatraz post office stamps: "Alcatraz Landing," 17 Dec. 1898 to 24 Sept. 1901, and "Alcatraz" established 6 March 1874.
Bottom left: Alcatraz chapel.

From that point on, Alcatraz became more of a secret to the world. Great efforts were constantly made to prevent publicity on either the prison or its inmates. This gave birth to a consistent growth of rumors. Rumors die hard and even today they linger on. Verrill Rapp, the first person paroled from Alcatraz to go to stand trial on other charges, did his share of starting the reputation that Alcatraz was the hell-hole it was intended to be. He spoke to a reporter on the way to his trial. Rapp said that Alcatraz was giving "inhumane treatment" to its inmates and that prisoners were going insane on "the Rock." San Francisco papers ran the story and the headline read: "Paroled Felon Raps Alcatraz."

Since Alcatraz was an experimental concept, all that was said or that did happen was of great interest to Washington. The bureau director, Bates, got wind of these stories and started to think in terms of what direction should be maintained for Alcatraz. He was of the opinion that inmates should not be paroled from Alcatraz directly. They should be transferred to another penitentiary from which they then could be paroled: "Even for these few the door of hope is not to be forever closed. If any of them can demonstrate that continued detention at Alcatraz is not necessary, the Bureau of Prisons is prepared to retransfer

them to one of the regular penitentiaries, where, in accordance with the law and regulations, the way may be opened to ultimate consideration for parole." He also expressed full confidence in the staff on Alcatraz. He wrote, ". . .but Warden Johnston can be relied upon to carry out the instructions of the Bureau that no brutality or inhumanity shall be practiced. Sustaining food and adequate medical attention. . ."

There was no question as to what Alcatraz was to be among those in the power structure. Warden Johnston, James V. Bennett, Sanford Bates, when it came to Alcatraz, spoke from one mouth. The purpose of Alcatraz was so different from that of other institutions that there was a degree of flexibility, allowing for adjustment. There were 16,500 prisoners in the Federal system, and of these, 270 were on Alcatraz. These 270 prisoners needed that special discipline Alcatraz was designed for. The Federal Prison system comprised the following:

1. Super-maximum security for incorrigible and long-term offenders — Alcatraz Penitentiary — 260 inmates.
2. Maximum security for prisoners serving more than one year — Atlanta Penitentiary — 2,800 inmates, and Leavenworth Penitentiary — 3,000 inmates.
3. Maximum security for drug offenders — Leavenworth Annex Penitentiary — 1,600 inmates.
4. Near-maximum security for long-term prisoners of a more hopeful type; special emphasis on education and training — Northeastern Penitentiary — 1,320 inmates.
5. Medium security; prison-farm activities — McNeil Island Penitentiary — 1,000 inmates.
6. Reformatories of medium security type — Chillicothe, Ohio — 1,500 inmates, and El Reno, Oklahoma — 800 inmates.
7. City jails of strong security — New York — 150 inmates, and New Orleans — 350 inmates.
8. Detention farms for short-terms — Milan, Michigan — 550 inmates, and La Tuna, Texas — 500 inmates.
9. Reformatory camp, minimum security — Camp Lee, Petersbury, Virginia — 550 inmates.
10. Reformatory for women — Alderson, W. Va. — 500 inmates.
11. Work camps, minimum security — Tucson, Arizona — 200 inmates, Kooskia, Idaho — 100 inmates, Dupont,

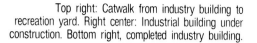
Top right: Catwalk from industry building to recreation yard. Right center: Industrial building under construction. Bottom right, completed industry building.

Washington — 200 inmates, and Montgomery, Alabama — 250 inmates.

12. Sick and insane medium and maximum — Springfield Hospital, Missouri — 600 inmates.

Punishment for violation on Alcatraz was swift. There was the one form of punishment that was a clearly established and written down procedure; and added to this were the procedures that never went recorded. Small extensions of the established forms of punishments — the ones we hear about from word of mouth and are never the same twice. Stories, rumors and exaggerations are the ones that usually find their way into the press. Probably the most popularized and mistitled tale of punishment was the locking up in the Spanish dungeons, a medieval concept for a place on Alcatraz. The ground floor of the old U.S. Army Citadel, now the basement of the main prison building, was what was referred to as the dungeons. These basement rooms were used, and Johnston wrote that he did not like the dungeons, but admitted using them in the first few years of his administration. Rumors have it that they were used for many years.

The Army had a few cells on the east side by the cistern, but the brick was so soft it could be dug through. Johnston kept his prisoners that needed to be put in those cells in chains. Finally, in 1940, these cells were torn down. The rumors and stories still continue to spark the most vivid mind today. Johnston had to deal repeatedly with people who believed that the island had been occupied by Spain, who built elaborate dungeons. He writes: "They were dungeons, but they were not Spanish. We used them when we had strikes in 1936 and 1937. I did not like these cells; in fact, I was ashamed of them and used them only under necessity."

When the chief of the Federal Prison system, James Bennet, visited Alcatraz, he was given the tour. Standing in front of these dungeon cells, Johnston told him he could use these cells in an emergency, but that he was ordered "not to do things like that." This implies that it was the chief himself who told Johnston not to use those cells.

Besides the main population of Alcatraz, the prisoners, there was a fairly large prison staff with families on "the Rock." The Treasury Department, in September of 1937, reported that Alcatraz had 158 adults and 64 children living in 51 sets of family quarters. 36 bachelor apartments were then in use. There was a recommendation for the building of new residences, but that did not happen until 1940. All the Army offices and non-commissioned officer quarters were used, as well as the old quartermaster building near the wharf.

In the annual reports of Warden Johnston, we can read the addition made to the operational aspect of Alcatraz. The work areas and corresponding structures were of concern to the warden, and many improvements were recommended and made. In 1936 we find the addition of some important necessities for the full operation of Alcatraz.

On the roof of the industries building, we now can see a guard tower. This tower is connected with a catwalk to the nearby "hill tower." The prisoners' recreation yard received

118

the concrete seats, referred to as the grandstands. A clothing factory had been added to the prison industries. It made prison uniforms both for Alcatraz and other prisons. The model shop had begun the reconditioning of discarded furniture by federal agencies. All the buildings on the island were painted inside and out.

Transportation on "the Rock" changed. Horse and mule were now replaced by a fleet of trucks. The July 1936 inventory shows the following transportation assigned to Alcatraz: a total of seven trucks and a 1934 Chevrolet passenger car, that was kept at Fort Mason, and used to transport prisoners to their court appearances. The trucks were fairly new: three 1934 Reo Motor ¾-ton trucks; a 1936 Chevrolet 1½-ton truck; a 1934 Diamond-T Howe 3-ton firetruck; and two leftover Army trucks, a 1929 Chevrolet ¾-ton truck and a 1932 Ford 1½-ton truck.

One of the major improvements desired by Johnston was the building of a new industrial complex. After some delays and chance that Alcatraz would be closed as a

prison in 1939, he finally got the OK for the project. The contract for a 306-foot-long, two-story building was awarded to Louis C. Dunn of San Francisco. In 1940 the funds were made available through the Public Works Administration (P.W.A. program). "I put a lot of thought into the planning," states Johnston. There were special features, such as an arrangement allowing the foreman guards to view and observe what was going on in two shops at the same time. New machinery with safety valves. Light, air, toilet facilities and special blowers to carry off dust were carefully considered. The antiquated laundry building was torn down and the new facilities occupied on July 1, 1941.

This new building, according to Johnston, was directly responsible for interest and better efficiencies on the part of the prisoners. He writes very enthusiastically about this phase of Alcatraz. "We began to solicit government departments for more work. We increased the amount of laundry processed for the Army. We purchased discarded automobile tires by the ton and converted them into rubber mats for the Navy."

If the new facilities indeed did boost the morale it is not measurable by us today, but in a place such as Alcatraz with no reform policy, anything must have been welcomed. Any diversion from confinement, and long hours of boredom. Some of the products did not give the prisoners a skill to take into civilian life, but that was not Alcatraz' intention.

Sunday morning, December 7, 1941, Pearl Harbor, was a special day for Alcatraz. First, the warden made a very rare announcement on the bulletin board in the mess hall. The next move was much more significant for Alcatraz and that was the process of converting the industries into a war support effort. The first job received on Alcatraz was due not only to the fact that Alcatraz wanted the job, but also that the Army had a problem situation with a civilian manufacturer who could not honor his contract with the Army. This was a test for Alcatraz and the small tailor shop on Alcatraz became a major garment producer. Many thousand herringbone twill and khaki trousers were made by the prisoners.

The next major industry was that of net manufacturing. The Navy sent over some people to teach the prisoners to make Navy cargo nets. Navy submarine net buoys weighing 400-600 pounds were brought to Alcatraz for maintenance and repair. The Navy crew from the submarine net depot delivered the damaged buoys to Alcatraz where they were transported to an open yard area.

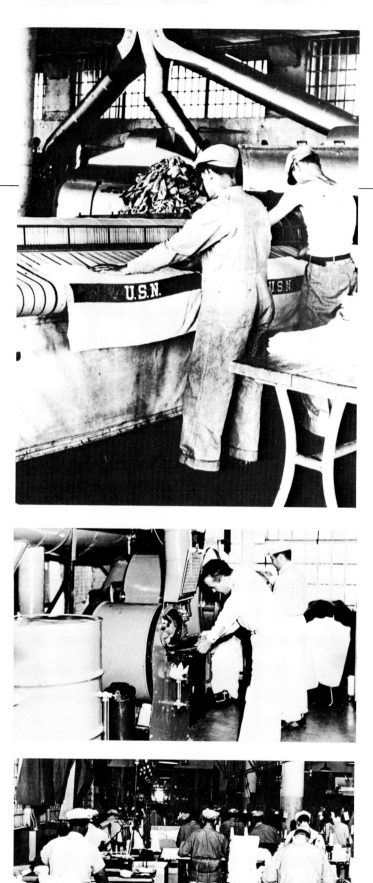

Inmate workers at various
equipment in the
laundry room, sewing room
and in the yard

The area was located on the northeast side of the island.
The men working in this open-air court could see the warships pass by on the way to the Pacific. Much conversation
must have taken place, for this was some spectacle. This
work continued throughout the war.

Warden Johnston wrote: "They realized that what they
were doing was important. They had a part in the war. They
were helping to win the war." As in Army days, their free
labor was used to defend this country. This time, however,
there was an enemy directly engaged against the U.S.

In 1942 a plan was put into effect to pay the men for
their work. One really cannot put the finger on the exact
reason as to why they now decided to pay the men.
Johnston writes: "We told them that we were doing it to
stimulate, encourage and reward industrious and co-
operative inmates." Could it be that at that time the inmates
did not fully cooperate? There was a lot of sabotage and
sloppy work. There are a few reports from inmates that
attest to just such a condition. We will discuss this in the
section dealing with the individual prisoners. Whatever the
reason, it was a change from the established pattern of no
rewards, no privileges. The first pay scale was based on a
skills classification. The degree of skill and knowledge was

120

announced to the prisoners and the pay scale was established as follows:

Men on 1st Grade jobs . . . . . 12 cents per hour
Men on 2nd Grade jobs . . . . 10 cents per hour
Men on 3rd Grade jobs . . . . . 7½ cents per hour
Men on 4th Grade jobs . . . . . . 5 cents per hour

Of interest here is the fact that each prisoner earning a wage was questioned as to his home situation and was made to send a percentage of what he earned to his dependents. Johnston's final opinion on the pay plan: "The pay plan was a good move. It gave the men the feeling that they were doing something useful and important and it helped them in personal adjustment. It benefited the institution and the government."

Construction changes were ongoing and even though the industrial complex was the major one, many others occurred. There was a "complete" renovation of the powerhouses in 1940. Two new boilers were installed. A new steam turbine, a diesel engine, a seawater pump and a new fire and sanitation pump were all part of this upgrading. Old quarters were demolished and repairs made to the other ones. For the inmates, new stainless steel trays, cups and bowls were provided. The mess hall received a new bulletin board. But the change that delighted the warden the most was the remodeling of D block.

D block throughout the history of Alcatraz would play a major role. This area of cells was designated as solitary confinement and would have different routines from the cells in the main population. The "dungeon," ruled out as a safe place, was replaced by D block's six cells on the ground tier. That was the place of ultimate confinement for those who violated any Alcatraz rules. Each cell was 6 feet 3½ inches by 12 feet 9½ inches by 7 feet 7½ inches high. These cells were built to be totally dark upon closure of the door. They were referred to as the "solitary cells." Each cell had two doors. The inside door was a bar stool of tool-proof steel. This door was a few feet away from the outside solid metal steel door. This outside door had a window, a pull-down panel. The guard could open up this panel from the outside and talk to the prisoner.

Inside, these cells were, with the exception of one, outfitted with a bed, toilet and wash basin. The sixth cell was totally bare of comforts. This cell was referred to as the "Oriental" or "Strip Cell." This area of confinement will become the subject of a later part of this book. Ironically, at the same time, just on the side of these cells, an area was developed into the library. A door from D Block leads into the library. So the most confining, depressing and damaging aspect of Alcatraz was directly next to the most refreshing and productive part of confined life on this "Rock," the library.

Now that we have all the major structures and departments in place, we need to focus our attention on the aspect of daily life on "the Rock."

THE END OF AN ERA

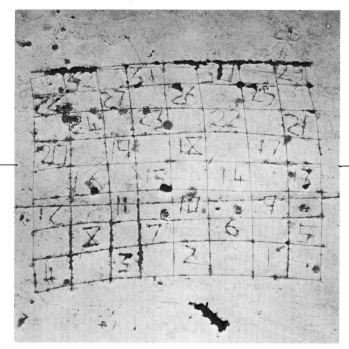

Playboard found in cell under the paint.

With the last step off the gangplank on March 21, 1963, the grim history for America's incorrigibles on Alcatraz came to an end. Frank C. Weatherman was the last inmate to leave Alcatraz. Twenty-nine years of Alcatraz Federal Penitentiary now became history. It is a relatively modern piece of history and one would think easy to document or record. Not so. These 29 years can never fully be recorded for history. The concept behind Alcatraz at that time made it impossible to accurately record its daily life. All was closed to the outside world, and the few who gained freedom were not the most reliable source for historians.

What these 29 years of Alcatraz history mean to us today can never be fully realized. Most of that history went with the people who occupied the island. The structures today reveal very little of the feelings, impressions, expressions and effects of the people who lived on "the Rock." The official records of those individuals are all over the place and, after tracing them down, we find them incomplete and pilfered. Connecting the remaining living individuals with the place and its events is a lifelong task in itself. The proverb, "the more you learn, the less you know," certainly applies to this time in the history of Alcatraz. Word of mouth, memories, fantasies, exaggerations and cover-ups make it very hard to find the real, true story of life on Alcatraz.

This life, though governed by very strict rules and regulations, still moves with the heartbeat of every individual; the intellectual luggage of each individual changed or added to the interpretation of what normally would be common facts. The perceptions of Alcatraz by individuals who lived on "the Rock" are very different from anybody else's perceptions. The meaning of life, its value structure, all rested with a small group of people whose life was governed by the reality of Alcatraz, a real place exclusive to a few.

Each prisoner on Alcatraz was given a book of rules and regulations. He was to read and know every aspect of this booklet. This was his life, on paper: what he could do, what he could not do. All aspects and variables of his daily life were covered in one paragraph or another. These prisoners had created their own rules in their civilian life. No rules, no laws, just action, leading to the next set of actions. Now the rules, on paper, were inflexible and binding —

Overleaf (pages 122-123): Impressions left behind by inmates in A-block. These graffiti are small in size and large in message and meaning. NR 127 represents the identification of an inmate that spent time on Alcatraz for post office robbery, conspiracy and violation of the Drug Act. He left Alcatraz to go to Texas 8/4/1936 and was returned on 9/29/1936.

hard-hitting for most, painful for some and unabidable for a few.

The hardest thing for anybody to realize who was not on Alcatraz or in any sort of confinement is the significance of trivial things. Something that would go totally unnoticed to the rest of the world may become a life-or-death matter for these few. Where else would an individual have time to cultivate a friendship with a cricket, fly, or roach? Where else would the playing of checkers or chess require an elaborate sign language system? The full understanding of the importance of trivia can only come from having the experience of total, isolated confinement. That experience was Alcatraz and was reserved for a few. Most of those individuals no longer are around to share this part of their experience.

Sometimes one cannot find an explanation for the importance of trivia, but must deal with the reaction it triggers. The following account best illustrates this point. A former inmate was asked: "What is the most humorous thing you can remember that stands out in your mind?" Here is his response: "There was an inmate named 'Abie' who never combed his hair and wore it in a snarled up mess on top of his head, with some of it hanging down the sides and front; his shirt was usually buttoned wrong, and there would be food particles on his pants and shirt front. This went on for months. Then one day, for a reason nobody ever discovered, Abie cleaned himself all up, combed his hair first-class, clean shirt and all, and strolled in for the noon meal. Well, when he walked in the mess hall and all the inmates saw his hair really combed, they let out such a roar of applause, screams, cat calls and whistles that it was heard all the way out to the front of the prison. Thinking a riot was in progress, the Captain and a number of guards came rushing to the mess hall, out of breath, to ask the guard on duty at the front door what was happening. All he could sputter by way of explanation was, 'Abie combed his hair!' "

Abie combing his hair in the context of Alcatraz at that

Top left: Inmates at dining table. Note band in background.
Bottom right: Original seating arrangement.

time could have been the spark that touched off a riot. Would anybody else understand that reason? Would it make sense? No. But to the people on Alcatraz that was life, their life, and very real to them. Many actions would be impossible to explain, yet lives depended on the reactions to these actions.

The meal is the single most important aspect of our daily lives. In all cultures, any place at any time, life revolves around the meal. When people are together, be it with family, friends, companions, in ceremonies, in celebrations of an event, or in confinement, the main event is the time reserved for the meal. Some meals are in celebration, some for survival, but all are the vital links of our daily lives. This point is no different for the people confined on Alcatraz.

It is well documented that one of the major causes in prison riots and rebellions is the dissatisfaction with the food. On Alcatraz a special effort was made to have meals that were better than any of those of other institutions. The reason is very simple: reduce the chances of a riot over the food. One must understand that even if the food had been prepared by the leading chefs of the world, somebody would find displeasure and complain. On Alcatraz this was held to a minimum by the fact that all the inmates could compare their meals in previous institutions with those on Alcatraz. And most of them would admit that the meals were indeed better.

The rules governing the mess hall and the meals were given to all inmates upon arrival. These, then, were the rules:

Dining Room Rules:

Meals are served three times a day in the dining room. Do not exceed the ration. Do not waste food. Do not carry food from the dining room.

Wear standard uniform.

Conduct yourself in a quiet, orderly manner. You may converse in normal tones with persons near you.

Boisterous conduct will not be tolerated in the dining room.

Observe the ration posted on the menu board and take all that you wish to eat within the allotted amounts, but you must *eat all that you take.*

You may go to the coffee urn on your side of the dining room only when no other inmate is there. Do not go to the urn for the purpose of visiting with others.

Do not pass or exchange food, cigarettes, notes, or any other items, anywhere in the dining room.

You will be given ample time to eat but no loitering will be permitted.

Shortages of silverware at the tables must be reported to the officer immediately before beginning to eat.

After you have finished eating, place your silverware in the right hand compartment of your tray. Empty bread, cake or pie trays and pitchers will be passed to the end of the table toward the center of the dining room. Inmates seated at that end of the table will arrange them for inspection by the officer assigned to the table.

When all inmates on a table have finished eating, the inspecting officer will give the signal to rise and leave the dining room. Proceed in single file directly to your cell. Enter your cell without delay. Do not loiter or visit on the galleries. Do not enter another inmate's cell at any time. Cell door will be locked as soon as you enter your cell.

Even with these firm rules in place, we know of several disturbances that occurred in the mess hall. However, the quality of the food was, with one exception, not the cause of these disturbances. One disturbance that took place because of the food occurred in 1954. The reason: lasagna had been served for the third time in eight days. This led to a spontaneous food riot. One of the 10-men tables was thrown over with food and utensils flying every which way. Before this had completely settled, every table in the mess hall was overturned. In a few minutes, guards outside began breaking out the glass panes in the mess hall windows and pointing their submachine guns into the mess hall. All was settled before shots were fired or the tear gas turned on.

In talking to former inmates, the general opinion is that the food was ample and good. Everybody had his favorite meal, but the spaghetti and meatballs had the best rating. Steak was next on the list. One inmate related his feelings somewhat differently. "As for favorite meals, there weren't any; we had to eat what garbage the steward dished out, most spaghet, gravy and spuds, starch, starch and more starch. The coffee lived up to its name of 'mud.' And the cold tea was equal to any paint remover. We had food strikes on the average of five or six a year. That's when we'd be dispatched to 'A' block, to enjoy the concrete floor coated with dust."

Most of the inmates liked the breakfast. The standard breakfast consisted of hot cakes, syrup, oatmeal or dry cereal, bowl of milk toast, butter, jelly, coffee, frequently a sweet roll with eggs, grapefruit.

The rules of having to eat all the food on the tray did change in the 50's. The inmates served themselves cafeteria-style from the steam tables at the front of the dining room. The only restriction was the number of servings with items such as meat and dessert. The warden on some occasions would step into line and test the food, in front of the inmates.

The mealtime normally was 15 to 20 minutes. As each man finished his meal, he passed the eating utensils to one end of the table. As soon as the guard accounted for the utensils of all 10 men at the table, they were allowed to return to their cells. In the event that a knife or spoon was missing, all the men at the table in question were searched before returning to the cells.

Since Alcatraz had no commissary where inmates could buy food, candy was a rare commodity. At times some food items would be smuggled out of the dining hall and it is understood that in some cases the guards looked the other way. At Christmas some candy was given to the inmates. If you had a sweet tooth, you had to suffer for the rest of the year. An ingenious way was devised by some inmates to sweeten their coffee. An inmate working in the kitchen would soak cigarette paper in liquid saccharine. He would let it dry during his shift, pack it into his cigarette paper holder and take it to his cell. This item was passed to other inmates as a trade item or just as a gift. To a new inmate, it must have looked strange to see some men dropping pieces of cigarette paper into their tea or coffee. As one

Dining room looking west toward steam-heated serving table and kitchen.

inmate recounts, "One day they were sitting there and a guy offered me a piece of this paper, and I said, 'No, thank you.' I thought they were nuts. Then I found out what they were doing."

The violence in the dining room was not so much directed at individuals but at the system and (used for release of group frustration) done in groups. There is a story that is told by an inmate that describes Burton Phillips slugging the warden in the dining room: "Through some queer mental quirk, Phillips conceived the warped idea that Warden Johnston was personally responsible for his trouble. After brooding many months over that obsession, he suddenly stepped out of line one day in the dining room and knocked the warden cold with one desperate smash. When the Warden fell, Phillips had time to kick him twice in the face before guards got to him. A guard by the name of Steer was the first to reach the spot, and he stiffened Phillips with one blow of his club. Associate warden Miller then straddled Phillips and continued to club him. We could see Phillips' body almost slide on the floor each time Miller brought down his club."

It was a miracle that Phillips survived the clubbing he underwent. Undoubtedly Phillips was mentally haywire when he attacked Warden Johnston, but he is more than haywire now.

The contact between inmates in the dining room was minimal, especially during the time of silence. In later years some of the inmates would drop back in line to the dining room so they could sit with their friends. The dining room did represent the time and place where most inmates would be together at one time, and it is natural that this time and place would be of special attention to the adminis-

tration.

The inmates who worked in the kitchen had special schedules for work and recreation. Instructions for those workers were especially different in regards to bathing. The regular population had their laundry exchanged on Tuesday afternoon and Saturday morning. The inmates on culinary detail got to bathe on Monday, Wednesday and Friday, in two groups as designated by the steward. During normal operations in 1937 and 1948, we find the following jobs and men assigned to the kitchen:

	1937	1948
Cooks	5	4
Bakers	4	3
Vegetable room	3	2
Butcher	3	0
Mess Hall	4	4
Kitchen Storage Room	1	3

The instructions to the guards on duty at the dining room gate read as follows:

This duty, like any other to which you may be assigned, is important, even though it may not seem so. Be alert for any trouble in the dining room, and in the event of trouble, it is your duty to aid in getting all officers out of the dining room, and to keep the inmates in the dining room until signals are given for them to leave.

Gas masks are located in the west gun gallery, and, in the event that gas is fired in the dining room, these will be passed down to the officers on this duty. Adjust the mask quickly and rush in to aid in getting the

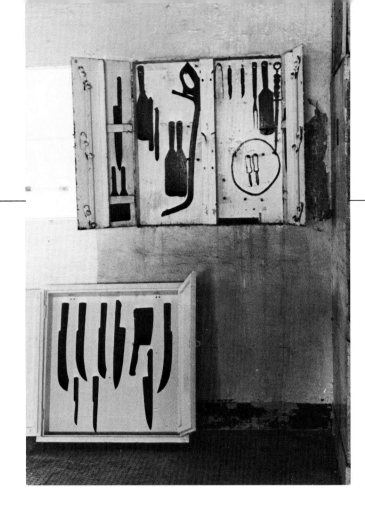

Top left, kitchen tools cabinet; bottom right, Warden Johnston with Edward G. Robinson, famous "tough guy" actor

officers out of the dining room.

The gas was never used in the dining room on Alcatraz. One inmate did not feel it could be used because they had been painted over so many times that he felt the canisters could not be broken.

The daily routines and privileges to the outsider stayed pretty much the same during the entire time Alcatraz was open as a federal penetentiary. To the inmate there were major changes in all aspects. Some of these occurred with the changing of wardens, often changed because of some incident that would affect all, such as the 1946 riot. To the inmate who spent time under several wardens, the changes would reflect the character of that man.

A general consensus of all who served time on Alcatraz was that of the effect of eternal boredom and monotony — the endless, repititious, nothing-filled days in that life. Everything that a mind could attach itself to would become important and necessary. The sounding of a boat whistle could be taken as a personal message to an individual, a look on a guard's face might trigger the rumor that Alcatraz was about to close. The rules and privileges are very clear: "You are entitled to food, clothing, shelter and medical attention. Anything else that you get is a privilege. You earn your privileges by conducting yourself properly."

As if the written rules weren't enough, the inmates, upon arrival, were marched into the mess hall where Warden Johnston got up and told them plainly what they were up against: "The rules have been laid down by the government in Washington, and there will be no deviation. I did not make the rules, but as long as I'm here I'll enforce them."

For sure some of the inmates had heard this line before, but for Alcatraz these words came to mean something special. Roy Gardner wrote what these words really meant to him:

1. Lost hope. The backbone of the hardest con melts to jelly under the lash of discipline without hope.

2. The rule of silence. No talking in the cell house or in the mess hall; mute men alone with their thoughts.

3. Complete isolation from the outside world. No newspapers, radio or any other means of knowing what's going on outside.

4. The brand of hatred — a hatred peculiar to one small rock alone that brews in the minds and hearts of men this shut up.

5. Over and above all, discipline. Rigid, severe, unre-

lenting. Rules on Alcatraz, like the bars, are steel, both are inflexible, neither bends.

The feelings ran deep and the mood of all concerned was tense. The idea was to break these men, render them mute and keep them from others in society.

Warden Johnston, "Saltwater Johnston," did want everybody to believe that it worked on Alcatraz — the tough stand, the rules, his system. It was Johnston who figured out most of the manners in which business was to be conducted on Alcatraz. Many VIP's toured that place under his rule: senators, local officials and movie stars. The country needed to know that it had a final, safe place for the gangsters who created such havoc in those days.

To remove them from all this attention, most-wanted status, public enemy No. 1 and financial power figures, would only be confirmed for the VIP's by actually seeing these men confined for most of the 24-hour day to a 13´x9´x7´ cell. Their new home.

In July, 1937, the VIP visiting was none other than the Director, James V. Bennett. On this visit, Bennett gave some serious thought as to the definitions of "privilege" and what was the right degree for those on Alcatraz. The stories that came to the surface were grim. Probably the worst part was that some of the stories had reached the eager press. A story that was written in July of 1935 told the first-hand news from behind the walls. William Henry Ambrose was released for deportation. A Chicago gangster, he gave the press its first view behind the walls of Alcatraz. The headlines read: "Alcatraz Silence Awful"; "Inmate Tells How Hard Boiled U.S. Is"; "Al Capone 'Burning Up' at Curb on Talking." Ambrose is quoted in the article: "Not a word can be spoken by any of the convicts in line, at the table, at work, or in their cells." He had once tunneled out of Leavenworth and was considered incorrigible. The last part of his story may well sum up the feelings of most of those on "the Rock": "It's the toughest pen I have ever seen. The hopelessnss of it gets you. Capone feels it. Everybody does."

Alcatraz water tank, built 1939

Washington got wind of all this news and asked the warden for a new resumé of the regulations, but it was not until after this VIP visit by Bennett that something firm took place. There was a strange relationship between Washington and Alcatraz. On one hand they wanted a place of no privileges, etc., but did not want to look as if they were in violation of human rights. Johnston wanted to run his own show. He was supposed to send a list to Washington twice a year, naming inmates who he thought could be transferred to other institutions for parole. He was asked several times, but not until October of 1935 did Washington receive the first list of 10 prisoners, falling into this category. All ten were former Army prisoners Johnston had inherited.

Bennett listed some very specific concerns regarding Alcatraz:

> I feel . . . that it is unnecessary to impose quite such rigorous rules with respect to talking in the mess hall and when the men are walking into the cell blocks from the work yard details. . . .

> I think you agreed that your present censorship of magazines was too rigorous and I suppose you will gradually make such changes in it as seems to you to be reasonable . . . .

> We shall also provide you with a better grade of issue tobacco and I want the library facilities expanded so that every man can have all the books of the proper kind and all the right sort of magazines to read when-

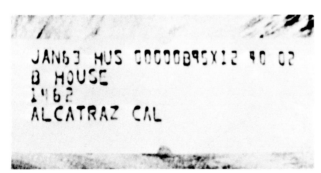

JAN63 HUS 0000089SX12 90 02
D HOUSE
1462
ALCATRAZ CAL

ever he wishes.

The chaplain was in charge of the library, and he reported that each prisoner drew an average of seven books and three magazines per month. It was not until 1938 that a printed library catalog had been placed in each cell and at that time the circulation increased to 8.2 books per man per month.

The inmates had no direct access to the library. They selected books from the lists available to them. "To request

delivery of library books to your cell, refer to the catalog for 'call' or identification number of the book you want and place that number on your library card. Place the card on the table at the entrance to the dining room on your way to breakfast. Return books in the same manner." So reads rule NR. 1 of 8 library rules. A designated inmate would then bring the book to the cell. At one time Capone delivered library books.

The Chaplain was in charge of the educational materials as well. In 1935 one of the improvements listed was that of the availability of correspondence courses from the University of California Extension Division.

Eighty-one inmates took advantage of this offer the first year. By June, 1936, they had completed 42 courses, but the enrollment was then down to 53. Not too many of the participants took those courses to help them when they got out, but merely to break the monotony in a legal way. The courses offered ranged from beginning algebra, English literature, beginning civilization to poultry husbandry.

By the end of 1960, the library boasted some 15,000 volumes. Nine thousand volumes had been left behind from the Army days. The rest of the books came from various donations. The largest donated part of the library were the law books. The inmates were allowed to purchase law books, and when they wanted to, would donate them to the library. Some who continued their legal battles, took the books with them, provided they had been listed on the personal property cards. The big book donors were Robert Stroud, Robinson and Tex Fleck.

The library rules spelled out very carefully what could be done with these books:

1. The library books you request are checked out to

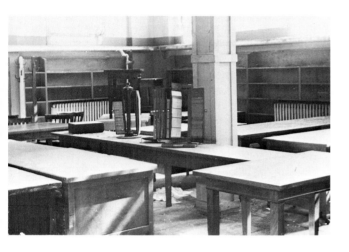

you and must be returned within the time limit shown on the date-due slips inside the back cover of the book. Failure to return the book to the library prior to or on the date due, may result in forfeiture of library privileges.

2. You are permitted to have not more than three circulating library books in your cell at one time. Keep your books and magazines neatly arranged on the shelf in the cell when they are not being read.

3. In addition to the circulating books, you are permitted to have a Bible, dictionary, and study books up to a maximum of twelve (12) in your cell at one time. This includes all books, personal, library, and study course books. Books beyond the maximum of 12 will be confiscated. A maximum of 24 pamphlets may be kept in your cell at one time. Pamphlets beyond this maximum will be confiscated.

4. Handle library books carefully. Many of the worn-out books, especially fiction books, cannot be replaced since they are out of print. You are cautioned not to loan or exchange books with other inmates or to toss books to other tiers. Defacement, mutilation or destruction of books will be cause for disciplinary action even to the extent of forfeiture of good time.

The library was considered, by most inmates, the highlight of their daily routine, and this was one privilege they did not want to lose. In 1937, four inmates were assigned to the library. By 1948, the number changed to two.

In those early years one could see the forming of patterns and systems that would for the most part remain until the closing of Alcatraz. Some of the rules and privileges were changed by the administration, but some privileges were not carried out to the end. Take for instance the formation of a musical group in 1936. Alfred M. Loomis, a counterfeiter from Southern California, in an interview on February 25, 1936, told of the formation of a musical group on Alcatraz. He said they would rehearse in the barber shop during the weekend recreation period. Some members of the band included Harman Whaly, 1935 kidnapper of George Weyerhauser in Tacoma, Washington, on saxophone, and Welton Sparks, former Dillinger associate, on the cornet. All the instruments were bought by the inmates. The chaplain was trying to arrange a string orchestra: mandolins, banjos and other strings. Al Capone was to be one of those; and it was during the time he was practicing on his banjo in the music area that he was attacked by Jimmy Lucas, who stabbed him in the back. Capone used his banjo to knock Lucas over the head, wrecking the banjo and knocking him out cold.

Al Capone claimed he talked Alvin Karpis into joining the band, on the guitar. Now the band had 12 members and two alternates. November was the target date for the first concert. By April, 1937, the band had produced three regular Sunday afternoon concerts. In 1938, there were 33 men practicing on musical instruments; and the monthly band of 10 men gave monthly concerts in the cell house. In the late 40's there was a small group in existence: "A group

Top left: Guitar player in his cell
Bottom left: One of the Alcatraz Bands
of the 50's. Bottom right: Typical radio jack
installed in each cell

of guys, whom we named 'Gangsterettes,' did form a git-fiddle band to serenade us on Sunday and holidays, but this didn't last long, for the local gentry at large cheered them with boos."

In the early 50's, there was a small combo that played for special occasions, such as Thanksgiving and the Fourth of July. Nobody seems to remember a band after 1953 up to 1959. One inmate in the mid-50's did buy a guitar and, after finding himself not to be a Les Paul, gave it away.

Music was becoming a part of Alcatraz. In 1940, an electric record player had been purchased, and the federal music project of the Work Projects Administration had donated many recordings. This music library soon grew to a thousand records, and musical programs were provided three times a week. The music was piped to the yard and a loudspeaker was put into the cell house in between the cells. Inmates complained that they practically had to lie on the floor and listen through the air vents to hear the music. This first-hand accounting of music on Alcatraz is interesting and reveals the feelings of one inmate:

When I first went to Alcatraz (1950), the only music to be heard was played over a loud speaker in the yard for approximately two hours on Saturdays and Sundays. It was anything but high fidelity, and sounded similar to a 1924 phonograph. Most of the records played were from 10 to 15 years old. Then the warden (E.B. Swope) was ordered by Washington, D.C. authorities to install a radio system. This was in 1954, as near as I can recall. However, he took so long preparing it (estimating wire needed, etc.) that some 18 months later the same authorities finally gave him the equivalent of an ultimatum . . . whereupon he

reluctantly installed a loudspeaker among the plumbing pipes in the passageway between cells. Unfortunately, to hear it you had to get down on the floor next to the toilet and listen through a ventilator located there. Before the speakers were turned on for the first time, a lieutenant passed around from cell to cell inquiring of each inmate whether he wished to hear a daily half hour of news, or a half hour of music . . . it cannot be said of Warden Swope that he favored coddling prisoners with such nonsense as radio. Eventually, the radio system progressed into a set of earphones for each listener.

Each cell received a two-channel jack into which the earphone could be plugged. The radio was controlled from outside the cell house. Each day from 6:00 p.m. to 9:30 p.m. programs were played for the inmates. Weekends and holidays gave them extra time — from 1:00 p.m. to 9:30 p.m. Each inmate signed for the tamper-proof headsets and this issue was noted on his property card. No headsets were allowed to remain plugged in if the inmate was not in his cell. Headsets found plugged in or hanging on the outlet box were picked up. Any loud laughter, yelling, cheering, or clapping was not tolerated. The temptation

Joseph Bowers

was there, especially during a sports event, when the favorite team scored.

For some, this relief from monotony was probably the only thing that kept them sane. Many accounts are given of inmates cracking up under the pressure of silence and monotony. During the daylight hours the prisoners had something to do to occupy their minds, but in the hours between 5 o'clock in the evening and 7 o'clock in the morning came the time that taxed men's souls. For most people it is hard to imagine what goes on during that time, but everybody at one time or another experiences a sleepless night. A night of tossing and turning, under the conditions encountered on Alcatraz, became especially difficult.

A man would sit on his bunk and brood and worry over his troubles until sleep was an utter impossibility. He would concentrate his thoughts upon the topic uppermost in his mind. To some, the thoughts were of wives or sweethearts. One inmate recalls: "I got a mental picture of my wife. Although in reality she may be entirely blameless, she would appear in another man's arms."

Some inmates named this experience "hell-nighting." The images formed by the "hell-nights" were often more than merely mental images. They often took shape and substance in an actual picture on the dim, bare wall of the cell. That picture resembled a cartoonist's drawing, in which the thoughts of the person depicted seemed to appear worded in a hazy "balloon" over the head of the person. There have been reports of hearing actual voices and sounds.

This experience takes place once or twice a week; and when the bell is rung to get up in the morning, that inmate is of the ugliest frame of mind. His eyes will be red and bloodshot, and he will be quarrelsome and disagreeable.

After a year of this type of experience, the "hell-night" may enter a different stage of "hell-nighting." This stage was when he got up in the morning and the image would not disappear from his vision. Looking at the wall, the image would still be there. He could no longer laugh it off. One inmate describes this state as, "He becomes reduced to a mental and moral pulp — a docile creature easier to handle because his mental condition deprives him of the ability to plan intelligently, or a raving maniac."

It must have been difficult for all concerned to assess the mental condition of the inmates. Their actions could lead to a death, and one would not be able to tell if it was a "put-on" or really a mental condition. One of the best examples of this problem was that of the death of Joe Bowers, listed as the first escape attempt.

Joseph Bowers, a violator of the Postal Law, as told by other inmates, was on the verge of a total mental breakdown. A smuggled letter to a San Francisco newspaper tried to bring attention to this problem, and specifically refers to Joseph Bowers. He was so far gone that he tried to cut his throat in a suicide attempt. He failed but not without a long scar on his neck. He struck a guard without provocation just three weeks before he was shot. Joe's duty at the time of the incident was around the incinerator. He was working alone. His orders were to keep the place impeccably clean. The garage truck arrived at the incinerator. The wind blew some paper over the fence and some against the fence. The paper against the fence was what Joe was after, so he climbed on the fence.

The tower guard questioned Joe. And after Joe told him he was going to pick up the paper, the guard shot him twice. One will never really understand the action of Joe. Nobody in his right mind would scale a fence in full daylight under the full view of a guard with escape in mind. On the other hand, one would not climb any fence in a place where everybody was out to bust a convict.

No doubt the guard thought he was doing his duty, as he

San Francisco news
San Francisco Cal

Please investigate criminal cruelty practices on prisoners at Alcatraz Prison. A few of the cases are (1) Edgar Lewis, age 28, serving 3 ys sentence, kept in dungeon for a total of more than 6 wks, starved, shot in face with gas gun, beaten over head with clubs by three guards (names will be given to investigating committee). He is now insane and is kept in a cage in the hospital. No hope for his recovery. His family lives at Los Banos, Calif. They don't know about it yet. The warden naturally wont give out information that will hang himself, but if an investigation is made and the inmates are questioned you will get the evidence. Another case is Jos. Bowers also insane from same cause, but not as bad condition as Lewis. James Grove is also insane and is under mental observation. John Stadeg is

A smuggled letter to a San Francisco newspaper

View from west gun gallery, through a gun port, into the hospital corridor

saw it. However, he may have acted overzealously in firing the fatal shot. The mood on Alcatraz was so bad that for the safety of the guard, he was transferred. Some inmates voiced some form of amazement at the incredible accuracy of his shot.

The official records show this was the first escape attempt from Alcatraz as a federal maximum security prison. Like so many incidents in this kind of environment, the real stories will remain untold.

The issue of mental health falls into a very vague category. Records of events, diagnosis and treatment related to mental health are far from complete. It's very difficult to make conclusive statements on the condition of some inmates who for some reason or another were called "crazy."

The problem of mental health was not totally ignored. The U.S. Public Health Services provided a psychiatrist for the examination of the Alcatraz prisoners. At that time, some inmates were diagnosed as having mental disorders and were sent to the Leavenworth Psychiatric Ward for observation. Some inmates did not get the "classification" of having a mental disorder and remained on Alcatraz. We find behavior by some that later would give them the classification of a mentally ill person.

One must realize that the mental issue became a way or a game for some inmates to change their current predicament. For some just to go to the hospital ward on Alcatraz was a welcome change of routine. The game that could be played with the staff provided some change of pace and some variation on the daily routine.

Rufe Persful pushed the issue to the limits by cutting off the fingers of his left hand with a fire ax. The publicity of this case led to the statement of the Director of Prisons, James V. Bennett, that Rufe Persful was mentally deranged.

We have several reports of actions and incidents of Alcatraz inmates that would lead one to make the statement, "Well, he is crazy." But it was not until several such incidents leaked beyond the confines of Alcatraz that the Director of Prisons, Bennett, asked for the addition of psychiatric services on Alcatraz.

A question can be raised in regard to the practices used on Alcatraz to deal with mentally unstable inmates. Very little reliable information is available. Two rooms in the medical ward called the "bug cage" were specially designed for this purpose. One room, entirely made of ceramic tiles, had nothing in it except a hole in the floor to be used as a bathroom. One former inmate recounts, "For a toilet stool one could enjoy himself trying to hit the little hole in the floor. A straight-jacket would be provided for those who thought they could stay a bit violent. And a big bang in the arm with some bug-juice (I call it 'Twilight' sleep juice) would put the guy in the arms of Morpheus for the whole night."

These bug cages were seen only by a few inmates on their way to some sort of psychiatric treatment. An intense description of the second bug cage is given by an inmate

Top right: Psychiatric ward called "the Bug Room."
Bottom left: Robert Stroud's individual hospital room.
Bottom right: Isolation hospital room.

who was sent there after an escape attempt. He tells, "Although it wasn't a cage per se, it was a room with a stark mattress on the floor, a toilet and wash basin, approximately 8´ by 8´ by 10´, the interior of which was completely surfaced in ceramic tile. Set in one wall was a translucent glass block window which had some kind of electric light outside to simulate daylight. The opposite side had a door with no handle or knob on the inside and a small glass panel to observe the bug. Pills and food were dispensed through a slot that could be locked or opened. It was artificially ventilated. Special care consisted of a 5-minute conversation with a psychiatrist, perhaps once a month. This room cured many a would-be psychotic after a month or two. It was shrouded in an air of mystery for the population (all inmates) since the only occupants it held usually were sent to the mental hospital."

What would get an inmate to the bug cage was not always clear, but it was usually related to some clear action on the part of the inmate. Words alone did not really trigger a stay in the bug cage. One explanation as to how an inmate got to be put into the bug cage is given to us by a former inmate: "Of men going insane on the island . . . usually they would become quietly deranged. Starting with a few odd statements and/or moves, these would develop and increase in their irrationality until it was difficult for officials not to notice. That is precisely what the officials did in most cases (not notice) . . . until some kind of bizarre *action* occurred — such as breaking a toilet, throwing pieces of it out of the cell and over the gallery, drinking

from the toilet, licking the floor clean, smearing the walls and their face with shit, and so forth. Then such a person would be whisked up to the hospital to a room within a room that was completely isolated from the population called the bug cage."

At that time, psychiatrists were brought in to examine and test the inmates. Such an encounter was recalled by an inmate, ". . . then to the bug cage as a possible psychotic. After regular interviews with a psychiatrist (ordered by the San Francisco federal district court), one day there appeared three psychiatrists, and the 'possible' psychotic became an 'undoubted psychotic! In very short order I was sitting in a compartment on the City of San Francisco (a Santa Fe train) en route to the medical center for federal prisoners, in Springfield, Missouri . . . better known as the 'funny farm.' I suppose you could say it was a case of extreme depression." This inmate had spent 30 days in the bug cage after starving himself in Cell 10 of D Block (total isolation).

Even in the best of circumstances, such analysis would prove difficult, but especially here on Alcatraz when some inmates would try to fabricate such mental conditions in order to get off "the Rock," it proved extremely difficult.

The fabrication of physical conditions that would send you up to the medical ward was part of the games attempted by some. The medical facilities on Alcatraz were sufficient, but by no standards a luxury place. The setup was such that an emergency could be handled on Alcatraz and for a special case one just brought in a doctor from the

mainland Marine base. There was a medical staff on Alcatraz and some had their families on the island as well.

A main function of the medical facility, other than emergencies, was to provide a secure place to conduct routine examinations and to dispense medication on a daily basis. The hospital had an operating room, X-ray rooms, diagnosis room, photo darkrooms, bug cages, and ward rooms. The first room in the medical facilities, after entering the iron gate, was the clinic. This room was for treating minor injuries and dispensing medications; across from it was the main operating room. On the same side of the hallway as the operating room was the pharmacy, and the two rooms designated as the bug cages. Farther down the hall, on the same side, was the room that housed Robert Stroud, the "Birdman," in isolation. The room, about $15\frac{1}{2}$ by 8´, with a high ceiling, had two doors. The outer door was solid wood and the other door was the regular cell bars. Stroud could open or close the outer wooden door for privacy, but could not open the inner iron bars.

Past his ward came the main wards, which were divided into three on each side, with a rather large hallway between them. Inmates moving from the clinic to the wards could and did stop and converse with Stroud, but the correctional officers would separate them in a short time. The only inmates capable of doing this were inmates committed to the hospital ward. The three wards on each side took up the rest of the floor and had concrete separations between them and a totally-barred front.

Many VIP visitors would want to see the medical facilities. Warden Johnston, in his one book, gives the impression of great pride over the facilities. The medical facilities and staff on Alcatraz were rated by the American College of Surgeons. Everybody entering the hospital could see the framed certificate issued by the College of Surgeons. Warden Johnston states, "I shared the pride felt by Dr. Ritchey when we were able to meet all the tests and requirements in order to secure the certificate."

The dental room had two chairs and its own X-ray equipment. Johnston refers to this room as a "modern dental parlor."

The question of fake sickness was always in the mind of anybody who saw the total picture of Alcatraz life. That question came up at one of those Johnston VIP visits. Dr. Ritchey, in charge at that time, told the visiting doctor, in so many words, that there were not that many out-and-out malingerers who consciously and deliberately faked illness just to get out of work. He did mention, however, that he had many inmates that were medicine takers. Some inmates apparently did develop a pill, aspirin, cold tablet or

ointment habit. Those mixed in with the hypochondriacs and neurotics, having no organic or functional difficulty, would keep them busy. Much of this ties in with the need by individuals to have some form of chemistry in their system, if not for physical reasons, at least for psychological ones.

We have an intense account of the opposite design by an inmate who did not want to get addicted to heavy drugs. This inmate spent some time in the medical ward and managed to attract the interest of an intelligent, well-educated male nurse. As the account goes, this man lightened the inmate's physical pain, cut some corners to ease his darkening days. Some of the other inmates would do anything to get some guard to get anything — benzedrine, "goof balls," alcohol, etc., but this inmate who had access to medicine was concerned with avoiding getting into taking morphine or atropine. He wrote: "I can get treatment at once now, so that if a nurse is not handy, all I have to do is call a guard and he can hand me the things that have to be kept under lock and key. Milder drugs, I keep within reach at all times. If an attack hits slow, I take liminal and tresentin. If it hits faster, I take panegoric and elixir of nembutal; but if it hits faster, I take codeine and atropine. That failing, morphine and atropine. The more powerful drugs mean a more powerful hangover, so I avoid them if possible . . ."

The drugs were kept in the pharmacy, a room described by Johnston as an old-fashioned drug store with all those medicine bottles on shelves behind the marble-topped counters. This room had a double-locked depository for the safe keeping of alcohol and opiates. Even so, there were some incidents of alcohol and drugs reaching some inmates. In April of 1951, a guard had been sentenced to five years in prison for smuggling letters, money, alcohol and drugs and the situation was termed "very explosive" by an assistant U.S. attorney. Even the prison's banker told of the availability of "goof balls" on Alcatraz.

Some inmates looked towards the medical ward as a place to obtain drugs. They would try in some cases to fabricate illness in order to obtain drugs. This practice was carefully watched by the officials and was handled with as much control as possible. There are some accounts of drugs getting into the main population through the medical facilities (but that was not commonplace). At times, in the late 50's, one inmate recalls, "When I first went there, they had the MTA's come around and they gave out something to the individuals, purely voluntarily. They were not making them take it, but they gave the individuals something, some kind of medication or whatever it was. At times there was quite a bit of confusion, with the pounding on the bars and rattling of the doors and that sort of thing when they were late, around 8:00 p.m. They would go to individuals and give them whatever it was, and, of course, I never did taste it or partake, but the rumor was that it was some kind of medication. It may have been a psychological thing, diluted aspirin or something. I don't know. But it wasn't hot milk."

Top left: Operating room
Bottom left: Alcatraz pharmacy
Bottom right: Hospital bathtub in therapy room

On Alcatraz the drugs and alcohol part of the individual's habits, practices or desires was very hard, if not impossible, to fulfill. However, where there is a will there is a way, and it is clear that one can make something happen to one's body with practically anything. To what point the effect is psychological or actually physical is hard to determine. "I did notice some of the 'bugs' smoking powdered aspirins, and orange peels. What kick they got out of this is just a guess. I may add this: the laundry did washing for the Army transport, and, in shaking down the clothes, uniforms, duffel bags, the cons found syringe needles and perhaps some 'goof-balls,' " recalls a former inmate. That practice did change and all the laundry did get searched by the guards on the dock.

At other institutions there was a commissary from which the inmates could buy items and then in some way use them to get some kind of "high." One account mentions the use of shoe polish to get a "buzz." Well, on Alcatraz there was no way an inmate could buy anything from a commissary, for Alcatraz did not have one. "I never saw any hard drugs (heroin, cocaine, 'grass,' etc.) while I was there, but barbiturates were easy to come by. The hospital gave them out by the handful until about the mid-50's. This was luminal, pill form at first, then for a time it was given in liquid form, and finally no one could get anything of that kind at all. Several inmates got so stoned on them; they couldn't find their way to the mess hall. And that was the reason for stopping the dispensing of this drug," recalls an inmate of the 50's.

There are some reports of guards giving pills and other substances to inmates, but one will never know how

credible these reports are. The punishment for this violation was severe and only the doctor was unquestioned in this practice. He did give the inmates "yellow jackets" on a trumped-up pretense. The inmates would save them, collect the powder from the capsules and roll it into the issued cigarette paper. Some would have contact with the kitchen personnel and would obtain baking soda to fill the capsules.

The rules given each prisoner in the 50's state clearly the procedure for medical attention and the handling of drugs (medication):

Medical Attention: Medical attention is available to all inmates. A member of the hospital staff conducts a daily sick-call line in the cell house at about 12:30 p.m.

To attend sick call, proceed directly to the west end of the cell house and stand quietly in line until called. After consultation, return directly to your cell. Do not loiter or visit on the gallery.

If you become ill at any time, notify an officer and you will receive medical attention. Do not make unnecessary disturbances.

When you receive a medical lay-in, you will remain in your cell except for religious services, meals and movies.

If you are notified by the medical officer of sick-call to remain in your cell for hospital call-out, you must do so.

You are allowed to keep in your cell only those medications issued to you by the hospital staff. Empty and unused bottles are to be returned to the west end desk. No medication will be kept in your cell longer than 30 days.

Today it would be hard to recreate the mood and atmosphere in the medical ward, for it was a prison with no privileges. The treatment received did not always proceed with great efficiency or speed. Was there understanding, caring and compassion in the medical center? That will never be

Top left: Building number 66, "The Morgue." Photo circa 1910-13.
Top right: Building number 66, "The Morgue" as seen in 1979 from guard walk on northeast side of recreation yard.
Bottom right: View looking into the morgue. Photo 1979.

clear, for it depends on whom you ask. Some inmates feel that they were greatly mistreated in the medical facilities and, on the other hand, some medical staff feel that the inmates treated them with contempt and that they were the recipients of the anger and frustration of the inmates. Some medical personnel were on Alcatraz as part of a tour of duty and the stay varied in length. The contact was with a few of the inmates, and some came to the medical ward as a result of an escape attempt, or as a result of a violent attack by another inmate. So the mood of the patient was not the best and sometimes would be reflected in the behavior in the medical wards.

Dr. Ritchey told a visiting doctors group that, after all, they could not send their patients elsewhere, and that's why they had such good facilities. The medical staff was provided by the United States Public Health Service and that fact would almost guarantee the access to anything medical needed.

Alcatraz had its own morgue. A room that was once used as a storage room for military ammunition now had a power generator mounted between the entrance and the four compartments designed to hold the bodies. This room was complete with a marble slab table used by the coroners to examine the corpse.

Life on Alcatraz certainly represented the ultimate confinement. But nowhere was it felt more than in the individual cell. Ironically, that cell represented to the inmates the only place of individual, personal, safe feeling.

The arrangement of cells on Alcatraz was such that maximum overview and control could be guaranteed to the guards. The main cellblocks were in constant use and the part referred to as "A" block or military cells were used only

for special occasions. Holding prisoners for short periods due to strikes or disciplinary reasons was common practice. Prisoners were also held in "A" block waiting for an interview by federal officials or a meeting with other prison officials for various reasons. Confiscated instruments were stored in "A" block. "A" block had cells equipped with typewriters (late 1940). Prisoners who worked in industry could go to "A" block on the weekend to use typewriters provided by the institution for the typing of legal material. Those who were not assigned to industry could use the typewriters during the week.

From all evidence, it is clear that "A" block was not as tightly controlled as the rest of the cells. One can find much information that revealed the actions on Alcatraz during the early years. In the first year, the military structures under the cell house, still called the dungeon, were used for the

most severe punishment. In 1940, cellblock "D" was completed and Warden Johnston tore out the basement cells and converted them to storage. Many stories and rumors evolved around the dungeon and, again, many will be lost to all forever. The stories would come from the prisoners confined there, and most of those would be denied by the officials. Most stories, by the time they got out, could not be regarded as factual. Even Johnston addressed himself to the question of the dungeons. He corrected the visitors on the question of the existence of Spanish dungeons by explaining that the Spanish never occupied or fortified Alcatraz and that prisoners were not kept in the dungeons.

The area referred to as the dungeons is the remnant of the old military citadel under the modern cell building. The building, as it stands today, was built on top of the foundation of the fortified citadel that was erected in the 1850's. The foundation was never considered safe for the housing of inmates. "They were badly located, poorly constructed and unsafe because they were easy to dig out," wrote Johnston.

There is, after sifting through many stories, enough evidence to confirm that, indeed, the basement under the cell blocks was used to confine inmates. Those inmates were kept in chains and the conditions were in violation of all standards set up by the Bureau of Prisons. A few accounts are available, such as the account of an inmate in the early days: "They used to put leg irons on the men in the dungeon. But most of the cons found ways to slip them off. Then the inmates would throw them out, so the guards quit the leg irons and took to handcuffing the prisoners to the bars. That was the way it was the first time I made the dungeon. That wasn't so funny," recalls the inmate.

The inmates would make a lot of noise and holler at the top of their lungs. The guards would show up, and on some occasions beat them silent. There were accounts of rats: "Some of them rats looked like they was two feet long, running across your legs." The inmates had to sleep on the floor with only a blanket, but most of them could not sleep, for the stink and the noise were unbearable. Not enough exercise, so the body was always cold. One inmate tells, "There was a lot of guys died right there in the dungeon in the five years before they abolished it."

One inmate who had a lot of publicity and who wrote his own story was Alvin Karpis. We will discuss him in a later

A-block isolation cell. Note graffiti near floor by grill. A close-up can be seen on next page, top left.

chapter, but his account of the dungeon is included here. He writes: "The dungeon lies deep beneath the cell house of Alcatraz and is entered from eight 'D' or 'A' blocks. It is unofficially used for prisoners not intimidated by the hole, and during the strike there are many of us." Karpis was sent several times to the dungeons, and he recalls his first visit. "I'm escorted down the steep steps leaving daylight, humanity, and civilization above. Flashlights jerk roughly across ancient slabs of stone cut by primitive Spanish instruments in another century." Even then the misconception of Spaniards on Alcatraz was firm in the dialogue of those telling the stories. "A moment later, I'm alone in the darkness. Water is running off the walls, continuously, keeping the cell damp. There is no toilet. At noon I receive two slices of bread which is the only meal a day. One of my greatest fears during the three days in the barren tunnels is that I'll fall asleep and wake up, my body covered with large rats whose green eyes sparkle from jagged recesses."

In the later years the dungeons were used for storage. Inmates on a wash detail or fetching a mattress did get to see parts of the dungeons. One inmate recalls, "I've never resided in its cubicle, but have been down there when we had a strike (which was a sort of agenda program). I went down there to get my musty mattress to rest my weary body at night. Geez, the Feds were kind to us, not wanting us to sleep on concrete floors in 'A' block, just above the dungeon. In the morning we had to return the mattress to the confines of the dungeons. The floors down there were covered with sawdust, no lights and no sound, just thick walls and seats made of stone."

An inmate in the late 50's on a wash detail recalls, "On the far side of 'A' block was a stairway that led down 15-20 steps to a locked massive solid steel door. The hack (guard) in charge had us carry down some surplus iron bed bunks. These were stored in the old dungeon along with obsolete machinery, filing cabinets, pipes and conduit, etc. On entering, the first thing I noticed was that it wasn't your everyday-garden-variety of dungeons . . . although it smelled like one . . . kinda dank, musty, potato cellar odor, you know? Torquemada would have picked it as an ideal spot for a ball, and I half expected any minute a bat would snarl itself in my hair. We were not down there too long and didn't venture very far into its depths — which made the crew happy — but we did see what was apparently a couple of cells. The Spanish didn't care too much for standard 6-8 inch walls and iron bars — the masonry was 2-3 feet thick, and for looking out of cells, as windows opening onto the corridors, there were slots 3 or 4 feet vertical by 5 to 6 inches wide cut through the thick masonry. You could poke your arm through it, but not your head — so no need for bars. These rooms or cells probably held 4 to 5 men. If I recall correctly they were perhaps 10x10 feet. There were no doors left — probably they had been solid iron — but only a kind of archway remained as the entry to them."

One wonders what an inmate that did get to go into the dungeon would tell the rest of the population. The official verson is that in 1940, with P.W.A. funds, those dungeon cells were torn down and the two rooms were converted to storage areas. The new disciplinary unit was built at that time and became known as the "D" block. This area of cells still receives the most publicity. "D" block was referred to as the solitary confinement unit. The reason for that name is logical since it is in those cells that we find the six solitary

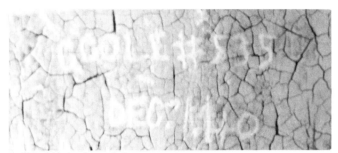
Graffiti in A-block solitary cell of an escape artist

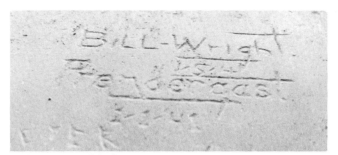
Graffiti scratched into A-block solitary cell floor

View of A-block cells with entrance to "the dungeons" visible

cells, with the rest of the cells designed to isolate the inmates from the rest of the population.

The six solitary cells hold the most fascination for the tourists today. Maybe it's because of the impact they have on anybody confined in them. These cells, N.R. 9-14, are used today to put some tourist in for a short time. Most express fear and discomfort of these experiences with total darkness, total confinement. The possibility of 10, 15, 19 days' stay in these cells is unthinkable to the tourist today, but that was a reality for many inmates who violated the "Alcatraz Laws and Rules."

Regardless of when the inmate was in the cell house, he had to follow very stringent rules. No caps could be worn in the cell house. Smoking was only allowed in his cell, in the library and in "A" block. "Do not smoke or carry lighted cigarettes or pipes on the galleries or flats in the cell house at any time." Specially-assigned orderlies completed the janitorial work. The orderlies swept the galleries, wiped the rails, washed the windows, dusted the side wall and polished the floors. The main cellhouse has large windows, forty-six on one side and fifty-two on the other. Large skylights, approximately 372 feet long, 4½ feet wide, admit additional lighting. From an engineer's study, we see that there are approximately 3,800 square feet of light space in the cell house, not the dark, musty chambers described in some news stories.

The traffic in the cell house was always swift and short. From cell to mess hall, to yard or to the showers, became the regular routine for the inmates. The guards in the cell house performed all supervisorial duties without weapons and were responsible for each inmate moving swiftly from one point to the other.

Upon entering the cell house, remove your cap and

walk directly and quietly to your cell. Loud talking, loitering on the galleries, stairs or aisles are not permitted. Don't enter any other inmate's cell at any time.

So read the second paragraph of instructions to each inmate. Each living being wants to claim a space of his own, a house, a room, a chair, a corner, all depending on his individual circumstances. There was no exception for the inmates. To the inmate, the only place to claim as his own would be his cell. This would be his home, his retreat, his personal space. That area, too, would be subject to rules, rules not always written down. "Your cell is subject to search at any time," seems like a simple rule. But considering that it could be done at any time, with no explanation, or as many times as it fitted the searcher must have been one of the most frustrating aspects of cell life.

"At the wake-up bell in the morning, you must get out of bed and put on your clothes. Make up your bed properly (as shown in the diagram) with your pillow at the end near the bars, blankets tucked neatly under the mattress, and extra blankets folded neatly at the foot of the bed. Sweep your cell and place the trash in the trash basket. Don't attempt to flush it down the toilet. Don't sweep trash or dirt out onto the gallery or off the gallery." These rules did not change much over the years, but the smallest change would be a welcomed change. The most insignificant thing can become a major problem under these conditions. "Contraband items found in your cell will be confiscated and a disciplinary report will be placed against you for possession of same."

Under normal circumstances, we would consider contraband items to be weapons, drugs, etc., but here on Alcatraz it could be an extra paper clip, shoelace or any

Graffiti, A-block cell bars

143

item not listed on the personal property card. Items issued and not used during a specific time became contraband, such as cigarettes or the candy received at Christmas. As a former officer tells it, "candy and 'tailor-made' cigarettes, given to inmates, must be used up in a short time or become contraband." In the late 40's, the utility officers would make the cell searches. The shake-downs were made at random and the officers would only know that morning that a shake-down would be made. They kept a list on every cell. There was no pattern to this searching, but some inmates' cells were searched more than others. The main reason would be to search for contraband, saw marks, graffiti, and anything not listed on the property card. This search was also used to harass the inmate. That, however, is denied by the officials.

It's hard to imagine what that means to a person who already has no privacy or any other way of feeling a sense of having his own place. Everybody would react differently: some would get used to it (at least, give that impression) and others would react violently to it. "One day a colored fellow marched down to the desk and inquired who in the hell shook down his cell. He had in tow his tenor sax. So Guard Fisher reared back on his heels and said loudly, 'I.'

The next thing he knew was that the colored gent crowned him over the head with the sax, fracturing the skull of 'I.' There went a good sax."

The procedure for getting the men into their cells was designed to give the guards maximum control. The men were lined up in front of the cells, the cell doors were opened and the men waited in the rear of their cells for the doors to be shut. The men then went to the front of their cells and stood there while the guards took the head counts. In the late 30's all cells were closed at 5:00 p.m., and they were never opened until the next morning. Should an inmate become critically ill, the cell door would be opened, but only in the presence of three officers: the doctor, the captain, and a guard.

In the early days of this institution as a federal prison, no games, cards or checkers were allowed. The rule of silence was in force and each person was alone in the cell. All the inmate was able to do was stare at the walls. Some inmates out of necessity to keep their sanity devised a very elaborate system to communicate and pass the time.

A language, made up of signs and signals, was developed to the point that inmates could play chess, checkers and other games from cell to cell. Some inmates even taught the game of chess via sign language. The players were surrounded by the supporting players. These players would control the times. What does that mean? Well, as we know, there was a head count every 30 minutes. The guards would walk in front of the cells and count the inmates present, walk to the end of the tier, and report the numbers to be called in to control. The supporting players would signal the approach of the officers as

144

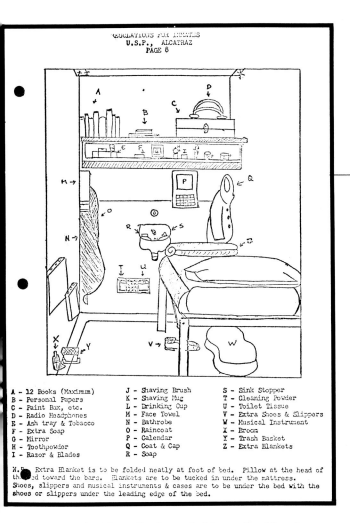

A - 12 Books (Maximum)
B - Personal Papers
C - Paint Box, etc.
D - Radio Headphones
E - Ash tray & Tobacco
F - Extra Soap
G - Mirror
H - Toothpowder
I - Razor & Blades

J - Shaving Brush
K - Shaving Mug
L - Drinking Cup
M - Face Towel
N - Bathrobe
O - Raincoat
P - Calendar
Q - Coat & Cap
R - Soap

S - Sink Stopper
T - Cleaning Powder
U - Toilet Tissue
V - Extra Shoes & Slippers
W - Musical Instrument
X - Broom
Y - Trash Basket
Z - Extra Blankets

N.B. Extra Blanket is to be folded neatly at foot of bed. Pillow at the head of the bed toward the bars. Blankets are to be tucked in under the mattress. Shoes, slippers and musical instruments & cases are to be under the bed with the shoes or slippers under the leading edge of the bed.

they approached from the far end of the galley. The players then would have time to retreat from the bars and rearrange the cell to make it look like normal. In some cases the playing boards would be matches on the floors, marking on the wall, or any other imaginary pattern with squares on it. One inmate used his hair as his pieces, cut to different lengths and laid on the bed. The game was not visible from the outside, since the hair blended with the blanket. One inmate actually asked another inmate for some light-colored hair to offset his dark hair.

There is the story that one inmate took 45 minutes to explain via sign language that, indeed, he had not flipped the other player off. Other inmates took sides and the silent argument went on. The incident does attest to the tense frustration of a situation wearing on anybody that exposed or forced into this situation.

In the 40's these strong rules changed and the inmates were allowed to "play games *quietly* with your adjoining neighbors *only*."

Playing cards was not allowed, and many different inventions were used to simulate cards. The bridge players would use either bone or ivory dominoes that had standard playing card faces on one side (instead of the white dots), something like a "Bicycle" deck, only in miniature: Aces, Kings, Jacks, etc., in color. They would turn all the "cards" face down and mix them around like dominoes, then each player would draw out his hand and set them in a wooden rack in front of them, made especially for that purpose.

The cells, basically, were all the same: a bed, bedding, small folding table, and a seat attached to the wall opposite the bed, electric light bulb with shade, shelf with clothes, books, identical toilet bowls, wash basins and ventilators under the wash basin. The differences in a tier of cells would be noticeable to the visitors in the colors of the cells or some extra items in the cells. The extra items, such as books, pictures, drawing boards, correspondence course texts, were accumulated due to the inmates' long-term sentences. All items had to be approved and were included on their personal property cards.

The change of colors in the cells stems from several sources: one, from the administration. Warden Johnston told a visitor in the early part of his term as warden that they were interested in the "color psychology." He pointed out that the different colors on the walls in the large rooms had such a good effect that he wanted to experiment with different colors in the cells. He felt that by using dark green on the back wall around the wash basin and light green on the side walls, the effect would be that the cell would look larger than if it was painted all white. The cells in later years did take on a large variety of painted decor. Checkered floors, patterned walls and pin-striping can still be found by a visitor today. It is not clear who got to paint his cell and what the fad was in which they were painted. Painting of subject matter on the walls was never permitted.

We see many ways the inmates made devices that would become hooks on walls, enabling them to hang things on walls. The cardboard material of matchbooks was commonly used.

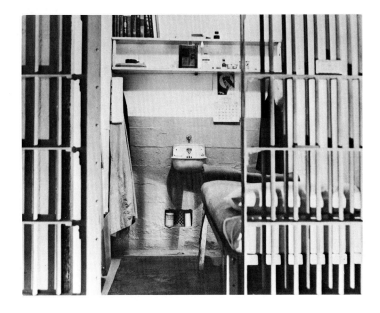

Top right: Pinstripe border on all floors. Top far right: Checkerboard pattern painted on floor. Bottom right: View down "Seedy Street" aisle between C and D-block toward the recreation yard.

One must wonder about the specific rule that states: "No fires are permitted in the cell for any purpose whatsoever. Do not attempt to heat water in your cell." Why would an inmate start a fire in his cell, especially when he could not get out, should it get out of hand? Well, there are many ways fire can be used to offset the routine.

The most likely way would be for the inmate to heat up any materials in order to create a fume that he would inhale and give him a "buzz." They would try anything. Torching of an inmate was of great concern to the officials, but especially to inmates not liked by the general population. Torching was simply setting on fire the cell of an inmate while he was in it and watching him burn to death. The time it took the guards to notice, rush to the cell and put the fire out was not fast enough to prevent death. There were two such threats known to the inmates, but it never happened. Instead, it was decided to poison the inmate.

At any given time there were riots and the inmates in their cells would start to make noise by banging their bunks on the floors, screaming and making an incredible amount of noise. Many thought for sure it could be heard in San Francisco. Imagine how a couple hundred men in the middle of the night making all that noise must have worked on the nerves of everybody. One single man could create a massive disturbance if he so chose. One evening, as the Director of Prisons, James V. Bennett, sat beside a fire in the home of Warden Johnston, they heard a loud shriek from the direction of the main cell block. This action would trigger the response of the other inmates who would scream, "Shut up," "Dummy up," "Knock it off," and a whole collection of obscenities. Bennett wrote: "The noise was deafening."

The other disturbance was created from the cells by every inmate throwing everything out of his cell into the main gallery. Paper was put on fire, toilet paper was lit and even the mattress was dumped.

The reason for these disturbances varied from time to time, and never really brought any changes. From a therapeutic sense, it was a good thing: letting off steam, expressing frustrations. The one inmate who shrieked assured the warden that he did not want to start a riot, but wanted to force a Congressional investigation of his imprisonment.

Some of the riots and disturbances were planned, but most of them were spontaneous outbursts, usually triggered by something that happened in the cell block. The close supervision and lack of privacy could have been sufficient to start something. One incident that could give some insight into the cell block mood at a given time would be the one that occurred around Christmas time. At Christ-

mas the inmates were always given a small one-pound bag of candy and some nuts. This was paid for by the Federal Bureau of Industries. One year the officer, who apparently had a natural paunch, and thus did not need the additional padding, entered the cell block dressed as Santa Claus. He was the Alcatraz Santa and had made his rounds for the children on the "Rock." He came in the door as Santa — jolly ol' Saint Nick — Ho, ho, ho — Merry Christmas — and walked up to the cell of one inmate, put the bag into the cell and proceeded to the next one. One of the inmates yelled out, "Who is that nut?" And the rest of the inmates responded by yelling, "It's old Saint Nick," and started to scream and cuss out this Santa Claus. The officer quickly realized he was not welcome and left. So, even though it was based on good intentions on the part of the officer, it was not welcomed and could have triggered disturbances.

146

This incident can be regarded either as humorous or sad but, either way, it reveals the mood at a given time in the cell block as totally unpredictable.

The cell blocks, until 1940, consisted of "A" block, the oldest part of the cells, "B" block and "C" block. The bottom level was referred to as "the flats," and the two levels above them as "tiers." At this time it still has not accurately been determined as to where the names for the aisles came from, but they were used throughout the life of the prison. The aisle between "A" and "B" blocks was called "Michigan Boulevard." The aisle between "B" and "C" blocks was named "Broadway," and is the main way between the administrative part and the west wing, hospital, kitchen and mess hall through the cell blocks. The logic behind the naming of this aisle as "Broadway" would surely be linked to New York's "Broadway." In the 30's, probably the most known and popular street in the United States was Broadway in New York. The traffic on Broadway was always heavy. On Alcatraz, the aisle with the most traffic was also "Broadway." The end of "Broadway," the area in front of the mess hall, was the busiest place and was named "Times Square." The aisle between "C" and "D" blocks, constructed in 1940, was named "Seedy Street." This name must have come about by the relationship of some inmate in that part of the building, possibly linked to Chicago.

Even though all the cells were the same in construction, the location of each cell would create some feeling of preference by the inmates. All top tier cells were warmer because the heat from the steam radiators rose to the top of the building. All cells on "Broadway" were considered too noisy and always exposed to the traffic and VIP tours.

A-block cell

Sink in A-block cell

A-block shower

These "Broadway" cells were the least desirable. The preferred cells were all the outside cells. Two reasons contributed to their popularity: one was the fact that they were opposite the windows and thus would enable the inmates to read past the time the lights were turned out (the moon provided just enough light for reading); the second factor is that there was a view of the city and the Golden Gate Bridge from the top tiers.

These factors became major points in the cell change requests from the inmates. The cells on "Broadway" were divided into several categories. All black and ethnic minorities were housed on the second tier of "Broadway." The top tiers were reserved for homosexuals. It is not clear as to how they made these distinctions. Not all homosexuals had been previously identified, and it must have been that the pattern fell into place as the inmates requested transfers in order to get away from that environment. This kind of pattern all of a sudden can be stated as fact, but one can never really document the process that created this situation.

New inmates and those assigned to the kitchen detail were housed on the flats of "Broadway" (bottom tier). It took six months before a new inmate could ask for a transfer.

Johnston, at first, requested that the cells be rotated frequently. His reasoning was the prevention of escapes. In later years inmates did get to stay in the same cell for many years.

The selection of a cell almost always became a major issue with the inmates. The reasons for either wanting a different cell or not wanting to be moved varied greatly, but never was that a light issue. One must realize that the working inmate spent 14 or 15 hours a day in this one place. The inmates who did not work spent 23 hours a day in their cells; and, except for the time used for meals, went nowhere. Those cells were searched as the inmates were in the shower or at meal times. Each prisoner had his cell searched at least once a week for contraband; and, as we stated earlier in this chapter, this caused great aggravation.

Reading through the special search instructions for the officers, one quickly can pick up the mood and feeling of their action and search. Consider these instructions: "Formulate a plan of search that will cover every square inch of the cell and its contents," and: "The mark of a good shake-down officer is his ability to make a thorough search and yet leave the cell in the same condition it was in when

A-block solitary door mechanism. Note vent holes above door.

A-block solitary cell door locking mechanism

148

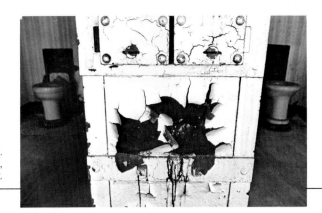

he began the search. Do not mess or upset a cell. Do not leave it in such condition that the inmate will know from its appearance that it has been searched." For the bars there was a totally prescribed way of searching — a big difference from the "formulate a plan" instruction. It would look worse and certainly become more public if bars had been cut through. After all, they were supposed to be tool-proof. The three things the officers were to look for were: broken welds, cracked and cut bars. Here is how they looked for those facts:

1. Tap ends of bars, and listen for distinctive rattle of bar ends striking against spreader plates.
2. Tap bars along length, and listen for dull ring.
3. Pass a thin metal instrument, such as the back of a knife blade, along the length of bar, feeling for cuts and depressions in the bar.

These instructions were followed with a word of caution: "A bar which has been cut is likely to have the cut filled with soap, putty, etc., to conceal the cut. If you find such a spot, dig into it and immediately report to the lieutenant, captain, or associate warden."

Each cell had the same inventory and anything found not part of the inventory was confiscated and would get the individual additional punishment. A new arrival in 1956 would find the following in his cell: Eighteen inches from the ceiling a shelf against the back wall, supported by three pegs, one in the center and one on each side of the cell walls. On that shelf he would find his aluminum cup for drinking water, a safety razor, an aluminum cup with a cake of Williams shaving soap in it, a shaving brush, a metal mirror, a toothbrush, tooth powder, a comb, a pair of nail clippers, a bar of soap, a sack of stud smoking tobacco, a corncob pipe, a roll of toilet paper, a can of brown shoe polish, a whisk broom, a green celluloid eye shade and the rule book.

When asking a former inmate his first impression of his cell, the first comment had to do with the size of the cell. All

149

Alcatraz inmates had spent time in some other joint and, thus, could compare the size of the cells. An impression related by a former inmate reveals a funny-looking picture. He states that after he had finally looked around his new home, he sat on the toilet, reaching for his toilet paper, and was struck by the view. As he looked out of his cell, he saw many other inmates sitting on their toilets. He expressed the strange situation for all of them: sitting on the toilet while staring at someone else a few feet away doing the same.

Getting used to his home is a process that never is completed. There is a constant adjusting to the total environment and, even though most things become familiar, one always reacts to the new reality of this environment. One of the most noticeable factors is that of the various sounds — these sounds, some of them regular, such as the opening or closing of a gate door or one's own cell door, and some of them new and unexpected, such as a plane overhead or the opening of a cell door at an unscheduled time. Anything like that creates a lot of questions in the minds of these inmates; and, until they have the exact reason or source, their thoughts work overtime sorting out all the variables. Each sound becomes an integral part of the environment. The way they heard certain walks could tell them exactly who entered the cell house and, probably in that short time, could determine the actions that would follow. We take sound for granted. But when confronted with a situation such as Alcatraz offered, they no longer just remained unnoticed sounds. They became the most valuable reference as to what was going on in their environment.

Today, in the totally empty Alcatraz, the tour guides demonstrate the sound with the opening and closing of the cell doors. It is hard to describe that sound, but a word that could be used would be "final." The sound is so hard, cold and final. It would be safe to say that no inmate ever became used to that sound, to the point of not hearing it. In a particularly tense moment in a movie, the director always uses the special effect of sound to heighten the drama or to force a certain mood. Well, on Alcatraz, that mood was forever the same: that of final hopelessness.

The need for self expression and sense of achievement was not always fulfilled with violence, frustration or defiance. Some inmates looked towards the arts to achieve this. The music band was part of that accomplishment, but there were others, such as writing, sports and painting. In

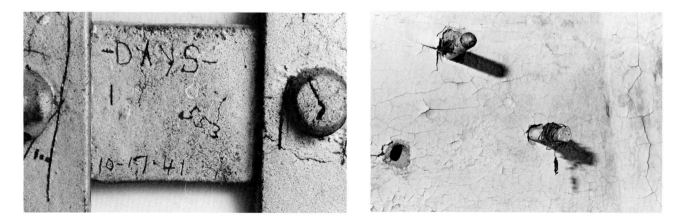

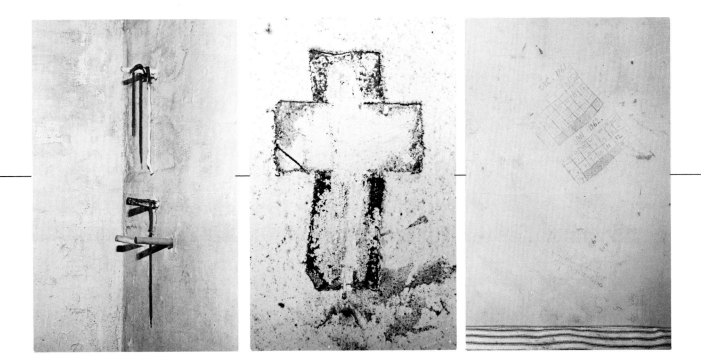

looking at the works of inmate artists, we not only see amateur dabbling, but, in some cases, we see professional-type work.

In their cells the inmates were allowed to have painting materials. Those painting materials would be especially ordered for them, and some inmates had large set-ups. The savings from the work in the industries were used to purchase the materials. An inventory of the cell of an artist revealed the following: ten small canvases, two boxes of paints, thirty-five assorted paint brushes in a wooden holder, three easels, one drawing board, a number of tubes of paint, a color wheel and numerous sketches. The subjects varied. Some of the art work dealt with religious themes, Alcatraz, copies of images, such as those of Norman Rockwell, or others seen in magazines.

One noted inmate artist was John Paul Chase, the partner of Baby Face Nelson, who painted scenes of the inside of Alcatraz. After his death in 1973, he was remembered by many through his paintings: "One of the most successful was John Paul Chase, who sold in the $300-$400 range," recalls a friend of his. Another noted Alcatraz artist of later years was Hayman, who did portraits in pastels. These portraits would be sent home and, through

an elaborate network, would reach the proper persons who, in turn, would transfer monies to pay for the work. All this was done through the mail, despite censorship. There was even a story on "the Rock" in the 50's that Henry M. won a commutation from a life sentence, as a result of an excellent portrait of the then Governor, Frank Clements, which was presented as a gift. Of course, that was not the official reason stated on the commutation, but Henry felt that was what did it.

The themes varied from landscapes, still-lifes, surrealism, etc., but the one most attempted was the portrait. Father Clark, the Catholic Chaplain, took some of the inmates' creations to show to a Mr. George Harris, a San Francisco artist. This artist was very much impressed by the work and offered to come to "the Rock" and give the painters advice and suggestions. Interest was high among the Alcatraz artists, and that led to the forming of an art class on Saturday and Sunday afternoons, during the regular recreation time.

"One of the painted scenes I remember best was by John Paul Chase, which depicted a view through barbed wire of the Golden Gate Bridge and a part of the San Francisco shoreline — a wistful prisoner/painter's view from "the

Top right: A typical Alcatraz cell on Michigan Ave.
Bottom left: A poem on a wall close to the bed

Rock" that spoke more than all the words," recalls a class participant.

After the meals before the cell doors were slammed shut, there was a short time of grace, when the inmates could look into another inmate's cell. During that time several inmates would go to the artists' cells to view their work.

The Alcatraz artist was allowed to give artwork to relatives, attorneys and people on the inmate's visiting list. Those people, in turn, could exhibit or sell the works. The inmates could not make direct sales.

The need for self expression cannot be taken away from an individual. One can only control the manner in which it is manifested. In any confinement, and especially on Alcatraz, that need to express oneself is the prime occupation of the individual. All is regulated; all falls into rules and the problem is finding the space or the time to express oneself.

Actions are a main form of expression — actions to try to create or maintain an image as to who one is, and on Alcatraz that was precisely what was to be broken down. Probably the individual who had the biggest image to maintain was Al Capone. Here was an individual who totally put himself beyond the law, beyond any rule — a snap of his fingers and things would fall into place. "I don't think he had guts enough to kill anybody. He always hired all that kind of work done," recalls an Alcatraz laundry partner of his. "Here he was a nobody and had to wash the dirty laundry, just like the rest of us."

His image, the big dealer, tough and controlling characters, was stripped down to nothing.

This single fact must have been more devastating for Al Capone than for any other inmate. On Alcatraz, the place where all the "Who's Who" in crime resided, it was terribly difficult to claim a "big shot" status. All inmates knew who did what, and telling stories would not go far.

Many of the stories told in the mail that went out would fill in for some of the needs of image-making. The letters and notes to various people, such as relatives, preachers and lawyers, would attempt to create a situation on Alcatraz that was just that — something created. The understanding of that need and the fact of self expression opens a much deeper reality of life on "the Rock."

This need is not just limited to the inmates. Anybody dealing with any part of that environment, such as Alcatraz offered, left some form of evidence of self. Some are more documented than others, for a lot of personal accounts are lost to us today; however, the part that is documented speaks loud and clear.

152

One of the forms of expression by the guards that is not as clearly documented is their physical abuse of some of the inmates. Their anger or frustration at times became expressed in physical acts against the inmates. Eyewitnesses were few when it came to the actual acts but some were witnessed and the evidence at times was ample. In a scuffle at one time an inmate broke his leg under the weight of a fat guard. There are many stories and claims of physical abuse but the most notable form of self-expression between guards and inmates on the "Rock" was verbal. "The deputy warden was a good one for cussing back and forth for any takers. One convict threatened to beat him up, to which the deputy (Miller) replied: "You might be able to whip me, but I'd give you a good go." Naturally, this was an unacceptable way of dealing with each other and at times would lead to a hearing, such as in the case of "the Dutchman (Roedel) who was put on court for calling a tower guard an S.O.B. At the hearing he denied it and claimed that he didn't know the guard could hear it. The deputy dropped the charges."

The interaction went on and, depending on who talks, the point of view of the facts changes. Most inmates be-

lieved that some guards took great pleasure in depriving an inmate of some luxury or privilege. "Just love to tear up a con's cell and pages out of magazines," recalls one individual. "Some of the guards inadvertently addressed me as Mister S. For the moment they still thought of me as a human being — not something inferior, with a number. In due time this error was corrected," states this inmate who tells us the following in regard to guard harassment: "On occasions, I would come back to my cell to find my pictures crumpled and in the toilet. A guard who had shaken down my cell must have been annoyed that he could not find any contraband, and reacted in a way that he knew would disturb me. I would have been laughed at if I had complained."

An inmate on Alcatraz in the mid-50's relates a different feeling towards the guards. "The mentality of the guards was far superior to the state prison guards. The officers here did not carry clubs and did not walk around striking inmates as occurred in the state prison. Here the guards spoke to the prisoners courteously. There were exceptions, of course. I did not find the brutality, the degradation that existed in the state prisons."

Today we hear more about how good the relationships were between the guards and inmates. The facts point in a different direction. Reading the personal accounts and records, the image of harmony is a faint veil over the true feelings that guided the men on Alcatraz through their daily routine.

Graffiti found scratched on glass in a guard cage

The graffiti reads:

— DAILY PRAYER —
...SE "DEAR LORD"
KEEP MY DAM NOSE
...HER PEOPLE'S BUSINESS —
"AMEN!"

A very complex means of achieving self-expression is the fostering and creating of interpersonal emotional and love relationships. The in-depth analysis of the homosexual society in prisons has been dealt with in numerous papers and books. This is not the place to pursue an in-depth search of this subject; however, the issue of homosexuality and its reality on "the Rock" must be mentioned.

The need for any human being to deal with his own sexuality is a foregone conclusion. The natural and most accepted way is not available for men in confinement. For some, the life style and actions of a homosexual become a permanent part of his makeup; for others, it is just a temporary arrangement while confined to prison.

Everybody in Alcatraz at one time or another had to deal with the issue of homosexuals. As mentioned previously, there was even a tier of cells set aside for homosexuals. Exactly how this was executed is not clear. There obviously were some blatant, admitted homosexuals; but that was not the majority of the population. We find all types of reactions to this fact. Some hated the identified homosexuals, others tolerated them, and others ignored them. The time and place for the sexual acts were very limited and always at great risk. The risk factor, to some, was part of the challenge.

The words used in describing homosexuality on "the Rock" were not much different from those of other prisons, but the reaction among a smaller, specialized population, such as was the case on Alcatraz, varied. The variation came mainly because of the desperation of the individual

confined to Alcatraz. This was not new for the prisoners of the Federal years. In an interview with an inmate of the military Alcatraz in 1925, he recalls, "I was only 18 years old. Rapes of inmates were very common. Some kids were severely beaten several times before they consented. Others were forced violently. A number of prisoners had several 5-year sentences added for sodomy. We didn't dare to inform the authorities because then they were put in an isolation, stool pigeon tier and went to the mess room in specially supervised lines and were often stabbed and killed. So I made up my mind I was going to die in the electric chair since I couldn't get help from authorities. I stashed bricks and bar, etc., around a rock pile and let the word out that I planned to murder any asshole who touched me. They had pulled kids under the rock quarry machinery and assaulted them. The most terror-stricken part of my life was that rock pile. Apparently I convinced those assholes that fucking me was going to be their death. I survived without any injury or molestation."

In those days there were more hours spent working outside and that made supervision more difficult. The cells in the 50's did not provide a good place for physical contact, for the only time the cell doors were open was when letting out one gallery at a time for work call or the mess hall. There was a certain amount of resentment from the other inmates toward the homosexuals but, as far as can be documented, most inmates held a neutral view. One inmate estimated 60% anti and perhaps 40% indifferent. "On more than one occasion some inmate, after being

154

Alcatraz officers' graffiti from various places in the main cell house

released by court order, would tell reporters in San Francisco that everybody on 'the Rock' was either a faggot or crazy. This would cause a lot of bitterness in the population," states one prisoner serving a 40-year sentence.

On Alcatraz, we did not really find the very young inmate, like in other federal prisons. Place on "the Rock," after all, was reserved for the hard-core criminal. "The great majority of prison inmates I have come in contact with in my 35 years of incarceration were hard types who worshipped physical strength and force. I may have a distorted view of this, since I spent most of my time in maximum-security prisons. Perhaps minimum- and medium-security prisoners lean more toward the so-called finer things in life as do most homosexuals," relates an inmate who tells of the tough act one puts on in order to be left alone, "as one who will take no shit." He felt the polite ways, such as, "pass the sugar, please," "excuse me," "thank you," would betray weakness. It was either that or get trampled on.

The activities would take place in the work area. The research on this topic alone was very difficult. It is not something related to others too openly. One story related to us, however, would probably sum up all that could possibly be said on such activities: "I never worked in the kitchen, so can't comment about what went on there. Most of those inclined would butt in at work (industry), although I can recall actually seeing only a very few incidents. Nothing was done too openly. There was a humorous incident when I happened to go up to the laundry one time. One of the

drying machines in the laundry stood about chest high and, because of its location, was a favorable assignation place for blow jobs. The blowee would stand behind the machine and look out over the top of it for any approaching hack (guard), while the blower would crouch down in front of him to perform where he couldn't be seen by anyone. On this occasion half a dozen of us cons knew what was going on. But when a hack approached and started to talk to this inmate standing behind the machine facing him, the inmate refused to break the 'connection' because he was right at the moment of truth, and so he tried to carry on a conversation with the hack while his eyes were rolling back and upward with a rigid facial expression in the throes of ejaculation. The hack finally walked off scratching his head, probably thinking, 'another stir-crazy con!' "

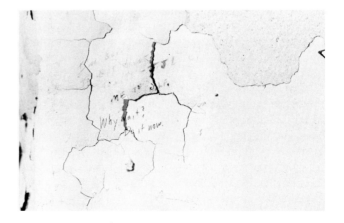

Top left: Drawing above cell door
Bottom right: Drawing on cell wall

The guards for the most part did not get close enough to the action to have to intervene. There are reports that some guards knew when not to walk by a certain place or just looked a little longer in the other direction. There are some stories that a guard was involved physically with an inmate. A guard states that he was propositioned twice. The guard, surprised, said, "Where would this happen?" upon which the inmate replied, "You are the guard. You can find the place." To this guard, that became the most disturbing incident. "Never heard of any guard and inmate being involved in any homosexual liaison — but there's always the possibility they could have," relates an inmate who was involved in robbing banks.

The only human contact these men had on "the Rock" was with other men. A woman was not to be seen on Alcatraz. When a former inmate was asked what was the most surprising thing that happened to you during your stay on Alcatraz, he replied, in a rather revealing way:

There were several surprising things that happened. But one of them was while I was living on the flats, which is the bottom gallery or ground floors . . . when suddenly, a woman walked by the front of my cell at 9:30 in the evening! She was accompanied by a deputy warden. That would not seem out of the ordinary to most people, but it was to me because I had not seen a woman or child in 7 years (excepting in magazines and movies). Turned out it was an emergency — that she was a marine nurse brought in to assist in a special operation on an inmate who had been stabbed that day. He died shortly after. You are probably wondering about this . . . thinking here is a

guy who spends 9 years on a prison island, and the only surprising thing he can come up with is seeing a woman walk by! It's hard to explain such things, how it affects emotions, but I had literally not seen any woman for 7 years . . . it was the way the island was set up. Just as I have not seen, petted, fed, or been around a dog or cat for 7 years. If I could have either a cat or dog around, believe me, it would get my full attention for an entire day or more. It is a lack, a void . . .something missing in a prisoner's life.

These words provide a great insight into the emotional domain of some individuals confined on Alcatraz. It is interesting for it reveals a different aspect than the usual one of lust and abuse. The lack of women on "the Rock" is a point mentioned by many inmates, and the following account reveals yet another incident dealing with women on Alcatraz.

The only women I even talked to in all the time I was there was a female judge and her secretary. That there was quite a caper. This woman parole judge, she was a battle-ax from away back. But when you don't see nothing with skirts on for years and years, even a battle-ax don't look too bad. The secretary, though, she was something else, again. Her legs was nice enough to make a silk worm happy to put in overtime. Gams. Real, live, genuine Hollywood gams, them legs was.

The individual was in front of this parole officer, discussing his parole. The irony was that there was no chance of a parole happening, and this individual knew it. So he did not

ttom left: The classification committee interviews an inmate.
ttom right: Head and names scratched into the
ncrete floor in solitary confinement

really feel too cooperative, and at one place his dialogue was to the point: "I ain't got no parole coming, and you know it and everybody else knows it. Besides, I'd rather look at your secretary's legs than talk to you." The conclusion of this was the reaction of the parole officer who "chewed me up in little pieces and spit me clean out of the office."

If an inmate had a woman friend he could correspond with, that would be the only contact with a woman. "After I had rested I tried to write Helen, but the letter didn't turn out as I had intended. I wanted so to write her a warm letter (probably to warm myself in the writing), but it just wouldn't come out."

For most, this privilege of letter writing was of utmost importance. That was one of the main privileges that the inmates cared about and took very seriously. The mail was very important, not only for the love emotions, but, after all, that was the only true contact with the outside world. So there were many stories about that mail privilege and many frustrations. The rules on mail privileges were clear:

Correspondence: Upon entrance to the institution, each inmate will be given a form to fill out, listing the persons with whom he wishes permission to correspond. After approval of the list, inmates may correspond only with approved correspondents. You will refrain from discussing other inmates or institutional affairs. Violent or abusive letters will not be mailed. Correspondence is limited to two (2) outgoing and seven (7) incoming letters a week. All regular inmate mail will be collected by the evening watch officer in the cellhouse. Writing materials are issued during the

Tuesday P.M. bathline, at the supply table in the clothing room.

The mail was censored and in some cases the amil never left Alcatraz. Some mail was not delivered, but put into an inmate's file for him to have after leaving Alcatraz. This is a sensitive issue since one could never really prove anything on either side of the argument. There was a "prisoner's mailbox," designed to provide any inmate the chance to write directly "without inspection by institutional authorities, to the Director of the Bureau of Prisons, the Attorney General, the Parole Board, the Surgeon General, Federal Judge, Department of Justice Officials, and in the case of military personnel to the Secretary of War or Navy, or the Judge Advocate General or the Adjutant General . . . the prisoner's mailbox is open to all inmates regardless of their status."

In cases of magazine subscriptions, many more problems plagued the system. The magazines were all censored and could only be subscribed to if they were on the approved list. On the list we find such magazines as *Life, Saturday Evening Post, Time, Newsweek, Sports Illustrated, New Yorker, Popular Mechanics, Scientific American,* etc. If something about any prisoner on the Rock happened to be printed in any of them, the page in question would be cut out. A correctional officer would be the appointed censor. This position would be rotated on a quarterly basis.

One of the inmates often mentioned in magazines was Robert (Bird man) Stroud, and he was always cut out. In some cases, they would just tape over a part they did not want the inmates to see. Most inmates thought that was

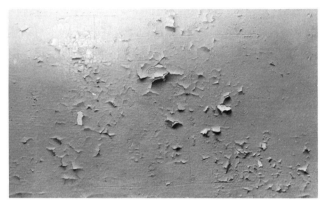

Top right: Small wooden pegs stuck to the wall to hang light things on. Bottom right: Hidden checkerboard, dark squares marked with a circle in the middle, hard to detect. Bottom left: Telephone directory issued to Alcatraz personnel.

Telephone
Directory

OCTOBER, 1951

Emergency } 2221
Fire Alarm }

UNITED STATES PENITENTIARY
ALCATRAZ ISLAND, CALIFORNIA

stupid, for all they did was hold it up close to their light and then they could see and read. One inmate relates, "The censorship was stupid in lots of ways. For example: a *Life* magazine came in on one occasion with a small circle cut out of the middle of one of the pages. The picture that remained was of a man standing up with an arm extended, but the circly cut out was of his hand. We later found out he was holding a .45 automatic pistol. On the other hand, *New Yorker* magazine ran a lengthy article on the life of Alfred Nobel. Among the paragraphs was a full and detailed description of the formula and chemicals required to make dynamite."

A magazine requested by an inmate, if rejected, would not be ordered. The inmates who would try to take the prison official to court for denying them access to the magazine would find that the courts rejected their claims on the grounds that the warden had the right to censor the reading material of inmates.

An interesting fact was that the pages torn out of one magazine for censorship would show up in another magazine, folded up. The inmates were sure it was a guard who would slip the article in the other magazine. It is said that the most prized illegal possessions by any standards were newspaper clippings that had mysteriously appeared on "the Rock." They would be folded into small squares and passed around. These newspaper clippings were guarded with their lives, since it was considered contraband and would cause a disciplinary report to be made, if discovered.

The regular periodicals would be circulated from cell to cell and would take several months to complete their rounds. But there was plenty of time on hand. One periodical found its way into Alcatraz in a most peculiar manner. A relative of an inmate ordered a subscription in the name of the parole officer librarian. After he would get his mail and place it on his desk, an inmate would steal the magazine and put it into circulation before the officer saw it. The inmate who ordered it would read it and then openly pass it on. The officers in the cell blocks were not aware of Washington's proscribed list. After their final use, they would be torn to bits and flushed down the toilets, so as to insure never having a full copy around after its use.

With all those hours to spend in the cell, reading material was of vital importance. Some of the inmates even became proficient in one or another subject. The area that stands out the most is that of law. Each inmate wanted to find a legal avenue to get out. The legal library was set up in accordance with several court decisions dealing with prisoners' legal rights. This was not fully established at the beginning of this institution but gradually, with the donations by the inmates, grew to several volumes.

This law library was located in "A" block during the 50's. A cell contained a typewriter and some well-used volumes of the United States Legal Code. What legal material the inmate could keep in his cell was never definitely established. The various briefs of one's own case could be kept in the cell. The "A" block cell had some of the materials used by the inmates over the years as they worked on their cases. Some inmates did write their own briefs.

The books were not provided for by the officials. The inmates could order them, pay for them and then donate them. Many did, including Robert Stroud, who had much material dealing with the law. Some inmates subscribed to the *United States Reports,* the *Federal Reporter,* and a couple dozen state reporters.

All of this was not just to keep the time passing. One inmate, when asked of the value of his time spent studying the law, had a very clear answer. "Yes, sir. I filed Section 2255 motion in the United States District Court. When the motion was denied by the District Court, I filed an appeal to the United States Court of Appeals for the Sixth Circuit, contending that 15 years of my 30-year sentence was illegal. In a 1956 decision written by the Sixth Circuit Judge (now Justice of the U. S. Supreme Court) Potter Stewart, my 30 years was reduced to 20, with the Court agreeing that my argument as to the other five years was not without some force. I typed the briefs in A-block on Alcatraz, mailed the typed copy to the clerk of the Sixth Circuit, Mr. Carl Reuss, with a request that he forward a copy to the printer for printing at my expense." Today this inmate is gainfully employed as a chief legal research associate.

This triumph is a very personal one. The system hated him, for he would create work for the system and help others who did not have the know-how. For him on

Alcatraz, there was a feeling of accomplishment. Even Warden Swope asked him to read the records of one inmate to see if he could do anything to help him obtain a new trial. This point varies from the official rules concerning legal help:

> "You are permitted to work on your own case or to hire a lawyer to represent you. . . . You are not permitted to work on another inmate's case or to give another inmate legal advice or instructions."

The institution required a copy of all materials typed in A-block. After the associate warden inspected the material, he would return one copy to the inmate.

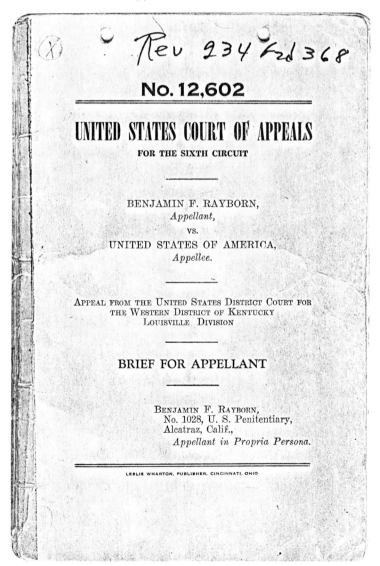

Appeal to the United States Court of Appeals by an Alcatraz inmate, asking reduction in sentence. The reduction was granted.

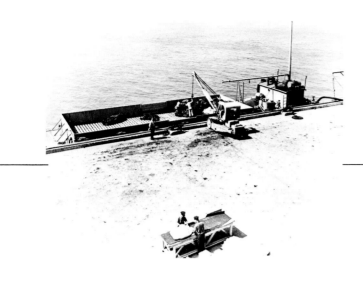

Naturally, all the inmates wanted out and they felt that maybe through their legal efforts there would be some chance. In just a very few cases did it have an effect. In general, the sentences held to what they were when they came in. But it never hurts to try and, especially, to break this devastating routine of life on "the Rock."

Most of the legal maneuvers were listed as the writ of habeas corpus. "That great writ has been relied upon for centuries to test the legality of imprisonment and to prevent the arbitrary, dictatorial, illegal deprivation of personal liberty as practiced before the Magna Charta was wrested from King John at Runnymede," writes Warden Johnston. Some prisoners would persue this avenue with great zeal. One inmate in the 40's had himself filed 15 petitions for writ of habeas corpus, seven appeals to the circuit court, three appeals to the Supreme Court, two motions for corrections of sentence and six petitions and other forms of writs, totaling 33. That was not even the top of the list. During the same time one inmate filed 56 statements and another prisoner 45, and another 36. So one can see that there was a lot of filing of writs. Judge A. F. St. Sure remarked, "Repeated filing of court petitions seemed to be regarded as an indoor sport on Alcatraz."

One inmate, Cecil L. Wright, did manage to gain release from Alcatraz on a technical point; and after serving his sentence at another institution, was sent back to Alcatraz, where he filed petition after petition until he was released from custody on grounds he did not have efficient assistance of council.

This activity related to the laws for some always presented some hope, some aim for future freedom. Other than the daily routine, all that is left is hope, though this environment and atmosphere is hopeless and very conducive to rumors.

Rumors went around on both sides. Both the inmates and the officers were subject to rumors. Some of them never die, no matter what happens. For the inmates the most dominant rumor was that Alcatraz was going to be closed. This rumor was part of the routine from the first day Alcatraz opened for business. This particular rumor was so much a part of the Alcatraz fabric that when, indeed, the information came in 1963 that Alcatraz would close, nobody reacted to it. It was not until it was confirmed by the

Attorney General, Robert Kennedy, that the inmates took it to heart. This account sums up the general feeling of that announcement. "We were out on the yard when the word came out over the speaker. (They had a speaker hooked up to a radio.) A lot of the guys said, 'Well, we heard this shit before.' There'd been rumors over the years. This time is different. This time it's the President's brother that's saying it, and he's not going to get out on a limb and let anybody cut that limb off behind him." This rumor did materialize into fact — one of the few. A prominent rumor in 1948 was that the cost of running Alcatraz would close it in three months; and in the same year the rumor that there was delegation from South Dakota parading in San Francisco demanding the closure of Alcatraz was attributed to some guards who "loved" to start rumors on Mondays. "It seemed that the convicts were told all that they would like to hear."

In the late 50's, an inmate relates, "Rumors were infinite. The most common one was that 'they are going to break the place up,' i.e., the government was going to discontinue the island as a prison. The rumor averaged twice yearly for all the years I was there. Every November the rumor would crop up that there was 'going to be' cigars, a box of chocolates, 20 candy bars, or similar claims as a gift for Christmas. The one-pound bag of candy never varied in my nine years."

On the other side of the rumor mill were those rumors that would affect the guards, such as a major breakout, rebellion, food fight or an industry breakdown. For the administrators, the situation was more difficult. There was no way they could ignore such a rumor; for if it was real or started as a decoy, it would create a situation beyond their control. So they would always be on the look-out and try to avoid a situation. One way was to change a pattern, move someone, or start a time check, etc. Even with all those safeguards in place, actions did materialize after they had supposedly just been rumors. The officials really could not do anything just on rumor. They needed some action.

One such action did evolve from a rumor started in December of 1935. January 20, 1936, marked the day the trouble began. That Monday in the laundry some inmates stopped working and moved toward the stairway, yelling for others to join them. After everybody in the front office had been alerted, the warden came to the industry building and lined up the prisoners who had quit work, gave them his speech, a warning, and marched them to their cells. The estimate of how many were part of this, again, depends upon who one talks to. It is safe to say that over 120 inmates were initially involved.

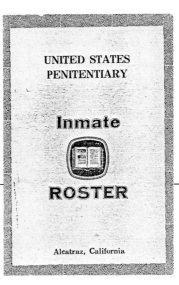

Inmate Roster given to the Alcatraz staff

At one point, it had been just a rumor, now a fact, a reality that had to be dealt with. The inmates were individually interrogated and an attempt was made to find the leaders. The individual grievances could be summed up as the following: Stop the rule of silence, nominal wages for industrial work, daily news, radio and magazines and a prison commissary.

The problem here is that the inmates could not really individually stop the stroke, for they would be classified as "rats" or "yellow" and suffer reprisals by the inmates. Some were classified as leaders and put into solitary. The next day more inmates joined the work stoppage, and prisoners working in the kitchen joined them.

This went on for several days, with many of the inmates put into solitary (dungeons) and all of them given only water, no bread. By the end of the week, 80% went back to work, but the rest were holding out and now were getting just bread and water. On Saturday they got a bowl of soup, scrambled eggs, toast and coffee. The rumor around this strike was that Al Capone "squealed" that the general strike was coming. Warden Johnston denied that account and stated that Capone had had no part in the strike.

Johnston reported to Washington that they had got through a trying time without shots being fired, no clubs or gas being used, and nobody being hurt.

There was great turmoil in those early days and it was difficult for everybody. The over- or under-reaction to rumors could trigger major conflict — constant little flare-ups, incidents, etc., until the inmates could organize. September, 1937, produced another major work stoppage. The routine was the same but a major incident that occurred during this strike was the assault on Warden Johnston by Burton Phillips. Over a period of several days, after a lot of noise and the leaders' demands on the others to stand firm, the men slowly came out of their cells and went back to work. The final major blow to the work stoppage came on Wednesday when 60 men agreed to behave and go back to work. The rest of the approximately 40 men, driven by hunger, soon dropped back into the work force.

At the same time the rumor of another strike was in the making. "The plan for the next mutiny at Alcatraz was diabolically clever." What they wanted was to have some leverage on the administration, and the only way they could achieve this was in stopping the work done on material brought to Alcatraz, such as the laundry. If nobody worked, the laundry would pile up and create pressure on the administration. "The mistake of the other strikes was in refusing to work and remaining in the cells. This time the mutiny will begin by wrecking the machinery in the shops."

The major difference from any strike in the cell house is the damaging of equipment not affecting the inmate. In his cell, any damage would affect his living conditions, and it was much easier to hold the individual responsible. If you had no mattress in your cell because you threw it over the railing, nobody else could be accused. In the industries, things would just happen and all workers came under suspicion. There were so many factors involved when dealing with rebellion that no formula could be developed for the prevention, only a reaction (punishment) afterward.

On Alcatraz, there was just so much you could do to an inmate. Physical abuse was common, but you could not kill an inmate. So the one thing that would prevent the whole situation from falling apart was human nature. In this situation, that nature takes on a different meaning. That the guards are only as effective as their informers is a fact of life. Why would there ever be such a thing as an informer? Well, it was always done with the hope of bettering one's own fate or out of vengeance or hate for someone in the prison population who did not fall into the same line of thinking. The motivation and reasons are many and very complex, and usually are directly related to the individual and his fate, not to a general pattern. All this leaves this aspect of prison life in a kind of secret, intriguing, cloak-and-dagger arena.

There were times where there was absolutely nothing pre-planned that triggered a situation of revolt or defiance. At times there was a "fun-and-games" element to all of this, especially in the industries. The following story reflects this point of the "fun-and-games" aspect. "I did know of the guard's stand in the laundry being torched (set on fire). In fact, I was accused of setting a guard's stand on fire. These stands are five-foot platforms standing on the floor, ladder leading to the stand, which had a chair and desk, plus a phone. From this high top spot the guard had a commanding view of the laundry. In fact, there were two stands in the laundry. So when one stand went on fire, the guards would rush to put it out; in the meantime, someone would set the other stand on fire. But before all this took place, it was made sure that the fire extinguishers were plugged! What a pastime!" This account dealt with an incident in 1949.

Alcatraz industry buildings as seen from the water on the NW end of the island

There are numerous accounts where some of the same style of activity was directed not against the system but against an individual inmate. In one case the damage was to be death by poisoning. Normally, an individual with a "beef" against an individual would create a one-on-one conflict. But there is a story of several inmates who wanted to poison another inmate: "The way it was told to me about trying to poison Gardner, it was to put [rat poison] in a sandwich and have it sent to his cell. Maybe he'd chomp on it and go to hell! I think that even a smuggled gun was to be used. So far, Gardner lived long enough to get out and commit suicide." Another Alcatraz inmate was caught up in a different institution, and he was burned to death in his cell.

The reason for those acts against inmates by a group of inmates rather than by one individual was simply that he was accused by the population regarding the individual as being a "snitch." A "snitch" is an individual who tells the authorities something which another inmate is doing against the rules. The hope of the "snitch" is to get favorable treatment. "Yep, there were quite a few snitches competing with one another. That's why escape plans went awry and contrabands were discovered — uncovered was the better term. The guards were only as good as their stool pigeons." There was nothing more objectionable and unforgivable than the act of "ratting" on some inmate. In some cases, "snitches" were settled with a knife. "It is the worst thing you can call a man (among prisoners, that is), and reflects extreme hatred for someone. The most out-and-out 'snitch' (at least he had this reputation) was a character called 'Stinky' Williams. Strangely enough, he was never bothered. He seldom talked or tried to talk to anyone; and perhaps, that was how he got off."

Some of these individuals would ask to be put into D-block isolation for their own protection. To what degree the system protected their sources is not really clear, but the facts support some such activities.

A very conducive place for any of this interaction, both positive and negative, was the industries. There was open contact between inmates and inmates, and inmates and guards. The tension was always high, and all that was needed was a spark to set off a hatred, friendship or suspicion. An incident that happened in the late 40's illustrates the varied ways events evolved. Some inmates were cleaning the machinery in the laundry. That was the normal procedure on Saturday. One inmate was using the prescribed caustic solution to clean the machinery. This solution looked like water; and just by looking at it, they could not be differentiated. The guard went over to the inmate and told him he had to wash these two suits of his officer friends. The inmate said, "I have strict orders from the deputy not to wash any clothes on Saturday." (With the treatment we was getting about that time, us inmates sure wasn't going to do anything we didn't have to do. Besides, when you're in prison, it's bad business to start something. If it works, they just make it part of the rules, and you got that much more to do from there on out. This is the same type of thing as the "never volunteer" when you are in the Army.)

The guard insisted and the inmate told him, "If you want them suits run through, run them through yourself. It's your baby. I go my orders," and walked away. (The guard, not liking the answer and needing to have them suits cleaned, just put them in the washer himself.) "He never asked me what was in that there vat, and it sure wasn't up to me to volunteer nothing." All that was left in the screen of the washer were a handful of buttons which the inmate dumped in the sewer.

Washing machine in the industry laundry room

Prisoners passing thru metal detector as they return from shops

The guard returned to find the machine empty and, until the last day of that inmate's stay on the Rock, figured he had stolen those suits and was hiding them for an escape attempt.

It was in the industries that the inmates would gather bits of materials which they would use for whatever needs not covered by the official supplies. It could be just a simple piece of leather or wood. In some ingenious way it could fit into something needed by an inmate. Metals were a more difficult proposition, since all of the inmates had to pass through a metal detector after leaving the industries. There is evidence that even metal got into the cells. The industry buildings were totally detached from the main building or yard. The workers had to leave the work place in a single file and march up a path to the bottom of the steps leading to a side entrance of the recreation yard. It was at the bottom of these steps that the inmates had to pass through the detectors.

There were many problems with those detectors, but, again, all this was not well documented. There were many repair orders that were made and the warden constantly tried to keep that part of the daily routine in top shape. The personal search was time-consuming and not the most desirable at times.

The inmate did try and found ways to beat the metal detectors. One way was to make sure that the metals were stainless steel. They claimed that this metal did not sound the alarm. Today it's just word of mouth that sustains this. However, there is an incident that happened in the 50's that makes just this point. "Eddie H. was a band member — guitarist — and one day in the yard Eddie asks me if I would carry a steel bar through the metal detector into the cell house for him. This metal detector was placed at the foot of some stairs leading up to the cell house entrance. It was in use when any inmate entered the cell house from

yard or work and it would make a buzzing sound when it detected metal. A search of the con's person then followed. The bar Eddie showed me and wanted me to carry in was about 6" long by 1 1/4" in diameter, weighing about 2 pounds. I took one glance of it and said, 'No. I'm sane.' So Eddie began a 30-minute discourse on how he had some other junk on him that might set the detector off and he would lose his bar in the shakedown. Further, that the detector would not ring on the bar, that he would go up right beside me and, if the buzzer sounded, he'd say the bar belonged to him and go to the hole for it. Well, after admitting to being insane, I thought, 'This, I've got to see,' but knowing full well Eddie's claim of its being his would be totally ignored. Sure enough! There was no buzzer that went off when I went through! That was how I discovered the metal detector would not detect stainless steel (which is what the bar was)."

Wood and leather probably were the materials they would find the most use for. A piece of wood could be shaped in such a way that it would fit between two bars and make a kind of platform. This little platform was used to put razor blades on as they were distributed and collected. Any book order forms, request slips, etc., could be put on those little pieces of wood. One inmate used some leather and wood to fill the holes created by slamming the bed on the floor. A lamp shade was created by a kitchen worker from the bottom of a tin can. A lot of inmates would collect things

and keep them hidden in industry and, to them, this became material for trade. It's hard for anybody else to fully understand the value that can be placed on a paper clip, rubber band, little wire, a nail, a piece of leather or wood. The objects in this confined environment take on a totally different meaning.

An inmate whose only job was to buff the floors for one hour a day tried everything possible to gain access to the industries. The main objective for this inmate was simply to be able to look out over the water as he walked down to work. That was the most important aspect. And he relates, "I was let out around 9:00 for my one hour stint with the floor-buffing machine and then I was back in my cell, my day's work done. After a couple of weeks on my floor-buffing job, I began attempts to be transferred to industries where, under a complicated formula, I would earn 'industrial good time.' After five months I was finally transferred to industry. I was glad to get out of my cell and expand my horizons. But the best part was going to and coming from work, twice each day. It was so lovely to go up and down the hillside where I could smell and see the shrubbery and not be continually faced with hard, cold concrete. Oh lovely freedom — be it ever so slight."

The work itself was routine and repetitious, but it made for a different environment and opened up the chances of something not covered in a regular routine to happen. There were some inmates who did not want to go to work and the reasons varied from individual to individual. But a major reason for some was the contact with a potential enemy.

After a disturbance where inmates broke government materials, such as toilet bowls, coveralls, mattresses, etc., some inmates were made to go to industry to earn the money to pay for the damages. The lever used to pressure

the inmates in controlling some of these disturbances was to gather the old-timers who had earned good time and were only one or two years from release and threaten them with the loss of that industry good time. This usually would move the leaders to stop their actions against the institution. So the industry work could be used for or against the inmates.

This was also true for the administration in its concern with meeting the production deadlines, especially in the laundry where Alcatraz was responsible for a large part of the military laundry. During the war this became a critical issue, since all the work was locked into the war effort. Johnston claimed that the war contract from the Alcatraz industries was good for the men, since it gave them a sense of patriotism. Well, that was a very unbalanced view, since most of the inmates never mustered up a great sense of patriotism, for their problems dealt with the federal government and most did not really have strong attachments to families of their own.

One must recognize, however, that the work of these men on Alcatraz did help and contribute to the U.S. war efforts. What the administration did not understand was the thinking of some of the inmates on the war. Their own

grapevine with the help of some guards worked well in advance of the official information delivered by the administrators. Take, for instance, 1941, when the warden posted the fact that Pearl Harbor had been attacked. The inmates, through their own radio receiver, knew about that event.

During the days with no news, radio, etc., being permitted, one inmate working in the machine shop over the years built one of the most powerful receiving sets in the Bay Area. It was hidden in a little cubby hole in back of a storeroom. "If you was a right guy, you could take turns sitting in there in the dark, listening. It was an all-wave set and we could pick up stuff from all over the world."

It is not clear who was in charge of that radio and how it escaped the "snitches," but it managed to last for some years. On the morning of December 7, 1941, the inmate monitoring the radio came running out, all "bug-eyed," and announced, "I have just picked up Honolulu — one of the military stations on the short wave. The Japs was bombing Pearl Harbor! It was several hours later that the official news came to us." That radio set ran during the entire war and nobody got wise to it. The information that the inmates were the most concerned with was what might happen to the inmates of Alcatraz if it became necessary to evacuate

San Francisco. One inmate recalls, "We knowed a lot of things that was going on around the world, long before the officials knowed them."

In more ways than one the industries were a closer link to reality, confirming that there is more to life than just the cell. For the alert warden it could be used to feel the pulse of Alcatraz. Depending on the production output, the assessment of the general mood of the inmates could be made. Sabotage of equipment was constant, but no one could tell what equipment would be affected, or if the sabotage was organized or just a disgruntled individual — valuable information in controlling such a place of confinement.

It was especially in the industry that the local "grapevine" came in handy. It was used by both sides. The administration used it to prevent a massive action or the destruction of equipment, causing a delay in delivery of material and it would indicate that all wasn't well on Alcatraz. The inmate side would use it to gather information on individuals. To the inmates, that information was vital in the understanding of their own environment. Many behavior patterns changed, based on information coming down the "grapevine."

The "grapevine" has the ability to furnish information that can certainly surprise most individuals. Such was the case to a new arrival on Alcatraz. "When I expressed amazement at their accurate knowledge of my actions and arrival on Alcatraz, a convict in a cell near me whispered, 'We knew you were coming last week and we knew you were a right guy because you wouldn't squeal to the screws on a pal; we got the word by grapevine.'" They did know of his coming to "the Rock," and for him there was a good welcome. That did not always turn out that way. Another inmate, even before he had properly moved into his cell, was told he would not be safe or welcomed here on "the

Guards walkway to industry building

Guards' door to the industry supervision corridor

Rock" by the inmates.

"Such is the mysterious 'grapevine' telegraph which does so many queer things in prison. The 'grapevine' works almost entirely through bribery of convicts who have privileges, or guards. And sometimes you'll find guards who will talk to make themselves appear big in the eyes of the cons. On Alcatraz, despite the restriction, we learned sometimes of news and changes in American prisons even before they were officially announced," responded one former inmate of the late 30's to the question of the reliability of the "grapevine." The privilege he refers to was the one in which an inmate got to work in the warden's house. "The guys in the warden's house told us less news from the outside world than the guards. And they got to see the newspaper. We got more information from the guards than the warden's houseboys," so tells an inmate of the 50's.

The "grapevine" was responsible for holding the escape attempts from the industry work area to four. Several had been planned and fell through because this "grapevine" had let the word out. If the guards did not get wind of it, the inmates would. The biggest problem for the inmates was that after the word was out, many wanted to be part of the escape attempt. Arguments would follow and would make it impossible to follow through with the plans. Materials were always needed, and that meant possible involvement of others, and nobody did anything for free.

Of the four escape attempts from the industry complex, two were from the mat shop, one from the wood shops and the last one from the laundry. The second escape attempt on Alcatraz came on the 16th of December, 1937, and originated in the mat shop. Neither the escapees nor their bodies have ever been located. This escape, even today, is laced with rumors and intrigue, especially of the whereabouts of these two Alcatraz inmates.

Theodor Cole, at 24, was serving a 50-year sentence for kidnapping. His partner in this escape, Ralph Roe, was serving a 99-year sentence for armed robbery. Both committed their crimes in Oklahoma. Their escape was not spectacular and took place at the point regarded by Warden Johnston as a weakest point on Alcatraz, for it could not be seen by any tower guard.

A window facing the water was broken and the metal sash was sawed. The two squeezed through the openings and made their way to the fence that surrounded that building, broke the lock with a Stillson wrench and entered the water. The tides were running at eight miles per hour. The City Engineer, Floyd C. Whaley, a specialist in local tides, was firm in his assessment that the stray tides that day and the 11:00 a.m. to 4:00 p.m. "run off" made it impossible to swim across to San Francisco. The story that they were aided by an oil can raft was told over and over on "the Rock," and the source was said to have been a woman contact who wrote to an inmate, in code, about this event.

It made good press and the local papers ran headlines, such as "Alcatraz Inmates Pleased with Success of Break," "Bank Managers Told to Have All Guards Alert," "Alcatraz Felons Alive, at Liberty, Prison Pat Says." The idea that they made it kind of played on the romantic notion of an escape succeeding from a place that was unbreakable.

The story of this coded correspondence to the inmate on Alcatraz was kept alive. The inmate who was reported by the inmates as having received this message told a good friend that it was "total B. S."

The second escape from the industry's mat shop was four years later and marked the fifth escape attempt from Alcatraz. On May 21, 1941, four individuals, all serving life sentences, seized several officers and, with a motor-driven emery wheel, proceeded to work over the bars on the mat shop windows. Those individuals never made it to the water. It is reported that a guard talked them out of following through on the attempt. Two of those attempting this escape became very involved in a major attempt in 1946. Both died in that second attempt.

The other two escapes from the industry building did not start in the mat shop. The third Alcatraz escape attempt started in the wood shop on April 23, 1938. This attempt was brutal and cost two lives: one inmate and one guard. Thomas R. Limerick, a bank robber and kidnapper from South Dakota, serving a life sentence with Rufus Franklin, a bank robber, serving a 30-year sentence, and James C. Lucas, a bank robber from Texas, also serving a 30-year sentence, left their jobs in the woodworking shop in the in-

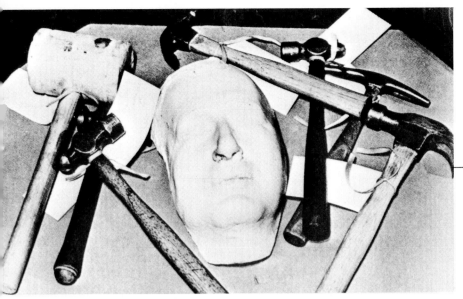

Tools used by James Lucas and Rufus Franklin in their escape attempt on April 23, 1938

James Lucas   Rufus Franklin

Ralph Roe

dustrial building. They had a hammer and a piece of iron as weapons. The hammer was used by Tom Limerick to strike the unarmed senior officer, Royal C. Cline, on the head. Officer Cline died the next day in the Marine Hospital. They made their way to the roof where they came into view of the tower guard, Officer Stites. All three men ran for the tower. Limerick went for the door, could not enter nor break the shatter-proof glass and drew fire from Officer Stites, the tower guard, which resulted in inmate Limerick's death.

Franklin was trying to bust his way and get the guard before he could do any more shooting. The glass didn't break, and the guard managed to shoot at Franklin, wounding him. Lucas had crawled under the roof tower and could not be seen by the tower guard. The alarm was sounded. And ten minutes after it all started, the third Alcatraz escape attempt was over: Two men dead and one wounded. In November, Lucas and Franklin were tried on first degree murder charges and given life sentences.

The last escape attempt from the industry was that of

Ted Walters on August 7, 1943. Walters was serving a 30-year sentence for bank robbing. His escape depended on timing, abundance of war work and a shortage of officers. Walters slipped out of the laundry and over the fence. The supervising officer in the laundry missed him right away and notified the proper people who gave the orders to start the search. The Coast Guard spotted Walters on the rocks, cold and, for unknown reasons, unable to take the plunge into the cold tidal waters. This escape attempt lasted one hour and ended the escape attempts from the industry building.

Over the years the industry served in a vital role for life on "the Rock." The best description of that simple but important role came from an inmate who worked in the industry: "At least it was something to do, other than staying in your cell." This opportunity to work was to be earned. The inmate, upon arriving, could be given work by the associate warden. "You are required to work at whatever you are told to do. Usually, your first assignment will be temporary maintenance around the cellhouse. Other maintenance jobs include the culinary unit, the clothing and bath room, the library and the yard detail. If you make a better than average work and conduct record while on your maintenance job, you may be considered for an assignment to a Federal Prison Industry Shop." One must remember, Alcatraz was not designed to give anybody a skill or hope for a future.

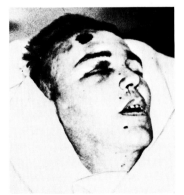

Theodore Cole   Thomas Limmerick

167

Fog rolling in on Alcatraz

In addition to being deliberately the end-of-the-line place, Alcatraz, by its location, also contributed to that designed plan, namely, with its fog. The fog that rolled in at times would necessitate the stopping of all outside activity and force a cell lockup. One cannot see the hand in front of the face, so thick is the Bay fog at times. Especially during those fog hours, the head counts were done with special attention.

The fog not only affected the pleasure crafts but, as we can see in this account, it affected all water traffic.

The most nervous hours for the wardens must have been those in which inmates were removed from the secure Alcatraz buildings. The removal, other than the dismissal of inmates, would only occur when an inmate had to go to court in San Francisco. A court case against an inmate on Alcatraz would usually include a collection of witnesses. All those came from "the Rock," and that meant they had to be transported to the mainland. On December 12, 1946, the warden was on the mainland with twelve prisoners. Four were heard in the morning and then returned to the prison, the rest were needed in the afternoon.

The warden was particularly concerned with extending himself to accommodate the attorneys and not giving them any cause to complain. Every effort was made to have an inmate witness in court on time. This took some planning, since there was a boat schedule to deal with.

On this day the warden and the eight prisoners were driven to the dock in a marshal's van and arrived ahead of the boat. The warden phoned the associate warden and ordered the 5:15 boat to return to the mainland to pick them up. The prisoners and the officer were now in a small waiting room on the dock. Normally, the wait would be 15 to 20 minutes. The guards were strategically placed in the room with the prisoners: one on the side of the building and two in the front doorway.

As time passed the 20-minute mark, the warden went to the phone and called to tell them to hurry this operation, only to find out the boat had been lost. He was informed that when the boat arrived at the island, the fog was so thick it almost ran into the rocks. It took two hours to guide the boat into the slip.

The Coast Guard was notified and the phone line between the island and a phone booth on the dock were kept open. The warden recalls not being able to see the end of the dock due to the heavy fog. Officers returning to catch the 7:15 boat to Alcatraz were immediately put to work guarding those eight prisoners. Around eight that evening the warden gave the order to send the boat for them, regardless of the fog. Guards were put on the dock and, at the fog bell, were ready to guide the boat. The warden states, "To recognize our officers who were guarding the prisoners in the waiting room, it was necessary for me to get very close and speak to them in order to make sure of their identity."

Late by three and a half hours, the port and starboard lights became visible. In great haste the men were loaded and the boat departed for Alcatraz. Only after the men were in their cells and counted by the officers on duty, did the warden breathe a sigh of relief. Those on board were not ordinary prisoners. They had previous records of escapes and some escape attempts on Alcatraz. Four of the men had life sentences, two were under sentence of 25 years, one in for 20 years, one for 19 years.

The news story on the radio on the night of December 12, 1946, was as follows: "A low-hanging fog clamped a

John Giles

Floyd P. Wilson

Escape was not only in the planning minds of the inmates, but in the preventing minds of the officials. And the fog would not be in favor of the officials.

There were two escape attempts from the dock itself. The first one occurred on July 31, 1945. John Giles was working on the dock when the laundry was being loaded and unloaded. His job was to sweep that one time, for apparently he was too weak to lift the laundry in order to load or unload it. Over a period of time he managed to steal and hide a complete uniform. One day he put the uniform on, pulled his prison clothes over it and proceeded to do his normal duties. Just as the boat, used by the Army Signal Corps to repair telephone cables, began to load up, Giles dropped his prison garb and walked onto the boat as a soldier. The 30-minute count instituted on Alcatraz revealed him as missing. An associate warden telephoned Angel Island, the next stop of the boat, and alerted the officials. Giles was greeted on his arrival and returned to Alcatraz, where an additional five years were added to his sentence. At his trial he asserted a legal defense that was interesting. He said he hadn't escaped. He went Pro Per at trial and in the Court of Appeals, claiming that he hadn't escaped and was always on government property. Clever, but he lost that appeal.

The second escape attempt from the dock was by Floyd Wilson on July 23, 1956. Wilson was on work detail on the dock and managed to hide a bundle of sash cord. His intention was to tie driftwood together and paddle to freedom during the night. He never got off the island, even though he managed to elude the officials for 12 hours.

The materials the inmates needed and wanted were so hard to come by that obtaining such necessities could and did take forever to gather. Even so, one would be amazed at the incredible things that turn up in a place such as Alcatraz. Everything found an important place in the life of someone, every cap, clip, string, nail, bottle, etc., and became a contraband trade item. One of the most valuable items was liquor — "booze."

Where could this "booze" come from? One place the "booze" could most logically come from was the kitchen. One inmate recalls, "I set myself up in the bootlegging business. It didn't last very long and there wasn't a cent of profit made. But a lot of the guys sure had themselves a time." A "snitch" told on him and got him sentenced to the dungeon. This inmate returned to work in the laundry at the same place as Al Capone. "They had switched Al Capone over on the presser by the time I returned, so the big alcohol king of Chicago didn't get cut in on this little bootlegging adventure of mine."

blackout over the peninsula and San Francisco, throwing rail, air and automobile transportation into a hazardous, slow-moving snarl. Alcatraz Island was blotted out from mainland view, delaying removal for two and a half hours of eight desperate cons from San Francisco, where they had testified at a trial. Guards had difficulty finding 'the Rock' on the return journey, despite many lights and flashing beacons." The warden retold this to many a visitor, and in his mind this incident stuck out for the rest of his life.

169

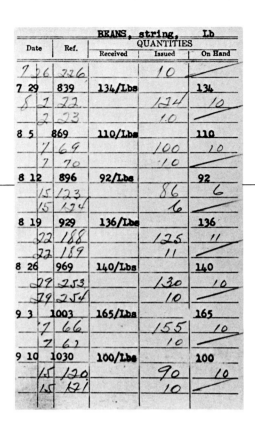

BEANS, string, Lb				
Date	Ref.	Received	Issued	On Hand
7 26	226		10	
7 29	839	134/Lbs		134
8 1	22		134	10
2	23		10	
8 5	869	110/Lbs		110
7	69		100	10
7	70		10	
8 12	896	92/Lbs		92
15	123		86	6
15	124		6	
8 19	929	136/Lbs		136
22	188		125	11
22	189		11	
8 26	969	140/Lbs		140
29	253		130	10
29	254		10	
9 3	1003	165/Lbs		165
7	66		155	10
7	67		10	
9 10	1030	100/Lbs		100
15	120		90	10
15	121		10	

After gathering information as to what was used to make alcohol, one must conclude that they could have made alcohol from anything. In the laundry they would make up a batch of what they called "alcohol soap." It was a mixture of some kind of chemical powder, ten gallons of gasoline and ten gallons of alcohol — pure grain. "We mixed it right in the vat, putting the chemical in first, then the gasoline, and on top of it all, the alky."

The inmate hid the 5-gallon can in the washing room and passed the word along. In a very short time many inmates from the industry walked over to where the can was and filled up their bottles: medicine bottles, ink bottles, even hot water bottles. As fast as they could bottle it, the inmates in the yard would drink it and come back for re-fills. At the time the inmates had to return to their cells, fifteen or twenty had to be carried back. Some had to go to the hospital. That's how drunk they were. The guards finally found a bottle on one of the drunks and could figure out that it was a combination of things found in the laundry. They could not find the source.

The next day the same story: a bunch of inmates decidedly drunk. This time the warden was able to trace it to the source and sent this individual to the dungeon. There was always an attempt at making "booze" and for every incident when the source was found, there were those bootleggers who were never discovered. There was even a blend that was called "rock juice" and the formula stayed the same for many years. The recipe came from an individual who bragged, "I done a little brewing and still-running back in them days when I was transporting liquor."

The recipe read: "Take a five-gallon crick and you put some figs, prunes and raisins in it. Then you toss in some sugar and add a cup of yeast. Then you set the whole thing in back of the kitchen range for a couple of weeks." The man in charge at the time was the head cook and he told the officials that the smell came from the yeast used for the bread. This, then, became a solid operation and business.

They would make this on a regular basis and even kept records. The place they chose to store the liquor was in a space created by two desks pushed together. The backs of the big file drawers, when knocked out and moved up, created a space in back of the last part of the drawer. The front was kept full of supplies and files, and the back provided the hiding place for the "rock juice."

This good little hiding place was discovered one day when a guard pulled the desks apart to find out why the mop of an inmate got stuck. There were the jugs, and the guard yelled, "Wait till I show this to the deputy." All the men rushed over to see what was going to happen. One of the inmates managed to sneak a jug of tea from the icebox. All knew exactly what to do, namely, switch the jugs. While the guard was pouring the juice down the drain, the last bottle was switched.

The next day, at the hearing, the officer presented the jug as evidence. The deputy found out that it was just tea. He dismissed the case, but told the inmates that he knew exactly what was going on.

Alcatraz had money and that would allow a business to flourish. "Booze," was the item bought the most. Cash was what was used and several inmates recall with amazement the amount of money on "the Rock." One inmate had four thousand-dollar bills, but never had to use them in 12 years on "the Rock." Money was considered contraband. One inmate recalls that after a shake-down his money was gone — $2,000.00 — but he was never called for having contraband. So he concluded that the security official just kept it. Claims were made that you could buy a lot of things on Alcatraz with money. "There was a price tag on almost everything an inmate might fancy to buy, and on 'the Rock,' at that time — all contraband. There were ways to get files and hacksaw blades smuggled in, if you were able to pay enough. Even dope. Most of the inmates had ways of getting hold of plenty of money. And money is what it took. Sometimes pretty big money. They say every man has his price. That was as true of guards on Alcatraz as it was of crooked cops in Kansas City. Anyways, that's the way I found it," emphasized a former inmate of the late 30's.

Some of the money and property changed hands as payments for bets. Gambling was illegal, but some of it would go on. The rules on money were clear and left no doubt. "You are not allowed to have money of any kind in your possession while in this institution. Use of cigarettes or other items as 'jail money' is forbidden." Yet there are accounts of gambling. Most of the betting and gambling was more man-to-man stuff. Most of that went on during the 40's. "In the late 50's there was no organized gambling on the island. By 'organized,' I mean football parlay tickets where you pick four winners and get odds of 8 to 1, etc., tickets which were put out by various inmates who collected the bets and paid off winners," recalls an inmate. The movement of inmates, that was kept to a minimum, could have been a part of the problem getting a regular betting operation going. The place where some betting was going on was the yard, the place where inmates could gather and pass information on.

The yard is located between the "top of the hill" main building and industry. The inmates going to industry had to pass through the yard. The inmates working in the industries or below the yard got the yard only on Saturday, Sunday and holidays. "All inmates in good standing are allowed the yard privileges on Saturdays, Sundays and holidays, if the weather permits. In addition, inmates who have completed their assigned tasks, or who have been 'laid in' by the detail foreman, or who have been 'held in' for hair cut, medical attention, interview or other official business, may be allowed the yard privileges on weekday afternoons if they are otherwise eligible.

"Inmates who are 'restricted' or who are in 'idle' status because they have quit a job, or refused a job, or were removed from a job for disciplinary reasons, are not eligible for weekday afternoon yard," so read the rules.

One of the main reasons for the yard was to be a place to get exercise. For the most part, that's what the yard was used for. Personal contact and recreation was also the reason for some inmates to go to the yard. Not all did and this account gives us a rare insight as to the feelings about the yard: "Saturday and Sunday mornings and afternoons we had yard for a total of about five hours each day. However, many men never went out except when the weather was ideal, and some never at all. One aspect of the yard I found most annoying was the loud speaker, continually blaring out country music. I suppose most of the men liked it, but I found it hard to take since there was never a moment of silence in the yard."

The yard provided several set-ups for various activities.

171

Top right: Guard cage viewed from top of water tower
Bottom left: Guard cage viewed from ground level
Bottom right: Handball game in recreation yard

For much of the time it was too cold just to sit around and play bridge or talk. The inmates could keep several items, such as handballs, handball gloves, and shoes in the cells. These men then went to the group of handball players, picked partners and played in small rivalry competitions. Handball was liked by about 20 to 25 inmates. The yard had two courts: "The best players held forth on the 'big court' — the 'little court' was used by beginners and had a shorter front wall. You had to win in order to stay on the 'big court' — if you lost you sat down and waited your turn again. As long as you won, you stayed on, game after game; 21 points made a game."

In the yard several unarmed guards stood by listening, looking and, with their presence, tried to prevent anything from happening. The tower guards were armed and kept a most alert eye on the yard. There never was an escape attempt from the yard, but there were several incidents when an inmate attacked another.

Now and then there was a softball game. The bats, bases, balls and gloves were left in a little alcove set back under the stairs. "The bridge tables were made of slabs of wood of heavy-duty construction with heavy wooden legs, which folded up something like a card table. I remember once when a race riot began. These tables were opened and the legs broken off by a lot of convicts for use as clubs. Some shots fired by the wall guard partially broke it up and the population spontaneously divided itself: blacks to one side of the yard and whites to the other — with 'no-man's land,' a strip extending length-wise down the middle of the yard." Considering the overall tension and frustrations on Alcatraz, there were relatively few such incidents in the yard. Many stories told about the steps in the yard being the power base of the inmates; the more power or leadership position the inmate held, the higher up he sat. Well, there are just as many claims by former inmates stating that this was not true. So, here again, it depends on whom one talks to.

Top right: Interior view of shower room
Bottom left: View of shower positions inside raised floor
Bottom right: Graffiti found in the shower room

On the average, about 30 to 50 inmates would go to the yard. Rain and fog would close down the yard. There was no real organization to the activities, but at times impromptu tournaments between the handball players occurred. The chess and bridge players, too, had a form of tournament, but not really on an organized level. Most of the men just walked up and down the yard in groups of two or three.

Personal confrontation was always a risk, and during the years did happen. The inmates in isolation D-block went to the yard in the mornings. One inmate who wanted to go to D-block to be close to his friend needed a good reason. So at the dinner table he said, "I think I will give it to Short Grass," meaning he would stab that individual in the yard. The other inmates at the table could not see why Short Grass was to be stabbed, so they said: "Why not give it to Dog Man?" This type of conversation was always regarded as "bullshit talk that doesn't exactly strike horror." On that given day those men at that table watched as this inmate indeed walked up "behind 'Dog' and hooked his arm around 'Dog's' neck as if to 'joke' him, but with a short-bladed knife was stabbing the throat around the lower chin and Adam's apple. 'Dog' finally wrenched free and took off running across the yard screaming like a stuck hog."

The guards on duty wrestled the individual, seized and held him under control. This individual did get to be confined into D-block, where his friend was. Most of the inmates in the yard claimed that they did not see this incident. They did not want to be involved with giving testimony.

Some of the inmates that feared being hurt or hassled just stayed in their cells. It was not so much that they feared being victims but being connected in any way with the action and, therefore, put into a position of being accused by the administration of being involved and losing good time. These individual conflicts at times would last over a long period of time and all concerned were just waiting for the right time.

Well, the right time for one inmate came in the shower room when he killed another inmate. These two, "G" and "S," were known to be lovers. Both were in isolation D-block. During the year or so they were there a violent "falling out" or feud erupted between them. The only way they could get at each other was by name calling, for in D-block the only time anyone was out of his single occupancy cell was to take a shower. D-block at the end of the bottom tier of cells had two showers. There was no personal contact between any inmates while there.

"S" was released to population first and a few months later "G" followed. "S" was a big man, 220 lbs. and 6' 2". As for "G," he was a slightly-built, 5' 5", 140-lb. youngster. "S" was working in the clothing issue section of the shower room. The basement shower room of approximately 40' by 90' had an area sectioned off where several inmates worked, issuing fresh, clean laundry to the showering inmates. The inmates would enter that room by descending the steps from the cell blocks. At the bottom of the steps was a table from which the inmates would receive soap and toilet paper, after their shower, before returning to their cells. Wooden benches were placed along the wall upon which the inmates could leave clothing and towels while showering.

The inmates would undress and then step into the

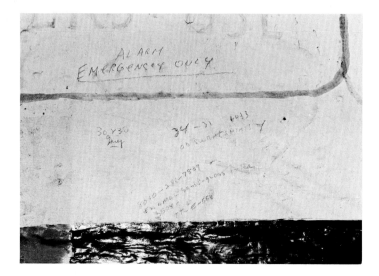

173

center of the room. There were no booths or stalls of any kind, but simply a six-inch curbing, forming a rectangle which enclosed the shower area and drains in the floor. The shower nozzles were four feet overhead in a double row. The inmates had no control over the water. It came out at about 100 degrees, and it was said that the water was extra hot so as not to get the inmates used to cold water. The assumption was made that they did not want to build up the tolerance to cold water and that was to make it more difficult in case of an escape attempt through the water.

The incident is recalled by one inmate: "S" was working in the clothing issue of the shower room the day "G" was released from solitary, and the moment "G" stepped under the shower with no clothes on, "S" charged out of his work area with a knife and proceeded to attack and stab him. The kid was game to the end and fought up and down the length of the curbed area, tooth and nail, but the inevitable resulted — bare hands and outweighed by at least 80 lbs, he was no match, and finally "G" crumpled and died. Again, several inmates watched all of this and what stood out in their minds was the action of one guard.

This 6' 5", well-built guard kept shouting, "Stop, stop, now," while throwing rolls of toilet paper at the combatants in the life and death struggle. "He was ever afterward known as "Shit Paper Slim" — the tag stuck."

There were several murders witnessed on Alcatraz and retold, but this incident tells more than just the fact that a man got killed. It provides us some insight into the action and thinking of individuals that, in turn, gives us a flavor of the life that existed on Alcatraz. "S" was subsequently acquitted of the murder by a San Francisco jury. The guard forever had to live with his new name.

"The killings among the cons on 'the Rock' were quite a few," tells an inmate of the late 40's. "We took them in stride as some sort of far-away news. There were some knifings, head crashing and stabbings. Over what? It was either one guy proving he's tougher than the other guy, and some said sex."

The physical violence was not just restricted to the inmates. There was a lot of corporal punishment by the guards. Today most former guards tell you that they were best of friends with all the inmates; as for the true story, it's different. Naturally, the guards figured that nobody would believe the cons; but if one listens to the various stories, and reads the files and court documents, it would take a blind person not to arrive at the conclusion of much physical action by the guards.

In order to expose these activities on "the Rock," Richard Numer wanted to take an English course to enable him to write. This was denied; and when he appeared before Federal Judge Roche, he stated that he needed this course to "fit myself to expose the brutality and vile conditions prevailing on Alcatraz." The court ruled that it had no jurisdiction over the prison's administration.

James Lucas, a participant in the brutal escape attempt of May 23, 1938, elaborated on the repeated physical abuse by the guards. In his court record one can read his persistent statement of those facts.

Guards sometimes ended up with broken bones and scars. Some even made the statement, "We are going to make it tough on you." And someone replied to the guard, "The tougher you make it, the better we'll like it." Blackie McKee told the deputy that he'd punch him silly, to which the deputy replied, "You might whip me but I'll give you a

Please investigate criminal cruelty practices on prisoners at Alcatraz Prison. A few of the cases are (1) Edgar Lewis, age 28, serving 3 ys

good go." "Some of those guards did fight pretty good. One black inmate by the name of Spinks fought a guard and got punched silly and it left him a bit on the goofy side." For sure there were many stories on the subject of physical abuse, and many of them were either not true or exaggerated. But, even so, the number of incidents is staggering, and that concern comes up all over the place. In the early days there were two inmates trying to get the word out. Nothing could leave the island and all mail was carefully censored. One note to a local paper did get out and pleaded for help: "Please investigate criminal cruelty practiced on prisoners of Alcatraz Prison." The writer of this note was concerned with the mental condition of the inmates. He lists the physical abuse as being starvation, being shot in the face with gas guns, and beaten over the head with clubs by three guards. The names of those three guards were known to the population, and that word was passed on for many years.

The cruelty went on and the files of the medical offices and chaplain are full of these incidents. The rights of the inmates were not as willingly supported, for at the time of the opening of Alcatraz the mood of all was to lock them up and throw away the key, so everybody would allow things to happen that normally wouldn't. The law in this matter reads: "The care, custody, contact, treatment and discipline of federal prisoners is vested solely in the Attorney General of the United States, or his authorized delegate, the Bureau of Prisons; and the exercise of that discretion will not be viewed by the courts in the absence of a clear-cut denial of federal rights, that is, the constitutional prohibition against cruel and unusual punishment in the 8th Amendment."

The major problem in the 30's, 40's and 50's with these words was the exact interpretation. We find the interpretation vague and can find almost no agreement by the courts to try a case of alleged prisoner mistreatment. The warden almost had his free way of interpreting these laws on Alcatraz, in particular, for it was designed for the worst, the ones with the least consideration by anybody. The question as to the right or wrong interpretation never really needed to be dealt with by the courts, so it lay dormant at the discretion of those in charge of the prisons. Even the basic civil rights were not enforced on Alcatraz — it had, for instance, open segregation of blacks, certainly not the way it was in the laws of the U.S. Who was to challenge these conditions? The word could not get out nor could anybody get in to investigate. Everybody knew this and all just coasted through the years, incorporating those facts into the daily routine.

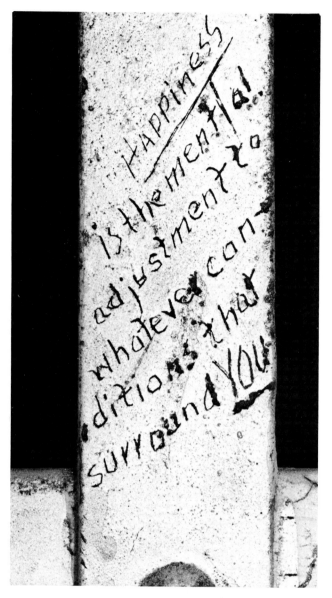

The official procedure in dealing with rule violation was written down to establish a clear way of dealing with the process of punishment. One part reads as follows: "The reporting officer is never permitted to personally punish a prisoner or to sit in judgment on the case of a prisoner he reported, . . . or to have any say as to the penalty to be imposed." The officer was to write up a disciplinary report and hand one copy to the deputy warden. A hearing was to be scheduled, at which the associate warden, the captain and the lieutenant were to be present in order to advise the prisoner of the charge against him. At that time the

prisoner could state his side. In most known cases the prisoner would just take the judgment of the panel without contesting it and the main reason was the concern of revealing something about activities in the environment or to implicate or involve others. All of this then would cause an endless chain reaction and unnecessary investigations, so he would just take the punishment.

For the officials that would cause some frustration. They wanted as much information on anything going on so as to anticipate or prevent any embarrassment. The guards needed and used the stool pigeon or snitches for most of their inside information, and they did not want to blow their connections. It was difficult to maintain secret connections, and to blow it just on a minor matter was not worth it. This would lead to some decision that would depart from the official instructions. There was a way that most men knew the delicate set-up. The warden didn't want his men to have any connection with the convicts and the convicts did not want other convicts to have connections with the administration. Should such a connection be known to the inmates, they would try to take immediate action. The most common way was just to isolate the individual and stab him. In one case they wanted to poison Gardner. Gardner fell under suspicion when he was left out of his cell to go to the hospital for supposed treatment. What actually went down was: he would go to the yard with his connection guard and talk over things about the activities, rumors, etc., from the population. One night the word got up to the hospital and those men in the ward had a look-out for him and, indeed, reported back to the population that Gardner did not come to the hospital, but was seen in the yard talking to the guard. They never managed to kill him, but he was under great psychological pressure on Alcatraz and was described by many inmates as a miserable character. Gardner did commit suicide and left these words to all: "I

hold no malice toward any human being, and I hope those whom I have wronged will forgive me for it." He was formally called a snitch and that probably was worse than anything else, bestowed on him by his fellow inmates.

This Alcatraz web network was a very intriguing set-up and one that will never fully come to light. Everybody was involved and nobody really could talk freely about that way of life, for he was not the last man alive. If a guard talked today, all the other living guards may take offense or try to discredit his story; the same, with just a different twist, would apply to former inmates. For the former inmate, the problem is of walking that tightrope between fellow cons and authorities, so, in the most cases, the rule of silence became the golden one, the one that helped in surviving.

Probably the toughest position must have been reserved for the chaplains, the men of spiritual values, men trained to deal with, help and console the spiritual needs of the individual human being. This area is the vaguest in all of the procedures and regulations. The prison chaplain on Alcatraz was in a category totally by himself. The idea of a chaplain in a place that had no provision for hope or improvement must have sounded as iconoclastic as anything.

"Catholic and Protestant services are held regularly on Sunday in the chapel. Jewish services are held on appropriate occasions. Religious advice and counsel are available by sending a request slip to the chaplain. The menu board in the dining room will indicate the schedule of the religious services," so read the rules in the inmate's instruction book.

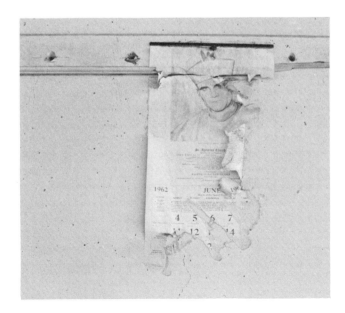

The room set aside for religious services and movies was located on the first floor in the administration building, the auditorium. "Use the east-end cellhouse stairs when going to and from the auditorium. Walk quietly and be co-operative if and when you are searched for contraband." The only items not considered contraband in the auditorium were a handkerchief and the inmate's glasses with the glass case. The inmate was not allowed to wear or carry a jacket, coat, cap, cushions, blankets or pillows. "The privilege of attending religious services and movies is important to you. These privileges may be withdrawn for violation of the rules."

The Alcatraz chaplains were the lowest paid members of the Alcatraz staff — $2,600.00 a year. And that was lower than the new clerk or guard in 1946. This fact must attest to the general feeling in Washington that the men on Alcatraz were considered lost even to spiritual redemption.

By the end of 1946 Alcatraz had its fifth resident chaplain. He was not exempt from the rumors and found that he was, indeed, the victim. The rumor was that the new chaplain would deprive the inmates of viewing magazines which had women in scanty attire and that he was going to censor the movies. So on Alcatraz even the chaplain fell into the mainstream of prison life, and found his clothes that he sent to the laundry damaged. Inmates took razor blades to his underwear and some of his shirts disappeared. As soon as the inmates found this to be just a rumor, the activities against the chaplain stopped.

The entire affair of religion, though available on Alcatraz, was not taken too seriously by anybody. The resident chaplain had other duties besides his Sunday sermon, which he gave every other Sunday. He was the librarian, education supervisor and social case worker. This gave him a chance to get to know some of the inmates from a different level. Even so, the participation at the Sunday services was low. Eight to twelve inmates would come to the ceremony, and that only if there was a special attraction, such as music or a movie. One chaplain recalls, "The men on 'the Rock' proved to be immature, neurotic, egocentric, defensive and lonely. To treat them as strong, able men who needed only to be cut down to size or bedgered into conforming seemed a sure way to deepen their immaturity and recidivism."

The chaplain on Alcatraz had access to every part of the institution. He would spend much time cultivating contacts with the individuals. One chaplain noted that since the men in D-block could not attend the services, he would go to them in D-block. He had long, mind-stretching debates with Robert Stroud just to accept Stroud's rejection of reli-

Alcatraz appears on the cover of the Knights Templar business meeting agenda of April 1, 1891.

gion. Other inmates felt the same; and in some cases their official records had entries in the classification summary that read: "He has never shown an inclination to discuss religion, and looks upon the subject as immaterial and irrelevant." This excerpt can be found in the files of Alvin Karpis.

Religion on Alcatraz was regarded as a privilege, but, even at that, it seems the inmate received a penalty for attending religious services. An inmate who attended the service had to give up equal recreation yard time. This was contested by a priest and finally was changed. However, what was devastating for the priest was that the attendance did not increase. Some of those who wanted could and did become altar boys. Machine Gun Kelly served as an altar boy. This point at one time or another may have given some favorable exposure to the character of the individual.

The chaplain, of all the people coming in contact with the inmates, was approached the most in order to make contact with the outside world. At times he would be asked to

Top right: View toward the altar as seen in 1981.
Bottom left: Recognition award for Alcatraz inmates from the United Bay Area Crusade, 1958.

take a letter to be mailed or would be asked about some news from the outside. Not much of this activity is recorded, for it would have jeopardized everybody. The chaplain, too, was instructed by the warden as to exactly how things would have to be on Alcatraz.

One of the chaplains could not understand why this inmate kept offering him a cigarette. The inmate kept insisting and finally the chaplain, a non-smoker himself, took the cigarette and put it into his pocket. Later that evening in his home he took the cigarette out of his pocket and noticed that it looked a bit different from a regular cigarette. After closer examination, he discovered that the cigarette contained a message: "Please call TO 29573. Urgent." The cigarette was used to pass messages back and forth and, too, would be used for storing money. Some inmates would roll up $100 bills and put them into the back of a cigarette, stuff tobacco in the front and forever move that cigarette to the back of the pack.

INMATES OF U S PENITENTIARY
ALCATRAZ

UNITED BAY AREA CRUSADE

HONOR
1958

IN RECOGNITION
OF OUTSTANDING
SUPPORT OF HEALTH
AND WELFARE
SERVICES OF THE
BAY AREA
COMMUNITY

The constant attempts to get something done — "Do me a favor, chaplain" — would create an air of suspicion even in the most trusting of the chaplains: a situation that did cause of degree of frustration, for some inmates knew how to play on that nerve of sympathy and thus tried to use the chaplain in the name of faith. Some inmates, however, felt that the chaplain was the same as a guard, and that he worked for the system and they were just as alert toward him as anybody else.

The feeling toward the warden and "the Rock" by a chaplain is well expressed in a letter to a member of the commission on the ministry in the institutions for the Federal Council of Churches: "The work here under the present warden has been somewhat more isolating and unconducive to significant program expansion and variation than under the former warden. But it has been no martyrdom, and I have been grateful for the experience. It leaves me, however, with a profound feeling as to the unnecessariness of this particular institution. . . . I should like to assist in gaining the dissolution of this monstrosity. . . ."

The Jews celebrated Passover. A rabbi would come to the island and gather the Jewish inmates in the same room where the other services were held and where the movies were shown. All inmates going to the services had to go through a thorough shakedown. The services were conducted under the watchful eyes of the guards. This rabbi was the same one who would perform these duties in San Quentin and for the San Francisco Fire Department, giving this entire service the institutionalized approach. "I don't think he could have been much of a human being even when he first started. Human beings do not turn into cold-blooded bastards." The Jewish inmates did get a couple of pounds of matzo, and that was it, for Passover.

The same room used for the religious services became the movie room or auditorium. This was one way for the inmates to let their minds, even for a short time, travel away

View in the chapel toward projection booth

Graffiti in chapel done by individuals during the Indian occupation, 1970.

from "the Rock." There is no record available of the movies shown and the reconstruction as to what was shown is very fragmented. At the start the movies were mainly westerns and cartoons. The movies never were of the latest run, and in the 50's consisted mainly of four- to five-year-old comedies. In the late 50's, one inmate recalls, "Being a movie buff, I went to all of them. There were two movies per month, or one shown every other week; although, sometimes a three-week span occurred between movies. Some of the better ones I recall were: 'The Rose Tatoo,' 'The Fugitive King,' 'Viva Zapata,' 'Cat on a Hot Tin Roof,' 'Come Back Little Sheba,' and 'Splendor in the Grass.'" Some other titles mentioned in prisoner surveys were: "Al Jolson Story," "Golden Earrings," "Eddie Cantor Story," "Moonlight Bay," "Cheaper by the Dozen," "One-Eyed Jacks," "From Here to Eternity," "Flower Drum Song," and "The Magnificent Seven." The family members of the officers of Alcatraz viewed the movies in the training building.

For some inmates there were the privileges of visitations to look forward to, but for others this was not possible, the reasons being different from individual to individual. Some had nobody to visit them and others could not afford a visit from relatives living on the other side of the country.

You are allowed to receive one visit each month from members of your immediate family or other persons approved by the warden. Visiting hours are approximately 1:30 p.m. to 3:10 p.m. weekdays.
In all personal visits you will confine your talk to personal matters and refrain from discussing other inmates, institutional matters, etc.
Visits with your attorney of record may be arranged through the office of the associate warden.

The visitors would write in advance to the warden and he would send a letter back that would read:

Back wall of cell in B-block painted by the inmate

Dear Mrs. S.:

If you will bring this letter with you, it will serve as a pass for you to visit your husband, Mr. S.-NRXXX-AZ on Wednesday, April 8, 1959.

Please arrange to board our prison launch leaving Dock #4, end of Van Ness Avenue, San Francisco, promptly at 12:55 p.m.

Sincerely,

P. J. Madigan
Warden

Some, even after traveling from the east coast, upon arrival at Dock #4, would be refused the visit with no explanation. After arriving on the island, all those visitors had to pass through the metal detector. The now-famous story of

the mother of Al Capone being stopped by the guards for setting off the metal detector remains a classic. After repeated times, it was discovered that the metal rods in her corset were responsible for setting off the alarm. After a visitor cleared security, he would be guided to one of the five visiting positions. These positions were a cut-out in the wall, about six inches by ten inches with a thick slab of bullet-proof glass. Communication was by phone that was being monitored. The officials, according to some inmates, did everything in their power to discourage visitors. One mother complained, "It is cruel, senselessly so. They punish not only my son, but those who love him. I go to see him, but I cannot touch him. I must speak to him over a telephone, and I cannot even see him clearly through the thick mesh of wire screen. What harm could there be to let me kiss him? To hold him?" The loved ones of every man on Alcatraz carried the same burden.

Most days there were no visitors and every once in a while one or two. It is estimated that only about 10% of the population received visitors. This is very low compared to other prisons. For the officers, family visitations were restricted only by the boat schedule. Usually, ten to thirteen minutes before the boat left, the wife of the guard would say, "Ten minutes till departure." And everybody leaving would start gathering their hats, coats, etc.

Life on the island was meant to be isolated from the rest of the world, and that feeling of Alcatraz life was described by an inmate in the following sentence: "The Rock, the fog, sand fleas everywhere, unnecessary scrutiny, censored mail, utter lack of hope, no amusement and no relief from boredom." There are men who feel that there was no need for this type of prison and that to make it possible, in the public's eyes, they kept some of the main characters there longer than needed. This, of course, could never be taken to court, for all was supposedly done by the book. There were so few things one could do on Alcatraz that the things defined were the don'ts.

The conditions affected every person who went through the system. One of the escape attempts that provides us with many aspects of Alcatraz life was the fourth escape attempt on the 13th of January, 1939. The first point of interest was that this attempt was started from within the

Top right: View of D-block cells.

cells. The five inmates were in isolation D-block as punishment for trouble in which they were involved in the 1937 strike.

D-block had not yet been remodeled and had the old bars made from flat steel. Over a period of time the men cut through the soft steel with an improvised abrasive. Considering the method used by the guards to inspect the bars, one must openly wonder about the possibility for five inmates to work their way through the bars. The next point of interest is that they managed to get into the cell an unknown tool, presumably a jack, that they used to work their way through tool-proof bars on the outside window.

These five men were Arthur "Doc" Barker, the youngest of four sons of the family known for crime and mothered by "Ma Barker," at 38 serving a life sentence for kidnapping; Rufus McCain, at 35 a kidnapper and bank robber from Oklahoma serving a 99-year sentence; Henry Young, 26, from eastern Washington, serving 20 years for robbing a bank; William Martin, an armed post office robber, serving 25 years; and Dale Stamphill, serving a life sentence for kidnapping.

On the foggy night of January 13, 1939, these five men reached the rocky shores: The alarm was sounded and all five were confronted on the beach, attempting to fabricate a raft. Two of the men gave the impression of fleeing, and the guard fired, killing "Doc" Barker and wounding Stamphill. McCain and Young surrendered peacefully and were kept in solitary. After their return to their cells in November of 1940, the two were known to be in a constant state of fighting. In December of 1940, while at work in the tailor shop, Young fatally stabbed McCain.

What followed probably was the event which affected Alcatraz the most. During the trial for the murder of McCain, Young's lawyer claimed he could not be held responsible for his actions due to the conditions on Alcatraz and the fact that Young was in isolation from 1937 to 1940. That defense prompted the courts to hear testimonies by Warden Johnston as to the procedures on Alcatraz. Several inmates were called to testify on the treatment and/or abuses of the officers on "the Rock." Nothing came of those allegations, but it did expose the courts to the life, held so secret, to which these inmates were subjected. It is certain that this put pressure on the warden and his staff at least not to repeat the same methods used in dealing with certain situations. Alcatraz got the funds at that time to upgrade D-block to modern standards.

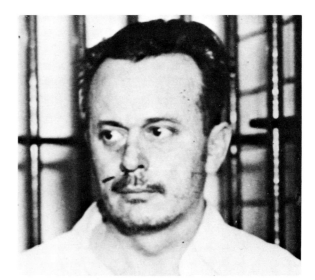

Arthur "Doc" Barker

William Martin

Rufus McCain

Dale Stamphill

Henri Young

181

WANTED BY THE FBI

ESCAPED FEDERAL PRISONER — BANK ROBBER
CLARENCE ANGLIN

FBI No. 4,731,702

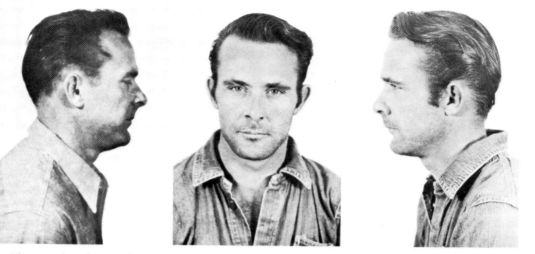

Photograph taken 1960   Photographs taken 1958

DESCRIPTION

Age: 31, born May 11, 1931, Donalsonville, Georgia (not supported by birth records)

Height: 5'11"

Weight: 160 to 168 pounds

Build: Medium

Hair: Brown

Eyes: Hazel

Complexion: Light

Race: White

Nationality: American

Occupations: Cabinet maker, farmer, laborer

Scars and Marks: Scar left side of upper lip, scar between eyes, scar right forearm, cut scar right ring finger; tattoos, "ZONA" and scroll left arm, "NITA" upper right arm

Fingerprint Classification: 18 O 27 W IOO 21 / L 27 W OIO

CRIMINAL RECORD

Anglin has been convicted of burglary, bank robbery and attempted escape.

CAUTION

ANGLIN HAS BEEN CONVICTED OF BANK ROBBERY AND WAS IN POSSESSION OF FIREARMS WHEN LAST ARRESTED. HE HAS A PREVIOUS RECORD OF ESCAPES. CONSIDER EXTREMELY DANGEROUS.

A Federal warrant was issued on June 13, 1962, at San Francisco, California, charging Anglin with escaping from the Federal Penitentiary at Alcatraz in violation of Title 18, U. S. Code, Section 751.

IF YOU HAVE INFORMATION CONCERNING THIS PERSON, PLEASE NOTIFY ME OR CONTACT YOUR LOCAL FBI OFFICE. TELEPHONE NUMBER IS LISTED BELOW.

DIRECTOR
FEDERAL BUREAU OF INVESTIGATION
UNITED STATES DEPARTMENT OF JUSTICE
WASHINGTON 25, D. C.
TELEPHONE, NATIONAL 8-7117

Wanted Flyer No. 305
June 14, 1962

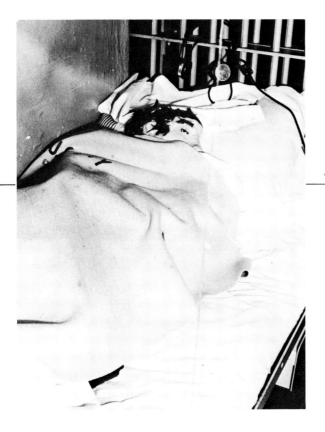

John William Anglin   Frank Lee Morris

Top left: Dummy head in place, as found by officer. Bottom right: The four dummy heads as displayed as evidence.

sleeping inmates to the guard who looked into the cells during the night. The materials they used to create their heads were gathered over a period of time and included real hair from the barber shops. Only at the morning count where the inmates were required to stand, was the discovery made. That gave the escaping inmates from 9:30 p.m. until 7:15 a.m., the standard head count time, to make it to the water.

They left their cells after 9:30 p.m., climbed up the utility corridor, using the drain pipes, and picked up some crude life preservers they made from stolen raincoats that they hid on top of the cell tiers. The bars leading through the ventilation to the roof were pried apart. The 12" opening was sufficient to allow all three men access to the roof. They let themselves down to the ground on the far end of the building, mastered a 15-foot fence and went to the water. That much is clear. What happened after that is anybody's guess. The officials, including Warden Blackwell, maintained that the trio drowned in the 34-degree water that was racing at eight miles an hour through the Golden Gate.

A watertight bag floating in the bay was found four days later by a patrolling Army Engineers debris boat. The contents of this bag was attributed to Clarence Arglin, whose name was on a receipt for a $10.00 money order. All the photos in the bag were of a woman. The search for the three bodies was on, yet, to this day, they have not been found.

The only other escape attempt is the now famous one of Frank Lee Morris and the Anglin brothers, Clarence and John Williams. On June 11, 1962, escape attempt number 13 went into action. This escape today is still "the" one. This escape had the long range planning that made it possible to be the success it was. All three were bank robbers serving long terms. The planning stages must have lasted several months, and exactly how long will never be known.

In order to get out of their cell, they chipped away at their ventilation shaft until the hole was big enough for them to crawl through. They chipped away patiently with some tool, possibly a spoon, until the actual metal could be removed. The holes were covered with painted replicas of the metal. After these holes allowed them to crawl through, they set up a regular workshop on top of the cell block tiers, where they worked at spreading the metal bars in the air vents leading to the roof.

To get around the time element of the constant visual count of all inmates, they created dummy heads as decoys to put into their beds. These heads gave the appearance of

Escape vent as found after escape

Escape vent after its reinforcement.

Top left: The story of the Anglin escape as told in a book and movie. Bottom right: Old military guard house, top floor, was used as a firing range.

This escape was dramatized in a book and made into a T.V. movie, and probably is the most responsible event for keeping the attention of the public at large on "the Rock."

The saddest part of a movie is that no matter who makes it and no matter what the original story line is, what we see is, for the most part, drama and not documentation. The impression it leaves upon the viewer can be carefully regulated. The producers say that they make movies which the public wants; the public, in many cases, take what they see on the screen as the truth. The portrait of one guard by one actor creates all the generalizations we so often hear: all the guards on Alcatraz were . . . ; all the guards felt this way, etc., etc. The truth is that the men working on Alcatraz fell into any and all categories in which one could place a guard.

The setup creates the fact that the inmates and the guards become natural enemies. There is no avoiding this. But what one must consider is that both are human in some aspect of their make-up. No difference on "the Rock." There were good and bad guards in the opinion of the inmates, and there were good and bad guards in the opinion of the warden and other guards.

Life and work on Alcatraz for the guards at least was "interesting and challenging." Some rejected the term "guard" and would want to be called correctional officer, custodial officer, or just plain officer. No inmate, in referring to these officers, used any other name but "guard," except if the inmates created a nickname. The regularly used names were: hacks, bulls, guards and screws. The personal names, for example, were for Warden Johnston, "Saltwater"; Warden Swope, "Cowboy"; Warden Madigan, "Promising Paul." For some of the guards the names were "Meathead" or "Jughead." The names for the Deputy Warden were: "Punch" (an ex-pug guard), "Masturbator," "Blue Bird," "Tillis," "Swash," and general names, such as "S.O.B.," "M.F.," "Bastard," and "Fruit." "That's how we showed our respect for the uniform," relates one inmate from the late 40's.

Most of these name (tags) stuck to the guards for their entire tour of duty. For some it was a name that directly related to a specific incident, such as "Shit Paper Slim," as described in a previous chapter. For the most part, one can say that the general population on "the Rock" did not have a friendly relationship with the guards. A friendly guard was one who did not go out of his way to harass an inmate. This guard would report the inmate for having a homemade knife in his cell, but would not report him for a contraband sandwich. There was a guard who would on occasion hide a candy bar in the desk of a con working in the library or toss a candy bar in the cell of an inmate. His nickname was "The Candy Man." And still, today, he is unknown — that being for his protection. Most of the good deeds or favors remain untold, but over the years there were guards who did a little extra.

There was a guard by the name of Miller who was well-liked by the inmates. During the '46 riot, an inmate relates how he pushed Barney so that he could not "fink" on this guard, E. J. Miller. He told this con that if he killed Miller, it would set the entire prison against him because Miller was well-liked by almost all the inmates. There were a few who would have been killed by almost any inmate. One that keeps being mentioned is a guard who, as mail clerk, would yell out in a loud voice that the wife of an inmate was divorcing him. "Well, old Joe D. Grinder has got your wife." Joe D. Grinder was a name that would describe a man who made love to a wife of an inmate. This guard went out of his way to torment the inmates. These types felt that they needed to go beyond just maintaining the discipline — the small man in uniform syndrome. The power of that uniform was then abused.

STOP

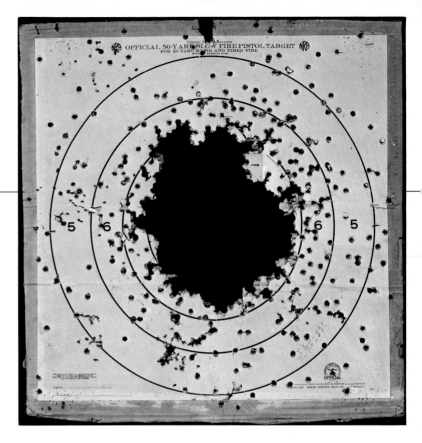

One of the activities of the guards that would bother some inmates was the routine of practicing with their weapons on the rifle range. There are reports that some of the bullet-riddled targets in man-form were left around for some of the inmates to see. But mostly what bothered the men was the noise of that activity — the "rat-ta-ta ta." Some felt that this was staged deliberately to create some fear in the men. Well, it didn't create fear, but became nerve-racking.

The four weapons that were fired on the range were the pistol, Springfield, Browning and Thompson. In the year of 1937 there were nine marksmen, five sharpshooters and seven experts. The person with the second-to-lowest score of 30 in the pistol had the biggest score in the Thompson of 684. That year the top man was a guard named Chandler, with 1,437 points in all four weapons. In the written instructions for armed officers on Alcatraz we repeatedly find the warning: "Aim to STOP, not to KILL." The arms were kept in the armory and issued by the armory officer. The armory officer had to issue the clearance for each officer to approach the armory. This was to ensure that there were no inmates present in the area through which the officer had to pass. The standard weapon used in the prevention of escapes was the U.S. carbine, caliber .30 MI. The revolver was issued to some officers to go with the carbine and could be issued under special circumstances. No firearms were allowed into the cell block at any time. Some of the guards' fear was that they would lose a bullet during their shift, especially in the gun cage in the cellhouse.

The dock tower had as its regular issue the Winchester rifle, caliber 30-60, model 70, this being an accurate long-range weapon. They myth that the officers were running around with submachine guns makes for a good movie script, but was not a reality on Alcatraz. The Thompson submachine gun, caliber .45 ACP model of 1928, was a reserve weapon and for use in special circumstances only, and then only by guards who had experience with it.

The officers on Alcatraz were under strict orders and firm, clear procedures when it came to the arms. And the abuse toward the inmates was in the rarest cases with the weapons issued on Alcatraz; and then only in a moment of personal judgment by the officers.

Alcatraz, like any other place with a chain of command, kept the contact by the officers with their superiors or commander at a respectable distance. The warden was in command, and he gave orders that had to be followed without question. If there was any doubt about that, the individual officer would be called on it. "You do as you are told, and that's it." The officers would generally fall into three categories when it came to the feelings about their warden: strong dislike for the warden, indifferent acceptance of him but respect for the position, and approval of him as an individual and tolerance of the rules and orders. Generally speaking, there was not a close relationship between the officers and the warden. Like in any com-

Mrs. Edwin B. Swope   Alcatraz Island, California

I have had beautiful flowers this Summer. My tuberous begonias in the greenhouse were a show worth seeing. I have an orchid in bloom now. With 5 blossoms on it. Its yellow - by cream & a little green in it & each flower about 4 in across.

Letter to a friend of Alcatraz warden's wife

mand type of situation, a special closeness would not allow the total operation to run as smoothly as needed. To check the alertness of the guard, the warden would go around and make some file marks on a bar, and ask for a written report on bar inspections. On that report there had better be some mention about the marks on the bars — sneaky but effective.

Some guards did get to see the inside of the warden's house at the time that they delivered and picked up inmates assigned to the warden's house for work. Those procedures were off the record and varied according to the personality or beliefs of the individual warden. The fact is that on Alcatraz there were inmates working in the personal services of some of the wardens. The jobs varied: cooks, gardeners, house boys, etc.

necessarily to the fact that they were on Alcatraz. Alcatraz contributed to this only by the fact that it was isolated from the mainland.

There are several reports as to the low morale of the officers. These reports could be found during any of the wardens' assignments. Generally, the morale would be the sum total of all the pressure and conditions, but could be affected by some single action by one of the wardens. According to the records and statements by the guards, the turnover was very high on Alcatraz. An issue always mentioned was their feeling that the salaries were insufficient. They would compare them with minimum security institutions and felt their salaries should be higher.

Warden house fireplace as seen today (1981)

Warden house. Notice snow on road.

The officers among themselves did have a fairly close community. Some had their families living on the island, and that created a more communal mood: children, home cooking, etc. There were single guards on Alcatraz, and they had their own social life on the mainland. This small community of officers on Alcatraz did have its own Peyton Place flavor — many stories of things going on and many stories of small conflicts between the guards — but this was due mainly to the character of the individual and not

View from dock tower of the officers' quarters

186

View of Alcatraz family residences built on the old parade ground

Some of their concerns were with some of the facts brought about by where Alcatraz was located: the terrible climate, fog and wind affecting their health; the boat home, requiring more time, should he miss a boat. They felt they put in more time than their counterparts at other institutions. All of these factors contributed to the low morale, and this would affect their behavior on and off duty. There was a high degree of alcoholism. It is hard at this time to re-create the total picture of those years past. But the reality of some of those facts should not be ignored in the attempt to write the overall history of Alcatraz.

A strange twist came when a guard felt a bit of compas-

Bathroom built in old military quarters. Note brick ceiling.

Bathtub in officers' quarters

sion for some inmates in solitary. This was during the holiday season, when this guard would give some sweets, tobacco and whisky to the inmates. One inmate by the name of Jimmy Groves, a reported snitch, supposedly told on the guard. There is also a report that a guard from the "graveyard" shift found out and told. The guard was arrested and expressed surprise, "I just did it out of the goodness of my heart. I wasn't the only guard who slipped stuff in to the cons. I didn't know it was against the law — just against prison regulation."

There was a guard who did not know much about the different leagues in sports. In order to get the scores to the inmates, he would write them on his hands, the left hand being one league, the right being the other. It is not known exactly what these scores meant to the inmates, but they could have been used for gambling.

The major problem with all this was that the moment a guard would do a favor for any convict, he would be "in the hold of the con." The convicts were always watching out for a chance to "get a grip on you." Not all were so bold about it as was Al Capone with Warden Johnston, but they tried. The guard had to watch himself in light of his colleagues. A smile or a friendly gesture could indicate some wheeling, dealing or favoritism. If an inmate got to a guard, that would mean the guard forever would be under his thumb. This did happen. And when discovered, could lead to a prison term

Fireplace in officers' quarters in old military barracks

187

for the guard. A guard in 1951 was removed from "the Rock" and sent to prison for 5 years for smuggling inmates' letters out and money in. The reason for this discovery was money found during a cell shakedown. Normally, the inmates would put the money into a cigarette or into the tip of their shoelaces.

To what extent this went on will never be exposed. The guards, like anybody else, were subject to human emotions that would allow them to break the rules of the very strict system. Men in uniform are subject to totally different human responses, and especially, in a place such as "the Rock."

"Officers are checked and rated regarding appearance, bearing, manner, speech, interest, ability, example, loyalty, courage, knowledge of duties and job performance. When the officer comprehends the purpose of the organization and how the work of each man fits into the whole plan, they are expected to put forth earnest, intelligent and forthright effort."

For some, Alcatraz was just another post in their tour of duty; but for some it gave them a special place in the system of prisons. Alcatraz was special, was different, and that made it almost impossible to be treated as "just another job."

To the families, this was not just another job. Especially for the children, the life style was different. The school-aged children had to take the boat to go to school and forever needed to answer questions in regard to their homes.

Most of them fell into the regular routine until something special happened. One boy remembered the good fishing on the island. They would go to the back of the island. Bass, striped bass, crabs and sharks would be the catch. He would go there with an adult and catch his fish, accepting the fact that he could not go beyond the fence. But on those special days, such as the riot of 1946, he could not go fishing. So he watched all the ships go by, including the aircraft carrier *Enterprise*.

These children knew where they were, and managed to create an environment for themselves that would allow them to grow up like any other neighborhood kid. The major restrictions prohibited them from possessing toy guns or pistols. They had a curfew of 9:00 p.m. on weekdays and 11:00 p.m. on Saturdays and Sundays.

For the most part, these children regarded their stay on Alcatraz as normal and did most of what other children their age would do. The children did feel like part of a community, and they would love the potluck dinners held once a month in the social hall. There were also special occasions for officials retiring or being transferred. There was a small grocery store, run by adults from Alcatraz, soda fountain, post office, and a baseball field. An upstairs apartment was converted to a chapel for the families. They had to obey very strict bicycle rules that read, in part: "The only place on the island where bike riding is permitted is on the big Parade Ground. The only time that bike riding is permitted is during daylight hours." This was followed by

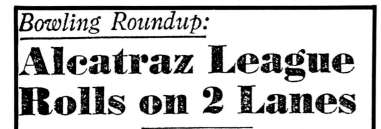

Bowling Roundup:
Alcatraz League Rolls on 2 Lanes

By Carl Reich

Alcatraz Island houses one of the most unique leagues in bowling.

Because the "tight little isle" has only two lanes, its eight team circuit must bowl in shifts, reports Secretary Billie Pepper. Two quintets bowl at 7 p. m. and two at 9 p. m. each Wednesday, and the others follow a similar schedule each Friday.

"You can imagine the rooting and rivalry we have, with members of the six idle teams kibitzing the bowlers," says Mrs. Pepper, a voluntary resident of the island for twenty years. (Her husband is a guard.)

Don Martin, another guard, is president of the league, and Kenneth Blair, custodial officer, serves as treasurer.

Bottom left: Bowling alley control box. Bottom right: Pin setting machine and a view of the two-lane bowling alley.

12 rules that all started by "No bike riding . . . ." These rules had to be signed by the child and the parent. The parent signed: "I approve of these rules and will encourage my child to obey them."

"I never felt different than any other kid. I enjoyed the boat ride and never felt scared," recalls one boy who was 16 at the time he lived on the island. He was the bowling alley pin setter and got paid for it. The island did have a league, and anybody bowling had to pay. There was no organized activity for the children on Alcatraz. The only things that were organized were the Christmas programs. Some classes were given to children, such as ballet dancing, which would be showcased during the Christmas programs.

The only possible contact the children could have with any inmates would be during transportation on the boat. The inmates were always chained and put into a different compartment. Once in a while the children would admire the get-up of some lady on the boat who was on her way to visit an inmate. The fancy clothes, furs and perfume were the dead give-away. They never knew who the person was.

The fact that the keys to the boat were attached to a wire and then were hoisted up to the "man with the machine gun" in the tower was a constant reminder that one could not leave this island at will. Even the guests visiting the families would notice this ritual with the keys.

The foghorns left a great impression on the children and are mentioned in every interview. "The view from the island on a clear day is something I will never forget," relates a

wife. She mentioned the fact that they had to pre-plan for the food, as there was no place to shop for a family on the island. The store on the island was stocked with the bare minimum for convenience, and was not intended to supply the families with their needs for daily living.

Probably the time that will be remembered as the most serious invasion of this regular daily routine for all families on "the Rock" was the 2nd of May, 1946. To many, this is the most noteworthy date in the entire history of Alcatraz. May 2, 1946, marked the beginning of events that would be remembered as the 1946 Riot. Two officers died and three inmates lost their lives. But the significance of this

period of three days was that it challenged, tested and violated all that Alcatraz stood for. These three days generated more rumors, stories, speculations, exposure, frustration and revenues from Alcatraz than any other time in its history.

Lengthy accounts of these days have been published, movies made and articles written; yet much is untold in a way that is far removed from the reality of events.

It is not very clear as to what originally had been planned, and all that we have is a reconstruction of events. A lot of what actually did happen did not seem to fit into a plan; but rather, was the result of impromptu actions that progressed from moment to moment. The characters involved all varied greatly in emotional stability, background and intelligence.

S. F. Red Cross Sent Supplies to Alcatraz Battle

Red Cross coffee and sandwiches were on the Alcatraz beachhead yesterday.

Answering a request for emergency food service from officials at the embattled island prison, the San Francisco Chapter of the American Red Cross sent supplies for 150 men to Alcatraz last night. They included hot coffee, sandwiches, food and cigarettes.

The supplies, according to Robert S. Elliott, manager of the San Francisco chapter, were delivered by a Coast Guard boat crew.

Dead and Wounded

Dead and wounded in the Alcatraz revolt are:

DEAD:
Harold P. Stites, guard, shot through the back.

WOUNDED:
Fred J. Richberger, guard, wounded in calf of leg.

Harry Cochrane, guard, wounded badly in upper left arm near shoulder.

Robert Sutter, guard, slight nose wound.

Elmus Besk, shot in both legs.

Herschel R. Oldham, guard, shot in left arm, hand and other parts of the body.

Henry Winehold, captain of the watch, serious but undetermined injuries.

Joe Simpson, lieutenant of the watch, serious but undetermined injuries.

A man identified only as Miller. Two unidentified guards.

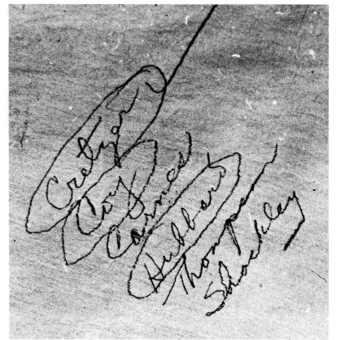

Officer wrote these names identifying the leaders of the 1946 riot on the cell wa

Clarence Carnes

Bernard Paul Coy

Joe Cretzer

Marvin F. Hubbard

Miran Thompson

Sam Shockley

The accounts of the events vary greatly in details, but it is still possible to reconstruct a fairly good picture of what happened. It started with the distraction of the officer in the gun galley. This officer walked over to the D-block side of the gun galley. The prisoner, Bernard Coy, a Kentucky bank robber, who was mopping the floor in the B and C-block area, joined Marvin Hubbard, who returned from the kitchen detail, in slugging Officer Miller. What they wanted was to get the keys from that guard. They did, and immediately unlocked the cells of two other prisoners, Joseph P. Cretzer and Clarence Carner. They dragged Officer Miller to a cell, Number 403.

Coy climbed to the top of the gun galley on the west side and managed to spread the bars of the top level with a "diabolically clever combination of toilet fixtures assembled in such a way that they could be used with the help of a pair of pipe pincers to spread the bars from the usual five inches to seven inches. The 'Rube Goldberg' contrivance consisted of two valve parts used in the toilets and two threaded pipe fixtures which could be rotated in such a manner that pressure would be brought to bear on the bars." This bar-spreader must have been surreptitiously fashioned in a prison workshop and then smuggled into the cell house in a false bottom of a garbage can. The report from Washington in the pamphlet claims "the plumbing parts had been locked in the utilities corridor where they were being used in repairing the smashed toilets in D-block. Once obtaining the keys from Officer Miller, it was possible to get into this utility corridor and secure the fixture." Had they been placed there by Coy during the week? He waited for Officer Burch to return, slugged him and captured the rifle, pistol, ammunition and keys. He threw the

ALCATRAZ REVOLT

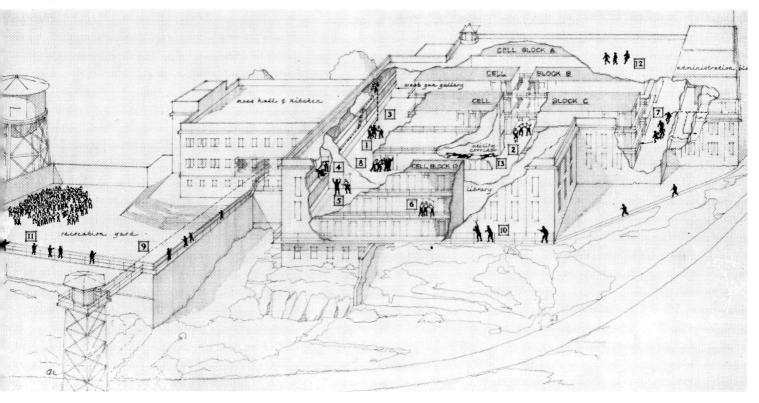

1. Coy and Hubbard slug and capture cell house officer Miller and take his keys. 2. Hubbard releases Cretzer, Carnes, and Thompson. 3. Hubbard and Coy monkey climb cage protecting armed officer while he is in "D" block and thus gain access by spreading bars. 4. Coy slugs armed officer Burch as he passes from "D" block to main cell house, captures his arms and throws pistol down to Cretzer. 5. With rifle Coy retained, he forces officer to open door between "D" block and the main cell block. 6. Cretzer pushes in with pistol and liberates thirty of worst prisoners segregated in "D" block. 7. Reserve officers on duty in administration building having been advised Officer Miller did not answer his call, enter main cell house to investigate. 8. They are captured and locked in cell where they were later shot by Cretzer. 9. Coy then attempts to shoot tower officer. 10. Officers run to rear entrance and this, plus Officer Miller's hiding of outside door keys, blocks escape from main cell house. 11. Other prisoners not participating in revolt are herded into recreation yard where they are guarded by Marines until prisoners in cell house are subdued. 12. Officers break through roof and drop grenades and bombs, finally dislodging Coy, Cretzer, and Hubbard from pipe tunnel where they were driven by officers after gun battle to regain west gun gallery. 13. Found dead in utilities corridor.

Top right: Telegram sent by Warden Johnston informing his superiors of the trouble on Alcatraz. Top far right: Electric control panel for some doors. Bottom left: Door that separates main cell house from D-block. Bottom center: Warden Johnston explaining security of door. Bottom right: Marine rifleman firing grenades into cell house during 1946 riot.

pistol to Cretzer with the keys to cell block D. Cretzer opened up the cells of some inmates in isolation, a reported total of twelve, including Sam Shockley. Miran Thompson was let out of C-block by Coy.

When this entire plot came to an end, many inmates were mentioned as being involved, but the testimony about them was not unanimous or conclusive. All involved were united in naming Coy, Cretzer, Carnes, Hubbard, Shockley and Thompson as the active armed conspirators.

These six men were holding their armed position in the cell house while the objective was to open the door to the yard. They did not achieve this. During this time, the attempt was made to kill some tower guards. Coy did manage to wound one of the guard tower officers. He was doing his shooting from the kitchen. Carnes was with him as Coy took aim at Officer E. J. Miller, who was approaching down the center corridor. Coy fired and Officer Miller ran toward the east entrance and reported to Warden Johnston, "Coy is armed; he took two shots at me. He's wearing an officer's uniform! I thought it was the captain till I saw the rifle!" An inmate working in the kitchen, who claimed to having refused an invitation to be part of the plot, recalls, "When the deputy seen the rifle, he broke and started to run back down the corridor. Coy fired and missed. It was

the first shot fired in the riot. Coy steadied the gun and squeezed off another shot. But just as he done it, Clarence Carnes knocked the gun barrel up. That there saved old E. J. Miller's life. Hadn't been for Carnes, Coy would have nailed him sure." As the officers entered the cell house, the inmates captured them and put them into two cells, #402 and #403. Half-crazed, Shockley egged Cretzer on by shouting, "Kill all the sons-of-bitches! Kill the bastards! Kill them all! Don't leave any witnesses!" Cretzer thereupon fired into Cells #402 and #403, critically wounding Miller and Corwin. Burdelle and Bristow played dead, and Lageson's cheek was grazed by a bullet fired from Cretzer's weapon. Simpson was shot in the back, Baher in the leg, and Officer Sundstrom was unhurt put pretended to be dead.

The fact that they could not get the key to open the door to the yard created a much more tense situation. The thinking did not follow the calculated way of doing business some of the convicts had used in pulling off some of their original crimes. Here they must have felt trapped and their actions became desperate. By that time, Officer Miller had hidden the key leading to the yard in the toilet bowl of cell No. 403.

The warden realized that this was a serious situation, so

Top right: 1946 riot bullet hole. Top far right: Door connecting main cell house gun galley to D-block gun galley. Bottom left: Key box in gun galley. Bottom right: Detail of key box with key hooks and keys visible.

he started organizing and mobilizing all the back-up systems. The Director, Bennett, in Washington started receiving teletypes from Johnston, informing him of the situation. A radio message was sent to the Coast Guard and to the San Francisco police, informing them of the trouble and asking that their boats circle the island. All officers were called to duty, and a message sent to the press: "Serious trouble. Convict has machine gun in cell house. Have issued riot call. Placed armed guards at strategic locations. Many of our officers are imprisoned in the cell house. Cannot tell extent of injuries suffered by our officers or amount of damage done. Will give you more information later in the day when we can control." Now the show was really on: the press and the people all became part, and for three days the headlines were dramatic, the public being victims of rumors and false statements, exaggerations and interpretations of what they, themselves, could see from the mainland.

The inmates in the industry area were gathered and headed into the yard, to be guarded, first, by the Alcatraz officers, and then by U.S. Marines, who offered help by sending a detachment. Fears and concerns did not just rest with the officials and inmates involved, but also with the inmates who by their own choice did not want to be involved. Once the alarm sounded, everything started to happen very fast and the inmates knew that there would be no careful selection of targets; all were in danger. At the sounding of the alarm, many of the convicts returned to their cells. The concern of one inmate is best illustrated by the exchange that occurred between Coy and a kitchen worker, "This thing's gone all haywire. You ain't going to make it. Quit now, you damn fool, before the big alarm goes and we all get killed." The total frustration at not being able to get out of the cellhouse may have been the reason for this response by Coy: "Hell with it. I'm going to make it cost them every life I can. I'm going to kill every man I can see that's wearing a uniform. I ain't got nothing to live for, because they'll kill me now, whatever happens."

One inmate at one time was concerned that Coy would turn on some of the inmates with whom he had bad blood.

Marines on duty during 1946 riot.

Top left: Blood-stained cell where hostages were kept
Bottom left: Coast guard boat used during the siege
Bottom right: The press, anxious to get close to Alcatraz for some pictures
Opposite page, top left: Bodies of Coy, Cretzer and Hubbard

recalls the inmate who at one time made coffee and gave it to the mutineers.

The guards, marines and special personnel were all over the place, keeping close aim at all the windows and doors of the main cell block. Gas was fired into the cells. Rifle grenades were fired into D-block; the ones that did not enter, fell to the ground and started the grass on fire. From San Francisco it looked like Alcatraz was on fire.

The plan was to drive these battling convicts into the cell corridors and then bombard them with demolition bombs. At 5:30 a.m., on Friday, officers started drilling the holes in the roof through which they would drop these bombs. After firing at the officers, Coy, Cretzer and Hubbard retreated into the corridor of C-block. The other participants had returned to their cells. The bombs were dropped. And in the morning the officers opened the door of C-block corridor, entered and found the three bodies. Coy and Cretzer, according to the doctor, had died before Hubbard, who was the farthest back in the corridor. The battle was over. The worst incident in the history of Alcatraz came to a dramatic end. Three inmates dead, two guards dead and many wounded. And a thousand stories as to what exactly happened. One such story that keeps coming up is that one guard died of a bullet from an officer's weapon, not from the inmates' weapons.

The headlines changed to other topics and life went on. For Alcatraz life never was the same. The '46 riot, the big one, a prison tragedy, was remembered by all. But for the families of Officers Miller and Stites no words or deeds could replace the loss. Director Bennett gave the following tribute to those two officers killed in action:

With that, he cornered Coy and told him to get out of that area. As he pinned him against an icebox, he said, "Do what you want to, but leave us be in here. The five of us don't want no part of this crazy caper."

The main effort by the warden at first was to get the officers from cell numbers 402 and 403. After that, he concentrated on isolating the armed inmates. After being kept in the yard all night, the inmates who had worked that day were brought back into cell block A. These inmates were cold, tired, and hungry. But, most of all, they were scared. "But they was more scared than anything else. They thought the whole place might go up in flames and smoke any minute. There was shrieking and cursing all night long,"

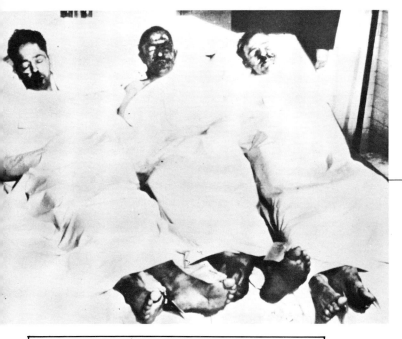

Thompson, Schockley and Carnes returning to Alcatraz after arraignment

Alcatraz, one could say the new Alcatraz, at least for a time period, however not clearly defined, it was a new Alcatraz. Oh, we are not talking of new buildings, new people, etc., but new feelings, destroyed connections, absent trust, modified work patterns, etc. The end was not with the removal of the bodies, that was the beginning.

One aftermath that kept all of this alive was the court process needed to punish the three remaining accused participants, Carnes, Thompson and Shockley. Inmates had to go to court to testify, including Robert Stroud (Birdman). It is reported that Stroud contributed money to the defense. The defense built its case around the argument of inhuman prison conditions and negligence of officers, medical treatment and deprivation of proper food. After 14 hours of deliberation, a jury of six men and six women returned its verdict at 12:40 p.m. on December 22, 1946, just about eight months from the day of the riot. Shockley and Thompson were to die in the gas chamber of San Quentin, and Carnes was given a life sentence because he showed mercy towards the captive officers before and after they were shot. "Thursday, May 2, 1946, was one of the fateful days of my life on Alcatraz," recalls Warden Johnston.

At this time the Director of the Bureau of Prisons, James V. Bennett, too, had a statement to make. The final paragraph of his document, in part, reads, "In a graduation system like that of the Federal Government, an institution like Alcatraz, for the desperate recalcitrants, is essential. There must be a place for those who are assaultive, riotous, and Alcatraz serves that purpose and will continue to do so."

Schockley and Thompson leaving the court room in chains and waiting for their appearance

Cell house being repaired after 1946 riot

View of San Francisco from Alcatraz — Photo by Laurie O'Grady

DISTINCT MEN OF ALCATRAZ

Bottom right:Warden Johnston guiding Attorney General Homer Cummings out of the Administration Building.
Bottom left: Johnston and Cummings inspecting the Alcatraz officers.

Alcatraz only had four wardens. The change between the wardens' way of running Alcatraz was minimal. The first warden was James A. Johnston, who must be called the founding father of Alcatraz.

Johnston, a young reform warden at Folsom and San Quentin, was asked by Attorney General Homer Cummings to create this escape-proof penal institution. At Folsom this young Johnston stood for the total opposite of what was to be the philosophy of Alcatraz. He stood for a rehabilitative system, and that was not to be the system on Alcatraz. He was a soft-spoken, be-spectacled, white-haired, slender, small man. When he took the job, he had to leave his current job of a senior banking officer.

His nickname, given to him by the inmates, was "Salt Water Johnston," and this came from the repeated practice of hosing down unruly inmates. This tag stuck with him until his retirement at 72 on April 30, 1948. Alcatraz was his system. It was what he designed to fulfill his orders of having an escape-proof, maximun-security prison to hold America's worst. In a way, during the early days, Alcatraz became a showplace, and many V.I.P.'s got the tour from Johnston. "Now take 'Salt Water Johnston.' He didn't bother about the condition of the joint, only walked around like God Almighty. Any time he came around with visitors, you can bet that the person was some real big-wig, some top movie star, senator, etc. As for guards, Johnston wouldn't let a guard walk up to him and talk. He'd motion them back." As we mentioned early in the text, Johnston did have some conflict with the Bureau of Prisons director. The main point of conflict was the cruelty practice. Under Johnston the inmates referred to the system as a "scientific stir." Attorney General Murphy termed "the Rock" a "hell-hole, a great injustice to both prisoners and San Francisco." Johnston knew of all the bad press, but continued to

run the island with a firm hand until April 30, 1948, when he retired at 72. He died in San Francisco in 1958.

The second warden of Alcatraz was Warden Edwin B. Swope. He was an unassuming grandfather-looking type of a man: soft voice, rimless glasses, gray hair, and he had a pleasant smile.

Swope came to Alcatraz from a position as Warden of New Mexico State Prison. On Alcatraz his nickname was "Cowboy." The way he got the name was very simple: the way he dressed, western hat and boots. He was considered by most a fair but firm warden. There were many reports by guards and other personnel that Swope was not good for the morale of the officers. At one time,

forgotten to order the full amount of an item. And when he wanted to go to the mainland to fetch it, Swope said, "Let the person who made the mistake face the angry convicts who would be minus this item. He will never forget to order anything."

Swope was much in favor of vocational option in the prison system. He worked at McNeil Island Prison, where the inmates had many possibilities to learn a vocation. After four years on Alcatraz, he said, "Science has done a great deal in certain fields, such as polio and other diseases, but not much about the human mind."

In contrast to Warden Johnston, Swope did not like parading V.I.P.'s down the cellhouse. One inmate recalls that the visitors of Swope were not "top brass." His wife and he had a dog (Irish setter) on Alcatraz. And, under his wife's care, the flowers were well kept. A personal visitor to the Swopes recalls an incident: "I asked the warden how many prisoners were on the island, and he replied '150.' As we stood at the bottom of the movie room, I only counted 110. A few inmates were here and there, but not to make up 150. So I asked the warden. His response was 'down there,' meaning the dungeons."

A story relating to George "Machine Gun" Kelly exposes a very different side from any official story. "Kelly used to pull Swope's leg by telling him, 'The reason that I'm working is that my grandmother lost her job taking tickets at a St. Louis burlesque house. Now I've got to support her.' " Then,

during a kitchen strike, he made guards wait on the tables of the inmates. One officer recalls, "Working as a waiter on the cons put us all in a menial position and therefore, losing the respect of the inmates." The chaplain at that time states, "He galvanized the faltering public concept of the institution." He resigned as chaplain and made it clear he could not work with Swope. Another incident that caused problems was that Swope ordered the stools to be removed from the guard towers. The guards rebelled, and the stools were returned.

There was an incident where the mess steward had

Top left: Warden Edwin Swope inspects a typical cell. Bottom right: Commendation given to Alcatraz officers by Warden Swope. Bottom of page: 1954 Christmas program and menu for the Alcatraz officers and families.

too, Swope had the habit of going around telling some of the guys, "That's a nice-looking pair of shoes you've got. I wish that I could get a pair like those." An inmate by the name of Ed Murphy told the warden he was in bad shape if he could not get a new pair of shoes. One time Swope went up to an inmate, Clyde Nimrick, and called him "son." Clyde was in his sixties, and let the warden have it (with words). "In my estimation, Swope had no style at all," recounts a former inmate. "He'd go around testing benches and tables for dust. Boy, only a lackey would do that."

Alcatraz boat
Warden Johnston

He left Alcatraz on January 20, 1955, to be replaced by the third warden, Paul Madigan. Madigan had the advantage of having served on "the Rock" as lieutenant, captain and associate warden. He said he found his career by chance. "I needed a job during the depression and became a guard at Leavenworth. I had no idea I would like it." He took several positions outside Alcatraz, the last being the warden of Terre Haute, Indiana.

UNITED STATES DEPARTMENT OF JUSTICE
UNITED STATES PENITENTIARY
ALCATRAZ ISLAND, CALIFORNIA

May 16, 1950

Correctional Officer Frank J. Heaney
Alcatraz Island, California

Dear Mr. Heaney:

This is to commend you for your extremely cooperative attitude in responding immediately to the emergency situation created by the inmates of this institution during the dining room disturbance on the evening of May 15, 1950. There is no doubt in my mind that your quick response, along with other members of the staff, prevented the disturbance from becoming a truly serious situation.

It is thought fitting that a copy of this letter be placed with your personnel records for future reference.

Sincerely,

E. B. SWOPE
Warden

The Entire Staff Wishes You a

Merry Christmas

and A Happy New Year

PROGRAM
Christmas Eve 1954

The following recordings will be played in the cell house:

O, Come All Ye Faithful
I'll Be Home For Christmas
God Rest Ye Merry Gentlemen — Bing Crosby
Silent Night Holy Night — Charles Paul
O, Holy Night — Kenny Baker
Hark! The Herald Angels Sing
Christmas Carols — Fred Waring

Christmas packages will be distributed, courtesy of the Director, Prison Industries and the Warden.

Christmas Day

CATHOLIC MASS .... 8:30 A.M.
Father Richard Scannell, S. J.

MOTION PICTURES ...... 1:30 P.M.
SECRET OF THE INCAS
Also
Shorts: CANINE I.Q. & CARTOON

MENU

Stuffed Celery   Ripe Olives
Roast Tom Turkey
Oyster Dressing
Giblet Gravy
Snowflake Potatoes   Buttered Peas
Cranberry Sauce
Parkerhouse Rolls
Bread and Oleo
Pumpkin Pie   Fruit Cake
Coffee

ADMINISTRATION

Herbert Brownell Jr., Attorney General

James V. Bennett
Director of Prisons

Edwin B. Swope *Warden*	Joseph B. Latimer *Associate Warden*
P. R. Bergen *Captain*	Gerald C. Hill *Chief Medical Officer*
R. A. Lewis *Assoc. Supt. of Industries*	A. C. Kaeppel *Chief Clerk*
Richard Scannell *Catholic Chaplain*	George De Roo *Protestant Chaplain*
P. A. Michaud *Chief of Mech. Service*	G. W. Stouder *Culinary Supervisor*
Rupert H. Sutton *Culinary Instructor*	Frank Peire *Culinary Instructor*
Clarence V. Bray *Culinary Instructor*	Leroy Mc Creary *Culinary Instructor*

United States Penitentiary
Alcatraz, California
1954

NOTICE OF OFFICIAL
EFFICIENCY RATING

REGULAR (X)   SPECIAL ( )
PROBATIONAL ( )

As of ___6/20/49___ based on performance during period from ___12/20/48___ to ___6/20/49___

Frank J. _____   Correctional Officer, Cpc-7
(Name of employee)   (Title of position, service, and grade)

__Justice-Prisons__   US Penitentiary, Alcatraz, Calif.
(Organization—Indicate bureau, division, section, unit, field station)

Efficiency rating: _____G_____

E. B. Swope(signature)

6/20/49   Warden
(Date of notification)   (Title)

Interpretation of Efficiency Rating

Your efficiency rating is an official record of the way you are doing the work of your job.

Excellent (E) means that performance in every important phase of the work was outstanding and there was no weakness in performance in any respect.

Very Good (VG) means that performance in at least half of the important phases of the work was outstanding and there was no weakness in performance in any respect.

Good (G) means that performance met requirements from an over-all point of view.

Fair (F) means that performance did not quite measure up to requirements from an over-all point of view.

Unsatisfactory (U) means that performance in a majority of important phases of the work did not meet job requirements.

Inspection

You are entitled to inspect your efficiency rating sheet (Standard Form 51), or a copy of it, upon request to your supervisor or personnel officer. You are also entitled to inspect the final ratings (not the rating forms) of all employees in your office or station.

Significance of Efficiency Ratings

An efficiency rating of "Good," "Very Good," or "Excellent" is necessary in order to receive a periodic within-grade salary advancement.

An efficiency rating of "Fair" requires a one-step salary reduction if an employee's pay rate is above the middle rate for his grade (the fourth step in six-rate grades).

An efficiency rating of "Unsatisfactory" requires that the employee be dismissed or reassigned to other work in which he could be reasonably expected to render satisfactory service.

Efficiency ratings are a factor in determining the order in which employees are affected by reduction in force.

Appeals

If you believe your rating is wrong, you should first discuss it with your supervisor or personnel officer. You have the right, if your position is subject to the Classification Act, to appeal your rating within certain time limits to a board of review established for your agency. Appeals or requests for additional information concerning appeals should be addressed to the Chairman, Board of Review, care of Civil Service Commission, Washington 25, D. C.

Official efficiency rating for Alcatraz officers in 1949

AGENCY Justice-Prisons | PAY ROLL PERIOD 9/17-30/50 | BLOCK NO.

NAME AND NO.
FRANK J.

| | TAX CODE | DIVISION | SLIP NO. |
| | 1 | CUSTODIAL | |

DESIGNATION: Correctional Officer | GRADE: Cpc-440-7 | SALARY RATE: $3225. | SECTION | UNIT

BOND AUTHORIZATION NO. | BOND PURCHASE PRICE $

Reg	80 hrs	124.04
ND	55 hrs	8.53
LSP	73 hrs	113.15
		245.72

APPROPRIATIONS

CHECK	CASH	EARNINGS			DEDUCTIONS					NET PAY	POS
X		Regular	Overtime	Gross Pay	Retirement	Tax	Bond	Other	Code		
Pay This Period		124.04	ND 8.53 LSP 113.15	245.72	7.44	39.50	-	-		198.78	
New Normal Pay											
Previous Normal Pay											

REMARKS: Separation- Military Service eod 9-30-50. Lump Sum Payment for 73 hours Accum. Annual Leave.

PREPARED BY
HGW

AUDITED BY

Official payroll slip for Alcatraz officers in 1949

ALCATRAZ

News Dealer Rates:

	DAILY	SUN.	MONTH
Examiner	$1.50	$1.00	$2.00
Chronicle	"	"	"
News	"	-	-
Call Bulletin	"	-	-

1953

Jan.	July
Feb.	Aug.
Mar.	Sept.
April	Oct.
May	Nov.
June	Dec.

DEPARTMENT OF JUSTICE
UNITED STATES PENITENTIARY
ALCATRAZ, CALIFORNIA

Date 6-30-54

To: Dr. Hill

SIR: Please grant me an interview regarding:

Could I please have an immediate interview with you. I hope you can find time

Thank you

P.S. I hope I can see you Thursday, if I don't, you may not be back
over

Reg. No. 1121 Cell Seg. Detail

Name Thomas Smith

State briefly exactly what you wish to discuss.
Do not use any other form.
Do not use an envelope.
Give this slip when filled out to orderly or guard.
You will not be called unless your request merits consideration.

STOCK RECORD — PILLOWS, FEATHER

(illegible handwritten stock record ledger)

UNITED STATES PENITENTIARY
Alcatraz, California

MINOR WORK REQUEST

Date January 30, 1962

Mechanical Service

You are requested to perform the following work: Could you please furnish me with 2 gallons of Dark Oak Varnish
1 gallon of White Enamel

I would like to varnish the floor of my living room and dining room and use the white to paint the fireplace in my living room.
My apt is 64 Bldg. apt 305. I can arrange to have this picked up myself if necessary. I can be contacted at 3121.

Requested by: R. A. WASZAK (Signature)   Authorized by: (Dept. Head)

Number: Priority: TO: Foreman: Paint Shop

Date: Approved: WMB. C.M.S.

Date Completed: 2-26-62   Shop Foreman

NOTE: List materials on back of request; complete form and return promptly to Chief. Mechanical Service.

Warden Paul Madigan at his desk on Alcatraz

Warden's house and lighthouse with residences

Warden Paul Madigan arrived on Alcatraz on January 30, 1955, and served until November 20, 1961. Madigan's nickname was "Promising Paul." He would always listen to the inmates' requests and then promise action, and most often nothing happened. He was a stout man, bald, wore glasses, and always chewed gum. He smoked a pipe. He was the guard in 1941 who talked Cretzer, Shockley, Kyle and Barkdoll out of a break attempt. The story that created an impression was the one of the "half potato." An inmate left a half of a potato on his plate. The guard had to report him: "I took him to Lieutenant Madigan's desk just outside the mess hall. I told Madigan he had left half a potato and explained why. Madigan said 'Hi, ya' to somebody passing by. I thought he hadn't heard me, and repeated the report. And he waved and nodded to somebody else. I finally got the pitch, led the prisoner away and told him to high-tail it on to his cell."

Warden Madigan managed to convince 50 inmates to donate a pint of blood each to the Irwin Memorial Blood Bank of San Francisco. One of the most memorable acts by Madigan was the adding of something extra to the Christmas gift of candy and nuts. He added six cigars in 1957. That was a major point for the inmates. On the other hand, in June of 1960, there seemed to be a flood of legal petitions reaching the courts. "Perhaps it's just a way of passing time," explained a surprised Madigan.

Madigan had the reputation of ruling with a fair but firm hand. He said about Alcatraz, "Our primary function is to house men who have proven difficult to handle in other federal prisons — the hostile, the assaultive, the trouble maker. The men who come here have less prospect for rehabilitation than the men in the rest of our prison system."

During Madigan's time as warden, there were only two escapes, involving only three men. The first escape happened on July 23, 1956. The attempt was made by Floyd P. Wilson, and his story is told earlier in this book. The second attempt occurred on September 29, 1958. Two men who worked on the garbage detail tried to escape by tying up the guard with them and going for the water's edge. The plan was to stay hidden in the water until dark and then slip by the circling boats to freedom.

This sounded simple, but the actual act took months of preparation and involved many risks during the planning stages. Clyde Johnson, a bank robber serving 40 years, and Aaron Burgett, a Post Office robber, teamed up for this attempt. All the planning was done by Johnson who, at the beginning of his planning, was not working with Burgett.

The planning took several months and consisted of collection of some plastic bags, to be used as a flotation device during the swim, the making of face masks from round plastic, cottage cheese containers to protect the eyes under water. The breathing device, a snorkel with extension tube, was made over a long period of time in the cell of the inmates.

Since this escape attempt took so long in planning, and these inmates wanted to wait until daylight saving time, the material had to be maintained and/or replaced. The hiding place for those plastic bags was in the water, and the salt deteriorated the plastic. Burgett was negligent in maintaining his plastic, and this is what cost him his life. Weighed down with a double set of warm underwear, he was found 13 days after the attempt floating in the bay near Alcatraz. Johnson heard a noise that could have been a call for help, but did not know if it was the call of the sea gulls, "Yellep, yellep," so could not give up his hiding position.

During the preparation phase, they made flower pots out of wood, the four sides of which, when taken apart, could be used as fins. After retrieving the body of Burgett, they did find these fins still attached to his feet. They tried to study the currents, but that, in itself, is a very difficult task. The thought process worked away on both individuals, a thought process that went in all the directions of speculation. "Most of my thoughts those summer nights

were on escape, and I tried to envision how it might go. When I got down to cases and got realistic about it, I'll confess, a lot of fear surged."

After both men were in the water, Johnson lost sight of Burgett. "I did not know what he was doing. I'm sorry to say, he was drowning. I did not know it at the time." To avoid being spotted by the circling boats, Johnson would go under water every time a boat approached. He could hear the noise under water of the propellers and knew when to come up for air. An observation made by Johnson: "One time, between boats, I broke the surface sputtering — it seemed like I'd swallowed gallons of sea water — when there, not four feet away, perched on a rock and looking directly at me as if I was crazy, was a tern. I almost had to laugh at the way that bird studied me, and so close! Every since, I understand and identify with how a canary or parakeet feels when someone peers into their cage at them." The last time he came up for air, he was facing a Coast Guard man in a bright orange, iridescent "Mae West." The jig was up. "With water dripping off the end of my nose and draining off me elsewhere into a sizable pool on the floor, one of the agents kept repeating, 'You were in the water of the Bay, right?' (I suppose for an admission and court evidence.)"

During the last years of Madigan's rule, there was a group of inmates called "the Cutters" that presented much frustration to the warden. "The Cutters" started to slash their Achilles' tendons. These inmates, supposedly in protest to the problems in writing petitions, became the leaders of a general "lay in." This is a refusal to go to work. With broken pieces of eyeglasses, nine inmates in solitary slashed their Achilles' tendons. A few days later, five more followed the same procedure, except this time they used thin pieces of sharpened metal. Approximately two weeks later, ten of the original "Cutters" tried to cut the tendon of the other heel. All of this was called an "attention getter." This last time, however, they used razor blades. The warden and everybody else were surprised how these inmates in isolation in the "dark hole" cells could manage to get razor blades. One ex-inmate recalls, "The 'bulls' really shook. They walloped the 'bejesus' out of the guys, trying to find out where those razor blades came from, but nobody snitched."

That probably is the one mystery that stood out the most in Warden Madigan's mind. On Sunday, November 26, 1961, after attending Mass (Madigan was a devout Catholic and attended Mass with the convicts), he turned over the leadership of Alcatraz to its last warden, Olin G. Blackwell.

Body of Aaron Walter Burgett. Note the taped home-made swim fin.

Top left: Warden Olin Blackwell.
Bottom right, Warden's offices.
Bottom of page: Warden's offices reception area.

Warden Blackwell probably will be remembered for the "softening" of "the Rock." He, himself, gave the impression of a good-natured personality. The times had changed and the type of prisoner on "the Rock" took on, for the most part, a different character. The relentless monotony, so characteristic of Alcatraz, took on a more varied appearance. The major change was the implementation of the new purchasing rule. This rule expanded on the things an inmate could purchase with his earned money.

Immediately, we saw these hard-core criminals sitting in their cells and crocheting. To see these men with crochet and knitting needles must have shattered all images firmly implanted in the minds of the general public. Blackwell did ask for a special rule: "You may not use the bedspread on your own bed." All of the inmates' work went out as gifts, bedspreads, colorful booties, crocheted doilies and sweaters. Blackwell himself decorated his 18-room house with some of the doilies. Doilies could be found in his office, too.

There was a change in attitude, and it seemed more relaxed under Blackwell. It was under Blackwell that the two last escapes took place. The escape of the Anglin brothers with Morris was mentioned earlier in this book; and the last escape attempt took place in December of 1962. An escape attempt that never made the records or news was that of an inmate serving a 30-year sentence for bank robbery. The plot was to secure the early release of this bank robber via a forged court order, setting aside a portion of his sentence. It was Warden Blackwell who brought the matter to the court's attention. Upon checking the document number and the judgment order number and discovering they were not the same, the court order was identified as a forgery. The author and source of this document has never been apprehended.

Top right: Salt water intake valve. Top far right: Document advising non-arrival of parts for plumbing repairs.

The last attempt, where an inmate got off the island, was in December, 1962: John Paul Scott, serving 30 years for bankrobbing and Daryl Parker, serving 50 years for bankrobbing and an escape attempt. The prison was in the process of scaling down, preparing for eventual closure. The storage room window in the basement under the kitchen became the place for their exit from the building. Over a long period of time, the two used butcher twine, soaked in wax and covered with coarse scouring powder, as an abrasive, to saw through the window bars. A few minutes after a head count, they squeezed through the opening, climbing to the roof via some outdoor pipes, and lowered themselves to the ground on the other side of the main building. Parker could not handle the current and clung to some rocks, to be found later by the guards within the house. Scott, with the help of some inflated rubber gloves, did get as far as the Golden Gate Bridge, where he was spotted. He nearly died from exposure and exhaustion.

Warden Blackwell was the last warden of "the Rock" and on March 21, 1963, he watched the last prisoner leave.

Alcatraz had only four wardens to run this institution for 28 years. Alcatraz had only 1,576 inmates in that same time period, and that is a low number, considering the figures for other institutions.

These men for whom Alcatraz was designed, by all standards — at least in the first phase of its Federal Penitentiary life — were the "Who's Who" in mainstream U.S. crime. One cannot say that all these men on Alcatraz committed the worst crimes towards the public, but they certainly did towards the system. At first, as we discussed earlier, the men had to work their way through the system to land on Alcatraz. It will never be conclusive as to the effect of Alcatraz on crime as a deterrent. But we do have a record of men for whom crime was their life before they came to Alcatraz. Some men were sent to Alcatraz more than once, but for the most part the men on Alcatraz were chosen as the worst offenders by the other institutions' staffs.

John Paul Scott   Darl Lee Parker

U. S BUREAU OF INVESTIGATION, DEPARTMENT OF JUSTICE

F.B.I. criminal history sheet on Al Capone

CRIMINAL HISTORY

It would be an academic guess as to who was responsible for the notoriety. Did Alcatraz get famous because of the men who went there? Or did the men get famous because they were on "the Rock?" For one, the question is clear, a name that was famous before he arrived on Alcatraz. And that was Al Capone.

"Scarface" Al Capone, Alcatraz No. 85, was probably the most famous resident on "the Rock." Much has been written about this gang-lord chief who had the most control over Chicago's gangster era — the wide influence he had and the connections he constantly tried to make in order to better his life in prison. On "the Rock" this was to stop. He was to disappear from the public eye and news. Nobody will ever find out to what extent he controlled anything on Alcatraz. Every inmate tried to have some special connections, and most guards did make decisions as to when they would bend the rule a little.

Al Capone was in a position, financially, at least, to promise anybody just about anything. The way he entered Alcatraz is told early in this book and how he tried to make connections with the warden.

It must have been hard for him to fit into this total, "no privilege" situation. He used to just snap his fingers and things would happen. Here on "the Rock" he fell into a more lonely, isolated rank. Immediately upon the arrival of a new inmate, Capone would get close to him in order to gather information about the underworld developments. He spent a lot of time with Alvin Karpis, a big-time, notorious gangster. They managed to play in the band together, and that allowed them to pass information to each other. Capone's organization seemed to have stayed intact. Karpis was the first of several new arrivals who kept Capone abreast of developments in the underworld.

The new director of prisons visited Alcatraz and requested to have a chance to interview the inmates who wanted to talk to him. A table was set up in a dark corner, and one of the first inmates to be brought to Bennett was Capone. "I'm getting along all right," he said. "Capone can take care of himself. But I shouldn't be here. I'm here because of my reputation, because there's such a misunderstanding about me. People don't know the things I've done to be helpful." Capone told Bennett that if he would remain on the island for two weeks, Capone would reveal the workings of the underworld to him.

What finally brought Al Capone to serve time were various charges and convictions of tax evasions. He started serving his federal jail sentence on May 4, 1932, in Atlanta. It is now known that the reason for his transfer to Alcatraz was to isolate him. From the day he entered prison, he started arranging favors with guards and fellow inmates. It

Al Capone

JOHN EDGAR HOOVER
DIRECTOR

U. S. DEPARTMENT OF JUSTICE
BUREAU OF INVESTIGATION
WASHINGTON, D. C.

June 19, 1931.

Mr. William J. Froelich,
care United States Attorney,
Chicago, Illinois.

Dear Mr. Froelich:

I wanted to write and to extend to you my
heartiest congratulations upon the great accomplishment
which you have brought about in Chicago in the case against
Al Capone. I well know that this achievement was due
largely to your efforts at Chicago.

With expressions of my highest esteem and best
personal regards, I remain

Sincerely yours,

J. Edgar Hoover

J. Edgar Hoover thank-you letter to attorney

was rumored that Capone had more control of the prison than the warden. Alcatraz changed that. He said, "It looks like Alcatraz has got me licked."

On "the Rock" Capone had his share of enemies. One inmate stabbed him with a pair of shears; others hassled him just because he had been the "big man." Some inmates had lost partners or friends to the Capone gangs, and they did not forget that. He constantly had to defend such stories. One former inmate said, "Capone, while on Alcatraz, was one of the most hated men in the prison, and the best hater. He was not the toughest."

He was a big man, standing six feet, and weighing more than two hundred pounds. Many times two inmates would gang up on him. There was constant trouble for Capone. First, he had the job of mopping the floor; from that came the nickname, "the Wop with the Mop." While working in the laundry, he had problems with the crew on machines, who, at times, would throw wet laundry in his face. A fight would most always follow. In the cellhouse he got into a fight with an inmate about equal stature. The reason for the fight was that Al Capone had supposedly been responsible for the killing of Dion O'Banion. "I didn't know him, and the only thing I held against him was the killing of Dion O'Banion." "No, Ray, I didn't torpedo O'Banion," replied Capone. "And I don't know who knocked O'Banion off."

Capone had been involved with the authorities as far back as 1919 and until his final arrest in 1931, after numerous arrests.

The medical staff on "the Rock" knew of the past medical problems of Al Capone. One of the tests that needed to be done to determine the stage of syphilis was a spinal tap. Al Capone never wanted this to be true, and he told them it had been cured in Chicago. On February 5, 1938, the advanced degree of his syphilis became known to those who observed his behavior. Doctor Edward Twitchell diagnosed the symptoms as the premonitory signs of paresis caused by syphilis. Now Capone gave the permission for the vital spinal tap. The fluid was sent to the lab,

and after several checks the conclusion was drawn that the syphilis had progressed and caused injury to his brain. He had just about one more year to serve on Alcatraz, and then had to be transferred to a correctional institution for one year.

On January 7, 1939, Associate Warden Miller took him to Oakland to board the train for Los Angeles. They got off in Glendale, California, to transfer to a car that brought him to Terminal Island. After his stay there, he went to Lewisburg for final release. He was in bad shape and his relatives took him to a hospital in Baltimore. He died on January 25, 1947, in Florida. The headstone on Plot 48 in Chicago's Mount Olivet Cemetery simply reads:

Qui Riposa
Alphonse Capone
Nato: January 17, 1899
Morto: January 25, 1947

Even after his death, Capone had a spot in the eye of the public; so much so that the family, in order to avoid the tourists, moved the grave to a different cemetery.

Al Capone's home in Miami, Florida

LAST RESORT
on Alcatraz Island - Known as "THE ROCK"
FREE room and board - Bars in every room.
Guards on duty 24 hours a day for your protection
FREE transportation - one way only!
NO PARKING OR TRAFFIC PROBLEMS.
Natural swimming facilities - Plenty of time.
Musical fog horns to get you up. Good fishing.
A GOOD PLACE NOT TO BE. The Management

Postcard sold in San Francisco in 1952

Capone may have been the most famous criminal. He did not create his fame during his confinement. Robert Stroud, "the Birdman of Alcatraz," without a doubt is the most famous prisoner of Alcatraz. There are many reasons why he has that designation. He achieved his fame not with his criminal activities but with his accomplishments during confinement and not on Alcatraz.

As his name reveals, "the Birdman of Alcatraz" achieved his stature through the work he did with birds. The name is misleading, for on Alcatraz he never did anything with birds. A book and a movie by the same title probably coined that name forever.

Robert Stroud was born January 28, 1890, in Seattle, Washington, the first of two males born to Benjamin Stroud and Elizabeth McCartney Schaefer Stroud. The Strouds were of limited means. Robert Stroud's formal schooling ceased at the third grade. He was very protective of his brother, Marcus. He did not get along with his father, and one main source of friction was his bringing home of stray dogs.

Robert Stroud, Alcatraz 594

At the age of twelve he ran away from home, returning at intervals. At fourteen, he ran away all the way to Illinois, where the family originally came from. This trip was very significant in his life, inasmuch as he was attracted to a girl cousin. He was unable or unwilling to develop this relationship. According to him, this was a major turning point in his life. He had learned the practice of pederasty, in which he had several experiences. At home he worked odd jobs, but at the age of seventeen he signed on with a construction gang in Alaska. When the job ended after six months, he was in the town of Cordova sick with pneumonia. A dance hall "box hustler" nursed him to health. That was Kitty O'Brian, with whom he moved to Juneau in November of 1908.

In January, 1909, Kitty was sexually violated and beaten by a bartender by the name of Charles Von Dahmer. Stroud went to see Charley Von Dahmer, and after a struggle shot and killed him. He turned himself in to the marshal and was jailed. A fact not often revealed is that Kitty, with Stroud, was indicted for first degree murder. The circumstances of the crime are both controversial and obscure. Stroud did state, in later years, that he did not intend to kill the bartender; he wanted to just beat him up like Von Dahmer had beaten Kitty.

Stroud entered a plea of guilty to manslaughter, for which he drew a twelve-year sentence. His plea of manslaughter gained freedom for Kitty. In August of 1909, Stroud left Alaska for McNeil Island Federal Prison, leaving behind his mother and brother, who had moved to Alaska.

At McNeil Island Stroud worked in the laundry and became a convict foreman. After 28 months in McNeil, he stabbed a prisoner in a knife fight. He had six months added to his sentence. In 1912, McNeil Island Federal Prison became over-crowded, and because of the knife fight Stroud was included in the group of prisoners selected for transfer to the Federal Prison in Leavenworth, Kansas.

Stroud was in the maximum security part of Leavenworth, and only after the new warden, T. W. Morgan, brought prison reform to the prison, did Stroud start with his many correspondence courses. These courses included mathematics, astronomy, structural engineering, and a course called "Strength of Materials."

He was a "hard case" criminal and was caught making

210

knives and attempting an escape. He was caught in the sewer and placed into solitary for five days.

In March of 1916, Stroud's brother came from Alaska to visit him, but was not allowed to see him on some technicality. The same day a guard by the name of Andrew Turner, who had had bad feelings toward Stroud, reported him for talking in the mess hall. Normally, this would not have been reported unless it caused a disturbance. The next day, March 26, 1916, during the meal, Stroud stood in front of Turner. Bad words were exchanged, and Stroud stabbed the guard, who died. This occurred in front of eleven hundred prisoners. Stroud was placed alone in the isolation section.

The warden wanted to see Stroud hanged, and a guard who wanted to kill him was fired. This news reached the family. The father said, "Let him die." The mother sailed from Alaska and hired a leading Kansas lawyer, L. C. Boyle, to defend her son. Since the crime was committed on federal ground, it was tried in Federal Court, thus allowing a death sentence.

On May 23, 1916, the first trial was held and the Federal Judge, John C. Pollock, sentenced Stroud to be hanged on June 21, 1916. This case was appealed, and the Circuit Court affirmed error and nullified the trial in December of 1916.

The second trial opened on May 22, 1917. The verdict: guilty with life imprisonment. This trial, too, was nullified. The third trial in May, 1919, resulted in a third conviction, and Federal Judge Lewis sentenced Stroud to be executed by hanging within the walls of Leavenworth on November 8, 1919.

He was ordered to be put into solitary confinement until he was executed. This order was later interpreted to mean solitary for life. His mother, working relentlessly in Washington, managed to have President Wilson commute her son's sentence from the death penalty to life imprisonment. The order by the warden read: "Stroud will be kept in the segregated ward during his sentence, which is for life. He will never be permitted to associate with other prisoners and will be allowed only the customary half hour each day for exercise in the courtyard. . ."

His new home was a cell twelve feet long and six feet wide with a small, barred window. He started to draw and paint, and was able to sell some of his cards, through his mother. This did not last long. His interest was then directed toward two fledgling sparrows he found in the exercise yard. He kept them alive. And with that started his now-famous activities with birds. He managed over a period of time to obtain permission to have material and

Top left: Drawings made by Stroud to illustrate his book dealing with the diseases of birds.
Bottom right: Robert Stroud

tools that would allow him to breed birds in his cell. He put all his energy into the study of canaries, up to the point where he was one of the leading authorities on the diseases of canaries. He received extra privileges that would allow him to find a remedy for septic fever and septicemic disorder in birds.

All his findings were collected and eventually put into book form. And even today one can still find the book, "Digest of the Diseases of Birds," in bookstores. There was extensive scientific experimentation and writing on Stroud's part. His cell resembled a laboratory, and it is said that at some time he had up to 200 birds in his cell. Stroud gained the respect of bird breeders from all over the world. His fame as "bird doctor" created many complications for the administration.

After the new directive, prohibiting prisoners from conducting business with the outside world, Stroud, with the help of public pressure, managed to have the Federal Prison Bureau alter its position. He got to keep his operation, and even to expand it. He now had two cells at his disposition.

Family problems aggravated Stroud. The person who was helping him from the outside, Della Jones, faced increasing friction with Stroud's mother. His brother visited Stroud and asked him to drop the relationship with Jones. Stroud refused, and that broke the relationship between him and his brother for many years. At the same time Stroud, becoming an increasing source of irritation to prison officials, was concerned that he would be transferred to the prison being built in California, Alcatraz.

To create public notice, Stroud and Della Jones drew up a contract declaring them man and wife. This was what created the open break between his mother and himself. She left for her family located in Illinois and refused to back her son in any parole efforts.

For Stroud things became more of a battle now, and he began violating prison rules on a more frequent basis. Finally on December 17, 1942, he was transferred to Alcatraz.

Upon arrival on Alcatraz, Stroud was put into a solitary cell in D-block. This prison "climate" was punitive. Having no access to anything dealing with his birds, his interest shifted to the study of law. He was allowed to check out books from the library. He felt strongly about his stay in D-block and described it as "a private purgatory where a few carefully chosen victims can slowly be driven mad."

His tight confinement on Alcatraz led to poor health and low morale. During the 1946 riot, Stroud played a role in securing D-block. He was able to communicate with Lieutenant Berger, convincing him there were no arms or mutineers in D-block; thus stopping the bombardment. He also appeared as a witness in the court case that followed. Stroud lost some of his privileges and his health worsened. His kidney problems and gall bladder attacks caused him to be transferred to the prison hospital. Before that transfer, he befriended his cell neighbor, Clarence Carnes, whom he educated in many ways.

By October, 1951, Stroud was in bad shape. He had saved some of the medication given to him for his gall bladder attacks; and with it, tried to take his life. He had it carefully timed, and it was the acute alertness of a guard in

noticing his irregular breathing which saved his life. At that time they found a tube in his stool that contained a will bequeathing his prison manuscripts to a San Francisco attorney. The plan by Stroud was for this to be found in San Francisco during his autopsy — clever.

In January, 1952, he attempted to take his own life in a different way. This time he took a razor blade and cut the artery in the vicinity of the groin. In a letter to Fred Daw, the only non-family member he was allowed to correspond with, he wrote, after the second attempt: "Shortly after writing you, I tried to step out of the picture. There is nothing in the future worth looking forward to."

His biography was published in 1955, and it must have affected him deeply not being able to read it. This book was denied him because it mentions crimes, and the rule prevented anything on crime to reach the Alcatraz library. A pocket book copy was later smuggled in to him by persons unknown.

He was not allowed to exercise in the yard from 1948 to 1958. For eight years in his hospital room, he had no toilet facilities and had to use a bed pan. Warden Madigan finally had a toilet installed. From many bird lovers there was constant pressure on the officials to release him.

On July 12, 1959, Stroud was transported from Alcatraz to the Federal Medical Facility in Springfield, Missouri, ending 43 years in solitary confinement. He was 70 years old at the time. This transfer had a great effect on Stroud, for here, all of a sudden, he was happy and spoke in an uplifting manner: "I am feeling like a million dollars."

During the next three years, Stroud worked as a librarian, book binder, and a leather craftsman. His prison record was without any incident, except for a minor infringement relating to a homosexual advance to another inmate. What did appear to be different is that during this time a lot about Stroud was appearing in print. The movie, "Birdman of Alcatraz," was playing nation-wide, and that was sure to create more publicity for Stroud. Stroud knew this to be the best approach: Keep your name in front of the public and you will have a power base. He was not the only one who knew that. Edward Long, a Democratic Senator from Missouri, made a proposal to the 87th Congress:

Mr. President, during the week of July 15, 1962, the *Washington Post* carried a series of seven articles dealing with Robert Stroud, better-known, perhaps, as "the Birdman of Alcatraz." A movie with the "Birdman" title is currently being shown throughout the country. These articles, appearing in serial form, were written by Eve Edstrow, nationally-known, award-winning writer.

With the movie being shown across the country, undoubtedly we will be asked time and again why this prisoner is still in custody. In order for the entire nation to know of heretofore unpublished facts concerning this convict, I now ask unanimous consent that these articles be printed in the *Record*.

There being no objection, the articles were ordered to be printed in the *Record*. That was on July 25, 1962, just a little more than one year before Stroud's death. All along, the Director of Prisons, James V. Bennett, tried to stop the public exposure of Stroud. He went to great lengths to stop Thomas Gaddis from publishing Stroud's book through Random House, a New York publishing firm. In an effort to stop the movie, he went to the 20th Century Fox executive

HAROLD HECHT Presents BURT LANCASTER in
BIRD MAN OF ALCATRAZ
co-starring KARL MALDEN • THELMA RITTER • NEVILLE BRAND
with EDMOND O'BRIEN as Tom Gaddis
Directed by JOHN FRANKENHEIMER
Produced by STUART MILLAR and GUY TROSPER
A Norma Production • Released thru UNITED ARTISTS

Top right: Metal detector on the way to the industry building
Bottom left: Five inmates left their NR scratched in the cement under a toilet in the industry building.

in Los Angeles. According to the producer, Jack Cummings, Bennett found Stroud "rather dull" and "cunning." On Stroud's accomplishments, the Director of Prisons said, "He amused himself with those canaries." In his own book "I Chose Prison," Bennett quotes Attorney General Biddle, "Stroud loves birds and hates men." It is clear that Bennett did not want the name "Stroud" to go beyond the walls of the system.

Stroud, when he died in Springfield, Missouri on November 21, 1963, ended the longest incarceration of a human being. "I have never had any fear of death, probably because most of my life has been so miserable," wrote Stroud.

It is not exactly clear who labeled George R. Kelly as "Machine Gun" Kelly. Those words ran in all the headlines in 1933 and became the permanent identity of a blue-eyed, round-faced, six-footer. His life could best be described as a collection of public relations images, J. Edgar Hoover, head of the FBI, Kathryn Kelly and the press all taking charge of this man.

Until George Kelly met his wife, he was a small-time, amiable bootlegger in Oklahoma City. He came from a good family and was college-educated. He met Kathryn Shannon in 1927, and married her in 1931. The details of the private influence will never be known, but there is sufficient information available to state that it was Kathryn who made George into the Number One Public Enemy. J. Edgar Hoover understood that and wrote about Kathryn: "Kathryn Thorne Kelly was one of the most coldly deliberate criminals of my experience. Here was a woman who could conceive a kidnapping and force it through to a conclusion largely through the domination over her husband, who, in spite of his terrorizing name, could only bow before her tirades." She was attractive, well-versed in underground affairs and understood the art of promotion. At one time she gave cartridges from her husband's practice firing to people in the underworld bars by saying, "Have a

souvenir of my husband, 'Machine Gun' Kelly."

Kelly, for Hoover, was just what he needed to promote his own cause: the FBI. With this man, he could create a public relations campaign that would give him all the support and funds to run his department. Here was this dangerous machine-gun-carrying gangster who had to be caught at any price to protect the public. This made for good press; and with that name, the public was whipped up to a frenzy.

Kathryn bought him the machine gun and had him practice. It was in her mind that he was going to be the Number One gangster around. He worked his way into small gangs and pulled off some holdups of small banks in Texas and Mississippi. From all evidence, it is fairly clear that the only big crime — that of the kidnapping of Charles F. Urschel in 1933 — was conceived and planned by Kathryn.

On July 22, 1933, two men entered the home of the Urschel family. There they found Mr. and Mrs. Charles F. Urschel playing bridge with Mr. and Mrs. Walter R. Jarrett. The man with the machine gun was Kelly, and the other man with the pistol was Albert Bates. They took Mr. Urschel into hiding and started the process of obtaining ransom moneys. $200,000 in twenty dollar bills was delivered and Urschel was released. Kathryn wanted to "kill the bastard" but was overridden by the others. He was released, and it was his attention to details and his fabulous memory that led the FBI to the hiding place of George and Kathryn Kelly.

Hoover claimed that it was during the capture of George that the expression "G-Men" came to life. According to Hoover, George was in a corner pleading for his life, asking the agents not to shoot: "Don't shoot. G-Men, don't shoot." Later, an officer who was on the scene during the capture states that nothing of that sort had been said by Kelly. This was probably another way Hoover saw to enhance the image of the FBI, or possibly his own position.

Only Los Angeles Newspaper With All Leading News Services—Associated Press, International News, United Press, Dow-Jones

Los Angeles Evening Herald Express
AN INDEPENDENT NEWSPAPER

NIGHT EDITION

Reg. U. S. Pat. Office. Copyright, 1933, by Evening Herald Publishing Company
The Evening Herald and Express Grows Just Like Los Angeles

VOL. LXIII THREE CENTS   Hotels and Trains Five Cents   TUESDAY, SEPTEMBER 26, 1933   Two Sections Section A   THREE CENTS   NO. 158

SEIZE 'MACHINE GUN' KELLY IN RAID

Lamson Is Sentenced to Die on Gallows

'OUTLAW NO. 1' TRAPPED IN MEMPHIS 'HIDEOUT' WITH WIFE, TWO OTHERS

By International News Service

MEMPHIS, Tenn., Sept. 26.—George "Machine Gun" Kelly, America's No. 1 desperado, sought for a series of abductions, bank holdups and massacres that have terrorized the nation, fell into the clutches of the law today.

The man who had sent the organized forces of law of the 48 states and the federal government on the greatest man hunt in history, taunting his pursuers with scornful, threatening letters, surrendered meekly to department of justice agents who trapped him in a Memphis hideout.

'CRIMINAL OF CENTURY'

Here is George "Machine Gun" Kelly, notorious "criminal of the century," who was captured today in Memphis, Tenn., as a result of a great manhunt extending into 43 states. The desperado received his nickname from the fact that he always had a machine gun with him. But when he faced the muzzles of his captors' shotguns, his bravado wilted. The "arsenal" shown here was seized with the capture of Harvey Bailey, Kelly's pal. A sub-machine gun such as is pictured was found in Kelly's "hideout."

George "Machine Gun" Kelly arrived on Alcatraz on September 4, 1934. The other men involved with him, Albert Bates and Harvey Baily, came with him to Alcatraz. On Alcatraz, Kelly became an altar boy, worked in the industries offices, tended to business and gave no trouble to the authorities. The warden felt that he had never expressed shame and embarrassment to his family. "Yes, Warden, a very good person (referring to a family member), my people are good people, even if I turned out to be an awful heel."

Some people who talked to Kelly felt he was glad to be away from his wife. Kelly found a way to relate his feelings about Alcatraz in a letter to the director of prisons, Bennett. He wrote: "Maybe you have asked yourself, how can a man of even ordinary intelligence put up with this kind of life at Alcatraz? What is this life of mine like? To begin with, these five words seem written in fire on the walls of my cell — NOTHING CAN BE WORTH THIS. No one knows what it is like to suffer from the intellectual apathy, the pernicious mental scurvy, that come of long privation of all that makes life real. A prisoner cannot help being daunted by a vision of life as it used to be and at such times I pay, with a sense of delicious melancholy, my tribute to life as it once was."

215

Clarence Carnes

Kelly was very articulate and would express himself with well-chosen words. On one occasion, as he was standing in front of the new warden, he said about Alcatraz, "The people in Washington have kept a bunch of us here to make a justification for the place. . . When people ask 'Why do you need this fortress?' they can say, 'We've got Kelly out there, or we've got so-and-so!' " He did not consider himself a big shot, as he told the warden in 1949, "I hope you've got me wrong, Warden. I don't think I am a big shot, and I don't try to be one. But I know it's easier for the other person to see us as we are, and all of us appreciate good advice." That statement was in response to a warning that he should not try to help so many inmates with advice. Kelly was transferred to Leavenworth and died three years later of a heart attack. His wife, in a letter after her conviction, gives insight into his character and her own: "There is no bitterness or animosity in my heart toward anyone but the perpetrators of the terrible crime who dragged an honored, honest, respected family down into the depths of blackest despair. My mother ever has been a good, Christian, law-abiding citizen, and my love and marriage to a gangster plunged my family into bitter tragedy through their innocent, hospitable trust and faith in my husband."

Not all inmates on Alcatraz fell into the Public Enemy Number One category. Especially in later years, we find many inmates of lesser notoriety. For many of the country's wardens, Alcatraz became a tool to control their own population. Should an inmate not behave, he could be sent to "the Rock." Alcatraz, at times, became the dumping ground for the unwanted, not only inmates, but employees, too. The latter is a hard thing to prove, but many felt that they were sent to Alcatraz for personality reasons. Many guards considered working on "the Rock" as a status symbol. They then became Number One in the system, the toughest. Anybody who was on "the Rock" gained in stature in his peer group. Most inmates went from Alcatraz to other prisons and, after their arrival, carried a certain status. For some, it worked to their advantage; for others, it was a disadvantage. This disadvantage would create a stigma that could never be disregarded.

One could write much about every individual who spent time on "the Rock." Here is not the place, so only a few colorful characters are mentioned, and that just to give some insight into life on "the Rock."

The youngest inmate sent to "the Rock" was a Choctaw Indian by the name of Clarence Victor Carnes. His nicknames were "the Kid" and "Joe." The name "Joe" was given to him by a group of kids he went to the movies with. They saw a movie with Joe E. Brown putting a whole apple in his mouth. Carnes did the same and got the name "Joe" from the actor. Another version — at least from Alcatraz — is that all Indians were called "Joe," so they gave him the name.

Carnes was born in 1927 in the hills of Eastern Oklahoma. His father wanted him to go to school and sent him to the Jones Academy for Boys. At that school young Carnes associated with boys who exposed him to stealing and being the tough boy. For Carnes, this was the start of a long list of small thefts that eventually led to a gas station hold-up. He was 15 and, with his friend, Cecil Berry, attempted to hold up a gas station in Atoka, Oklahoma. The attendant, W. M. Weyland, saw the gun in Carnes' hand and attacked him with a coke bottle. The gun went off and Weyland was dead. Carnes was captured, jumped the jailer, stole a revolver and escaped. He was again captured and, on October 26, 1943, after pleading guilty, was sent to life imprisonment. After leaving a work gang and traveling across state lines with a farmer, whose car he had stolen, he received an additional 99-year sentence for kidnapping. This law was called "the Lindberg Act," and came after the well-publicized kidnapping of the child of Charles Lindberg.

Carnes, because he was a dicipline problem and escape risk in Leavenworth, was sent to Alcatraz on July 6, 1945. He was only 18 at the time and, therefore, the youngest inmate on Alcatraz. His number at Alcatraz was AZ 714. One year later, on May 2, 1946, Carnes was part of an escape attempt from "the Rock," which is now known as the '46 Riot. It was his friendship with Bernard Coy that supposedly got him involved.

He was not sent to the gas chamber for his involvement in the '46 Riot because he spared the lives of some captured officers. The details of what happened are only as accurate as to what was said in court. He was sent to life imprisonment and returned to solitary on Alcatraz. He made friends with Robert Stroud and was taught by him to play chess. Carnes was the chess champion for several years on "the Rock."

In the recreation yard he played on the big court, and that meant he was one of the better players. He had friends

Clarence Carnes with author
in San Francisco, 11/30/1980

and related well. His favorite way to get some information out or to someone else was by passing it to the chaplain during a handshake. This method was used extensively during his time in isolation. His personal, most precious possession was a family picture. His father visited him until the feelings changed, and then it was just letter writing. His sister wrote him regularly.

Carnes is the only surviving member of the '46 Riot, and that has brought him some fame. A TV movie was made of his life on "the Rock," and for a while he was on the pier in San Francisco, signing autographs. Many people would look at him and ask him the same questions over and over. His health is fading and he has to battle constantly the desire to drink. He is free now and living in Missouri. He spent the major portion of his life behind bars and he says, "I am very lonely out here — don't know anybody inside. Knew lots of people. It's hard." (Not to speak of the people who constantly try to exploit him.)

217

July 21 - 1939

Roy Gardner

Another big name associated with Alcatraz is that of Roy Gardner. He was called the last of the lone bandits of the Old West, the 20th Century Jesse James. Stealing a watch at 16 marked the beginning of his long career as a criminal. He served a term at San Quentin for stealing jewelry before he started smuggling munitions to the Mexican rebel, Carranza. He was caught red-handed and was sentenced to die before the firing squad. He escaped the closely-guarded jail and fled back to the United States.

Mail theft was his next venture, and it brought him a 20-year sentence in 1920. He never got to jail; he escaped en route. While loose, he held up a train and got an additional 25 year term. Again, en route, he escaped. Not until June of 1921 was he captured and sent to McNeil Island, where he broke out during a Labor Day ball game. He reached the mainland by stealing a boat. He was wounded, but managed to flee to Arizona, where he held up two more mail coaches. During the second hold-up, the mail clerk, with help, overpowered Gardner. He got 25 more years and was sent to Atlanta. A repeated rule violator, he had a stormy time and went on a hunger strike three times. In 1927 he tried to saw his way out; and in 1928 he tried to blast his way out, with the captain as his hostage.

The last hunger strike got him sent to St. Elizabeth's Hospital in Washington, D.C., for a mental examination. The reports show him as a trustworthy inmate after he arrived in the Leavenworth Annex in January of 1930. He was sent to Alcatraz in 1934 at his own request. The reason was to be closer to his family.

On Alcatraz there were some who wanted to poison him. He was called a snitch among the inmates, and that was sufficient for the call to go out to kill him.

His stay on Alcatraz was short, but left a solid impression. He was sent to Leavenworth just two years after arriving on Alcatraz. His wife had divorced him and remarried. He tried a number of ventures, none of which panned out. He wrote a pamphlet about his stay on "the Rock" and its effect on him. He called it "Hellcatraz." During the San Francisco World's Fair, he worked a booth, "Crime Doesn't Pay."

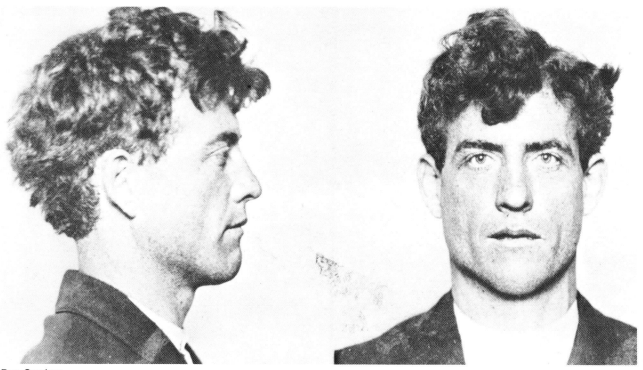

Roy Gardner

F.B.I. "Wanted" flier for Alvin Karpis.

In January of 1940, in a hotel room, Roy Gardner took his own life. By inhaling cyanide fumes in the room where he left his final note, he, himself, ended the Roy Gardner saga. The note had the following passages in it: "I hold no malice toward any human being, and I hope those whom I have wronged will forgive for I am old and tired and don't care to continue the struggle. Please let me down as lightly as possible." The note on the door read: "Do not open this door. Poison gas — call police."

A notorious gangster of the 1930's was Alvin Karpis. In the twenty years before his big crime he had to his credit fifteen bank robberies, two kidnappings, four murders and three jail breaks — a Public Enemy Number One.

Karpis at one time told Hoover to "come catch me if you can." Today that statement creates a lot of questions as to exactly what happened in the final arrest. The official version was that Hoover arrested Karpis and put the handcuffs on him. Hoover wrote: "We closed in swiftly. The wrists of Alvin Karpis were in handcuffs before he could even whirl for his gun." On the other hand, Karpis tells of mass confusion and that nobody even had handcuffs, so they finally used a necktie to tie his hands. Hoover may have directed the arrest, but even at that it is reported that only after many agents had caught Karpis, he emerged from a dark alley. A car pulled up and left with Karpis in the middle of the front seat. In the back seat was Hoover with Clyde Tolson and Connie. Karpis states, "The most obvious flaw in the FBI story, though, lies in Hoover's own character. He didn't lead the attack on me. He hid until I was safely covered by many guns. He waited until he was told the

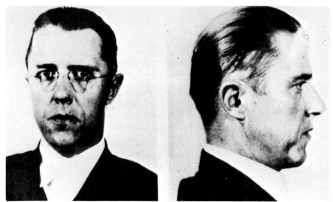

Alvin Karpis

coast was clear. Then he came out to reap the glory. The story of Hoover the Hero is false."

Who used whom the most is hard to tell, but today it is clear both used each other. Hoover's personal courage was under attack in 1936. The FBI operation was in danger and under attack by Congress. The only thing Hoover could do was use a case to get the headlines and create an impression on Congress that would allow the FBI to prosper. Karpis' case was the one and, as Karpis wrote: "I *made* that son-of-a-bitch"; but it was Hoover who told the world he had personally captured Karpis.

Karpis was born in Montreal, Canada, in 1908. At ten he had already stolen a gun. At eighteen he escaped from a reformatory in Kansas. The list of his crimes is long and varied: from bank robbing to murder to kidnapping. After three jail breaks he was sent to Alcatraz on August 6, 1936. His nickname given to him by FBI officials was "Creepy Karpis." His first name on "the Rock" was "Rat."

He was a medium-sized man, about one hundred and forty pounds, with a smooth way. At first he did a lot of bragging on "the Rock." He told a story that included a partner. At a later date that partner was sent to Alcatraz and told a different story. Karpis became the laughing-stock of the entire prison. One inmate told of his constant fistfights: "He was very belligerent and quarrelsome, which naturally resulted in fistfights."

Karpis was a member of the famous Ma Barker's Ozark Gang, and with that had the attention of Al Capone. Karpis, during an interview for a story on Capone's life, said, "Capone was a wonderful person . . . a real man . . . he always knew when we hit town and where we stayed, but he never tipped off the cops." On Alcatraz he had a chance to meet Capone, and the story is that Capone sent for him in the yard. Capone's reason was to gather information from the outside. The inside story on "the Rock" was that it was

Karpis who put up Jimmy Lucas to kill Al Capone.

An inmate at that time recalls, "Old 'Creepy' came to "the Rock" with a lot of national publicity hanging all over him, like decorations on a Christmas tree. He was a big shot, and he didn't want no one to forget it. 'Creepy' had the mind of a ten-year-old kid, and still has. I wouldn't trust 'Old Creepy' as far as a kid could throw him."

Karpis did manage, after 25 years on Alcatraz, to get a transfer to McNeil Island. He finished his sentence without an incident at McNeil, and this is probably due to the fact that he had a "friend" in the Warden. Warden Madigan had been the Warden on Alcatraz and supposedly helped Karpis get a parole opportunity. From McNeil Island he was deported to Canada. Karpis said about Alcatraz, "Alcatraz was the greatest fraud put on the American people. The American people were fooled. It was a bad place."

Karpis has two books to his credit, and the money from one of the books enabled him to move to Spain where he died in 1979.

Not all the Alcatraz inmates could rank as the Number One Public Enemy. To write about all the inmates on Alcatraz would be an immense task, to be reserved for a future publication. Most of the inmates were bank robbers, kidnappers and murderers, but many were not. There were some political prisoners with very small offenses and others who did not fit into the idea of an end-of-the-line prison. Why they were on "the Rock" is subject to speculation, and would require a lot of difficult research.

Mickey Cohen, a racketeer, was sent to Alcatraz for income tax evasion. William Cook, a 24-year-old mass murderer serving a 300-year sentence, served one year on Alcatraz before he was executed. Harmon Metz Waley was on Alcatraz serving forty-five years for the Wyerhause kidnapping. His partners Bill Dainard (alias Mahan), Herb Former, Fritz Malla and Gus Galates were involved in the

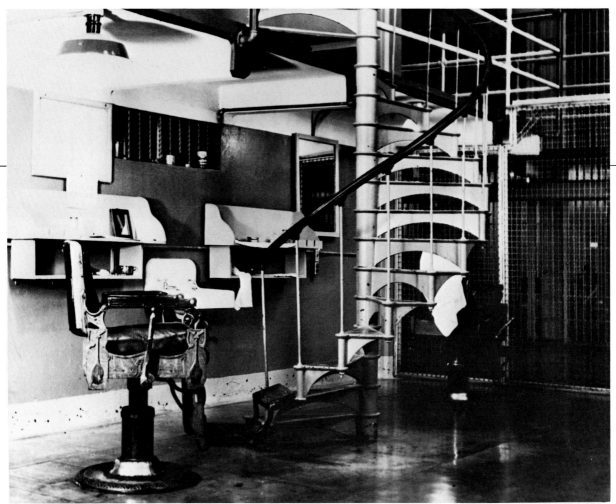

Barber shop in the late 30's.

Barber shop after close of Alcatraz

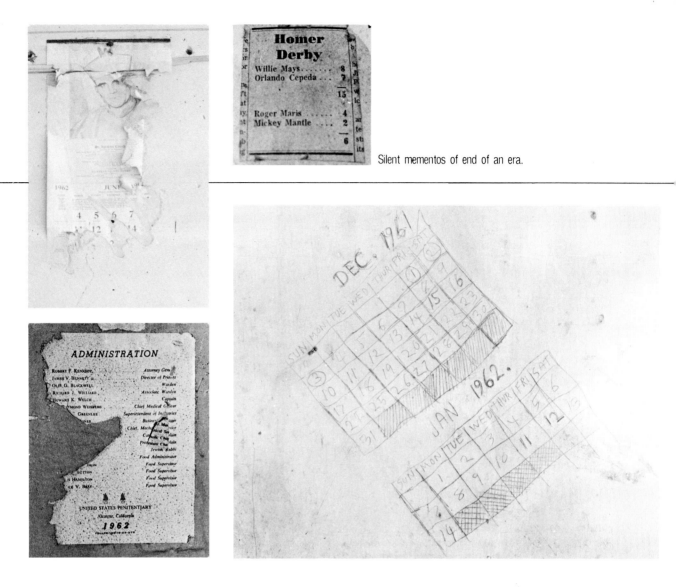

Silent mementos of end of an era.

Kansas City Massacre. Others serving time on Alcatraz were Sammy, Harry and Louise Fleisher, accused members of the famed Detroit Purple Gang; Floyd Hamilton of the Bonnie and Clyde outfit; John Paul Chase, partner of "Baby Face" Nelson; Mortay Sobell of the famous Rosenburge Spy Case. And the list goes on and on. "What a snake pit!" recalls a former inmate of "the Rock."

The effect Alcatraz had on these men will never be fully known. We have just a few testimonies or views on these stories, but it is so varied that no firm conclusion can be drawn at this time. There is an extensive study being conducted at this time, addressing itself to the question of the effect Alcatraz had on these men.

As mentioned before, the rumors of Alcatraz closing were constant, and when it came to be true, must have shocked everybody. But by this time, in 1963, the process of scaling down in preparation for closure became a reality.

Today it is widely accepted that the decision to close Alcatraz was based on two points. First and foremost: the cost of upgrading, maintaining and running Alcatraz weighed in favor of closing "the Rock." The estimate was $5,000,000 just to bring the buildings up to standard. The salt water and winds, combined with the constant moisture, caused the concrete to become brittle. Attention to that fact

was drawn to the public by the escape of the Anglin brothers.

The cost of maintaining the standard set forth at its inception was now running way ahead of any other institution. Alcatraz, by the government's own admission, was costing $13.79 a day to maintain each inmate, with only about four cents going toward his rehabilitation. This was compared with $5.37 spent for maintaining inmates at other federal prisons that had large rehabilitation facilities. Senator William Larger observed that: "It costs as much to house a man in Alcatraz as it would in the Waldorf-Astoria" ("Waldorf-Astoria" — the status hotel in New York during the 40's to 60's).

The second factor was that of a general feeling toward the rehabilitation of inmates rather than the fostering of the isolation concept.

Alcatraz was being phased out as a federal prison. Men were being transferred, personnel being reassigned, and this time "the rumor" became a fact. At 10:45 a.m., on March 21, 1963, the last 27 prisoners left "the Rock." The Press had been invited, and the 50 members of the Press Corps were clicking and writing away in the final attempt of capturing the historic moment: the closing of Alcatraz.

It was decided during the phase-out period to have the Press on "the Rock" for the final departure. According to

222

Top right: A collection of assorted contraband
planned for use in escape attempts.
Bottom right: Last prisoners leaving Alcatraz.

the Bureau of Prisons, they were swamped with requests by the media for a chance to document this event. Invitations were sent out to the Press; and on March 21, 1963, they were greeted on the mainland and then ferried to Alcatraz for a tour.

Several days before the closing, personnel from Washington came to help close "the Rock." The deputy director of prisons, Fred T. Wilkinson, took the time to talk to the remaining inmates. By now they knew that Alcatraz was closing, and their concerns varied, but again, permit us an insight into their thinking: "Can I make it in a big house with 2,500 people milling around and where the young troublemakers are?" "Will I have a single cell?" "Can I be able to make the right field on the baseball team?" "Do they have these Muslims there?" One inmate wanted to be the last man on Alcatraz, so he kept "bugging" Warden Blackwell with his wish. He did not get his request. Jack Rosenthal was the assistant director of the Press Information Office of the Department of Justice, and was by fielding questions from the Press Corps.

In a way, it all seemed a production. As the Press was touring the prison, the remaining prisoners were gathered to be paraded down Broadway, to be loaded on the boat that would take them to Fort Natham, to be sent in various directions. Some went to Atlanta, Leavenworth, Kansas, McNeil Island, Washington, and Lewisburg, Pennsylvania. One woman among the Press Corps recalls, "It was like something of medieval times. These men shuffling down the corridor in their leg irons. The sound was what I remember the most, a silence, but a strange sound from the shackles. Strange feeling."

The media members had been guided to the mess hall, given some coffee and doughnuts, and were told that this was "it" for Alcatraz. The Deputy Director of the Bureau of Prisons recalls, "At approximately 9:15 I announced to them that we had prepared the last 27 men of Alcatraz for immediate departure and that they would leave the island later that morning. There was a wild scramble to reach the telephones and other communication devices. We had thoughtfully closed off all telephones and the radio was enclosed in the control room, so this provided equal opportunity for all, rather than permitting some to score a beat." There was a security concern, too, and that concern centered on the possibility of the docks being invaded by people who would have heard or read the news, thus making it difficult to load the prisoners onto the buses.

A dramatic visualization of the end was the moment when the last tower guard asked for permission to abandon his post. Senior officer Gordon Gronzo lowered his

weapon, glanced at the boat leaving with the last inmates, waved to the associate warden, Dick Williard, to acknowledge his abandoning of the tower and descended for the last time. From the boats passing by, the view of an empty tower must have been surprising. But soon the world knew that Alcatraz stood empty of inmates. It was over. And even though the powerful chairman of the House Committee on Appropriations, Clarence Cannon, objected, the orders to close Alcatraz as a prison by Attorney General Robert F. Kennedy stood.

The words of the Deputy Director of the Bureau of Prisons, who was on hand for the closing, sum up the views of the officials in charge: "From the first 34 military prisoners received, and through the years, Alcatraz contained all manner of serious and violent offenders, helping, yet controlling them for the protection of society. I feel the task has been well fulfilled. It remains for history to make a more critical and discerning evaluation as time passes. I know the employees who worked there so unswervingly through many years under trying conditions will have many poignant moments in memory of Alcatraz."

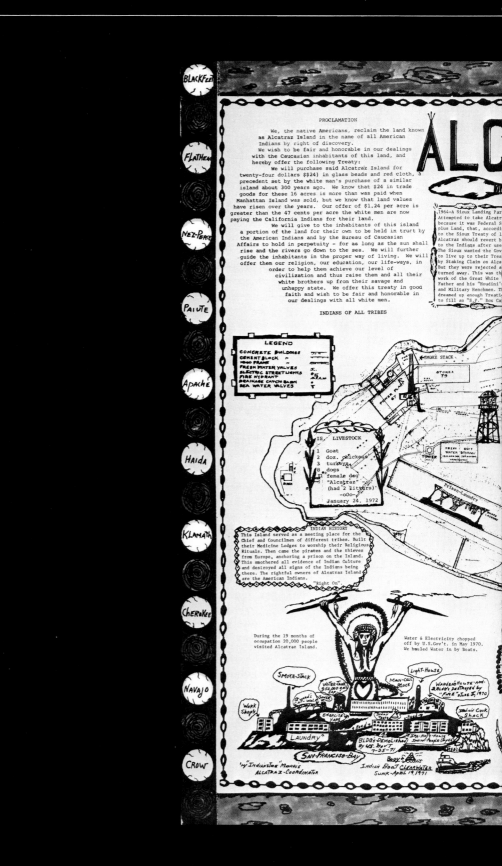

TRAZ INDIAN LAND

First Landing, November 14, 1969
Liberated on November 20, 1969
The "rip-off"--when Alcatraz
fell back into the hands of the
"Feds"--was June 11, 1971.

Credence Clearwater Revival
donated $15,000. We spent
$4600 for "Bass Tub I." Changed
the name to "Clearwater" on
July 25, 1970. Sank in launch
landing April 19, 1971.

Water Barge stolen by U.S.
Government, May 27, 1970

Indian recreation Bldy. 65
Burned-Aug 15, 1970

000 Gals. Water
lost during the
fire June 1, 1970;
due to broken water pipes

ALCATRAZ-I.S. PRNT-U
MAY 5.

Indio-Residents
"Crash-Pad's"

RECREATION GROUND

ALCATRAZ ISLAND BLUEPRINT # 2

Main-Cell-Block

TOWER

Island
Teepee

Light-House-Tower

"Fire" Destroyed Wardens Mansion
Bldy. 76 Doctors House Bldy. 7
gutted the light House-June 1, 1970

Indian
shack

APARTMENTS "A"

Fire Have
APARTMENTS
"Crash-Pad's"

S.S. Indian Hope
Searching-For-A-Short
Route-to-U.S. Indian
Land Claims, & Broken
Treaties-Dept.

BLACKFEET-SHIELD

ALCATRAZ
was just a start,
a squeeze-play to bring
you a point, enlighten-
ing the people of this country to the mistreatment the
Indian People have received, and
their valiant struggle for recognition. Non-Indian People should
assist us in preserving our Language and Culture, and in seeing
that the Indians receive justice
in the high courts in our fight
for our ancestral lands and
fishing rights, and Right
to Breathe!!!!!!!!!
"Right On!"

ALCATRAZ RECEIVING DEPOT
INDIANS OF ALL TRIBES
PIER 40, EMBARCADERO

HONEST PEOPLE
AMERICAN INDIANS

S: North American
South American
E: To enlighten the American
People of the Injustice done
to the American Indian by steal-
ing their land by Phony
Treaties.

Indian Joe Morris
Mainland Coordinator

DONATIONS

JANE PONDA - 8 portable
Honda generators and a
rototiller - May 1970

UNITARIAN CHURCH - 2½ T diesel
generator - 80 kw - Oct. 1970

Fuel Tank

JOHN TATE - 75 kw
air-cooled diesel, Dec.
1970

A SHORT HISTORY OF THE ISLAND AND PRISON,
ALCATRAZ

In 1775, Lt. Jacon Manuel de Ayala of San Carlos
sailed into San Francisco Bay. The Lieutenant named
the island Isla de los Alcatra, the Isle of the
Pelicans, and it remained practically undisturbed as a
bird refuge until 1846.

Pio Rico, the last Mexican governor of California
sold Alcatraz to Julian Workman. It was then resold to
Gen. John C. Fremont, a representative of the Federal
government, for $5,000. Fortification of the island by
the Federal government began in 1854.

In 1869 Alcatraz was a disciplinary barracks. In
the early 1870s Indian prisoners were sent there. Among
them were Lieutenants of Geronimo, the Apache who fought
from the Southwest.

Between 1854 and 1882 the government spent $1,697,
500 for guns and ammunition storage caves on Alcatraz.

The island continued to serve as a prison, mainly
for the military. It was designated a civilian prison in
1934. There, mobsters and gangsters were housed, among
them, Al Capone,' a Chicago hood.

Alcatraz was finally closed in early 1963; and
became surplus.

by "Indian Joe"
Morris

Mojave

Sioux

Hoppe

Miwok

Seneca

Modoc

Hoopa

UTE

Pawnee

TLingit

ALCATRAZ AND THE INDIANS

View of San Francisco from deteriorating Alcatraz

"The Rock" now stood alone against the elements: fog, wind, salt water and time. Man had left. A $24,000-a-year, rusting and molding albatross was around the neck of the U.S. General Services Administration (GSA) which was in charge of maintaining Alcatraz until the government decided what to do with the island. The helicopter pilot of San Francisco Radio Station KGO flew over the island daily to drop the newspaper for John and Marie Hart. The Harts, with Bill Doherty, were the caretakers of the island.

The public during that time viewed Alcatraz from a distance and, probably, with some relief. But from the time of closing,, various proposals came to the attention to those in charge. A gambling casino, museum of art, wax museum, and many other proposals for some form of tourism were considered.

On August 3, 1964, a presidential commission recommended that a peace monument be built on Alcatraz to direct world attention to the city which was the 1945 birthplace of the United Nations. This never became a reality.

Federal agencies were screened to find out if any would be interested in Alcatraz. None was. And so Alcatraz, on April 12, 1963, was officially accepted by the General Services Administration from the Department of Justice. The presidential commission met on the island on March 24, 1964, to determine the future of "the Rock."

On March 27, 1964, five Sioux Indians filed a claim for Alcatraz. The five were Walter Means, Allen Cottier, Martin Martinez, Richard D. P. McKenzie, and Garfield Spotted

Elk. These urban Sioux had occupied Alcatraz for several hours on March 8th. This claim was dismissed by the U.S. Attorney General as being without legal foundation. This same point would in a couple of years play an important role in the events on Alcatraz.

The General Services Administration assumed custody of Alcatraz in July of 1964. Again, the claim of Richard McKenzie in September of 1965 brought into focus the legal contention for Alcatraz. This suit, like the previous claim, was dismissed for lack of prosecution. The public was aware of this action, but did not really take note, especially since it lingered in the courts until July, 1968.

This situation changed rapidly when the City of San Francisco showed an interest in the island. The city wanted to use it for a park and recreation center. Ideas were solicited from the public, and many ideas kept coming in. Some wanted to keep the prison; some wanted it removed, some wanted gambling casinos, hotels, etc. There were all kinds of ideas. The most serious consideration was given to a plan by the oil millionaire, Lamar Hunt. His proposal offered the preservation of the current prison, the establishment of an 1890-flavor village theatre with galleries and restaurants. Hunt included in his proposal a 364-foot tower with a replica of the Apollo Space Capsule.

The commission accepted Hunt's ideas. This act so outraged a local citizen that he formed a campaign to "Save Alcatraz." Alvin Duskin, a dress designer, took out a full-page ad in a leading San Francisco newspaper. The ad made it clear that Hunt's idea was totally unacceptable and that the creation of a 1890 village was absurd and "that idea is in a league with plastic redwood trees." The ad headline read: "As Big a Deal as Manhattan Island." This ad generated 8,000 responses within four days. The momentum was with Duskin and, since it was an election year, some members of the committee changed their vote and the proposal was tabled for reconsideration at a later date.

This attention towards Alcatraz brought back the notion by a descendant of a pioneer California family, the Workmans. William T. Workman wanted to find a lawyer who would take on the case of his grandfather and restore the claim to his family for the Island of Alcatraz. The deed or grant has disappeared, but he was convinced it could be found in the Contra Costa records. Nothing came of this claim.

The claim for Alcatraz by the Indians was not such a silent matter. During the night of November 9-10, four Indians attempted to land on Alcatraz. They were not successful, but returned with 10 more Indians and did land

Oraibi prisoners at Alcatraz, confined on "the Rock" since January 3, 1895 with chief Lo-ma-hung-yo-ma in the center. Back row, left to right: Unidentified, Polingyouma, Hahvema, Masatewa, Quoyahoinema. Center row, left to right: Kochventewa, Beephongva(?), Poolegoiva, Chief Lomahongyoma, Lomanankwosa, Uochadah, Wongnehma. Front row, left to right: Komaletstews, Yoda, Nagvatewa, Kochyouma, Soukhongua, Sekaheptewa, Karshongnewa.

on the island. The following day, T. E. Harmon, Regional Administrator of GSA, managed to leave the island with the Indians. All was quiet for the next ten days.

The statement that appears all over the place asserting that the Indians were on the island before the white man is at this time totally unfounded. No evidence of such action can be found. In the early days of Alcatraz we do have evidence of Indians being held captive on "the Rock."

To reconstruct the history of those who were shipped to Alcatraz would demand a lengthy research into some very incomplete archives and records. The military on Alcatraz, as on any fort, had to provide the government with a monthly report. This monthly report accounted for the personnel at the fort and their condition. In the 1870's, much activity took place between the U.S. soldiers and the American Indians. To track down exactly all that happened in those years would be a task almost impossible for any one scholar and would not be appropriate for this text.

The first entry of any Indians on Alcatraz came in 1873 with the mentioning of Guiwhatanava, a Mualpai Apache Mohave chief. He was sent from the Department of Arizona and was delivered on Alcatraz by Lieutenant W. Fleming of the 12th Infantry on May 18, 1873, for safekeeping. The records of the keeping or releasing of Indians were not kept complete. In this case we do have the information that he was released to this tribe on October 25, 1873.

President Ulysses Grant commuted the death sentence of two Modoc Indians to life imprisonment at Fort Alcatraz. The official records indicate that on October 24, 1873, the Provost Guard delivered Barncho (Boncho) and Slolock, two Modoc Indians from Fort Klamath to Alcatraz.

The tribe they belonged to lived in Lake County on the border of Oregon and California. There was no war between them and the white men, but with settlers moving in, the mood changed. Soon the military set out to drive the Indians north to the Klamath Reservation. The Indian camp

227

421-F-15 26 (30a)
Copy Neg #22,490

Knch-i-wentiwa is one of the hostiles. A few years ago matters come to such a pass that the Conservative Element, (which was the stronger) said to the liberal Element: You have forsaken the gods of your fathers, you are no longer Mokis. You can hereafter have no land, & we will have no dealings with you." This taking away of their land, brought down upon the Conservatives the anger of the government, & Major Williams, the agent, took up a troop of soldiers, arrested nineteen of the ringleaders and sent them to Alcatraz Island as prisoners. There they were kept for several months, & then allowed to return. The feeling still continues though it is not openly displayed

was shot up and the few survivors, 52 braves, 150 women, children and old men, took to the lava beds, between Siskiyou and Modoc Counties. They set themselves up in a 50-square-mile area and fought. No soldier saw an Indian, but 38 soldiers lay dead and the Indians gained 150 horses, mules, Army rifles and plenty of ammunition.

Captain Jack, the Modoc chief, wanted peace with the government, and so did the government. Major General E. R. S. Canby was chosen to head the discussions. The sub-chieftain did not want peace and accused their chief of falling for the white man's tricks. After a long debate among themselves, the chief reportedly said, "It shall be as you wish. We shall make war."

There was a meeting between Captain Jack, the Modoc

chief, and General Canby. Captain Jack wanted Hot Creek as their home. General Canby said he could make no deal until the Indians surrendered. The chief gave a signal, and Boncho and Slolock burst into the tent and shot at the members present, and Captain Jack shot the general between the eyes.

They fled to the lava beds, where they fought a tough battle but, eventually, outnumbered and hungry, they were overpowered. Captain Jack and three sub-chieftains were hanged. Alcatraz became the home for Boncho and Slolock. On May 26, 1875, Boncho died of consumption, and Slolock was released in 1877. No details are available on the military report.

The Piute chief, Nutchez, was released from Fort

ATop left: Keint-poos, the Modoc chief called "Captain Jack."
Bottom right: Word "Free" painted into U.S. flag by Indian occupying Alcatraz.

Government personnel, at that time of Indian wars, did not feel the Indians needed to be accounted for; and for several Indians, that meant the total disappearance of their history. No records, unmarked graves and a terrible attitude toward the native Americans permitted a great gap to exist, even on a small place such as Fort Alcatraz.

At least one fact is sure, and that is that the white man never took the Island of Alcatraz away from anybody living on it. In 1969, the issue of surplus government property was at the core of the Indian occupation of Alcatraz, and the island did have people living on it. So, from a technical standpoint, the island was not abandoned.

At approximately 2:00 a.m., on November 20, 1969, the Indians returned to Alcatraz. The exact number is not quite clear, but a figure often used is that between 80-100 Indians arrived on Alcatraz. They were determined to stay. They called themselves "Indians of All Tribes," and immediately handed out press releases with their intentions, demands and conditions.

The spokesman for the group was Richard Oakes. He was very clear on what he wanted, and the list was handed to the officials. The purpose of the occupation was to gain a center for Native American Studies, American Indian Spiritual Center, Indian Center of Ecology, Indian Training

Alcatraz after having been there for only twelve days. He was received from Winnemucca, Nevada, on January 30, 1874, and released by orders of the Commanding General of the Military Division on February 11, 1874.

The largest shipment of Indians to Fort Alcatraz must be the 19 Mogui Hopi who arrived on January 3, 1875. There was a letter of instruction sent from Washington, D.C., on December 26, 1894, ordering the safekeeping of these Indians. On September 19, 1895, orders arrived requesting their transfer to Fort Defiance, Arizona. On September 23, 1895, these Indians left Fort Alcatraz.

A report to the Commission of Indian Affairs by Captain Constant Williams gives us a brief insight regarding the 19 Indians: "The troubles at Oraibi resulted from the disposition on the part of the hostiles to drive the friendlies from their fields. In the fall they drove the friendlies from the fields at Moencopi, and in the spring threatened to do the same thing at Oraibi. Nineteen ringleaders were arrested by U.S. troops and sent to Alcatraz Island, in San Francisco Harbor. This action settled the question, at least for the present."

The complete documentation of the Indians kept on Alcatraz probably will never come to light. The U.S.

Top left: Grace Thorpe on Alcatraz. Bottom left: Indian graffiti on Alcatraz. Bottom right: A Sioux Indian on his way to Alcatraz.

School and American Indian Museum. The following document was their explanation as to why they took "the Rock":

11/20/69

To Whom It May Concern:

We, the members of the Indian Nations and tribes of North America, in an attempt to secure this island; in our attempt at asserting our cultural heritage; in establishing on this island an Institute responsive to the religious diversity of this Indian Nation, in the creation of a viable program of higher education serviceable to the needs of the Indian people; respectfully solicit your cooperation and expertise.

Indian people are desperately in need of self-assertion for their way of life and their desperate needs, both economic and political. The move to Alcatraz symbolizes what American Indians can get with mind power.

We are asking you to give back our honor and we won't need jails; give Indians a chance to come up and not have to stand behind any more.

We have been in this land for thousands of years.

After a hundred years as prisoners of this country, we feel that it is time we were free. We have gone to Alcatraz Island to preserve our dignity and beauty and to assert our position with the new weapons we have come to learn how to use. These weapons are the same ones these invaders of our country used to take what they wanted.

These weapons are the laws and the lawyers, and the power of the pen to tell our real story.

But, in addition, we now have a more powerful weapon. The people of this country know a little of the real history and tragedy of the Indian people. What they do not know is the tragic story of the Indian people today. We intend to tell them that story.

Stella Leach, a licensed vocational nurse, came to Alcatraz at the beginning of the Indian occupation, to be the nurse. She set up the first medical clinic on Alcatraz for the Indians in the former hospital cell of Robert Stroud. Later they moved it to the old doctors' cottage which had electricity. In a speech, Stella clearly formulated the beginning of the occupation: "Why Alcatraz? Alcatraz, at the time of the invasion, had gained national publicity, due to the fact that all of the developers in the country were fighting over Alcatraz. They wanted to build a Disney-like creation out there. They wanted to build a tourist trap. They wanted to build various things on Alcatraz. But no one ever thought of preserving the beauty of Alcatraz. So we knew that within a couple of days Hunt was to gain control of Alcatraz, because the San Francisco city fathers were being approached; and, of course, as you know, most of these people have a price. And I think they were being able to name their price. We were afraid that Alcatraz was going to go down the drain. The students had discussed Alcatraz since the previous May, so they decided that they would

Top left: Indian writing on a cell wall. Bottom right: Indian children on Alcatraz. Note writing on wall made by the Indians.

take Alcatraz at that time; and this would stop the ecological disaster of a tourist-trapism-type thing on Alcatraz. So it was done on the spur of the moment, without too much planning, and perhaps that's why it was successful." Her statement demonstrates the depth of some of the concerns and frustrations involved in the Indians' stand on Alcatraz.

After the initial novelty of the occupation, the realities had to be dealt with. While the politics and dealing went on, the structure for the day-to-day life needed formulation. The children needed schooling, so schools were organized. A leadership structure needed to be created to run the affairs of this new Alcatraz community. A council-like government had been set up. Security and law and order was the concern of all, so there was created an Alcatraz "Police Force," which even had special jackets with a tee-pee design and the words "Alcatraz Security" hand-lettered in red paint on it. Intoxication was discouraged and liquor was officially banned from the island. There were, however, a lot of problems with intoxication and drugs reported throughout the occupation.

There was a lack of strong, organized leadership on Alcatraz. Several groups wanted to take power but none could muster enough support. Many came forward to claim leadership, appeared in front of the TV cameras and press, and then disappeared in the crowd.

There was very strong, sympathetic support by the people for the initial Indian cause on Alcatraz. Food supplies and needed materials of all sorts were delivered to the Indians. John Trudell, a member of the Indian Council, expressed on many occasions that what they really wanted was the help of the grass-roots Indians. "Support from the Indians is what we want. There are different kinds of support from different Indians. Some reservation Indians can't actively come out and support us because of the B.I.A. (Bureau of Indian Affairs) . . . Chicanos and others should always look out for their own needs first, because that's what we're doing. Be honest about it, Indians . . . we're

looking out for Indians first." Many groups felt they could get on the bandwagon. The Hell's Angels motorcycle riders, for instance, gave their support and organized a party in Oakland for the Indians. Some council members objected to their involvement.

The Black Panthers offered help, with movies and medicine. In the publication of the Black Panther organization the cry for help was printed. The Black Panthers brought 500 blankets. Money ($2,500.00) from the Jewish Women's Organization was received. First United Church of San Francisco donated a 30-kilowatt generator, and a second generator was donated by the United Automobile Workers. Restaurant owners supplied turkeys during Thanksgiving. A Chicano, who sneaked in with a boatload of food, lost his hand in the process of helping the Native Americans unload this cargo.

A different kind of help came to Alcatraz via a group called the Thunderbirds. This militant Indian group was very much involved in the trafficking of heroin and was known to be tough. At one point, when the fight for

Top right: Indians with full regalia involved in a dance on Alcatraz. Bottom left: Indian jacket with various symbols attached.

leadership was in full swing and a group led by Stella Leach was opposing the Oaks group, members of the Thunderbirds were brought to Alcatraz and housed in Building 64. They were armed with chains and pipes and beat up other Indians on Alcatraz. Eddie, on May 23rd, had his nose pushed clear over against his cheek. This account is particularly sad, for it was brother against brother and would give the white public just the kind of ammunition needed to discredit the very gallant, honorable and honest effort by some to establish pride and dignity in this Indian cause.

It may be pointed out that this same group, led by the island nurse, was dispensing pills (narcotics) and selling marijuana in her apartment. Some of the leadership objected to this, and that, again, created open conflict. The two sons of that nurse were identified by several sources as the main trouble-makers on Alcatraz. Her son, Mike, had a rifle and carried it around.

The council in February, 1970, consisted of Stella Leach, Lenado Means, John Trudell, Charles Dana, Eleanor Lopez and Al Muller. Most of the participants in the Alcatraz occupation were students; and one of them, John Trudell, came from Los Angeles. "I had freed myself from my responsibilities and went up to the island and met Mr. Richard Oakesand some of the people involved in the occupation. And I liked what they were doing. I was going to college at the time and I dropped out. I went to Alcatraz and joined what was called the Militants, and have been there ever since."

Besides being on the council, John became the voice of Alcatraz. At night, over the Berkeley KPFA-FM station, in 15-minute segments, John interviewed spokesmen for the cause, arranged dialogues about Indian culture and played recordings of typical Indian music. The effect of "Radio Free Alcatraz" was best summed up by John in the following statement: "The radio broadcasts reached the immediate Bay Area at that time, but I'm finding out now that quite a few of those broadcasts were taped. I heard that there might be nearly 10 or 15 hours of tapes just from my Alcatraz broadcasts. We had a good impact locally. What we had not counted on was that they were taped. In 1975 I ran into this guy in Oakland, who went to Evergreen State College in Oregon or Washington, and he said, 'Hey, I heard these Alcatraz tapes. They have them in our American studies.' So this is when I started to catch on that they did get out. So it had an impact. When I look at it, it was the very physical act˜ going in and occupying Alcatraz˜ that had the impact. And the rest were just supportive roles of the initial impact."

Both the impact of life and death affected the occupation on Alcatraz. Yvonne, the 12-year-old daughter of Richard Oakes the foremost leader of the Alcatraz occupation, fell over a railing and died on January 8, 1970. "One of the main reasons that Richard left the island was after the death of his daughter," recalls John Trudell. Richard lived on the mainland but was still connected to what was occurring on Alcatraz. Richard returned to Alcatraz on the 23rd of March, 1970, the same time the radical group, the Thunderbirds, were on the island. Richard returned with fifteen friends on May 2nd, and apparently was drunk and obnoxious.

232

Bottom left: Food donated to the occupying Indians on Alcatraz.
Bottom right: Indian assisting in securing a landing vessel.

The first baby born on Alcatraz was to an Indian couple on July 20, 1970. To the best of our knowledge, that was the only child ever born on Alcatraz. On several occasions, the Coast Guard was called to take Indians off the island for emergency reasons. Vern Conway's daughter was unconscious from a suspected dose of sleeping pills, and was rushed to the mainland on February 14, 1970. On March 23rd, the Coast Guard took to the mainland a 13-year-old with appendicitis and a 3-year-old who fell. A blood poisoning victim from dope injection was taken to the mainland on March 26th. And on April 10th, a 14-year-old who had a bad LSD trip was ferried to the mainland by the Coast Guard.

The Indians, in a public statement, said that it was an outside group that burned the buildings on Alcatraz. On March 8th, after returning to the island, some Indian boys, including Sonny, Mike and David Leach, told of the beating of 150 Indians at Fort Lawton by the government. They told the government official they were "going to burn everything on the island down and let San Francisco know how they felt about the treatment of the Indians at Fort Lawton." On June 1, 1970, the historic Alcatraz Island lighthouse and four other large buildings were destroyed by fire.

Ad that appeared in the "Black Panthers" newspaper asking for help.

233

Indian boys playing basketball on the old parade ground.

Alcatraz Indian Security Force identification jacket.

Against all of this background of activities, the process of negotiations carried on. The various Indian councils formed during that time tried to deal with their official demands.

"To have a voice in the government, you had to be 13 and live on the island a week. This means you had a voice. You could help pitch the council members. You had a vote. We had, I believe, a 12 member council, and then it went to nine and then to seven. We had to experiment with numbers on the council. Sometimes the council would grow bigger, sometimes smaller, according to the population. The council was structured so that every 90 days a certain percentage of the council seats were up. We could recommit ourselves to stay or get sent out, but this kept more participation within our government system," stated John Trudell.

The official proclamation was printed up and handed out.

PROCLAMATION:

To The Great White Father and All His People

WE, THE NATIVE AMERICANS, re-claim the land known as Alcàtraz Island in the name of all American Indians by right of discovery.

We wish to be fair and honorable in our dealings with the Caucasian inhabitants of this land, and hereby offer the following treaty:

We will purchase said Alcatraz Island for twenty-four dollars ($24) in glass beads and red cloth, a precedent set by the white man's purchase of a similar island about 300 years ago. We know that $24 in trade goods for these 16 acres is more than was paid when Manhattan Island was sold, but we know that land values have risen over the years. Our offer of $1.24 per acre is greater than the 47¢ per acre the white men are now paying the California Indians for their land.

We will give to the inhabitants of this island a portion of the land for their own to be held in trust by the American Indian Affairs and by the Bureau of Caucasian Affairs to hold in perpetuity¨ for as long as the sun shall rise and the rivers go down to the sea. We will further guide the inhabitants in the proper way of living. We will offer them our religion, our education, our life-ways, in order to help them achieve our level of civilization and thus raise them and all their white brothers up from their savage and unhappy state. We offer this treaty in good faith and wish to be fair and honorable in our dealings with all white men.

We feel that this so-called Alcatraz Island is more than suitable for an Indian Reservation, as determined by the white man's own standards. By this, we mean that this place resembles most Indian reservations in that:

1. It is isolated from modern facilities, and without adequate means of transportation.
2. It has no fresh running water.
3. It has inadequate sanitation facilities.
4. There are no oil or mineral rights.
5. There is no industry and so unemployment is very great.
6. There are no health care facilities.
7. The soil is rocky and non-productive; and the land does not support game.
8. There are no educational facilities.
9. The population has always exceeded the land base.
10. The population has always been held as prisoners and kept dependent upon others.

Further, it would be fitting and symbolic that ships from all over the world, entering the Golden Gate, would first see Indian land, and thus be reminded of the true history of this nation. This tiny island would be a symbol of the great lands once ruled by free and noble Indians.

Coast Guard patrol boat alongside Chinese "junk" intending to dock at Alcatraz.

John Trudell, Indian leader and radio operator on Alcatraz.

John Trudell in an interview with the author.

USE TO BE MADE OF
ALCATRAZ ISLAND

What use will we make of this land. Since the San Francisco Indian Center burned down, there is no place for Indians to assemble and carry on tribal life here in white man's city. Therefore, we plan to develop on this island several Indian institutions:

1. A CENTER FOR NATIVE AMERICAN STUDIES will be developed which will train our young people in the best of our native arts and works as well as educate them in the skills and knowledge relevant to improve the lives and spirits of all Indian peoples. Attached to this center will be traveling universities, managed by Indians, which will go to the Indian Reservations, learning those necessary and relevant materials currently available.

2. AN AMERICAN INDIAN SPIRITUAL CENTER which will practice our ancient tribal religious and sacred healing ceremonies. Our cultural arts will be featured and our young people trained in music, dance, and healing rituals.

3. AN INDIAN CENTER OF ECOLOGY which will train and support our young people in scientific research and practice to restore our lands and waters to their pure and natural state. We will work to de-pollute the air and water of the Bay Area. We will seek to restore fish and animal life to the area and the revitalized sea life which has been threatened by the white man's ways. We will set up facilities to de-salt sea water for human benefit.

4. A GREAT INDIAN TRAINING SCHOOL will be developed to teach our peoples how to make a living in the world, improve our standards of living, and to end hunger and unemployment among all our people. This training school will include a center for Indian arts and crafts, and an Indian restaurant serving native foods, which will restore Indian culinary arts. This center will display Indian arts and offer Indian foods to the public, so that all may know of the beauty and spirit of the traditional Indian ways.

5. SOME OF THE PRESENT BUILDINGS will be taken over to develop an American Indian Museum, which will depict our native foods and other cultural contributions we have given to the world. Another part of the museum will present some of the things the white man has given to the Indians in return for the land and life he took: disease, alcohol, poverty and cultural decimation (as symbolized by old tin cans, barbed wire, rubber tires, plastic containers, etc.). Part of the museum will remain a dungeon to symbolize both those Indian captives who were incarcerated for challenging white authority, and those who were imprisoned on reservations. The museum will show the noble and the tragic events of Indian history, including the broken treaties, the documentary of the Trail of Tears, the Massacre of Wounded Knee, as well as the victory over Yellow Hair Custer and his army.

In the name of all Indians, therefore, we re-claim this island for our Indian nations. For all these reasons, we feel this claim is just and proper, and that this land should rightfully be granted to us for as long as the rivers shall run and the sun shall shine.

Signed,

Indians of All Tribes
November, 1969
San Francisco, California

Indian graffiti inside living quarters.

True feelings expressed on a cell wall.

On the government side was Mr. Robert Robertson, Executive Director of the National Council of Indian Opportunity, and Mr. Thomas Hannon, Regional Administrator of General Service Administration. Mr. Robertson stated, "After two days of patiently listening to their ideas, I could draw no conclusion other than that safety and health requirements could not be met until the women and children are off the island and the Indian group is reduced to a sensible size." The government offered to keep a symbolic force of 5 to 10 men on the island on the federal payroll and then negotiate. This was fully rejected by the general membership as being "bought off." The government proposal reads as follows:

THE U.S. GOVERNMENT'S "MAXIMAL"
COUNTER-PROPOSAL

For: Indians of all Tribes, Incorporated
Alcatraz Island, California

From: Robert Robertson
For the United States of America

March 31, 1970

THE PROPOSAL

1. That the Department of the Interior, planning with Indian people and using the attached report as a point of departure in the process, develop a master park plan for the island, creating an outstanding recreation resource within reach of millions of urban dwellers.
2. In order to protect the symbolic value which has been effected on Alcatraz over these past months and to assure that the ultimate park plan will have a maximal Indian quality, an Indian Joint Planning Committee will be formed to work with professionals in the Department of the Interior. This Committee would be composed of Indian writers, historians, artists, religious leaders, "grassroots people," and so forth, and would be chosen by the Secretary of the Interior from lists supplied by Indian individuals and organizations throughout the country.

WHAT MIGHT RESULT

The following are thoughts and suggestions that the Indian Joint Planning Committee might consider in bringing about an optimum Indian quality to the Island. Let me stress that planning is a process and that this proposed process can evolve interesting results not even imagined at the beginning.

Here, then, are some planning ideas:

That the Indian planning group might suggest a new name for the Island, possibly from the ancient Ohlone (Costanoan) language or from a suggestion provided by Indians across the country.

That monuments commemorating noted Indians through history be located about the Island park.

That a cultural center and museum be an integral part of the park plan, allowing non-Indians an excellent opportunity to learn from Indians of the treasured culture and heritage of the "First Americans." It is difficult at this stage to conceptualize just what the cultural center should be in the final analysis, but Indian ideas would establish its parameters. A good number of those who would be park rangers could be Indians professionally trained by the Park Service.

As we have said, the Indian-Interior professional planning process will develop ideas which can be considered in putting together the ultimate master plan.

IN CONCLUSION

With respect to your educational proposal, you indicated the need for a university. We do not argue with this need. As you all know, the first Indian-run institution of higher education is now underway at Many Farms, Arizona-Navajo Community College. A number of major

236

Top left: Indian petition asking for support. Top right: Message on smokestack.

universities in the country now have courses in Native American studies and there is an obvious need for advanced educational opportunity for Indian scholars so that maintenance of Indian culture and heritage will be maximized. The Indian Planning Commission, meeting with appropriate federal agencies, could suggest how best this need can be met and where such an institution of advanced Indian studies might best be located. This Administration is very desirous of cooperating in this endeavor.

This, then, is the very best proposal we could evolve, keeping in mind, at all times, the best interests of Indian people and all other Americans. We hope that you will consider it fully and that you will see fit to give it your blessing.

In all of this, we have not forgotten the admonition given us by the Sioux medicine man who conducted the peace-pipe ceremony on the occasion of our last visit to the Island. He said that we should never utter that which we did not mean and that which would hurt others. We have abided by his admonition in preparing this proposal.

The shaky truce that had existed from the beginning between the government and the Indians fell apart when the Indians unveiled a "Declaration of Independence." It proclaimed: "We shall exercise dominion on all rights of use and possession over Alcatraz Island." This was the end of the truce. The caretaker on the island sent his helpers to the mainland, and on May 28th, the last white man left "the Rock." It was at that time that the government stopped the supply of water and electricity to Alcatraz.

Urgent cries for help went out to the public that at one time was totally on the side of the Indians. Support came from many sources but the most visible supporters were actors, such as Anthony Quinn, Jane Fonda, Ethel Kennedy, Shirley Temple Black and Jonathan Winters. Even Governor Reagan asked for help for the California Indians. In a letter to the Secretary of Health, Education and Welfare, Reagan asked for $1.9 million in funds. The support had dwindled to almost a stop. The public was exposed to the filth, vandalism, fighting and disease on Alcatraz; and probably the turning point in the support was with the sight of the buildings burning on Alcatraz. "The fires are just one more factor in the mounting problems of Alcatraz since they took over, and cause us to look at the

Indians there with suspicion," states a government official.

The Indians were angry and declared the island off limits to all government personnel. "The Coast Guard doesn't have to ask permission to go onto its own property. When they are ready, they will go on the island," so spoke Mr. Hannon, the government representative.

When the Indians lost Richard Oaks as their leader, something went with him that never was replaced. The cause, the idea, the energy something left with him. The end to his life was as tragic as the end of the occupation. "He was in a bar one night and somebody hit him in the head with a cue stick and it left him partially paralyzed for awhile. He never had the same use of his senses after that. My feeling is that he was assassinated. Some YMCA caretaker shot him and killed him. He was unarmed and I know he didn't have good movement. He lost his reflexes. The guy used some excuse that Richard tried to knife him or shoot him or some kind of lie like that. I'll always believe that it was just an outfront assassination, because of the politics that Richard represented at Alcatraz," recalls John Trudell.

On Friday, June 11, 1971, twenty armed federal

237

marshals went to Alcatraz and removed the last Indians from Alcatraz. Six men, four women and five children were on the island at that time. It was a non-violent removal but the marshals were ready for violence, believing weapons still remained on the island, based on eyewitness reports and testimonies. Some Indian leaders still deny this fact.

Much has been written and much has been said about that period of the history of Alcatraz. But the depth of the impact on the American people regarding Indian issues probably never will be measured. "In spite of the fact that the government removed the people from Alcatraz, one of the main implications of the whole Alcatraz occupation was that this was something like 15,000 runners going out into the general community. The influence of Alcatraz is still being felt. That's how we got together to talk about Alcatraz. So it never really went away," stated John Trudell in a recent interview with the author.

After the end of the nineteen-month occupation, the government secured the island. They built a fence all

Top left: A regional administrator for the federal General Services Administration inspecting the damage done by the Indians. Top right: Lighthouse with leveled family living quarters in foreground. Bottom right: Alcatraz cell building as seen from recreation yard.

around and posted guards. This was to prevent a similar incident from recurring. The last Indians did vow to return.

"Alcatraz may open to the Public," so read a headline in the *San Francisco Chronicle* on February 2, 1973. Just a year earlier, in February of 1972, legislation asking to establish the Golden Gate National Recreation Area as part of the President's Environmental Program was introduced in Congress. The bill establishing the Golden Gate National Recreation Area was signed into law on October 27, 1972, by President Nixon. One year later, in October, 1973, Alcatraz opened to the public.

At that time there was a return visit by the Indians. Thirty Indians, including some veterans of the occupation, led by Adam Nordwall, walked up to the main cell block and into the prison mess hall. The Indians were in full dress and began to sing and dance. This ceremony ended with the peace pipe being passed around and a moment of silence "for the three people who gave their lives fighting for us." "We are here proclaiming a victory," said Nordwall. "If the Indians hadn't taken over this place, it would now be part of Lamar Hunt's space museum."

Before the tours were conducted, a press preview tour was arranged for the 31st of May, 1973. Eighty-six reporters and camera persons descended upon "the Rock" and announced to the world the future of Alcatraz. Even the Australian press was represented.

The superintendent of the newly-created Golden Gate National Park Recreation Area led the tour and answered as many questions as possible at that time. David Ames, superintendent of the Fort Point National Monuments, made possibly the best statement when he said, "Little is known about Alcatraz, and one thing the Park Service will do is set historians to work in the National Archives, interviewing former guards, inmates and family residents to learn about the history." In 1983 Alcatraz is still San Francisco's biggest tourist attraction, with no signs of relinquishing that distinction in the future.

It is hoped that this book will help in this process and provide information, leads and resources that will establish the true history of "the Rock" — Alcatraz.

CATRAZ
San Francisco Bay

BUMPER STICKER
LUGGAGE, DENS, GARAGES
BEND BACK AND
PEEL OFF

© IMPKO
STRIPZ
MADE IN USA

CHILD $1.00

"I did my time on The Rock"

ALCATRAZ

HARBOR TOURS, Fisherman's Wharf, San Francisco, CA

35928

ADULT $2.50

"I did my time on The Rock"

ALCATRAZ

HARBOR TOURS, Fisherman's Wharf, San Francisco, CA

294071

"The Rock"

We, the students of Herbert Hoover High School's Advanced Photography Class wish to expand our individual learning experience through researching and documenting a California landmark.

Our interest in preserving and documenting Alcatraz started as an extension of previous activities in preserving and documenting local (L.A.) landmarks. Our most recent documentation was the "Lummis House" in Los Angeles.

We plan on producing a book that would be available to the public. In this book, we will give a full visual documentation of the island and include written research related to the history of Alcatraz.

We want to provide a visual record of Alcatraz's past and present and the effect and evidence for history. We feel committed to the concept of sharing with future generations a span of time of a historical place, building and concept.

We are going to finance this endeavor by soliciting sponsorship in our local area, from civic organizations, business and national corporations, as well as individual fund raising activities throughout the Los Angeles area.

We will be on the island for five days and nights to collect the visual and graphic documentation needed for this project. A research facility and state historian have been made available to us. Federal and State files and records are being used by the group to establish accurate fact documentation. Interviews with former prison officials, personnel and their children, as well as members of the Indians party that occupied Alcatraz (69-71) are being set up. The group of 12-15 senior high students and 1 instructor would be totally self sufficient and the daily routines and activity master plan will be available 7 days before arrival on the island. Our planning is broken down into the following time line:

November 1 to Nov 25- Research preparation, research and organization, documenting session.

November 25 to Nov 28- Travel preparation and travel.

November 28 to December 2- Photodocumentation on Alcatraz.

December 2 to April 29- Compiling layout and photo printing

April 29 to May 30- Publication at Printers and Binders

June 1 to June 15- Release to the public.

We thank you again for your support; if you have any further inquires feel free to contact us through Advanced Photography class
C/O Pierre Odier
Herbert Hoover High School
651 Glenwood Rd.
Glendale Ca. 91202

242

AFTERWORD

Each year offers the opportunity for a teacher and students to embark on something new, something unknown and something challenging. 1980 was no different. During a discussion with the students of my advanced photo class the idea of investigating and documenting a local jail came up. This discussion went in many directions and at one point the name Alcatraz came up. It was at that point that someone said, "There is no way we can document Alcatraz." Then the question came up, "Why not?"

The Alcatraz project offered an opportunity to weave together all these different individuals into a cohesive unit. The process itself, towards achievement, provided the perfect catalyst for each individual to take risks, make use of a chance, to challenge assumption, and to see things in a new way. He hopefully then would push himself to new levels of awareness and achievements. Each individual is the sum total of his experiences and achievements, and the more opportunities we can provide at the high school level, the further the individual can reach during his stay on this planet.

The objective to live on Alcatraz in 1980 for one week and photo-document the island came about very quickly. Within three weeks of the original thought we were on the island, alone and experiencing our own accomplishment. That self-accomplishment, "We did it," was quickly overshadowed by the evidence of the grim aspects of Alcatraz. The direct connection between the us and "the Rock"

affected all of us. Each student found one or more aspect that captivated him. For one it was the medical ward, for the other it was a particular cell, the sounds at night, the fog, the silent testimony of violence, the beauty and irony of the flowers growing, the rusting tricycle left behind by an Indian child, the many toilets, the mystery, the hopeless isolation, the beauty of the lights of San Francisco at night, and most of all the special feeling that of all the people in this world, we were here now and forever into a non-retractable personal expansion. Our lives now were part of "the Rock," and "the Rock" now a part of our lives.

For me personally the experience was just as intense and valid. For all this to stop upon returning home from "the Rock" was impossible. I, too, went home with a part of "the Rock." It had captivated me, and for two years there followed an investigation into all its aspects, the result being this book, a book that tries to hold together many pieces of "the Rock" not previously linked together. There is new material surfacing all the time, but I hope this book will provide a structured stepping-stone for the organization of all materials pertaining to "the Rock."

The message to you students who were on "the Rock" in 1980 must be that once you have an idea, a thought, a wish or a goal, you — and only you — can and must convert that thought into reality. No matter how absurd that thought may sound, no matter how impossible it seems, if you have the idea, get it done.

Standing, L to R: Steve Ovanessian, Louie Jimenez, Dave Goguen, Liz Colla, Danny Aragon, Pierre Odier, Mike Conway. Not pictures: Greg O'Loughlin.
Front L to R: Mike Geiser, Donna McDonough, David Wiggins, Laurie O'Grady, Donna Moore, John Rodiger, Michele Leffler.

Commanding Officers Stationed on Alcatraz, 1859-1916

Capt. Joseph Steward, Third Artillery, Dec. 30, 1859 to May, 1861. West Point graduate

Maj. Henry S. Burton, Third Artillery, May 1861 to May 1862

Capt. William A. Winder, Third Artillery, May 1862 to August 1864

Capt. Charles O. Wood, Ninth Infantry, Aug. 1864 to Oct. 1865

Capt. James M. Robertson, Second Artillery, Oct. 1865 to July 1866, brevet brigadier general, Civil War

1st Lt. John A. Darling, Second Artillery, July 1866 to Nov. 1867

1st Lt. John Fitzgerald, Second Artillery, Nov. 1867 to Feb. 1868

Capt. James M. Robertson, Second Artillery, Feb. 1868 to Dec. 1872

Maj. Charles H. Morgan, Fourth Artillery, Dec. 1872 to Dec. 1875. West Point graduate; brigadier general, Civil War

Capt. John Egan, Fourth Artillery, Dec. 1875 to Dec. 1877. West Point graduate

Maj. Albion P. Howe, Fourth Artillery, Dec. 1877 to June 1879. West Point graduate; brigadier general, Civil War

Capt. Henry C. Cushing, Fourth Artillery, June 1879 to Dec. 1879

Maj. LaRett L. Livingston, Fourth Artillery, Dec. 1879 to May 1880. West Point graduate

Capt. Edward Field, Fourth Artillery, May 1880 to July 1880

Capt. Arthur Harris, Fourth Artillery, July 1880 to Nov. 1881

Maj. Royal T. Frank, First Artillery, Nov. 1881 to Dec. 1884. West Point graduate; Medal of Honor, Civil War

Maj. Alanson M. Randol, First Artillery, Dec. 1884 to Oct. 1886. West Point graduate; brevet brigadier general, Civil War

Maj. John I. Rodgers, First Artillery, Oct. 1886 to Nov. 1887. West Point graduate, future brigadier general

Maj. William L. Haskin, First Artillery, Nov. 1887 to Oct. 1888

Lt. Col. Charles G. Bartlett, First Infantry, Oct. 1888 to Apr. 1889. Brevet brigadier general, Civil War

Lt. Col. William M. Graham, First Artillery, Apr. 1889 to Oct. 1889. Brevet brigadier general, Civil War; future major general

Maj. William L. Haskin, First Artillery, Oct. 1889 to May 1890

Maj. Abram C. Wildrick, Fifth Artillery, May 1890 to Nov. 1891

Lt. Col. Francis L. Guenther, Fifth Artillery, Nov. 1891 to June 1896. West Point graduate; future brigadier general

Lt. Col. William Sinclair, Fifth Artillery, July 1896 to Oct. 1896. West Point graduate; future brigadier general

Capt. James Chester, Third Artillery, Oct. 1896 to June 1897

Maj. David H. Kinzie, Third Artillery, July 1897 to Apr. 1898

Capt. Charles W. Hobbs, Third Artillery, Apr. 1898 to June 1898

Capt. Charles H. Dasher, Sixth Calif. Vols., June 1898 to Sept. 1898

Capt. George B. Baldwin, Eighth Calif. Vols., Sept. 1898 to Jan. 1899

Maj. David H. Kinzie, Third Artillery, Jan. 1899 to Apr. 1899

Capt. Ammon Augur, 24th Infantry, Apr. 1899 to May 1899

Maj. J. Milton Thompson, 24th Infantry, May 1899 to June 1899

Capt. John D. C. Hoskins, Third Artillery, June 1899 to Sept. 1899. West Point graduate

Capt. George T. Bartlett, Third Artillery, Sept. 1899 to Apr. 1900. West Point graduate

1st Lt. Lyman M. Welsh, 28th Infantry, Apr. 1900 to May 1900

Capt. James O'Hara, Third Artillery, May 1900 to June 1900. West Point graduate

Capt. Henry C. Danes, Third Artillery, June 1900 to July 1900

Capt. Benjamin W. Atkinson, Sixth Infantry, July 1900 to Sept. 1900

Capt. Charles W. Hobbs, Third Artillery, Sept. 1900 to Mar. 1901

Lt. Col. Sumner H. Lincoln, 30th Infantry, Mar. 1901 to Apr. 1901

Capt. Charles B. Hardin, 18th Infantry, Apr. 1901 to May 1901

Maj. George S. Young, 18th Infantry, May 1901 to Oct. 1901

Capt. Elon F. Willcox, Sixth Cavalry, Oct. 1901 to Nov. 1901

Lt. Col. Abner H. Merrill, Artillery Corps, Nov. 1901 to July 1902

Maj. Bernard A. Byrne, 13th Infantry, July 1902 to Feb. 1903, Medal of Honor, Philippine Islands

Maj. Cornelius Gardener, 13th Infantry, Feb. 1903 to Mar. 1903. West Point graduate

Maj. Alexis R. Paxton, 13th Infantry, Mar. 1903 to Oct. 1905

Maj. George W. McIver, Fourth Infantry, Oct. 1905 to Jan. 1906

Maj. Abner Pickering, 22nd Infantry, Jan. 1906 to June 1907. West Point graduate

(In June 1907 the official post designation was changed from "Alcatraz Island" to "Pacific Branch, U.S. Military Prison, Alcatraz Island," and the title "Commanding Officer" was changed to "Commandant.")

Maj. Reuben B. Turner, Eighth Infantry, June 1907 to Nov. 1911. West Point graduate

Col. Robert C. Van Vliet, Infantry, Nov. 1911 to June 1913

Col. Charles M. Truitt, Infantry, June 1913 to Sept. 1914. West Point graduate

Capt. Charles R. Howland, 21st Infantry, Sept. 1914 to Dec. 1916

Army Units Stationed on Alcatraz, 1859-1916

Regiment/Unit	Company/Battery	Years
Regulars:		
First U.S. Artillery	A, B, C, D, H, I & M	1881-90
Second U.S. Artillery	B, E, F, G, K & L	1865-72 and 1859-64
Third U.S. Artillery	A, B, D, E, H, I, K, L, N and Band	1896-1900
Fourth U.S. Artillery	C, D, E, F, G, H, K & L	1872-81
Fifth U.S. Artillery	A, B, C, E, H, I & K	1890-96
	63, 64 & 71, Coast Artillery	1901-02
First U.S. Infantry	C, E & Band	1888-89 & 1897
Fourth U.S. Infantry	B, C & D	1905-06
Sixth U.S. Infantry	G	1860
Seventh U.S. Infantry	H	1900-1901
Ninth U.S. Infantry	F, G, H & K	1862-1865
Tenth U.S. Infantry	M	1905
12th U.S. Infantry	C, E, F, G, H & M	1902-05
18th U.S. Infantry	A & C	1901
22nd U.S. Infantry	A, E, F, G, H & K	1906-07
24th U.S. Infantry	H (Black troops)	1899
U.S. Engineers	Detachment, Co. A	1861
First Dragoons	Recruits	1861
First Dragoons	Confalescent Co. No. 2	1900-01
U.S. Military Prison Guard	Cos. 3 & 4	1907-15
Disciplinary Battalion, Pacific Branch, U.S. Military Prison		1914-16

(Fifth, Sixth, Seventh and Eighth Companies and Second Disciplinary Band, all composed of prisoners)

Volunteers:

Second Infantry, Calif. Volunteers	G	1861-62
Fifth Infantry, Calif. Volun.	H & K	1862
Sixth Infantry, Calif. Volun.	A	1864-65 & 1898

THE ESCAPE ATTEMPTS

1—April 27, 1936

JOSEPH BOWERS: He was shot during attempt and fell to his death.

2—December 16, 1937

THEODORE COLE, RALPH ROE: Believed drowned. To this day they are still listed as unaccounted for

3—April 23, 1938

RUFUS FRANKLIN, THOMAS LIMMERICK, JAMES LUCAS: Brutal attack with hammer on officers. Limmerick died of gunshot wounds and Franklin and Lucas both received life sentences.

4—January 13, 1939

ARTHUR "DOC" BARKER, WILLIAM MARTIN, RUFUS McCAIN, DALE STANPHILL, HENRI YOUNG: Barker died on way back to the prison; the rest were all captured and stood trial for their escape attempt.

5—May 21, 1941

LLOYD BARKDOLL, JOSEPH P. CRETZER, ARNOLD T. KYLE, SAM SHOCKLEY: All four surrendered before reaching the water.

6—September 15, 1941

JOHN R. BAYLESS: Escape attempt from the garbage detail. Captured before reaching the water

7—April 14, 1943

JAMES BOARMAN, HAROLD BREST, FLOYD HAMILTON, FRED HUNTER: Boarman drowned and all the others were captured.

8—August 7, 1943

TED WALTERS: Captured before he made the water.

9—July 31, 1945

JOHN GILES: Escaped to Angel Island via the army launch. Captured on Angel Island and returned to Alcatraz.

10—May 2, 1946

CLARENCE CARNES, BERNARD PAUL COY, JOE CRETZER, MARVIN F. HUBBARD, MIRAN THOMPSON, SAM SHOCKLEY: This attempt is referred to as the 1946 Riot. Found dead in a utility corridor were Coy, Cretzer and Hubbard. Shockley and Thompson died on December 3 in the gas chamber at San Quentin. Carnes was given a second life sentence.

11—July 23, 1956

FLOYD P. WILSON: After disappearing from the dock crew he was captured on the island before he could enter the water.

12—September 29, 1958

AARON BURGETT and CLYDE JOHNSON overtook a guard while on the garbage detail. Burgett drowned and Johnson was captured in the water and returned to Alcatraz.

13—June 11, 1962

CLARENCE ANGLIN, JOHN WILLIAM ANGLIN, FRANK LEE MORRIS: This escape was made famous with the movie escape from Alcatraz. They escaped via the roof and have never been found.

14—December 14, 1962

JOHN PAUL SCOTT, DARL LEE PARKER: Parker was found on a rock near he island and Scott near death at Fort Point.

BIBLIOGRAPHY

1. Books

AINSWORTH, F. C. *Regulations for the Government of the United States Military Prison and of any Branch Thereof.* Washington: Government Printing Office, 1909.

AUDETT, BLACKIE. *Rap Sheet,* Williams Sloane Assn. Inc. New York 1954.

BANCROFT, H. H. *History of California.* 7 vols. San Francisco, 1884-1890.

BARNES & TEETERS. *New Horizons in Criminology.* Prentiss-Hall 1943.

BATES, SANFORD. *Prisons and Beyond.* The MacMillan Company, New York. 1936.

BEILHORZ, FELIPE DE NEVE

BENNETT, JAMES V. *I Chose Prison.* Edited by Rodney Campbell. New York: Alfred A. Knopf, 1970.

BLUE CLOUD, PETER. *Alcatraz Is Not an Island.* Berkeley: Winglow Press, 1972.

BOLTEN, HERBERT EUGENE. *Father Escobar's Relations of the Onata Expedition to California,* 1919.

————. *Crespi, Missionary Explorer, 1769-1774.*

BROWN, DEE. *Bury My Heart at Wounded Knee.* New York: Holt & Rinehart, 1970.

BRUCE J. CAMPBELL. ,
A Farewell to the Rock, Escape from Alcatraz. New York: McGraw-Hill Book Co., 1963.

CHESSMAN, CARYL. *Cell 2455 Death Row.* New York: Prentice-Hall, Inc. 1954.

THE CORPS OF ENGINEERS MUSEUM. *Genesis of the Engineers . . . From 1745 to 1966.* Fort Belvoir, BA: n.p., n.d.

CROOK, GEORGE. *Resume of Operations Against Apache Indians, 1882 to 1886.* Reprint, 1886. London: Johnston-Taunton Military Press, 1971.

DAVIDSON, GEORGE. *Sir Francis Drake's Anchorage, 1579.* Vol. 1.

————. *Discovery of San Francisco.* San Francisco: F. F. Partridge, 1907.

DELORIA VINE, JR. *God is Red.* New York: Delta Book, 1973.

DE NEVI, DON, & BERGEN, PHILIP. *Alcatraz '46, The Anatomy of a Classic Prison Tragedy.* San Rafael: Leswing Press, 1974.

DUFFY, CLINTON. *The San Quentin Story,* New York: Doubleday & Company, 1950.

EGAN, FEROL. *Fremont, Explorer for a Restless Nation.* New York: Doubleday & Company, 1977.

ELLIS, STEVE. *Alcatraz Number 1172.* Los Angeles: Holloway House, 1969.

FRAZER, ROBERT W., ed. *Mansfield on the Condition of the Western Forts, 1853-54.* Norman: University of Oklahoma Press, 1963.

FREMONT, JOHN CHARLES. *Memoirs of My Life.* Vol. 1. Chicago, 1887.

GADDIS, THOMAS E. *Birdman of Alcatraz: The Story of Robert Stroud.* New York: Random House, 1955.

GARDNER, ROY. *Hellcatraz.* No publisher, 1939.

GILLAM, HAROLD. *San Francisco Bay.* Doubleday, 1957.

GODWIN, JOHN. *Alcatraz: 1868-1963.* New York: Doubleday & Company, 1963.

GRIVAS, THEODORE. *Military Governments in California, 1946-1950.* Glendale, CA: Arthur H. Clark Co., 1963.

GUDDE, ERWIN G. *California Place Names, The Origin and Etymology of Current Geographical Names.* Berkeley: University of California Press, 1962.

FORBES, ALEXANDER. *California History, 1778-1862.* 1839.

HANSEN, GLADYS. *San Francisco Almanac, Everything You Want to Know About the City.* San Francisco: Chronicle Books, 1975.

HARLOW, NEAL. *Maps of San Francisco Bay.* The Branding Iron, 1975.

HART, H. *Old Fortress of the Far West.* Seattle, 1965.

————. *Pioneer Forts of the West.* Seattle, 1967.

————. *The U.S. Army on Alcatraz, A Report to the City of San Francisco.* Tampa: n.p., 1969.

HEITMAN, FRANCIS B. *Historical Register and Dictionary of the United States Army from 1789 to 1903.* 2 vols. 1903. Reprint. Urbana: University of Illinois Press, 1965.

HEIZER, R. F. *Francis Drake and the California Indians.* Berkeley: U.S. Press, 1947.

HOLLAND, FRANCIS ROSS, JR. *America's Lighthouses, Their Illustrated History Since 1716.* Brattleboro, Vermont: The Stephen Greene Press, 1972.

HOOVER, J. EDGAR. *Ten Thousand Public Enemies.* New York: Blue Ribbon Books, 1935.

————. *Persons in Hiding.* Boston: Little Brown and Company, 1938.

HOWARD, CLARK. *Six Against the Rock.* New York: A Jova HB Book, 1977.

HUNT, A. *Army of the Pacific, 1860-1866.* Glendale 1951.

JAMES, HARRY C. *Hopi History* (pages from). University of Arizona Press, 1979.

JACKSON, BRUCE. *Killing Time.* Cornell University Press, 1977.

JOHNSTON, JAMES. *Prison Life is Different.* Boston: Houghton Mifflin Co., 1937.

———. *Alcatraz Island Prison (and the Men Who Live There).* New York: Charles Scribner's, 1949.

KARPIS, ALVIN, with BILL TRENT. *Public Enemy No. 1: The Alvin Karpis Story*

———. *On the Rock: Twenty-Five Years in Alcatraz.* New York: Beaufort Books, 1979.

KEMBLE, JOHN HASKELL. *San Francisco Bay: A Pictorial Maritime History.* New York: Bonanza Books, 1957.

KIRKPATRICK, ERNEST. *Voices from Alcatraz.*

———. *Crimes Paradise.* San Antonio: The Taylor Co., 1934.

KOBLER, JOHN. *Capone: The Life and World of Al Capone.* Greenwich: Fawcett Publications, 1941.

LAWES, LEWIS. *Life and Death in Sing-Sing.* New Yori: The Sun Dial Press, 1937.

———. *Twenty Thousand Years in Sing Sing.* New York: The New Home Library, 1932.

LEIBERT, JULIUS. *Behind Bars.* New York: Doubleday & Co., 1965.

LEWIS, EMANUEL RAYMOND. *Seacoast Fortifications of the United States: An Introductory History.* Washington: Smithsonian Institution Press, 1970.

———. *A History of San Francisco Harbor Defense Installations: Forts Baker, Barry, Cronkhite, and Funston.* State of California, Division of Beaches and Parks, 1965.

———. *The Ambiguous Columbiades.* 1964.

MANUCY, ALBERT. *Artillery Through the Ages.* Washington: National Parks Service, CNPS Interpretive Series History No. 3, 1949.

MARCH, RAY A. *Alabama Bound.* University of Alabama Press, 1978.

MARSHALL McDONALD & ASSOC. *Report and Recommendations on Angel Island, 1769-1966.* (n.p. 1966).

McCAIN, H. P. *Regulations for the Government of the United States Disciplinary Barracks and Its Branches.* Washington: Government Printing Office, 1915.

McDOWELL, IRWIN. *Outline Description of Military Posts in the Military Division of the Pacific, 1879.* San Francisco: 1879.

McKELVEY, BLAKE. *American Prisons.* Patterson Smith, 1977.

MERCER, JOHN D. *Alcatraz Island, California.* Creative Eye Press, 1976.

MILLIS, WALTER. *Arms and Men: A Study in American Military History.* New York: G. P. Putnam's Sons, 1956.

———. *American Military Thought.* Indianapolis: The Bobbs-Merrill Co., 1966.

MINTON, ROBERT J., JR. *Inside Prison American Style.* New York: Random House, 1971.

MOONEY, MARTIN. *The Parole Scandal.* Lyman House, 1939.

NEEDHAM, TED, & NEEDHAM, HOWARD. *Alcatraz.* Millbrae, CA: Celestial Arts, 1976.

NEESE, ROBERT. *Prison Exposures.* Rahway, NJ: Quinn & Boden Comp., 1959.

NEVINS, ALLAN. *Fremont: The West's Greatest Adventurer.* 2 vols. New York: Harper & Brothers, 1928.

O'BRIAN, ROBERT. *This is San Francisco.* Whittlesey House, 1948.

OLMSTEAD, R. R., ed. *Scenes of Wonder & Curiosity from Hutchings' California Magazine, 1956-1961.* Berkeley: Howell-North, 1962.

ORCHARD, HARRY. *The Man God Made Again.* Nashville: Southern Publishing Association, 1952.

PAEZ, JUAN. *Cabrillo Log, 1542-1543.*

PAURODE, RICHARD F. *The Summary Call to California, 1968.*

PHILLIPS, CATHERINE COFFIN. *Through the Golden Gate.* Sutton House, 1938.

PRISONER X. *Prison Confidential.* Los Angeles: Medco Books, 1969.

RICHMANN, I. B. *California Under Spanish & Mexico, 1535-1847.* Boston: Houghton Mifflin, 1911.

RIESENBERG, FELIX, JR. *Golden Gate: The Story of San Francisco Harbor.* New York: Tudor Publishing Co., 1940.

RUSSELL, T. C. *Razanov: Voyage to Nueva California, 1806.*

SCUDDER, J. KENYON. *Prisoners Are People.* Garden City, NY: Doubleday, 1952.

SHANKS, RALPH C., JR., and SHANKS, JANETTA THOMPSON. *Lighthouses of San Francisco Bay.* San Anselmo: Costano Books, 1976.

SHINDLER, HENRY. *History of the United States Military Prison.* Fort Leavenworth: Army Service Schools Press, 1911.

SMITH, EDGAR. *Brief Against Death.* New York: Alfred A. Knopf, 1968.

SOBELL, MORTON. *On Doing Time.* Bantam Books, 1974.

SPENCE, MARY LEE, and JACKSON, DONALD. *The Expeditions of John Charles Fremont.* Vol. 2. *The Bear Flag Revolt and the Court Martial.* Urbana: University of Illinois Press, 1973.

SQUIRE, AMOS O., M.D. *Sing Sing Doctor.* New York: Doubleday Doran Co., 1935.

STANGER, FRANK M., and BROWN, ALAN K. *Who Discovered the Golden Gate? The Explorers' Own Accounts, How They Discovered a Hidden Harbor and at Last Found Its Entrance.* San Mateo: San Mateo Historical Association, 1969.

STANTON, WILLIAM. *The Great United States Exploring Expedition of 1838-1842.* Berkeley: University of California Press, 1975.

STROUD, ROBERT. *Digest of the Diseases of Birds.* 1936.

TEGGART, FREDERICK J. in Academy of Pacific Coast History. Vol. 2, No. 4, 1911.

THOMAS, GORDON, and WITTS, MAX MORGAN. *The San Francisco Earthquake.* New York: Stein & Day, 1971.

TREUTLEIN, THEODORE E. *Discovery and Colonization, 1769-1776.* California Historical Society, 1968.

TULLY, ANDREW. *The FBI's Most Famous Cases.* New York: A Dell Book, 1965.

TOTTEN, JOSEPH GILBERT. *Report of General J. G. Totten, Chief Engineer, on the Subject of National Defences.* Washington: A. Boyd Hamilton, 1851.

[U.S. ARMY], Office of the Adjutant General. *The Army Correctional System.* Washington, CA, 1952.

————. *Outline Descriptions [of] Military Posts in the Military Division of the Pacific,* 1879.

————. Quartermaster General. *Outline Descriptions of Forts and Stations, 1871.* Washington: 1872.

————. ————. *Outline Description of U.S. Military Posts and Stations in the Year 1871.* Washington: Government Printing Office, 1872.

————. ————. *Revised Outline Descriptions of Posts and Stations of Troops in the Military Division of the Pacific.* Washington: 1872.

————. Surgeon General. *Report on Barracks & Hospitals with Descriptions of Posts.* Circular No. 4. Washington: 1870.

————. ————. *Report on the Hygiene of the U.S. Army with Descriptions of Posts.* Circular No. 8. Washington: 1875.

U.S. CONGRESS. House Documents, House Executive Document No. 1, 40th Cong., 3d Sess. (Serial 1367), Annual Report of the Adjutant General of the Army, 1868.

————. *The War of the Rebellion: A Compilation of the Official Records of the Union and Confederate Armies.* 73 vols., 128 pts. Washington: Government Printing Office, 1880-1901. Of use in this report was Series 1, vol. 50, in two pts.

U.S. DEPARTMENT OF COMMERCE AND LABOR, Lighthouse Board. *Annual Reports.*

————. *Report of the Operations of the Light-House Board* in *Reports of the Department of Commerce and Labor, 1910.* Washington: Government Printing Office, 1911.

————. ————. *Revised Outline Descriptions of Posts and Stations of Troops in the Military Division of the Pacific.* Washington: 1872.

————. Surgeon General. *Report on Barracks & Hospitals with Descriptions of Posts.* Circular No. 4. Washington: 1871.

————. ————. *Report on the Hygiene of the U.S. Army with Descriptions of Posts.* Circular No. 8. Washington: 1875.

U.S. CONGRESS. House Documents, House Executive Document No. 1, 40th Cong., 3d Sess. (Serial 1367), Annual Report of the Adjutant General of the Army, 1868.

————. *Report of the Commissioner of Lighthouses* in *Reports of the Department of Commerce and Labor, 1911.* Washington: Government Printing Office, 1912.

U.S. DEPARTMENT OF THE INTERIOR, National Park Service. *National Park System Plan: History.*

————. *Historic Structure Report, Fort Point, Historic Data Section, Fort Point National Historic Site, California,* by Edwin C. Bearss. Denver: National Park Service, 1973.

————. *Historic Resource Study, San Juan Island National Historical Park, Washington,* by Erwin N. Thompson. Denver: National Park Service, 1972.

U.S. DEPARTMENT OF JUSTICE, Bureau of Prisons, *Alcatraz.* n.p., n.d.

————. ————. *Annual Reports, 1933-1964.* Called *Federal Offenders* to 1941, then called *Federal Prisons.* No report was published in 1942.

U.S. DEPARTMENT OF THE TREASURY, Lighthouse Board. *Annual Reports.*

VINCENTE, SANTA MARIA. *The First Spanish Entry into San Francisco Bay.*

WAGNER, R. HENRY. *Drake On the Pacific Coast.* 1970.

————. *California Voyages, 1537-1541.*

WEIGLEY, RUSSELL F. *History of the United States Army.* New York: The Macmillan Co., 1967.

WILSON, DONALD POWELL. *My Six Convicts.* New York: Rinehart Co., 1951.

2. Manuscript Materials

Berkeley. University of California. Bancroft Library: George H. Mendell, Letterbooks. 2 vols. 1872-1884.

————. ———— Edward J. Maybridge Photograph Collection.

California Historical Society Quarterly. The Mythical Johnston Conspiracy. June 1949.

Denver. National Park Service. Denver Service Center. F. Ross Holland, Jr. "Lighting the West Coast: The Story of the Building of the Pacific Coast's First Sixteen Lighthouses." Typescript.

————. John A. Hussey. "Fort McDowell, Angel Island, Marin and San Francisco Counties, California. Report on application by Board Supervisors, County of Marin, State of California, for Transfer of Surplus Properties for an Historical Monument." Typescript. Prepared for Region 10, War Assets Administration, 1949.

————. Lawrence Kinnard. "History of the Golden Gate and Its Headlands." Typescript. 1962-1967.

San Bruno. Federal Archives and Records Center. Record Group 26, Records of the United States Coast Guard, 15 sheets of plans of First and Second Lighthouses and Fog-Bell House, Alcatraz Island.

————. ————. Record Group 77. Records of the Office of the Chief of Engineers:

Journal of the Operations connected with the Fort on Alcatraz Island, 1853-1876. 2 vols, series 1955.

Register of Materials and Services Received and Their Cost for Fortifications at Alcatraz Island, San Francisco Bay, 1854-1861. Series 1919 and 1920.

San Francisco District. Letters Sent July 1858 to February 1861. Series 1921.

San Francisco District. Letters Sent by Engineer Officers Gilmer and De Russy Relating to Fortifications, January 1861-December 1864. Series 1922.

San Francisco District. Register of Materials Received 1858-1863, Series 1927.

San Francisco. Western Regional Office. National Park Service. Roger E. Kelly, "Cultural Resources of Golden Gate National Recreation Area." April 1976.

Washington, D.C. The National Archives. Record Group 26. Records of the United States Coast Guard:

Correspondence of Maj. Hartman Bache, June 1855-December 1858. 8 vols.

Lighthouse Board Journal, October 9, 1852-August 11, 1854.

Lighthouse Board. 12th District. Engineer's and Inspector's Reports February 1853-June 1856.

Lighthouse Board. 12 & 13th Districts, Engineer's and Inspector's Reports, July 1868-May 1869.

————. ————. Record Group 77. Records of the Office of the Chief of Engineers:

Letters to Officers of Engineers, March 1848-February 1869. 40 vols. This report used vols. 16-40.

Letters Received 1838-1866. Arranged alphabetically by the names of the engineers in the field.

Official Papers, Colonel Totten's 1860-1861 (including his communications to the Secretary of War on his visit to the Pacific Coast). Vols. 8 and 9.

Correspondence Relating to Fortifications. Letters Received by the Chief Engineer (Third Division) December 5, 1866-December 31, 1870. 2 vols.

Correspondence Relating to Fortifications. Letters Sent by Chief engineer 1866-1870. 3 vols.

Correspondence Relating to Fortifications. Letters Received (A File) by Chief Engineer, 1867-1870.

Correspondence of the Fortifications Division. Letters Received by the Chief of Engineers, 1871-1886. 77 feet.

Board of Fortifications. Miscellaneous Papers, 1885-1887. (Endicott Board).

Letters Sent, Office of Chief of Engineers, 1886-1889. 13 vols.

Letters Received Relating to Fortifications, Administration, and Explorations and Surveys, 1888-1889. 40 feet.

General Correspondence 1890-1892. 148 feet.

General Correspondence and Record Cards 1893-1894. 88 feet.

General Correspondence 1894-1923. 3,041 feet.

Land Papers (Alcatraz Island).

————. ————. Record Group 92. Records of the Office of the Quartermaster General:

Consolidated Correspondence File 1794-1890. (Alcatraz Island).

General Correspondence 1890-1914.

————. ————. Record Group 94, Records of the Adjutant General's Office:

Military Prison Record Division. Letters Sent 1875-1889. 5 vols.

Military Prison Record Division. Letters Sent 1881-1890. 11 vols.

ACP File for Col. George Mendell.

————. ————. Record Group 129, Records of the Bureau of Prisons: U.S. Penitentiary, Alcatraz Island. 1933-1938.

————. ————. Record Group 393, U.S. Army Continental Commands:

Alcatraz Island. Register of Prisoners at the Military Prison, October 18, 1870-March 24, 1879.

Alcatraz Island. Medical Department, Orders and Letters, 1873-1896. 4 vols.

Alcatraz Island. Descriptive Book, Officers and Men, January 9, 1883-August 19, 1905 (nearly all enlisted men in Hospital Corps).

Alcatraz Island. Medical Department, Register of Patients and Consolidated Report, U.S. Army Hospital, January 1884-September 1891. 2 vols.

Alcatraz Island. Record of Medical History of the Post, February 1873-August 1877 and July 1884-October 1898. 2 vols.

Alcatraz Island. Return of the Personnel and Equipment of the Hospital Corps, January 1890-April 1898.

Alcatraz Island. Deaths & Burials, Military Hospital, January 1875-June 1891.

Alcatraz Island. Deaths & Interments, USA Post Hospital, March 23, 1893-July 24, 1910.

Alcatraz Island. USA Medical Department, Records of Letters and Endorsements Sent January 1, 1897-January 24, 1905.

Alcatraz Island. Monthly Sanitary Reports, November 30, 1898-July 4, 1913.

Department of the Pacific. Letters Sent 1848-1866, also known as Department of California.

Department of Pacific. Special Orders 1858-1863.

————. ————. Microcopy 617. Returns from U.S. Military Posts, 1800-1916, Rolls 14-17. Post Returns, Alcatraz Island 1859-1916.

————. ————. Microcopy 661. Historical Information Relating to Military Posts and Other Installations ca. 1700-1900. 8 rolls. Roll 1 Alcatraz Island.

————. ————. Cartographic Archives Division.

————. ————. Audiovisual Archives Division, Motion Picture Branch. "Alcatraz Prison Open for Public View"; and Still Picture Branch.

3. Newspapers.

Daily Alta California, San Francisco.

Evening Bulletin, San Francisco.

San Francisco Call.

San Francisco Chronicle.

San Francisco Examiner.

Los Angeles Times.

Newsweek.

Time Magazine.

4. Articles

Bechdolt, Frederick. "The Rock." *Saturday Evening Post,* November 2, 1935, pp. 5-7 and 85-6.

Babyak, Jolene. "Alcatraz Was My Home," *TWA Ambassador, The Trans World Magazine* 8 (August 1975) 20-22.

Conway, Bryan, No. 293, as told to T. H. Alexander. "Twenty Months in Alcatraz," *Saturday Evening Post,* February 19, 1938, pp. 8-9, 31-2, and 34.

Costo, Rupert. "Alcatraz," *The Indian Historian,* 3 (Winter 1970) 4-12 and 64.

Cummings, Homer. "Why Alcatraz Is a Success." *Collier's,* July 29, 1939.

Fries, Amos A. "Maj. Gen. James Birdseye McPherson." *Professional Memoirs, Corps of Engineers, United States Army,* and *Engineer Department at Large.* 7 (May-June 1915) 378-82.

Holland, Francis R., Jr. "Notes and Documents, Lighting Alcatraz: The West Coast's First Lighthouse." *The Western Explorer.* 2 (April 1964) 30-38.

Kock, Felix. Escape from Alcatraz Federal Prison. Overland Monthly V:57.

Lewis, Emanuel Raymond. "The Ambiguous Columbiads." *Military Affairs.* 28 (Fall 1964) 111-22.

Strobridge, William F., ed. "California Letters of Major General James McPherson, 1858-1860," *Ohio History.* 81 (Winter 1972) 38-50.

ALCATRAZ CONVICT SLANG GLOSSARY

ACADEMY — jail

ARCTIC — isolation, solitary confinement

APE — derogatory term for a black male

B & W — bread and water

BARGAIN — reduction of an original sentence

BEATING THE GUMS — talking, screaming, shouting

BLAST — shoot with firearm

BOOGIE MAN — turnkey, "screw"

BROADWAY — wide east-west aisle between B and C cellblocks

BUG JUICE — a liquid mixture of sodium luminal given to disturbed types

BUM RAP — unfair or excessive sentence

BUTCHER — captain of the guards

CELL — an inmate housing unit

CELLBLOCK — two or more cells, in one section or "block"
   Note: at Alcatraz there 124 cells in A-block, 168 cells in B-block, 168 cells in C-block and 42 cells in D-block.

CELLFRONT — front wall of a cell, usually barred

CELLHOUSE — a room enclosing one or more cellblocks

CLEAN — free from contraband articles

COLD STORAGE — solitary confinement

COMING OUT PARTY — discharge

CON — a convicted criminal

CROAKER — a prison medical officer

DECK — steel floor of gun galleries, towers, etc.

DOG BLOCK — D-block (segregation and isolation

DOUBLE TEAM — two officers guarding an inmate

EASY GO — easy prison job

FAIRY — a sexual pervert

FATHER TIME — prison court

FINK — contemptuous term for a law enforcement officer

FLATS — the ground floor of the cellhouse

FOOD PASS — an oblong 4x12-inch opening in a cell front

FRESH FISH — a newly arrived prisoner

FRISK — a quick, superficial body search

GENERAL POPULATION — majority of inmates not in isolation or segregation

GO ON THE GREEN CARPET — appear, as in prison court

GRADE — lesser form of punishment

GUN BULL — armed guard

GUN CAGE — gun gallery

GUN GALLERY — a secure, elevated, enclosed walkway from which an armed officer supported unarmed officers

HACK — prison guard, officer

HIT THE BRICKS — escape to San Francisco

HOLE — solitary confinement cell

HOLED UP — hidden in a defensive position

HOT BOX — solitary confinement

ISOLATION — housed apart from other prisoners. In most instances, a synonym for segregation.

JIGGERS — keeping a watch against officers

JUG HEAD — a derogatory term for a stubborn, unyielding official

JUNGLE — recreation yard

KING SCREW — warden

KITE — an illicit communication, usually a letter

LAG — "jailbird" of long standing

LIFEBOAT — bardon

LIFE ON THE INSTALLMENT PLAN — series of prison sentences

MEAT HEAD — synonym for jug head

MICHIGAN BOULEVARD — inmate nickname for the A-B aisle in cellhouse

MONKEY SUIT — a prison officer's uniform

ON THE CARPET — disciplinary action

PAPER HANGING — passing bad checks

PEKIN PLACE — inmate nickname for the north-south aisle across the east end of cellhouse. The visiting area.

PIG STICKER — a knife

PISS & PUNK — bread and water diet

PUNK — an inexperienced criminal and/or a young male playing the female part

QUARANTINE — segregation

QUEER — a sexual pervert

RACK — operate a mechanism to open or close a cell door

RAIN CHECK — parole

RANGE — a row or tier of cells

RAT — an informer

RIDGE RUNNER — a woodsman or "hillbilly"

RUMBLE — rumor

SALLYPORT — a specially designed and safely controlled entrance/exit

SCRAPPLE — prison food

SCREW — a prison officer

SCREWDRIVER — a prison official, usually the captain

SEEDY STREET — inmate nickname for C-D aisle in cellhouse

SEGREGATED — confined apart from others

SHAKEDOWN — search

SHITTER — a water closet, a cell toilet

SHOOTING GALLERY — term for gun gallery

A SHOT — disciplinary report

SOFT TIME — easy jail sentence

SOLITARY CONFINEMENT — housed apart from others, usually in an unlighted cell

STOOLIE — stool pigeon, an informer

TAKE A FALL — be imprisoned

TICKET — inmate's record or discipline report

TIER — a row of cellblock cells, constructed atop another row of cells

TIMES SQUARE — the north-south aisle, across the west end of the cellhouse, where cellhouse clock was located

TRACK 13 — life sentence

TOUGH TIME — difficult jail sentence

UNDERDOGS — inmates

UNDERGRAD — convict

UPPERDOGS — officers

VALENTINE — short sentence

WALKAWAY — the elevated pathway in front of a tier of cells on the upper tiers of a cellblock

WOLF — an aggressive homosexual

YARD BIRD — cleanup man assigned to prison yard

INDEX

A

ABIE124
ACAPULCO 11, 12
ACHILLES' tendons 205
ALABAMA 118
ALASKA 14, 210, 211
ALBION NOVA 11
ALCATRACES (pelicans) 23
ALCATRAZ Island 23
ALCATRAZ Prison 87
ALCATRAZ Prison Press 79
ALCATRAZ Register
ALCATRAZ, The Indian Council 53
ALCATRAZOS 33
ALDERSON, W.VA. 117
ALEXANDER, Edward Porter 48
ALGIERS & West Point Foundries 59
ALLEN, David 78
ALTA CALIFORNIA 10, 14, 24, 25
AMBROSE, William Henry 129
AMERICAN College of Surgeons 136
AMERICAN Indian Museum 229, 235
AMERICAN Native 22, 25
AMES, David 237
ANDRES, Fray Juan 18
ANGEL ISLAND 16, 23, 29, 33-35, 40,
    48, 57, 62, 66, 93, 85, 87, 169
ANGLIN brothers 206, 221, 222
ANGLIN, Clarence 183
ANGLIN, John Williams 183
AÑO NUEVO POINT 15
ANSON 11
ANZA, Juan Bautista de 21, 24
APACHE 227
APOLLO Space Capsule 226
APPEALS Court 169
ARGÜELLO, Luis Antón 24 25
ARIAN, Straits of 11
ARISTA, Mariano, President 29
ARISTOCRACY 25
ARIZONA 117, 218, 229
ARIZONA Department 227
ARIZONA-Navajo Community College
    236
ARIZONA Territories 72
ARMY and Navy Journal 73
ARMY Board of Engineers 32
ARMYEngineers 68, 183
ARMY, U.S. 84, 93, 95, 118-120, 169
ASIATIC Coast 10
ATLANTA 101, 109, 112, 223
ATLANTA Penitentiary 117
ATLANTIC Coast 68
ATLANTIC Ocean 11
ATOKA 216
AUSTRALIAN 237
AYALA, don Manuel de, Lieutenant 22
AYALA log 22
AYALA map 22

B

BAHER 192
BAILEY, Harvey L. 112, 215
BAJA CALIFORNIA 17
BALTIMORE 209
BARCHO 227
BARKDOLL 203
BARKER, Arthur (Doc) 181
BARKER, Ma 181, 220
BARNEY 184
BATES, Albert L. 112, 214, 215
BATES, Sanford 98, 99, 101, 110, 112,
    114, 117
BAY AREA 47, 48, 99, 165, 232, 235
BEAR, Grizzly 26
BEECHEY, Captain Frederick 24
BECH, Elmis 190
BELFOST 34
BENDER, George 83
BENICH, Arsenal 48, 58
BENICIA, California 41
BENNETT, James V. 117, 118, 129, 130,
    134, 146, 193-195, 208, 214, 215
BERKELEY 85, 232
BERNARD, John G. 38, 40, 44
BERRY, Cecil 216
BIDDLE, General A. 214
BIRDMAN 136, 157, 195, 210, 213
BLACK PANTHERS 231
BLACK Warrior, U.S. Ship 41
BLACKSTONE 92
BLACKSTONE, Nathaniel 50
BLACKWELL, Olin 183, 205-207, 223
BLAIR, Kenneth 189
BLIENT, Simon F., Lt. 33
BLOOD BANK 203
BOARD OF ENGINEERS 33, 63, 66
BODEGO QUADRA, Juan de 21
BOLAÑOS 13
BOLSHEVILLE 85
BONCHO 227, 228
BONITA POINT 51
BONNIE & CLYDE 221, 222
BORD, enrollment 85
BOSTON 25, 58
BOWEN, Hugh A. 112
BOWERS, Joe 133
BOWLING 189
BOYE 11
BOYLE, L. C. 211
BRISTOW 92
BRITISH Corvette, Satellite 45
BRITISH Pacific Squadron 59
BRITISH Steamer 56
BRITISH Warship Sutlej 59
BROADWAY 147, 148
BROWN, John H. 27
BROWN, L. G. 163
BROWNIE, Frank B. 112

BROWNING 185
BUCARELI, Viceroy 22-24
BUCH, Franklin A. 34
BUENO, Admiral Cabrera 12, 14, 16, 19
BURCH, Officer 191, 192
BURDELLE 192
BUREAU of Immigration 87
BUREAU of Indian Affairs 231
BUREAUS of Prison 95, 98, 99, 117, 141
    157, 223
BURGE, Robert C. 99, 101
BURGELI, Aaron 204
BURKE, Martin 78
BURTON, Henry, Capt. 57
BUTTERWORTH, Thomas F. 100

C

CABO de San Francisco 11
CABRILLO, Juan Rodriguez 10
CACAFUEGO 11
CALIFORNIA 10, 14, 24, 85, 131, 227
CALIFORNIA Constitution 32
CALIFORNIAFlower Assn. 95
CALIFORNIA History 11
CALIFORNIA Indians 234
CALIFORNIA missions 25
CALIFORNIA Republic 26
CALIFORNIA, Spanish 21
CALIFORNIA, Upper 18, 21
CALIFORNIA Volunteers 80
CAMBON, Father Pedro Benito 24
CAMP, Lee 117
CANADA 200
CANBY, E. R. S., Maj. Gen. 228
CANIZARES, don José 14, 22, 23
CANNON, Clarence 223
CAPE de las Almejas 9
CAPE Horn 33
CAPE of Good Hope 11
CAPMAN, Frank 112
CAPONE, Al 112, 113, 129-131, 152,
    161, 169, 180, 187, 208-210, 220
CAPONIER 36, 41, 42, 65
CARLOS, San (packet boat) 22
CARNES, Clarence 91, 192, 195, 212,
    216, 217
CARRANZA 218
CASEY, Thomas 68
CASSIN, Michael 50
CATHOLIC 151, 176, 205
CATHOLIC Church 24
CAUCASIAN 234
CAVENISH 11, 12
CEDAM 44
CEMETERY 209
CERMEÑO, Sebastián Rodrigues 12, 13
CHAMBER of Commerce 10, 98
CHAMISSO, Adalbert von 24

CHANDLER 185
CHANTILLY, Virginia 58
CHOPLAIN 130, 146, 151
CHAPMAN, J. M. 72
CHAPMAN, schooner 57
CHARLES II, King of Spain 14
CHARLESTON, South Carolina 40
CHARTA, MAGNA 159
CHASE, John Paul 151, 221, 222
CHEVROLET 119
CHICAGO 147, 169, 208, 209
CHICANOS 231
CHILD, George R., Mrs. 95
CHILLICOTHE 101, 117
CHINAMEN 45
CHINESE 84
CHINESE Consul General 78
CHINESE granite 44
CHINESE population 78
CHINESE servants 78
CHOCTAW Indian 216
CHOLOS 25
CHRISTIANS 14, 21, 216
CHRISTIAN Indians 14
CHRISTMAS 126, 160, 189, 203, 220
CHRONICLE, San Francisco 83, 84
CITADEL 57, 67, 72, 80, 81, 118
CINCINNATI 99, 101
CIRCUIT judge 159
CIVIL Service Commission 101
CIVIL WAR 42, 56, 57, 62, 68, 69, 72, 76,
  80
CLARK, Father 151
CLEMENTS, Frank 151
CLINE, Royal C. 167
CLIPPERTON 11
CLOVER 65
COAST GUARD 111, 167, 168, 193, 204,
  233, 237
COCHRANE, Harvey 190
COHEN, Mickey 220
COLE, Theodor 166
COLUMBIA 85
COLUMBIA River 57, 64
COLUMBIADS 41, 47, 58
CONCEPCION, Francisco de la, Fray 12,
  24
CONFEDERACY 72
CONFEDERATE States of Mexico 48, 49
CONFEDERATE sympathizers 57
CONGRESS, U.S. 32, 42, 43, 50, 87, 213,
  220
CONSTANSO 17
CONSTANSA, diary of 17
CONSTANSO, Miguel 14, 15
CONSTITUTION, California 32
CONTRA Costa County 40, 226
CONWAY'S, Vern 233
COOK, Dalmer Company 29
COOK, William 220
CORDOVA 210

CORTES 10, 14
CORWIN, Thomas 51, 192
COSTANOAN 236
COTTIER, Allen 226
COURT, Appeals 169
COURT, Circuit 211
COURT, Federal 211
COURT, Supreme 159
COY, Bernard 190-194, 216
CRALLE, Maury G., Col. 91
CRETZER, Joseph P. 190, 194, 203
CRESPI, Father 14-19, 21
CRESPI, map 21
CROIX 18
CROWDER, Enoch H., Maj. Gen. 86, 89
CROWN of Spain 21
CRUZADO, Fray 18
CUBA 41, 92
CUMMINGS, Homer S. 98, 101, 112, 196
CUMMINGS, Jack 214
CUSTER, General 235
CZAR 24

D

DAILY Alta California 50, 64
DAINARD, Bill 220
DALY, Dennis J. 78
DANA, Charles 232
DAPHNE, patrol boat 111
DARIN 11
DAVIS, George B. 83, 84
DAVIS, Secretary of War 41
DAW, Fred 213
DEFENSIVE expansion 21, 22
DEFIANCE, Fort 229
DEMOCRATIC State Committee 72
DEPARTMENT of California 75, 76
DEPARTMENT of Interior 236
DEPARTMENT of Justice 99, 223
DE RUSSY, Rev. E., Lt. Col. 40, 41, 43, 61,
  62
DERN, George H. 98
DESIRE 12
DETROIT 221, 222
DEVILS Island 90, 99
DIGEST of the Diseases of Birds 212
DILLINGER, John 131
DISCIPLINARY barracks, U.S. 87, 88, 91
DISNEY 230
DOILIES 206
DOLORES Mission 25
DOUGLAS, David 24
DOUGLAS fir 24
DOUGLAS spruce 24
DRAKE'S Bay 12, 13
DRAKE, John 11
DRAKE, Francis G. 11
DRAMATIC Association 74, 75
DUTCHMAN 153
DUNN, Louis C. 119

DUPONT 117
DUSKIN, Alvin 226

E

EARTHQUAKE, San Francisco 10
ECETA, Bruno de 21
ECOLOGY Center 229, 235
EDSTROW, Eve 213
EGALITE, French Corvette 38
EGAN, John, Capt. 66
EGYPTE 10
EIFFEL Tower 10
EL AGUADOR 82
EL PRINCIPE 19
EL RENO 117
ELIZABETH, Queen of England 11
ELIZABETHAN Age 11
ELK, Grfield spotted 226
ELLIOTT, George Henry, First Lt. 49, 57-
  60, 62
ELLIOTT, Robert S. 190
ELLIS, William J. 98
ENDICOTT, Board 68
ENDICOTT, William C. 68
ENGINEERS, Board of 33, 63, 66
ENGINEERS, Dept. 62
ENGLAND 11
ENGLISH, the 11, 12
ENROLLMENT Board 89
EMMA, Queen of Hawaii 62
ESPLANDIAN, Los Sergas de 10
EVERGREEN State College 232

F

FAGES, don Pedro 14, 18, 19
FATHERS 25
FARALLONES Islands 29, 32
FARM Colony 94
FEDERAL Bureau of Investigation 214,
  219, 220
FEDERAL Bureau of Prison 95, 117
FEDERAL Reporter 149
FETON, John B. 29
FIGUEROA, José, Gov. 25
FILLMORE, Millard, Pres. 32, 33
FLEISHER, Sammy Harry Louise 221,
  222
FLEMING, W., Lt. 227
FLEXITED 130
FLOWERS on Alcatraz 95
FOLSOM 101, 196
FONDA, Jane 237
FORD 119
FORMER, Herb 220
FORT Alcatraz 46, 227
FORT Barry 83
FORT Delaware 43
FORT Defiance 228
FORT Klamath 227
FORT Lawton 233

FORT Leavenworth 94
FORT Natham 223
FORT Point 33, 36, 38, 40, 42, 43, 51, 60, 61, 63, 65, 72, 237
FORT Pulaski 60
FORT Sutters 26
FORT Sumter 58
FOX, 20th Century 213
FRANCISCANS 14, 24, 25
FRANCISCAN Order 14
FRANKLIN, Rufus 166, 167
FREMONT, John C. 29
FRENCH 38
FRENCH Corvette 38
FRENCH Police 83
FRESNEL light 51
FULLER, Capt. A. M. 80, 81
FUNK lamp 51

G

GADDIS, Thomas 213
GALVEZ, José de 14
GALATES, Gus 220
GARDNER, Roy 112, 128, 162, 76, 218 219
GASPER, Don 18
GERMANS 45, 84
GERMANY 11
GEMS of the Pacific 45
GILES, John 169
GLASGOW, Scotland 24
GLENDALE, California 209
G-MEN 214
GOD 15, 16
GOLD rush 26
GOLDEN GATE 13, 16, 33, 35, 44, 69, 234
GOLDEN GATE bridge 148, 151, 183, 207
GOLDEN GATE National Recreational Area 237
GOLDEN GATE, ship 44
GOMEZ 14, 17
GORDEN, H. T. 27
GOVERNMENT, Mexican 26
GRADED School Dept. 88
GRAND, Ulysses, U.S. President 227
GREAT Meadows 94
GRINDER, Joe D. 184
GRONZO, Gordon 223
G.S.A. 226, 227
GUIWHATANAVA 227
GWIN, Hon. Wm. M. 43

H

H., Eddie 163
HALLECK, Henry W. 38, 58, 62, 64, 72, 83
HALSTEAD, Lt. lawrence 83

HAMILTON, Floyd 221, 222
HAMMACK, W. T. 101, 102
HANNON, Thomas 236, 237
HARDBURG, Lt. Col. Thomas H. 81
HARMON, T. E. 227
HARRIS, George 151
HARRISON Street 60
HART, Marie 226
HAWAII 62
HAYWARD 16
HAZELTON, Capt. Reginald 11
HEARN Light 52
HELLCATRAZ 218
HELLS ANGELS 231
HIND, the Golden 11
HONOLULU 165
HOOVER, J. Edgar 182, 214, 219, 220
HOPI 229
HOSPITAL COVE 22
HOT CREEK 228
HOWITZER 47
HUBBARD, Marvin 190, 191, 94
HUMPHREYS, Gen. 72, 73
HUNT, Lamar 226, 230, 237

I

IDLE, William B. 26
IDAHO Territory 72
IMMIGRATION 87
IDAHO 117
ILLINOIS 210
INDIAN Council 231
INDIAN Reservation 234, 227
INDIAN Spiritual Center 235
INDIAN Center of Ecology 235
INDIAN School 235
INDIANS, Modoc 227
INDIANS, Sioux 226
INDIANS, Mualpai 227
INDIANS, Apache 227
INDIANS, Mohave 227
INDIANS, Hopi 228

J

JACK, Captain 228
JAIL, Broadway Street 84
JAPANESE 165
JAPANESE Navy 66
JAPANESE stowaways 84
JARRETT, Walker R. 214
JESUS CHRIST 21
JEWISH 176, 178
JEWISH Women's Organization 231
JOHNSON, Clyde 204
JOHNSTON, Brig. Gen. Albert S. 48
JOHNSTON, James A. 98, 101-103, 110, 113, 116-120, 129, 130, 136, 141, 146, 148, 161, 166, 84, 187, 192, 195, 196

JONES Academy for Boys 216
JONES, Della 212
JOURNAL, Army & Navy 73
JUDGE Advocate 157
JUNEAU 210
JUSTICE Dept. 99, 157

K

KANSAS 94, 110, 210, 223
KANSAS CITY 171
KANSAS CITY massacre 221, 222
KANSAS State Prison 83
KARPIS, Alvin 131, 142, 177, 208, 219, 220
KELLY, George (Machine Gun) 112, 177, 214, 215
KELLY, KATHRYN 214
KENNEDY, Ethel 237
KENNEDY, Robert 160, 223
KENTUCKY 191
KEWEN, E. J. C. 72
KGO Radio Station 226
KING, John 191
KING Philip II of Spain 10-12
KING of Spain 14, 24
KINGDOME, Rear Adm. John 59
KLAMATH Reservation 227
KNIGHTS Templar 177
KOOSKIA 117
KYLE 203

L

LA SALUD 15
LA TUNA 117
LABEARE, Napoleon 78
LAGER, William 221, 222
LAGUNA de los Dolores 24
LAKE County 227
LAND Commission 29
LASY, Conte de 21
LAWTON, Fort 233
LEADBETTER, First Lt. Danville 33, 34
LEACH, David 232
LEACH, Mike 232
LEACH, Sonny 232
LEACH, Stella 230, 232
LEAVENWORTH 94, 101, 103, 117, 210, 216, 218, 223
LEEDS, Capt. 51
LES Paul 132
LEWIS, Edgar 175
LEWIS, Judge 211
LEWISBURG 107, 209, 223
LIFE 57, 158
LIMANTOUR, José Ifes 27, 29
LIME, Point 33, 36, 60, 65, 67, 79
LIMERICH, Thomas R. 166, 167
LINDBERG ACT, the 216
LOGAN, U.S. Transport 84

LONDON 83
LONG, Edward 213
LOOMIS, Alfred M. 131
LOPEZ, Eleanor 232
LOS ANGELES 209, 213, 232
LOST PORT 12, 14
LOWDER, Sgt. John 77
L.S.D. 233
LUCAS, Jimmy C. 131, 166, 167, 174, 220
LUZON 85

M

MacARTHUR, Maj. Gen. Arthur 69
MacARTHUR, Gen. Douglas 69
MADIGAN, Paul J. 180, 184, 203, 204, 205, 213, 220
MAGELLAN 11
MAGNA CHARTA 159
MALLA, Fritz 220
MALLIARD, J. W., Jr, 98
MANHATTAN Island 226, 234
MANILA 10-14, 80
MANILA ships 13
MANILA trade route 11
MANSFIELD, Maj. Gen. Joseph King 58, 59, 62, 64
MANZANILLO 44
MARINES, U.S. 136, 191, 193
MARIANE, San Diego de 22
MARTIN, Don 189
MARTIN, William 181
MARTINEZ, Martin 226
MAP, WARNER 32
MASON, Capt. James J. 34, 36
MASSACRE 110
MASSACRE, Wounded Knee 235
McCAIN, Rufus 181
McCLELLAN, Maj. Gen. George Briton 58, 61, 66
McCULLOGH, Samuel 78
McDOWELL, General (boat) 82, 99
McELROY, Lt. 84
McKEE, Blackie 174
McKENZIE, Richard D. P. 226
McKINSTRY, Maj. Charles M. 52
McLEOD, Doris 98
McNEIL 101
McNEIL Island 101, 109, 111, 117, 210, 220, 223
McPHERSON, Lt. James Birdseye 44, 46-50, 58, 62, 77, 78
MEANS, Lenado 232
MEANS, Walter 226
MEDICAL Corps 93
MEDICAL Facility, Federal 213
MENDELL 63-68, 73
MERCHANT, Lt. Col 72
MERITT, Ezekiel 26
MEXICAN 25, 38
MEXICAN Government 25, 32, 44

MEXICAN Rebel 218
MEXICAN Viceroy 13, 18
MEXICAN War 34
MESICO 13, 14, 34, 44
MICHELTORENA, Manuel 27
MICHIGAN 117
MICHIGAN Boulevard 147
MILAN 117
MILITARY Department 29, 32, 72
MILITARY Prison 84
MILLER, E. J. 108, 153, 184, 190-192
MILLER, William A. 194, 195
MILLS, L. O. 102
MILLS, Brig. Gen. Nelson A. 76, 80
MINDANAO 85
MISION Dolores 25
MISION San Antonio de Padua 19
MISION San Francisco 17
MISSISSIPPI 214
MISSOURI 135, 213, 214
MODOC 227, 228
MODOC chief 228
MOHAVE 227
MOENCOPI 229
MONTANA Mountain 16
MONTEREY 13-19, 24, 26, 32
MONTEREY Bay 13-16
MONTEREY, Port 17-19, 21, 23
MONTEREY, Royal Presidio 19
MONTGOMERY 118
MONTGOMERY, John 13, 26
MONTREAL 220
MORCADA, Rivera Y 14
MORDHEUS 134
MORGAN, Maj. Charles Hale 66
MORGANT, W. 210
MORRIS, Frank Lee 183
MOUNT OLIVET Cemetery 209
MOVIES 179
MUHLDAI 227
MULLER, Al 232
MUSLIMS 223

N

NAGASAKI 84
NATIONAL COUNCIL of Indians opportunity 236
NATIVE Americans 239
NATIVE American studies 229, 231
NATIVE American Studies Center 235
NAVY 119, 156
NEGRO 25
NELSON, Baby Face 151, 221, 222
NEVADA 72
NEW ORLEANS 117
NEW SPAIN 10, 13, 25
NEW JERSEY 98
NEW YORK 44, 98, 117, 147, 221, 222
NEW YORK Arsenal 41
NEW YORK Magazine 157, 158

NIXON, Richard 237
NOBEL, Alfred 158
NORTH AMERICA 10
NORTH CAROLINA 34
NUMER, Richard 174
NUTCHEZ 228

O

OAKLAND 91, 209, 231, 232
OAKS, Richard, 229, 232, 237
OAKS, Yvonne 232
O'BANION, Dion 209
O'BRIAN, Kitty 210
O'FARRELL, Philip 98, 99
OGDEN, Maj. Cornelius A. 33, 34
OHIO 117
OHLONE 236
OKLAHOMA 117, 166, 216
OKLAHOMA City 214
OLD WEST 218
OLDHAM, Herschel R. 190
ORAIBI 229
OREGON 50, 61, 64, 72, 227, 232
ORIENTAL 121
ORO, Toisón de (Golden Fleece) 22
ORTEGA, Sergeant José 14, 16
OZARK Gang 220

P

PACIFIC 11
PACIFIC Board 43, 66
PACIFIC Branch, U.S. Disciplinary Barracks 88
PACIFIC Branch, U.S. Military Prison 81
PACIFIC Branch, U.S. Military Prison, Alcatraz 81
PACIFIC Coast 29, 33, 34, 42, 57, 59, 63, 67, 72
PACIFIC Coast Board of Engineers 63
PACIFIC Coast of Panama 44
PACIFIC Division 84
PACIFIC Mail Steamship Company 44
PACIFIC Northwest 46
PACIFIC Ocean 57
PAITA 11
PALO ALTO 16
PALOU, Father Francisco 15, 16, 22, 24
PANAMA 11, 68
PANAMA Fever 36
PARIS, France 10, 51
PARK Service 236, 237
PARKER, Daryl 207
PAROLE Board 157
PARRON, Fray Fernando 18
PARROTT guns 58
PAULY, Jail, St. Louis 83
PAYTON PLACE 186
PEARL HARBOR 119, 165
PEÑA, Faher 22

PENITENTIARY 83
PENNSYLVANIA 223
PEPPER, Billie 189
PERSFUL, Rufe 134
PEREZ, Juan 21
PETERSBURG 117
PEWTER, Daniel 94
PHILLIPS, Burton 127, 161
PHILIPPINES 10, 12, 13, 41, 85, 92
PHILIPPINE insurrection 80
PICO, Gov. Pio 27, 29, 49
PICKERING, Maj. Abner 81
PIUTE Indian chief 228
PLUMPER, British steamer 56
POINT Blunt 65
POINT Bonita 51, 83
POINT, José 33
POINT Pines 3, 15
POINT Reyes 12, 13, 16, 18, 19, 21, 40
POKEBERRY juice 26
POLICE chief 98
POLICE force 231
POLICE, French 83
POLICE, San Francisco 193
POLLOCK, John C. 211POST, Alcatraz
   Island 46, 60
POST, Exchange 188
POST surgein 59
POSTAL Law 133
POPE 24
POPULAR MECHANICS 68, 157
PORTLAND cement 82
PORTLAND, Maine 36
PORTER, Albert J. 52
PORTOLA, Gov. 14, 15, 17, 18
PORTSMOUTH, U.S.S. 26
PRATT, W. H. 27
PRESIDIO 72
PRESS, Australia 237
PRESS Corps. 221-223
PRIME, Frecerick E. 36, 37, 44, 58, 62
PRISON Equipment Bureau 99
PRISON Press 74
PROTESTANT 176
PROVINCE (New Spain) 21
PROVOST Guard 227
PUBLIC Works Administration 119, 142
PUGET Sound 57
PULASKI, Georgia 60
PUNTA de los Reyes 18
PURPEL Gang 221, 222
PYRAMIDS 10

Q

QUARRIES 40
QUEEN Elizabeth of England 11
QUENTIN, San 101, 178, 195, 196, 218
QUINN, Anthony 237
QUINN, William J. 98, 112

R

RACCOON Straits 34, 59
RADIO Free Alcatraz 232
RADIO Station KGO 226
RANDAL, Maj. 75
RANDOM House 213
RAPP Verrill 117
REAGAN, Ronald 237
RED CROSS 190
REICH, Carl 189
REO Motor 119
RESERVATION Indians 227, 234
REUSS, Carl 159
REVOLUTIONARY Party 26
REYES, Los 11
REYES, Point 18, 19, 21, 40
REZANOV, Count Nicolas 24
RICKBERGER, Fred J. 190
RILEY Channel 35
RINCON Point 35
RIOT (1946) 216, 217
RITCHEY, Dr. 136, 140
RIVERAD Y MONCADA, don FERNANDO
   de 14, 15, 122
ROBERTSON, Capt. James Madison 61-
   64, 66
ROBERTSON, Robert 236
ROBINSON, 130
RICKWELL, Norman 151
RODMAN, 57, 59, 64, 68
ROE, Ralph 166
ROEDEL 153
ROGER, D. 11
ROSECRANS, Maj. Gen. William S. 58, 62
ROSENBURGE Case 221, 222
ROSENTHAL, Jack 223
ROSSI, Mayor 112
ROSTER, inmate 161
ROYAL Presidio 19
RUNNYMEDE 159
RURIK 24
RUSSIAN 14, 45, 84
RUSSIAN Frigate 24, 38
RUSSIAN propaganda 85
RUSSIAN settlements 24

S

SACRAMENT 15
SACRAMENTO 40
SACRAMENTO River 32
SACRED expedition 14
SAINT FRANCIS 24
SAN AGUSTIN 12, 13
SAN ANTONIO 14
SAN BLAS, Port of 23
SAN CARLOS (Boal) 14, 22
SAN DIEGO 14-19, 38
SAN FERNANDO Apostolic College 19

SAN FRANCISCO Bay 10, 11, 21, 24, 34,
   36, 57, 67, 69, 90
SAN FRANCISCO Board of Supervisors
   98
SAN FRANCISCO Call 51
SAN FRANCISCO Chronicle 83, 84, 98
SAN FRANCISCO, City of 10, 12, 13, 24,
   27, 36, 44, 45, 59, 60, 62, 68, 89, 90,
   91, 98, 116, 135, 160, 165, 166, 168,
   174, 178, 213, 217, 226, 230
SAN FRANCISCO Harbor 42, 51, 56, 229
SAN FRANCISCO market 34
SAN FRANCISCO paper 79
SAN FRANCISCO, Port of 11, 12, 16, 17,
   19, 21-24
SAN FRANCISCO Resident 67
SAN FRANCISCO Town Council 32, 33
SANDUSKY County, Ohio 44
SANSWICH Islands 45
SANTA ANNA 12
SANTA CLARA Valley 18
SANTA FE train 135
SARMIENTO, don 11
SATELLITE, British ship 46
SATURDAY Evening Post 157
SAUSALITO 48
SAUTLERAND Co. 51
SCIENTIFIC AMERICAN 157
SCIGLIANO, Gloria 98
SCOTLAND Yard 83
SCOTT, John Paul 207
SCOTT, Maj. Gen. Winfield 48
SEATTLE 210
SECRETARY of War 43, 48, 68, 69
SEEDY Street 147
SENATE, U.S. 43
SEDOYS 45
SERAPHIC, Father San Francisco 19
SERRA, Fray Junípero 14, 18, 21, 22, 25
SETTLERS 24
SHAFTER, Maj. Gen. William 80
SHANNON, Kathryn 214
SHELVOCKE 11
SHENANDOAH Valley 60
SHERIDAN 60
SHERMAN 60
SHOCKLEY, Sam 191, 192, 195, 203
SHRUBS on Alcatraz 95
SHUTTLEWORTH, Deputy Warden 112
SIMON, Stevens 29
SIMPSON, Joe 190
SING SING 94
SIOUX 226
SIOUX medicine 237
SISKIYOU 228
SITKA, Alaska 24
SLOAN, John 50
SLOLOCK 227, 228
SMITH, Caleb B. 32
SMITH, Capt. Frederic A. 34

Smith, Maj. John L. 33, 34, 36
SOBBELL, Mortay 221, 222
SONOMA 26
SONOMA (steamer) 79
SONORA 22
SORROWS, Lady of 24
SOUTH DAKOTA 160, 166
SPAIN 10, 12-14, 24, 41, 118, 220
SPAIN, King of 24
SPANIARDS 12-14, 24, 25, 27, 142
SPANISH 69, 81, 142
SPANISH-AMERICAN War 67, 68, 80, 84
SPANISH Crown 25
SPANISH dungeons 118, 141
SPANISH Empire 65
SPANISH galleon 10
SPANISH Inquisition 87
SPANISH sails 11
SPANISH warships 41
SPITFIRE 11
SPORTS ILLUSTRATED 157
SPRINGFIELD 118, 135, 185, 213, 214
ST. ELIZABETH'S Hospital 218
ST. LOUIS 83
ST. PETERSBURG 24
ST. PETERSBURG, Russian court 21
ST. SURE A.F. 160
STAMPHILL, Dale 181
STANTON, Edward M. 29
STARS and Stripes, U.S. 26
STATE Assembly 72
STATE Penitentiary 83
STEVENS, Maj. Gen. Isaac Ingalls 58, 62
STEWART, IRON Comp. 101
STEWART, Capt. Joseph 48, 56
STEWARD, Potter 159
STITES, Harold P. 167, 190, 194, 195
STRAITS OF Magellan 33
STRIP cell 120
STOCKTON 29
STOUT, John Drake 26
STROUD, Elizabeth McCartney Schaefer
  210
STROUD, Marcus 210
STROUD, Robert 116, 130, 136, 157,
  159, 177, 195, 210, 212, 213, 216,
  230
SUBMARINE (Navy) 119
SUMTER, Fort 49
SURGEONS 136, 1570
  SUTLEJ (British warship 59
SUTLER, Robert 190
SUTTER'S Fort 26
SUTTER'S Mill 33
SWAN, Edward E. 50
SWOPE, E. B. 132, 184
SWOPE, Mrs. E. B. 185
SWORDS, Lt. Col. Thomas 47

T

TACOMA 131
TELEGRAPH Hill 72
TEMPLE, Francis 27
TEMPLE, Shirley Black 237
TERRITORIES, Arizona 72
TEXAS 85, 117, 214
THANKSGIVING 231
THAYER, Walter N. 98
THOMAS, Brig. Gen. Lorenzo 72
THOMPSON Gun 185
THOMPSON, Miran 191, 192, 195
THORNBURG, Lt. Thomas TI 64
THUNDERBIRDS 231, 232
TIME 157
TOLSON, Clyde 219
TOTTEN, Joseph 29, 34, 36, 41, 42, 48,
  57, 58, 60
TOWER, Zealous Bales 29, 36-38, 40-43,
  58, 61, 63
TREASURY Dept. 50, 60, 118
TREASURY Secretary of, U.S. 51
TREES on Alcatraz 95
TRIM, Corporal 73, 74
TRUDELL, John 231, 232, 234, 237
TUCSON, Arizona 117
TURNER, Maj. Reuben B. 81, 82
TWITCHELL, Dr. Edward 209

U

UNITED Automobile Workers 231
UNITED Bay Area Crusade 178
UNITED Church 231
UNITED Nations 226
UNITED STATES arsenal 34
UNITED STATES Congress 33
UNITED STATES Court of Appeals 159
UNITED STATES Disciplinary Barracks
  87, 88, 98
UNITED STATES District Court 27, 159
UNITED STATES Federal Government 32
UNITED STATES flag 26
UNITED STATES General Services
  Administration 226
UNITED STATES Government 27, 77,
  229
SPANISHGovernment 27, 77, 229
UNITED STATES Legal Code 159
UNITED STATES Marshal 72
UNITED STATES Military Academy 56
UNITED STATES Military Prison, Pacific
  Branch 81
UNITED STATES Penitentiary 95, 102,
  103, 112
UNITED STATES Public Health Services
  134, 140

UNITED STATES troops 229
UNGER, Jacob 44
UNION, the 49
UNION Army 58
UNION demonstration 49
UNIVERSITY of Calif. Berkeley 85
UNIVERSITY of Calif. Extension Div. 130
URSCHEL, Charles F. 214
URSCHEL, Mrs. Charles 214
URSCHEL family 214
U.S. (see United States)

V

VALLEJO, Mario 26
VANCOUVER, George 24
VAN WAGNER, Underhill 50, 51
VAQUEROS 24
VERGER, Father Rafael 21
VICEROY 18
VIZCAINO, Fray Juan 18
VIZCAYNO, General don Sebastián 19
VIRGINIA 92, 117
VISAYAS 85
VOCATIONAL training 88
VOCATIONAL training department 88
VOLUNTARY conversion 21
VOLUNTEERS 19
VON DAHMEN, Charles 210

W

WAGNER, Henry A. 11
WALDORF Astoria 221, 222
WALEY, Harmon Metz 220
WALTERS, Ted 167
WAR, Civil 42, 56, 57, 62, 68, 69, 72, 76,
  80
WAR Claims Board 92
WAR Department 32, 41, 60, 61, 68, 80-
  82, 85-87, 92
WAR Secretary 98, 157
WAR, Spanish-American 67, 68, 80, 84
WARNER, Lt. William Horace 32, 35
WARNERS map 37
WASHINGTON, D.C. 34, 47, 48, 112,
  130, 132, 161, 193, 218, 223, 229
WASHINGTON, George, Pres. U.S. 49
WASHINGTON Post 213
WASHINGTON State 118, 131, 181, 210,
  232
WASHINGTON Territory 57, 72
WEATHERMAN, Frank C. 124
WEBB, Col. 102
WEEKS, Col. 102
WEINHOLD, Capt. H. W. 108, 190
WEST Coast Arsenal 41
WEST POINT 44, 81, 92

WESTERN Military Dept. 72
WEYERHAUSER 220
WEYERHAUSER, George 131
WEYLAND, W. M. 216
WHALEY, Floyd C. 166
WHALY, Harman 131
WHITE Father 234
WILBES Expedition 33
WILKINSON, Fred T. 223
WILLIAM, Capt. Constant 229
WILLIAMS, Stinky 162
WILLIARD, Dick 223 ˙
WILMINGTON, Delaware 44
WILSON, Floyd 169, 204
WILSON, W., Pres., U.S. 211
WINCHESTER 185
WINDER, Capt. William A. 57, 58, 61, 72
WINTERS, Jonathan 237
WOOD, Brig. Gen. John E. 11, 37
WORKMANN, Julia William 27, 29, 226
WORLD WAR I 84, 92
WORLD WAR II 67
WOUNDED Knee 235
WRIGHT, Cecil L. 160
WRIGHT, Gen. George 59

Y

YANKEE Doodle 26
YERBA Buena 16, 23, 26, 29, 33, 67
Y.M.C.A. 237
YOUNG, Henry 181
YOUNG, Maj. Gen. S. B. M. 80

Acknowledgments:

Many thanks to the following, without whose help this publication would not have been possible.

Associated Press
Michael Aun
Clarence Carnes
Judith Craemer
Pete Dracopoulos
Yumi Gay
Lee Geiser
Frank J. Glover
Golden Gate National Recreation Area
Herbert Hart
F. H.
Bob Kirby
Joan Knudsen
Ray Logan
Ray March
Frank A. Norick
Erwin N. Thompson
San Francisco Chronicle
San Francisco Examiner
San Francisco Public Library
United Press International
United States Park Service